W9-AZU-575

The War in the Air
1914–1994

American Edition

Edited by
Alan Stephens
RAAF Aerospace Centre

In cooperation with the
RAAF Aerospace Centre

Air University Press
Maxwell Air Force Base, Alabama

January 2001

Library of Congress Cataloging-in-Publication Data

The war in the air, 1914-1994 / edited by Alan Stephens ; in cooperation with the RAAF Air Power Studies Centre—American ed.
    p. cm.
    Includes bibliographical references and index.
    ISBN 1-58566-087-6
        1. Air power—History—Congresses. 2. Air warfare—History—Congresses. 3. Military history, Modern—20th century—Congresses. I. Stephens, Alan, 1944-II. RAAF Air Power Studies Centre.

UG625.W367 2001
358.4'00904—dc21   00-068257

Disclaimer

Opinions, conclusions, and recommendations expressed or implied within are solely those of the author and do not necessarily represent the views of Air University, the United States Air Force, the Department of Defense, or any other US government agency. Cleared for public release: distribution unlimited.

Copyright © 1994 by the RAAF Air Power Studies Centre. No part of this book may be used or reproduced in any manner whatsoever without written permission except in the case of brief quotations embodied in critical articles and reviews. Inquiries should be made to the copyright holder.

Contents

Essays

Foreword

This book is the Air University Press edition of the proceedings of a conference on aerial warfare held by the Royal Australian Air Force (RAAF) in Canberra in 1994. Because of the stature of the contributing authors and the excellence of their essays, the original publication by the RAAF's Air Power Studies Centre has been in great demand and increasingly short supply. This American edition is essentially a reprint, although it is a somewhat shortened version with stylistic changes. Its publication will allow a wider audience access to an important segment of airpower literature.

Among the book's virtues are the high levels of expertise of its contributors and the diversity of their backgrounds. Here the American student can sample the views of Australian and British airmen and scholars, as well as some perhaps more familiar American vistas. Each of the book's contributors speaks with authority, and each discusses a specific area or period in the evolution of air and space power from World War I to the near future. Essay subjects include World War I; doctrinal development in the interwar period; strategic bombing and support of surface forces in World War II; and airpower in the Korean War, Vietnam War, Arab-Israeli Wars, Falkland Islands War, and Persian Gulf War. They also include coverage of airpower in such peripheral conflicts as Operation El Dorado Canyon, the Malayan Emergency, and the Israeli raid on the Osirak nuclear reactor in Iraq.

We at the Air University Press are pleased to republish this important work and are grateful for the opportunity. Special thanks are due to Dr. Alan Stephens, who not only edited the original book but who did it again for our edition; the Aerospace Centre for allowing us to publish this work; and Professor Dennis M. Drew of Air University's School of Advanced Airpower Studies, who recognized the value of the original work and the need for a new edition.

Shirley Brooks Laseter

SHIRLEY BROOKS LASETER
Director
Air University Press

About the Authors

Professor Robin Higham

Professor Robin Higham was born in the United Kingdom and educated on both sides of the Atlantic. He served as a first sergeant pilot in the Royal Air Force (RAF) from 1943 to 1947, ending up in Southeast Asia Command on Dakotas with No. 48 Squadron and then as an airfield controller. He graduated cum laude from Harvard in 1950 and received his PhD there in 1957. He has taught military history at Kansas State University since 1963.

Professor Higham has been the editor of *Military Affairs* (1968–88) and *Aerospace Historian* (1970–88), and remains editor of the *Journal of the West* (1977–). He has published a number of books, including *Britain's Imperial Air Routes; The British Rigid Airship, 1908–1931*; and *Air Power: A Concise History*, and many papers and articles. He is currently researching a book on the RAF and its preparation for war in the period 1933–41.

Dr. Alan Stephens

Dr. Alan Stephens is a senior research fellow at the RAAF's Aerospace Centre. Before joining the center, he was a principal research officer in the Australian Federal Parliament, specializing in foreign affairs and defense; prior to that he was an RAAF pilot, where his postings included the command of No. 2 (Canberra) Squadron in 1980–81.

Dr. Stephens is the author or editor of numerous books and articles on security and airpower. He is currently writing an official history of the RAAF from the end of the Second World War to the withdrawal from Vietnam.

Associate Professor John McCarthy

Associate Professor John McCarthy has been a teaching fellow at the University of New South Wales, resident scholar at the Australian National University, lecturer and senior lecturer in history at the Faculty of Military Studies, and associate professor at the University College, University of New South Wales. His work includes the publication of such books as *Australia and Imperial Defence, 1918–1939; Australian War Strategy, 1939–1945;* and *A Last Call of Empire,* and numerous articles on defense and foreign policy. He was the foundation president of the Association of Historians of Australian Defence and Foreign Policy and is a member of the Australian Institute of International Affairs.

Dr. Vincent Orange

Dr. Vincent Orange was born in England and served for three years in the Royal Air Force. For many years he has been a New Zealand citizen, and since 1962 has taught at the University of Canterbury where he is a reader in history. He is also a member of the Royal Aeronautical Society.

Dr. Orange has written four biographies of New Zealand airmen, including *Sir Keith Park* and *Coningham.* With the cooperation of family members he is currently preparing a book on the life of Tedder.

Professor Richard Overy

Professor Richard Overy is professor of modern history at King's College, London. He moved to King's in 1980 after teaching for some years at Cambridge. He has written extensively on the history of airpower, the Third Reich, and the Second World War. His books include *The Air War, 1939–1945; Goering: The "Iron Man"; The Road to War;* and *War and Economy in the Third Reich.* He is currently completing a history of the Nazi economy and has been commissioned to write the Oxford history of the Second World War.

Dr. Jeffrey Grey

Dr. Jeffrey Grey is a graduate of the Australian National University and the University of New South Wales, and currently is a senior lecturer in the Department of History at the University College, Australian Defence Force Academy. He is the author or editor of half a dozen books, including most recently *Australian Brass: The Career of Lieutenant General Sir*

Horace Robertson and *Vietnam: War, Myth and Memory.* He is an author in the current series of official histories, *Australia's Involvement in Southeast Asian Conflicts, 1948–1975;* he has completed the volume on Konfrontasi and is now engaged in a volume on the Royal Australian Navy.

Dr. Chris D. Coulthard-Clark

Dr. Chris Coulthard-Clark is a former army officer and public servant who is presently working as consultant on a history of Australian Defence Industries Ltd. He received his PhD from University College, Australian Defence Force Academy, in 1991.

Dr. Coulthard-Clark has authored, edited, or contributed to 16 books, mostly in the field of Australian defense studies, and has written numerous journal and newspaper articles. His contribution to air history includes *The Third Brother* and a volume of the official war history series covering the RAAF's involvement in Vietnam. He is also working part-time on a biography of F. H. McNamara, Australia's only Victoria Cross winner in the air from the First World War.

Air Vice-Marshal R. A. Mason

Air Vice-Marshal Tony Mason is the Leverhulme airpower research director of the United Kingdom-based Foundation for International Security. He retired from the RAF in 1989, where his last appointment was air secretary.

Over 20 years he has written several books and many articles on airpower, including *Airpower in the Nuclear Age* with M. J. Armitage, *The Soviet Air Forces* with J. W. R. Taylor, *War in the Third Dimension,* and *Airpower and Technology.* He has recently concluded "Aerospace Security in the Middle East," a study for agencies in Israel and Jordan. His next book, *Airpower in International Security, A Centennial Appraisal,* is being published by Brassey's.

Air Vice-Marshal Mason lectures internationally to military colleges and universities on airpower and is a regular defense analyst for the British Broadcasting Corporation. He is a consultant to the Society of British Aerospace Companies on the European Fighter 2000 program. He is a senior visiting fellow to the Post-Graduate School of International Security Studies at the University of Birmingham and to the Mosher Defense Institute, Texas, and is a senior research fellow at the Conflict Studies Centre, Sandhurst.

Air Marshal R. G. Funnell

Air Marshal Ray Funnell was educated at the Brisbane State High School. He entered the RAAF in January 1953 as a cadet at the RAAF College and graduated as a pilot in December 1956.

His early career was spent mainly in fighter flying and in flying instruction. In midcareer he occupied numerous staff positions in the RAAF, in the central defense staff, and on exchange with the United States Air Force (USAF). Operational commands were held with No. 79 (F) Squadron at Ubon, Thailand, in 1966; and No. 6 Squadron at Amberley from 1972 to 1975 when it converted from the F-4E Phantom to the F-111C.

His appointments at air rank included director General Military Staff, Strategic and International Policy Division, Department of Defence; chief of Air Force Operations and Plans; vice chief of the Defence Force; and chief of the Air Staff.

Air Marshal Funnell retired from the RAAF in October 1992. In January 1994 he was appointed as the first principal of the Australian College of Defence and Strategic Studies.

He is a graduate of the RAAF Staff College, the USAF Air War College, and the Royal College of Defence Studies. He holds a master's degree in political science and a graduate diploma in administration. He has written and spoken extensively on military issues both in Australia and overseas.

Col Dennis M. Drew

Col Dennis M. Drew is professor of military theory, strategy, and doctrine, and associate dean, School of Advanced Airpower Studies, Air University, Maxwell Air Force Base, Alabama.

Colonel Drew retired from the United States Air Force in 1992 after 28 years duty, including war service in Vietnam and Thailand during 1966–67. He was an intercontinental ballistic missile (ICBM) combat crew commander with Strategic Air Command (SAC), and also held several staff appointments at SAC Headquarters. For the last 15 years of his USAF career, Colonel Drew was on the faculty of the Air University, attaining the academic rank of full professor. After retirement from the military he joined the civil service in his present position.

He was the project director and coauthor of Air Force Manual 1-1, *Basic Aerospace Doctrine of the United States Air Force* (1992 edition). Other publications include *The Eagle's Talons: The American Experience at War; Making Strategy: An Introduction to National Security Processes and Problems* (both with Donald Snow); and *Nuclear Winter and National Security: Implications for Future Policy*. His book *Lexington to Desert Storm* has recently been released.

Dr. Benjamin S. Lambeth

Dr. Benjamin S. Lambeth is a senior staff member of the RAND Corporation, with principal interests and background in the Russian military field. He received his doctorate in political science from Harvard University.

His articles on Soviet military doctrine and strategy have appeared in numerous journals and symposium volumes, and he has lectured widely on these subjects. Prior to joining RAND in 1974, Dr. Lambeth served in the Office of National Estimates at the United States Central Intelligence Agency. He is a member of the Council on Foreign Relations and the editorial board of *The Journal of Slavic Military Studies*.

In addition to his work in the Soviet military area, Dr. Lambeth has written extensively on tactical airpower. He is a licensed pilot and has flown over 20 different fighter types with the United States Air Force, the United States Navy, the United States Marine Corps, the Air National Guard, the Canadian Forces, and the Royal Australian Air Force. In December 1989 he became the first American citizen to fly the Soviet MiG-29 fighter and the first Westerner invited to fly a combat aircraft of any type inside Soviet airspace since the end of World War II.

In recent years Dr. Lambeth has been working on an official study of Soviet airpower for the Russian Air Force.

Air Chief Marshal Sir Patrick Hine

Air Chief Marshal Sir Patrick Hine became military adviser to British Aerospace and a director of British Aerospace Defence in January 1992. Prior to his retirement from the RAF in September 1991, he was commander in chief of United Kingdom Air Forces (NATO) and air officer commanding-in-chief of the Royal Air Force's Strike Command.

Sir Patrick joined the RAF as a trainee pilot in 1950 and throughout his career flew fighters—Meteors, Hunters, Lightnings, Phantoms, and Harriers—in addition to three years as an instructor at the Central Flying School. Staff appointments included senior air staff officer at Headquarters Royal Air Force, Germany, and assistant chief of the Air Staff (Policy) in the Ministry of Defence.

Sir Patrick is a liveryman of the Guild of Air Pilots and Air Navigators, a fellow of the Royal Aeronautical Society, and a graduate of the Royal College of Defence Studies.

In 1990–91 he was joint commander of all British forces involved in the Persian Gulf crisis and war, exercising overall command from the war headquarters at High Wycombe but regularly visiting Saudi Arabia throughout.

Gen Charles A. Horner

Gen Charles A. Horner is commander in chief of North American Aerospace Defense Command and the United States Space Command, and commader of Air Force Space Command. He was awarded his pilot wings in 1959 and has since commanded a tactical training wing, a fighter wing, two air divisions, and a numbered air force. A command pilot on F-100, F-105, F-4, F-15, and F-16 aircraft, he flew more than 100 combat missions over North Vietnam. While commander of the Ninth Air Force, General Horner also commanded US Central Command Air Forces, in command of all US and Coalition air assets during Operations Desert Shield and Desert Storm.

Dr. Richard P. Hallion

Dr. Richard Hallion has been historian of the United States Air Force since December 1991. After obtaining a doctorate in the history of aerospace technology at the University of Maryland in 1975, he worked as a curator at the Smithsonian Institution's National Air and Space Museum and, between 1982 and 1990, he held chief historian appointments at Edwards, Wright-Patterson, and Andrews Air Force Bases. He has also been Charles A. Lindbergh professor of aerospace history at the National Air and Space Museum and a visiting professor at the United States Army War College.

Dr. Hallion is the author or editor of 14 books, including *Storm Over Iraq*, *Strike From the Sky: The History of Battlefield Air Attack*, *Test Pilots: The Frontiersmen of Flight*, and *The Wright Brothers: Heirs of Prometheus*. He is also a practicing pilot.

Preface

This book contains the proceedings of a conference held by the Royal Australian Air Force (RAAF) in Canberra in 1994. Since its publication by the RAAF's Air Power Studies Centre in that year, the book has become a widely used reference at universities, military academies, and other educational institutions around the world.

The application of aerospace power has seen significant developments since 1994, most notably through American-led operations in Central Europe and continuing technological advances with weapons, uninhabited vehicles, space-based systems, and information systems. But notwithstanding those developments and the passing of six years, the value of this anthology of airpower in the twentieth century seems undiminished. I am pleased that the RAAF has been able to join with the Air University Press to produce this reprint. Together with the AU Press, I should like to thank my fellow authors for allowing their work to be reprinted.

Alan Stephens
RAAF Aerospace Centre
Canberra
May 2000

Acronyms and Abbreviations

AAA	antiaircraft artillery
AAM	air-to-air missile
AAP	Australian air publication
AAR	air-to-air refueling
ABC³	airborne battlefield command and control center
ACP	air campaign plan
ACTS	Air Corps Tactical School
ADF	Australian Defence Force
Adm	admiral
AFB	air force base (USAF)
AFFE	Army Forces Far East
AIM	air intercept missile
AMC	Air Mobility Command (USAF)
AMRAAM	advanced medium range air-to-air missile
AOC	air officer commanding
APEC	Asia-Pacific Economic Cooperation (forum)
APSC	Air Power Studies Centre
ASEAN	Australia and South East Asian Nations
ASW	antisubmarine warfare
ATACMS	Army tactical missile system
ATO	air tasking order
AWACS	airborne warning and control system
BBC	British Broadcasting Corporation
BDA	bomb damage assessment
Brig	brigadier
C²	command and control
C³	command, control, and communications
C³I	command, control, communications, and intelligence
CAP	combat air patrol
Capt	captain
CINC	commander in chief
CINCFE	commander in chief Far East

CINCUNC	commander in chief United Nations Command
Col	colonel
Comdr	commander
CNN	Cable News Network
CRAF	Civil Reserve Air Fleet
CT	communist terrorist
DRV	Democratic Republic of Vietnam
EAF	Egyptian air force
ECM	electronic countermeasures
ELINT	electronic intelligence
EUSAK	Eighth United States Army in Korea
EW	electronic warfare
FAC	forward air controller
FEAF	Far East Air Forces
FPDA	Five-Power Defense Arrangements
GBU	guided-bomb unit
Gen	general
GHQ	general headquarters
GQG	Grand Quartier General
GPS	Global Positioning System
GWAPS	Gulf War Air Power Survey
HAS	hardened aircraft shelter
HMS	Her Majesty's Ship
IADS	integrated air defense system
IAF	Israeli Air Force
IDF	Israeli Defense Force
INS	inertial navigation system
IR	infrared
JFACC	joint force air component commander
Joint STARS	Joint Surveillance Target Attack Radar System

JSTARS	Joint STARS
km	kilometer
KTO	Kuwait Theater of Operations
lb	pound
LGB	laser-guided bomb
LSL	landing ship, logistics
Lt	lieutenant
MACV	Military Assistance Command, Vietnam (US)
Maj	major
MCP	Malayan Communist Party
MIA	missing in action
MLRS	multiple launch rocket system
MOOTW	military operations other than war
MPAJA	Malayan Peoples Anti-Japanese Army
MRAF	marshal of the Royal Air Force
MRC	major regional contingency
MV	motor vessel
NADACS	National Air Defense and Airspace Control System
NavFE	Naval Forces Far East
NATO	North Atlantic Treaty Organization
NBC	nuclear, biological, and chemical (weapons)
NCO	noncommissioned officer
OCA	offensive counter air
OODA	observation-orientation-decision-action
PAVN	People's Army of Vietnam
PGM	precision-guided munition
PLO	Palestine Liberation Organization
RAA	Royal Australian Army
RAAF	Royal Australian Air Force
RAF	Royal Air Force

RAN	Royal Australian Navy
RFC	Royal Flying Corps
RN	Royal Navy
RNZAF	Royal New Zealand Air Force
ROE	rules of engagement
ROK	Republic of Korea
RTAF	Royal Thai Air Force
RVN	Republic of Vietnam
SAAS	School of Advanced Airpower Studies
SAC	Strategic Air Command (USAF)
SAD	surface-to-air defense
SAM	surface-to-air missile
SAS	Special Air Service
SCAP	supreme commander Allied Powers
SEAD	suppression of enemy air defenses
SHAPE	Supreme Headquarters Allied Powers Europe
SIGINT	signals intelligence
SS	supply ship
TAC	tactical air control
TMD	theater missile defense
UK	United Kingdom
UN	United Nations
UNC	United Nations Command
US	United States
USAAC	United States Army Air Corps
USAAF	United States Army Air Forces
USAF	United States Air Force
USMC	United States Marine Corps
USN	United States Navy
USS	United States Ship
USSPACECOM	United States Space Command
USSR	Union of Soviet Socialist Republics
VSTOL	vertical short takeoff and landing

Airpower in World War I, 1914–1918

Robin Higham

World War I broke out in 1914 only a decade after the Wright Brothers first flew in late 1903. In that short time, gentlemanly experiment had evolved into the aircraft and engine industry with ancillary services. Concurrently, the world's armed forces had begun to take a rather skeptical interest in aircraft, both lighter- and heavier-than-air, for naval and military purposes.

As befitted the nineteenth century legacy of cartels and cross licensing, there were many international linkages between the firms involved, through both commercial contacts and international aviation meetings.[1]

But there were also inherent tensions in this early stage of a technological and military development. Although there were links to the nascent automobile industry, especially in the development of engines, on the whole the aviation industry would continuously go through all the trials and tribulations of a new technology, compounded by venturing into a medium of which very little was known. There was little knowledge of the aerodynamics of control, of the importance of weight, or even of drag and streamlining. This lack often produced disappointing, if not tragic, results and frequently created difficulties between the optimistic advocates and the pessimistic bureaucrats, whose cooperation was so necessary for the success of aviation itself.

Another tension in this new industry, felt especially keenly in relations with the military, was not linked to the secrecy that was just beginning to muffle intelligence, but to the desire of the military to standardize a weapon which was not sufficiently tested for such standardization to be wise.

Capt Murray Sueter, RN, in prewar days the inspecting captain of airships Royal Navy, early on noted that each new design needed to have three prototypes—one for production, one to further develop that model, and one to provide data for the next design. He was quite correct, for outside of the rigid airship field, aircraft could be designed and made operational

1

within six months, meaning that the four years of the First World War would see some eight generations of aircraft design. At the same time, aeronautics, civilian production, and military attrition would grow astronomically and come both to be accepted and to cause noticeable changes in the political, economic, social, and ideological forces of the nations engaged in the conflict, whether in the end victorious or defeated.

In assessing aviation in the 1914 war, it must also be borne in mind that at the start of the war, airpower was virtually impotent, with neither a civilian managerial structure nor an experienced military command. By the end of the war in 1918, a little over four years later, however, airpower had been organized both in its infrastructure and at the front. But it had taken time, and it was only in mid-1917 that airpower had become effective enough to begin to merit respect over land and sea. Airmen started the war burdened with their own and their superiors' preconceptions of the coming conflict. That short-war syndrome deterred planning and preparations, which by 1918 had become so pessimistic as to bound to a long-war concept, seeing maybe the end in 1920.

The 1914–18 war saw the rise of airpower from a fad to a land and sea battlefield force, with the added possibility of becoming a grand-strategic weapon independent of the surface forces, but nevertheless subject to political control.

The Great War in the air exhibited traits and trends that would be evident in the subsequent evolution of this highly technical, consuming, new military arm. It did then, and it continues today, to require very skilled professional management to make it efficient.

* * *

In order to provide a framework for an overview of the aeronautical proficiency of the world military powers, American naval historian of the 1890s, Rear Adm Alfred Thayer Mahan's criteria provide a yardstick against which to measure Russia, Austria-Hungary, Italy, Germany, Great Britain, and France— the air powers of 1914–18.

Though Mahan's *The Influence of Sea Power Upon History, 1660–1783,* was about the technologically well-established

Royal Navy in its mature sailing-warship days, the work is also a resource, as air history falls into the regular patterns of history in general.[2] Mahan's definition of sea power is applicable to the air—the ability to go where you wish, when you wish, and to prevent the enemy from doing likewise. In addition, it may be added that airpower is based upon technology, terrain, thought, training, and tactics.

Mahan's criteria for military success were:

- Geographic position
- Physical conformation
- Extent of territory
- Number of population
- National character
- Character of the government

In terms of their geographic position in relation to possible enemies—the ability to undertake the offensive or remain successfully on the defensive and always maintain security—the following can be said about the powers.

Russia was a vast land mass stretching from the German border to the Pacific, linked only by a thin ribbon of steel.[3] The tsarist empire had recently been humiliated by the Japanese in the war of 1904–05 and faced enemies on three frontiers—German, Japanese, and Austro-Hungarian. The distances, by European standards, were immense and the country was haunted by the memory of 1812. In addition Russia had undeveloped resources. It is generally accepted that while the Industrial Revolution had come to Britain about 1760, it had not reached Russia until 1895, when her newfound French ally began to pump in capital to develop manufacturing. But the extent of the tsarist domains were such that agriculture remained dominant; there was only a small middle class to develop commerce, and it was spread too thin, lacked capital, a vigorous internal communications system, and warm-water ports.

One result of these deficiencies was that Russia had virtually no aircraft industry and little that could be done to develop one. Thus, it relied heavily on imported French air materiel, and although it had a large population scattered about, it was generally not skilled enough for aviation ground crew, and aircrews were limited to the aloof aristocracy, which abhorred commerce. And finally, it was not the autocratic nature of the Russian government that made the country virtually impotent, in spite of the work of Igor Sikorsky in creating 36 long-range heavy bombers, it was that the rulers did not understand the management of war. That led the middle class to revolution in March 1917, only to be overthrown by the Marxist intellectuals in November. Thereafter, Russia dropped into civil war and outside intervention until 1922. If only the Dardanelles could have been opened and Western arms supplied to the available, but unarmed, manpower, Brusilov might have been successful in 1916 in driving the Austro-Hungarians out of the war, with interesting consequences that might sometime be war-gamed.

Austria-Hungary at this time had a constrained geographical position with the distinct possibility of three and possibly four fronts to be defended. Although the mountains surrounding the country in most directions provided both defensive positions and offensive sally ports, Vienna lacked natural resources for war production, especially in the area of aeronautics. Critical to the Dual Monarchy's success in war was a numerous and reliable population. But the empire was divided, not only into the two major semistates of Austria and Hungary with their two separate capitals and administrative centers but also by a potpourri of minorities. Under those circumstances, the management of war required strong and prescient leadership as well as imaginative control of production and of resources. But that was not to be. Vienna not only got very limited production from its few aircraft and engine firms but also found itself increasingly in thrall to Germany for both raw materials and aeronautical supplies in general. As with Russia, the people were not commercially inclined, but were agricultural peasants ruled over by an aloof aristocracy not professionally interested in war. The navy, moreover, was confined to the almost landlocked Adriatic, where its bases were ultimately within range of Italian airplanes, as was Vienna itself. And lastly, the autocratic government was lethargic under Franz Joseph I, who had come to the throne in 1848 and would die in 1916. Thereafter, control began to ebb until the multinational forces took control at the end of the war.

4

Italy at this time had an important geographic asset in the Alps, which allowed an essentially defensive stand until the Austrians and Germans broke through at Caporetto in October–November 1917, after a long series of indecisive battles on the Isonzo. With its flanks protected by the sea and Allied naval power, Italy could turn its attention to activating the air arm as an offensive weapon.[4] For this task it had developed automobile, engine, and shipbuilding industries, as well as a skilled population—who had cheered the early aviators both over Turkish Libya in 1911 and over holiday crowds at home—to man both the front and the infrastructure. Italians liked aviation, and they were fortunate that the many governments of the day supported its development while limiting competition.

Germany had all the territorial disadvantages of Russia, including a two-front threat to its security.[5] But even though its land frontiers were vulnerable, it had little seacoast and few harbors that could be attacked by the great rival across the North Sea or by the lesser one in the Baltic. Moreover, although Germany lacked some desirable resources for war production, it had a strong chemical industry that could and did produce substitutes. In addition it had not only a plentiful, skilled people but also a commercially and industrially minded population who accepted the need for military preparedness in the face of enemies both to the east and the west. And finally, the kaiser's government, although it may not have funded the war sensibly, was very much attuned to the professional conduct of war and to technology. Germany's aeronautical difficulties came eventually from the conservative development of engines and a shortage of manpower, even though it was sophisticated in the evolution of airframes.

Great Britain, of course, was Mahan's ideal. It was situated off the coast of Europe in such a way that it could undertake the offensive easily, yet was well protected from attack by the English Channel and the North Sea. In the security created, Britain was able to develop commerce and industry to dominate the world, in part because its rivals had other distractions and weaknesses. However, the rise in 1870 of a fiercely competitive Germany challenged Britain's commercial and naval supremacy. And the technological revolutions at the turn of the century would enable Germany to strike both under the seas at British commerce and through the air at its industry. Three-dimensional war became a real challenge for the island kingdom.

To meet this challenge, Great Britain had a physical conformation that provided coal and iron, but it lacked petroleum, bauxite for aluminum, and spruce needed for wooden warplane construction. It also lacked the ability to feed itself. Still essentially immune to invasion, though not to fears of such, in addition to ports well served by railways, the British acquisition of land for aerodromes further exacerbated the shortage of sufficient acres upon which to grow food.

The country was densely populated with people who had taken to commerce and industry; however, the 1914–18 war would scrape the bottom of the manpower barrel, force the creation of the Ministry of Health, and require the dilution of skilled labor with unskilled men and women. And that would necessitate rethinking the way in which goods were produced.[6] As the short, victorious war slid into an indefinitely long one, skilled labor had to be recovered from the armed forces, if still alive.

Finally, in Britain, the character of government was favorable to industry, though paradoxically the rulers did not understand its nature. The "amateur gentleman" concept of a people who prided themselves on being able to "muddle through" blinded them to the necessities of applying the principles of war also to the whole of the national economy—concentration and economy of force being especially important. Casual habits of wealth and reluctance to talk about money created inefficiencies and, in the Royal Flying Corps (RFC), lack of training led to high casualties of men and materiel.

The quintessential aeronautical power of the First World War was France.[7] Though a land power with numerous borders, it was only faced with the German enemy and was only vulnerable along the northeastern frontier, essentially from Verdun northwest. Although the French had lost their vast iron and coal resources in Alsace-Lorraine in 1871, this did not seem greatly to handicap the war effort. Coal was imported from Britain, to whom, in turn, the French supplied large numbers of aircraft engines. And although France had a shrinking population and had lost a fair proportion of its 1870 population to Germany, nevertheless, it had adequate skilled manpower, if not enough soldiers and sailors. The French, moreover, were more skilled in industry than the British gave them credit, and their factories turned out more aircraft and engines than anyone else during the war. Not only had they pioneered in aviation, but they were also able to mobilize their automakers, so that there was a concentration of the aviation industry around Paris. Furthermore, the French army air service was dominant, in contrast to Britain where there was a rivalry between the Royal Naval Air Service and the RFC for materiel. This rivalry led to the formation of the Air Ministry early in 1918 and the amalgamation of the rival air arms into the Royal Air Force (RAF) in April. In France, the tensions were between the Grand Quartier General (GQG) at the front and the bureaucrats in Paris, stresses caused in part by the problems of total and continuous war and in part by the very evolutionary nature of airpower.

Judging by Mahan's criteria, the course of the war in the air was preordained on the eastern and Italian fronts by the paucity of aeronautical resources, amongst a number of other factors.

The issue was much less clear on the western front where geographic position was to the advantage of the Allies in that they could tap world resources, notably the United States and Canada. Extent of territory put Germany at the disadvantage of having to fight major wars on two fronts and because it lacked some essential resources and did not have the means to reach beyond its European position for its needs. On the other hand, Germany was prepared for war and to mobilize what it did have to fight efficiently and professionally on interior lines. In terms of population and skills, the opponents were about equal with the most critical matter being the management of manpower, in order to strike a balance between the needs of the fighting fronts and of the infrastructure, especially where skilled labor was concerned.

Although the principles of war were bruited about from time to time before the Great War, they were not written down, at least in Britain, until 1920. At that time, Col J. F .C. Fuller, then an instructor at the Army Staff College at Camberley, gave them as follows:

7

- the principle of the objective
- the principle of the offensive
- the principle of security
- the principle of concentration
- the principle of economy of force
- the principle of movement
- the principle of surprise
- the principle of cooperation

*   *   *

Both sea power and airpower operate in a fluid, three-dimensional medium; both need bases and an infrastructure. However, there are three important differences. First, sea power is constrained by coasts, whereas airpower—technology and diplomacy permitting—can operate over land or sea. Second, naval vessels can stop their engines and remain stationary without consuming fuel. Only airships can do that. Third, naval vessels can enforce a blockade indefinitely by their mere presence if the opponent has no counter weapons. On the other hand, subject to limitations of time, place, and technology, aircraft can appear anywhere, but cannot remain.

Although it had been possible in the past for a sea power to obtain virtually absolute control of the waters, an air power could not completely dominate more than a limited area. In the past, a fleet in being could remain in port and always be a potential threat. The air equivalent was the withdrawal of air forces to airfields beyond the reach of the enemy. In both the cases of sea and airpower the *de facto* realities of the pre-radar First World War were that control was limited. In the case of airpower, control of the air—or air superiority—was only achievable for very limited periods and over small areas. Only after mid-1918 were the Allies so dominant in the air that the German air force was increasingly unable to intervene in the ground battles. Yet even in the vital matter of photographic reconnaissance, German technology and chemistry prevailed, allowing their planes to operate at 24,000 feet, quite above the ceiling of Allied fighters and the pilots manning them.

In a far distant theater such as Palestine, a very few aircraft on either side made a significant difference. The British achievements in 1918, especially, were due to the successful exclusion of Turkish observation aircraft and the use of a combination of armored cars and aircraft to isolate the Turkish headquarters and cause the disintegration of the Turkish front, already weakened by the Arab revolt and the shortage of food.[8]

Not only did the ability to achieve air superiority depend upon the stage of the war and whether by day or by night, but it was also closely linked to the logistics organization, including that of salvage and repair, a topic very largely neglected in the literature.

The air war at sea, which started out being dominated by Zeppelins, saw a battle for air superiority develop over the Heligoland Bight between long-range flying-boats from Britain and German defensive forces, which involved evolution and invention on both sides. By the end of the war, short-range British fighters were being transported to the area and then flown off, while the British Grand Fleet never went to sea without some 150 aircraft of both lighter- and heavier-than-air types, the latter operating from flight decks fitted to a variety of warships. But even this exercise of airpower was hampered by production shortfalls on both sides.

The other use of airpower was in the grand-strategic realm. There the ephemeral nature of airpower was clearly demonstrated in the ping-pong of attack and defense, if on a miniature scale. Zeppelin attacks on Britain began in daylight until forced to shift to night by the rising success of the defenses and the vulnerability of the hydrogen-filled airship as a weapon.[9] The same was to be seen when the giant airplanes came into the picture. On the other hand, neither the French nor the British grand-strategic attacks were physically devastating, nor were they beaten off by the defenses within Germany. Their most notable difficulties were encountered in the few short-range daylight raids conducted by unescorted medium bombers countered by German fighters.[10]

Both sides showed that grand-strategic bombing was possible if conducted at night, especially by aircraft operating independently. But far more significant was the response of those attacked to the psychological threat of feeling naked at home; that would create a legacy that would seriously divert attention from the real lessons of the 1918 tactical use of airpower.

*   *   *

The creation and employment of airpower in the Great War was a matter of management—a form of command, control, and communications.

It required the assessing of needs, the drafting of specifications, planning, and approval, as well as the accumulation of resources and their coordination and direction to obtain the desired end result. In other words, ends had to be matched to means and vice versa, the whole being based upon a reasonable forecast of likely action by both Allies and opponents for the next year, taking into account seasonal patterns, production possibilities, and other variables.

Table 1

Total Aircraft and Engine Production

Ratio of Prototypes to Service Types	
France	264:38
Great Britain	309:73
Germany	610:73
Airframes Produced	
France	52,000
Great Britain	43,000
Germany	48,000
Engines Produced	
France	88,000
Great Britain	41,000 (+16,000 French)
Germany	43,486

Source: John H. Morrow, The Great War in the Air (Washington, D.C.: Smithsonian Institution Press, 1993), 368–71.

Table 2

Aircraft Production and Consumption

Country	Produced	Wasted	Percentage
Austria-Hungary	5,431		
Germany	48,537	27,637	6.9
USA	15,000		
Italy	20,000		
Great Britain	58,144	35,973	61.8
France	67,987	52,640	77.4

Source: Enzo Angelucci, *The Rand McNally Encyclopedia of Military Aircraft* (Chicago: Rand McNally, 1981), 29 (Plate 7). See also figures in John H. Morrow, *The Great War in the Air* (Washington, D.C.: Smithsonian Institution Press, 1993).

Table 3

Losses of Manpower

Country	Air Force Size 1914	Air Force Size 1918	Casualties
Germany		80,000	16,054
France	3,500	90,000	7,259
Great Britain	2,073	291,175	16,623
Italy		94,337	

Source: John H. Morrow, *The Great War in the Air* (Washington, D. C.: Smithsonian Institution Press, 1993), 364–67.

What made this especially difficult in the aviation world was the nascent stage of technology in 1914, the fact that engines were generally behind airframes, the lack of training methods and knowledge of aerodynamics, demands upon manpower and resources, as well as the variable acceptance at the front of aviation itself.

The numbers employed in the industry rose so that by the war's end the French employed 183,000; the British 202,000 of whom 67,100 were women and boys (about 40 percent); and the Germans between 110,000 and 140,000. In contrast, at the time of the Armistice, the French air services had 90,000 officers and men and 11,000 aircraft; the British 291,200 and 22,000; the Germans 80,000 and 9,000; and the Italians 100,000 officers and men. Although these figures were minuscule as compared to the size of the armies, they could make for an interesting comparison in terms of the number of persons behind the men in an air force aircraft, if really reliable figures were available. Roughly it can be said that the French had 8.2 men per aircraft, the Germans 8.9, and the British 13.3 in November 1918.[11]

As the voracious demands from the front for a steady flow of manpower continued, aircraft firms and their protecting bureaucracies had an increasingly difficult time preserving the workforce. And women had always had a place in the manufacture of the wood and fabric aircraft, usually as seamstresses, but also in other work. By the end of the war, their participation had to be increased at both the airframe and the engine manufacturers. By the Armistice, dilution with women and boys in Britain had reached 50 percent of the workforce.

In every country from time to time there were labor disputes brought on in part by the need to raise wages to match inflation, yet opposed by the bureaucracies who did not wish to see prices rise or who were not yet into cost accounting. Craftsmen also objected to piecework rates versus wages. But labor unrest also came to the fore as a skilled craftsman's reaction to the simplification of tasks, which enabled unskilled labor to do the job. The development and use of manufacturing jigs enabled this simplification.

These labor disputes pitted workers against management in an industry that had a close, paternalistic ambience and a management opposed to the bureaucracy. In turn the officials responsible for aviation found themselves confronting both the military and naval ministries and those controlling manpower and materials, as well as having to contend with demands from the war front, from officers unfamiliar with manufacturing and too high in rank to have flown. Most actual flight experience was confined to those under 25 years of age and rarely, as the war progressed, from the select military academies or the aristocratic class.

Weather was also a significant factor in the success of the war; it affected not only flying operations and training but also manufacturing. Although we have no studies of the impact of weather upon operations, which would enable us to make precise statements about the frequency of fog, rain, snow, and high winds, we do know that in the principal area of operations, rainfall varied annually from 26 inches at Paris to 44 inches at Valenciennes on the Belgian border.[12] And in the British Ministry of Munitions, shell consumption or wastage was calculated on summer and winter rates.[13] Although there seems little such correlation in aircraft manufacturing, due to the high wastage rates (66 percent per month of all fighters produced in Britain—meaning that a squadron of 18 consumed 130 airframes every 12 months[14]), weather did affect production in Austria during the very cold winter of 1917–18 when the Germans refused to ship adequate coal to Vienna and the factories were freezing. This affected not only personnel but also gluing of wood and doping of fabrics.

Management of the war was influenced also by the constant tension between the needs for quantity and quality. This directly affected the seesaw battle over the front for air superiority. The standardized aircraft of 1912 with which the powers entered the war were rapidly being overtaken in 1915 by newer models, which could carry armament and were flown by pilots with hours and skills accumulated in an environment that was not yet lethal, except for ground fire and the usual accidents. Increasingly, by 1916 a renewed struggle for air superiority was created with a return to standardization, the greater availability of aircraft and crews, and the offensive-defensive demands for formation flying made possible by units being composed of the same type of aircraft (especially important with rotary-engine machines whose power was either on or off). But the benefits of all this were vitiated by the British. At least partly to blame was the lack of thorough testing of new aircraft types that were being rushed into service; and more importantly, blame could be attributed to the inadequacy of training. Pilots arriving at RFC squadrons had only 15 hours all told. Only those who survived to have some 400 hours had a chance of becoming aces. Unnecessary casualties were caused by the pilots' inability to command and control their aircraft, let alone fire the guns or drop the bombs effectively, and by lack of parachutes.

In all the air services there was the problem of feedback from the very junior officers and NCOs at the front to the procurement agencies, and from them on to the manufacturers. Although the normal flow was through reports, Rolls-Royce sent field representatives out, as they did for their luxury cars, to find out how their engines performed.[15] Various French and German aces went back occasionally to the factories to talk about their needs, and in 1918, the Germans even insisted that Gen Ernst von Hoeppner, the air director, hold a discussion and competition for a new fighter. Both Anthony Fokker and Geoffrey de Havilland were successful because they test flew their own designs.

In all of this the auto industry played an important part either directly as manufacturers or indirectly because so many of those engaged in the aero-engine industry had started in automobile factories or as mechanics and even drivers of racing cars.[16]

The military and naval management of aviation came from a variety of backgrounds and was inhibited by the experience, skepticism, and caution of the high commanders, and rightly so. If officers were only seconded to the air arm for a limited period before the war, it was for their own career protection, especially in regimental armies. Navies having just undergone the development of submarines were less skeptical and more technologically minded. Though in 1909 a spate of articles appeared on the new air arm and its potential, including one by the Italian Giulio Douhet, the military and naval services entered the First World War with very little idea of how aircraft could be used except as scouts. In part this was because they had little experience with reliable equipment and in part because they had not realized how the air gave a different perspective upon surface matters. Kite balloon observers had the advantage of pilots. Trying to jot notes on a knee pad while flying the machine and perhaps also uncertain as to its exact position made reports unreliable. It was not until the development of aerial cameras in 1915 that reconnaissance and observation became more dependable.[17] In fact, a specialization developed between photographic sorties and artillery observation. In part this was necessary as the training required was different and the hazards somewhat more varied. Training of observers was something that the French and Germans took seriously, because reconnaissance was important, making their backseaters professional observers, cameramen, and well-trained gunners.

Once it was realized that aerial observation was much more dangerous than most other forms of aerial activity because such flights tended to be followed by artillery bombardments (or if an attack was pending, because of the vitiation of the element of surprise), fighters were developed to deny that information. And in spite of their limited resources, the Germans at first created larger and larger units until they reached the "circus" of some 60 aircraft. Nevertheless, the German concern was less for absolute air superiority and fighting for the sake of fighting, or a battle of attrition, than it was for the destruction of weaker hostile units. (Thus Richthofen's picking upon stragglers and those obviously new to combat was a sound fighting tactic.) Indeed, the Anglo-German air battles, as well as those Franco-German affairs, also reflected the philosophies of the armies. The British attacked in a war of attrition, which, as on the ground, cost them more casualties than their opponents, especially as they refused to allow the use of parachutes and, with the prevailing wind and German doctrine, combats were often over the German lines. After Verdun, the French realized they could not afford that type of warfare and took a more conservative approach. The British did not learn from the battles above the Somme, also in 1916, and continued to treat air war as a hunting game with the emphasis upon the white feather award for lack of determination. The result was a fatalism and combat fatigue that gave an airman a life expectancy of three weeks.[18] The Royal Navy was more understanding than the RFC, of necessity. Ships spent much time in port and even flying-boat crews were rested because of bad weather and unavailability of boats suffering from being anchored out.

15

The demand for improvements went in different directions in the various countries and services. In Russia, Sikorsky's brilliance was countered by a lack of suitable targets for his Giants and the supreme headquarters' lack of faith. But what was wanted were tactical and strategic aircraft that could operate along and immediately behind the front. All aircraft were scarce imported machines or license-built in Russia. Austria-Hungary had much the same problems, though it could have used grand-strategic bombers against Italian industry in Milan, Turin, and Genoa. Yet design development was hindered by German control of engines and other resources. In Germany itself, improvements in aerodynamics were forced by the failure to develop higher horsepower engines. The result was that the Germans got outstanding results, as in the Fokker D-VII of 1918, using basically a 1914 engine. Strained resources and the desire to standardize for efficiency led to the production of only a limited number of types and a reluctance to sponsor Junkers' all-metal strafing plane, though Gothas and Zeppelins were encouraged for grand-strategic bombing of the British Isles. In Britain, the effort to get quality resulted in too many types being kept in production, but at the same time, in a quest for higher horse-power engines. Thus, while as many as 50-odd types were in production and many manufacturers involved, engine power improved from 120 to 450 horsepower in four years. However, production was circumscribed by disputes between the bureaucrats and manufacturers, and the British were only saved by the importation of several thousand rotary and in-line engines from France. On the whole, the French managed not only to keep many types in production but ultimately to create the world's largest air force of the day, while at the same time supplying the British, and after mid-1917 the Americans, with aeronautical materiel. Thus, French, as well as German, doctrine gradually came to reflect both the front and rear realities of the war. Given French politics, it was as nearly rational a system as could be managed.

All opponents developed some kind of antiaircraft defense, whether it was rifle fire or ack-ack or flak. The Germans appear to have paid the most attention to flak as part of their defensive strategy, while the British failed to learn from their experience in spite of a 1919 postwar survey, reissued in 1933 as SD80.

One area of doctrine that had great postwar influence was in grand strategy, where the argument was for an independent bombing force not under the control of Generalissimo Ferdinand Foch so that deliberate attacks on German industry could be undertaken. The force created under Hugh Trenchard in France did not interpret its mandate that way and spent the majority of its time bombing strategic targets in back of the front lines. The real grand-strategic force being developed to retaliate on Berlin was not yet equipped for operations from the United Kingdom when the war stopped.[19]

* * *

For the air services to be efficient and do their perceived work, they needed both the right equipment and properly trained air and ground crews. Unfortunately for us, very little has been written on the training of other than pilots and almost nothing on the education of fitters, riggers, armorers, and the like.

We do know that the naval services, with their higher interest in technology, their greater resources, and their concern with flying over the sea, paid more attention to these matters than did the armies. The fact that senior officers in their youth had to face the rigors of the sea seems to have contributed to this. Conversely, senior air service officers were almost exclusively transfers from infantry, artillery, engineers, or the transport corps. Important as well to an understanding of how the technical side of the air services developed is a knowledge of the training, experience, and the duties of senior NCOs, the rocks upon which the services were established.

As noted, observers were not navigators over land. In fact, it was not until 1942 that the RAF abolished the observer and replaced him with a trained navigator. The development of maps and techniques suitable for aerial work had to be evolved. Bombsights did not exist at the beginning of the war and were only developed to a crude level by 1918. Wireless had to be modified and lightened for use in the air, and radio-telephony (R/T) was only just becoming available for artillery spotting at the very end of the war. For a long time, gunnery training for both observers and gunners on the one hand and pilots on the other was limited to a few hours, often skeet or target shooting with virtually no air-to-air practice. And not only the development of cameras had to take place to provide accurate maps and intelligence of enemy activities but also the methods and staff to convert photographic evidence into useful information and assessments. Even when that was done, there had to be a proper channel to be certain that the commanders understood its significance. Ultimately, just as all new organizations tend to follow the extant manuals, and just as commanders had artillery and engineer advisers, so they acquired air commandants as well. But the effectiveness of these new commandants depended both upon their own knowledge and prestige and upon the efficiency of the infrastructure that supplied them with the sinews of power—the men and materiels. And into that category fell the maintenance and salvage and repair, or rebuilding, of aircraft and auxiliary equipment, for which large depots were set up behind the lines, especially in France. Probably 40 percent of the aircraft and equipment delivered to squadrons were rebuilds. This became of extra importance in 1918, when tactical aviation came into its own, with consequent high casualties and damage.

* * *

The impact of the theorists on the fighting from 1914 to 1918 was not nearly as great as that which they and their heirs exerted after 1919. While F. W. Lanchester, in his articles and in his 1916 book, *Aircraft in Warfare: The Dawn of the Fourth Arm*, had some impact upon the British leaders, on the whole his vision and knowledge as a practicing engineer outran the current conflict. Douhet's *Command of the Air* began to circulate in 1921, but his work was a polemic written from a very Italian viewpoint. The influential practitioners included Trenchard of the RFC, because of his close association with British commander in chief Earl Haig and because of his extraordinary tenure as chief of the air staff of the RAF—briefly in 1918 and then from 1919 to 1929. Trenchard's disciple was Billy Mitchell, or so he said, because both switched from being supporters of strategic and tactical aviation to proponents of grand-strategic bombing as the solution to the slaughters of the Great War. Like archaeologists, the theorists and their disciples interpolated from a very few incidents and produced a grandiose theory of airpower which remained unmatched by the men and materiel available. The ends far out ran the means.

Whether grand-strategic bombing would have become a success in 1919 remained an unanswered question. But it would have been interesting to history to know how the Germans—the pioneers in grand-strategic bombing—would have reacted if Berlin had been bombed, both then and in terms of postwar aviation development.

What is curious is the duration of the glamorous myth of the Red Baron and his cohorts, the aces of the Great War. They still fly with us in air shows, in advertising, and in "Snoopy versus the Red Baron." In fact, theirs was a brief, hazardous life at the front and frenetic behind it.

*　　*　　*

In conclusion, what can be said of the heritage and lessons of the first great air war?

The warring nations fought the air war as their Mahanian assets indicated that they would. But their natural and manpower resources combined with their technical and professional expertise and the nature of their governments determined their success.

The first difficulty was matching men and weapons and doctrine, always a prime problem in innovation. Close to that was the need to realize that the new weapon was not yet a war-winner, that it had severe limitations, and that air superiority, except in very limited terms, was not possible.

Second, the high command, in a time of revolutionary technological change, faced a daunting challenge. To exercise this managerial responsibility required not so much the ability to use power as the sense to understand the new system, to see its implications for the future, and to work with younger and more skilled officers and bureaucrats—men and clerks as well as women—to apply it.

Third, it was important to comprehend that war requires the simplification of tasks, rapid realistic training, and the application of the principles of war at all levels or at both the front and in the infrastructure. Gen Sir Archibald Wavell put it well in *Generals and Generalship* (1941) when he noted that a commander needs knowledge, the ability to combine arms, and an understanding of humanity. Moreover, Wavell added that the key to success is the thoughtful study of the past, an open mind, and the ability to understand others' difficulties.

Though casualties in the air arms were minute compared to those of the surface forces, especially the infantry, they were from the aristocratic and middle-class governing elite, thus making them part of the postwar "lost generation." Moreover, casualties in the air arms were reduced proportionately in the last two years to 18 months of the war as better aircraft and better training mitigated the earlier risks of being airborne, or almost so. Flying, in other words, ceased to be so hazardous, and thus combat also was reduced somewhat in risk. Formation flying and better discipline as well as more suitable training were also contributory.

The 1914–18 war saw not only the refinement of engines and airframes but also that of the aeronautical organization. In addition, enough examples were made available that tactical, strategic, and grand-strategic activities could be tried in combat. Thus, the Great War really was the prototype of future wars. The much vaunted days of the aces was really an aberration, just as the days of champions had been in medieval and other times, caused by the birthing process in which there was a lack of agreed or dictated doctrine, organization, command experience, and numbers at both the front and the rear.

The very officers who fought the air war as squadron leaders would be the air officers commanding (AOC) of the Second World War. Yet few drew lessons from the First World War, in spite of the slow, somewhat biased, and neglectful help of the official historians. Airmen were so arrogant, or unread, that after the war some insisted that history provided no precedents for their service. The 1918 tactical battles were not to their liking, and thus the airmen eliminated them from their memory. Others were not allowed to be so foolish and as a result developed blitzkrieg and other operations in which tactical and strategic air forces supported the surface arms.

The irony of the war at sea was that after the Armistice the Royal Navy lost the battle to the Royal Air Force and sent its experienced naval aviators to teach the Japanese carrier warfare.

It is all very well to talk about the flexibility of airpower, but the technical and political realities, amongst others, have to be kept in mind in terms of the objective, concentration, economy of force, and other principles of war.

Whether fighting a war of attrition over the front or bombing the infrastructure, the objective must be clear—force concentrated to achieve victory, and at the same time used economically in terms of manpower, materiel, and money.

Airpower in World War I was not unlimited in strength or activities, and it was governed by precedent whether airmen saw this or not.

Studying the 1914–18 war again through glasses tinted with both Mahanian principles and those of war can yet yield useful lessons.[20]

Discussion

Air Marshal Ray Funnell: Thank you very much Professor Higham. As you pointed out, there is still much to be learnt from conflict which occurred 80 years ago. Speaking of airpower theorists and theories, you mentioned F. W. Lanchester and Giulio Douhet, but when you think of the way in which, late in the war, an Independent Air Force was formed with a specific mission which in today's terms would be regarded as strategic, you would think that there must have been a body of thought behind that extremely significant development. What was the thinking behind the Independent Air Force?

Professor Higham: There is some doctrinal material in the archives and a couple of books have been written on the formation of the Independent Air Force. I think part of the answer

21

is that the independent force was created for political reasons. But I think what you also have to take into account is that this was a case where personalities came into play. Trenchard commanded that force, and he saw it basically as a strategic force in the army sense of operating just beyond the front line, but not really a grand-strategic bombing force. Apart from that, I'm not sure if the doctrine is really very clear. There was some idea of attacking enemy towns, but there was French resistance to that because of the fear of retaliation. I think the picture is not very clear at this point.

Professor Richard Overy: I was struck by the contrast you drew between the British, French, and German experiences in the use of fighter aircraft on the front line. It seems to me that much of that difference can be explained by the different relationships with the respective armies, and the fact that France and Germany had a large army tradition whereas Britain was developing a large army for the first time. Would you like to add some comments to that view?

Professor Higham: I think you've got a reasonable case there. The British organization grew almost in an amateur sense as it was expanded rapidly, and inexperienced people suddenly found themselves commanding very large forces. But I think the problem turns more on the fact that the British had done relatively little thinking about fighting a war on the continent. Before the First World War, the British army was very largely for the defense of the empire. You had a few regiments in England, but England relied on the navy. The French and the Germans expected to fight each other. The Germans particularly expected to also have to fight the Russians and so they were very interested in conserving their forces. I think that if you look at German air doctrine, it's very like the German army approach to pillboxes: they built them very strong facing the enemy, but with no back, so that if they were captured they were useless to the enemy.

I think that the Royal Flying Corps—more so than the Royal Naval Air Service—had to grow very rapidly under people who had very little aviation experience. And a number of those people like Trenchard had been in the colonial forces. He'd been in West Africa originally and then applied to go to the Macedonian constabulary, and then suddenly had to apply his thinking to the war in the air. I think you also can't leave out the impact of very high casualty rates. About 50 percent of pilots were lost, so there were very few experienced people who rose to higher ranks. And even those who did, like Keith Park for instance, who was a squadron commander at the age of 26, had very little experience to fall back on. Things were changing all the time.

Dr. Alan Stephens: Another question on Trenchard. You mentioned that British air forces over the western front adopted a highly offensive strategy which was in contrast to the Germans'. It's sometimes been said that Trenchard's approach in the air was simply a reflection of Haig's on the ground, a relentless offensive, and that it was not necessarily derived from an appreciation of the particular demands of air warfare. Could you comment please?

Professor Higham: I think that is true. It was perhaps the approach of a colonial army, which tended to take the view that you went on the offensive all the time regardless of the odds. If you look at colonial wars, they got away with it so often. It's only when they got involved in the Boer War that it became a real problem. I think Trenchard had the idea that you must fight all the time, just as he wouldn't allow parachutes because people might take a white feather and jump over the side. He and Dowding had a row over this in 1918, I believe, when Dowding insisted that people needed more training, which would pay benefits in the long run, but Trenchard couldn't see this. That's why I think we need to go back and look at squadron records and see how much these people flew. Have any of you seen the old Ronald Colman and Errol Flynn movie *Wings*, which was made around about 1928? You think it's appalling, but in fact that's the way it was. On those fighter squadrons, very few people survived the war.

Dr. Iain Spence: You talked about the influence of individuals. There were also institutional influences, such as creating an air force from scratch with a predominance of cavalry officers as opposed to infantry officers. That may have made a difference to the way in which air forces developed. Also, once they had their structures in place, those structures must have influenced the way the air war was fought.

Professor Higham: You have to remember that in the early days officers had to pay for their initial flying training, which meant that only the wealthy became pilots, and that obviously affected the early nature and quality of aviation. But as the war continued more people were recruited directly into the air services, which broadened its base. I'm sure both approaches affected the structure. But the structure of the air forces, I think, evolved in the same way as for any other new organization. People reached into their cupboards and pulled out the manual of organization they were familiar with, that they'd been using in the army or the navy. So you're right, familiar institutional structures were used at first. But they had become terribly diluted by experience by 1918.

Wing Comdr John Benjamin: I wonder if you'd share with us some of the early historical developments of single-role versus multirole aircraft and any of the lessons that might have emerged and any compromises that were made?

Professor Higham: Most of the aircraft that started out in the First World War really were single purpose. They started with reconnaissance and then they had to be armed, and so they gradually split into observation aircraft and fighter aircraft. Up until 1918, they really went on in those separate roles. Then in 1918 there were two developments: the two seaters were converted also into day bombers, and aircraft were converted for ground strafing. But even so I think aircraft remained fairly specialized because strafing aircraft like the Junkers, which was all metal and looked like a small gardening shed flying along, were not capable of mixing it with fighters at high altitude. So I think the specialization went on. The general purpose aircraft came in much more strongly during the financial constriction of the 1920s and 1930s when fewer aircraft were being built and so were required to do many things. When you look at that experience, I think one has to be rather skeptical about general purpose aircraft.

Mr. Peter Skinner: Unless I misinterpreted your remark, you seemed to have said that we in Britain didn't learn a great deal from the First World War. Would you agree that, in fact, it helped us very greatly in the preparation for the Second World War, bearing in mind that it was only 15 years before we started the rearmament program and set up the command structure which led to the success of the Royal Air Force during World War II?

Professor Higham: I think that's only partly true. In 1934 the Royal Air Force had really perfected 1917. It had forgotten 1918. It had biplane fighters that were not much better; they were just a little bit faster than those from the First World War. The heavy bombers weighed about 14,000 pounds with the same design basically as those of 1918. It's not even accurate, I think, to say that the command structure had improved. In 1936 the Air Defence of Great Britain—which provided a single command structure for the defense of the country—was broken up into Bomber Command, Fighter Command, Coastal Command, and Training Command, with Maintenance Command being added in 1938. With the result that Dowding fought the Battle of Britain able to control only Fighter Command. There was discussion in 1936 of creating an air officer commanding-in-chief Royal Air Force to be the field commander because the chief of the air staff was only adviser to the secretary, but it didn't wash. It disappeared, partly I'm told, because the only candidate was Dowding, and Stuffy knew too much to be liked by a number of the air force. So I think my argument holds.

I've just looked at the air exercises from 1933 and 1934, for instance, and they were set up exactly like the First World War. A line was drawn on the map with the enemies on one side and the RAF on the other. A force was to be taken to France, which for the exercise was named Gaul. All the attitudes were strictly from the First World War. There's a lot of continuity of the idea that World War II was simply going to repeat World War I. It was a tremendous shock when suddenly France fell, all of Europe fell, and commanders had to think totally differently.

Dr. Dan Keenan: One of the reasons the Royal Flying Corps had a forward air strategy to fight on the German side of the lines was that the British realized quite early the very great importance of photo-reconnaissance and artillery spotting. And of course those lessons were totally ignored after the First World War. Could you make some comment about the importance of this with regard to the land battle?

Professor Higham: Photo-reconnaissance, aerial reconnaissance, was very important. That was one of the big British contributions. But if they realized photo-reconnaissance was so important, then you have to ask the question, why didn't the British develop fighter aircraft with the ability to get to 24,000 feet to deal with the German reconnaissance aircraft which were at that height? After the First World War the RAF abandoned the idea of trying to fly at those altitudes. If you read the medical histories, one of the reasons why Royal Air Force bomber crews carried two oxygen masks was because they were wearing one and thawing the other in their armpit because somebody decreed in 1920 that nobody would ever fight above 20,000 feet. So medical research stopped on that.

Coming back to your reconnaissance point. The soldiers in the line I think realized the importance of reconnaissance aircraft because they knew it was they who were going to get bombed; they who were going to get shelled. The reconnaissance aircraft directed the artillery. The other reason why the RAF tended to fly over the German side of the lines was simply to do with wind. The wind tended to drift aircraft over the German side of the lines. The Germans had the advantage that not only did they fight over their own side of the lines, but they had parachutes.

Notes

1. As an example, see Robin Higham, *The British Rigid Airship, 1908–1931: A Study in Weapons Policy* (London: G. T. Foulis, 1961).

2. A. T. Mahan, *The Influence of Sea Power Upon History, 1660–1783* (Boston: Houghton Mifflin, 1890); (reprint, New York: Sycamore Press, 1957); and (reprint, New York: Dover Books, 1993).

3. *The Cultural Atlas of Russia* (New York: Time/Life Books, 1992).

4. On early Italian air warfare, see *Revista Aeronautica: I Priori Ciquant' anni dell Aviazione Italiana*, Anno XXXC, 3 Marzo 1959.

5. William Carr, *A History of Germany, 1815–1945* (New York: St. Martin's Press, 1969).

6. A. J. P. Taylor, *The Oxford History of England*, vol. 15, *English History, 1914–1945* (London: Oxford University Press, 1965).

7. Theodore Zeldin, *France 1848–1945*, 2 vols. (London: Oxford University Press, 1973).

8. F. M. Cutlack, *The Australian Flying Corps in the Western and Eastern Theatres of War, 1914–1918* (Canberra: Australian War Memorial, 1923), 8; (republished, St. Lucia: University of Queensland Press, 1984); see also Col A. G. Butler, *The Australian Army Medical Services in the War of 1914–1918*, 3 vols. (Canberra: Australian War Memorial, 1943), 405–24.

9. D. H. Robinson, *The Zeppelin in Combat: A History of the German Naval Airship Division, 1912–1918* (London: G. T. Foulis, 1962); Peter Grosz et al., *The German Giants: The Story of the R-Planes, 1914–1919* (London: Putnam, 1969); and Raymond A. Fredette, *The Sky on Fire: The First Battle of Britain, 1917–1918 and the Birth of the Royal Air Force* (New York: Harcourt Brace Jovanovich, 1976); (reprint, Washington, D.C.: Smithsonian Institution Press, 1991).

10. Malcolm Cooper, *The Birth of Independent Air Power: British Air Policy in the First World War* (London: Allen and Unwin, 1986); Barry D. Powers, *Strategy Without Slide Rule, British Air Strategy, 1914–1939* (London: Croom Helm, 1976); and Alan Morris, *First of the Many: The Story of Independent Force, RAF* (London: Jarrolds, 1968).

11. Manpower and war production figures are not easy to obtain. Even John H. Morrow in *The Great War in the Air: Military Aviation from 1909 to 1921* (Washington, D.C.: Smithsonian Institution Press, 1993), could not produce consistently comparable figures. Christienne, Groehler, and others all have slightly different ones. Charles Christienne et al., *Histoire de l 'Aviation Militaire Francaise* (Paris: Charles Lavauzelle, 1980); and Olaf Grohler, *Geschichte des Luftkriegs 1910 bis 1980* (Berlin: Militaruerlag der DDR, 1981). For dilution in the British airframe and aero engine industry, see *The History of the Ministry of Munitions*, vol. 12, pt. 1 (London: Her Majesty's Stationery Office [HMSO]), 84.

12. *World Atlas of Agriculture*, vol. 1 (Novara, Italy: Instituto Geografies de Agostini, 1969), 116–17.

13. *History of the Ministry of Munitions*, vol. 10, chap. 6, 73.

14. *History of the Ministry of Munitions*, vol. 12, pt. 1, 70; and Enzio Angelucci and Paolo Matricardi, *The Rand McNally Encyclopedia of Military Aircraft, 1914 to the Present* (Chicago: Rand McNally, 1991), 29. Morrow suggests that the Germans wasted or lost 56.9 percent of all aircraft produced, the British 61.8, and the French 77.4 percent.

15. Herschel Smith, *A History of Aircraft Piston Engines*, 3d ed. (Manhattan, Kans.: Sunflower Press, 1986), 31.

16. For instance, see Ian Lloyd, *Rolls-Royce: The Growth of a Firm*, 3 vols. (London: Macmillan, 1978).

17. For a brief history, see Roy M. Stanley II, *World War II Photo Intelligence* (New York: Scribners, 1981); and for a more detailed view, Peter Mead, *The Eye in the Air: A History of Air Observation and Reconnaissance for the Army, 1785–1945* (London: HMSO, 1983).

18. Denis Winter, *The First of the Few: Fighter Pilots of the First World War* (Athens, Ga.: University of Georgia Press, 1983), is an excellent portrait and should be read in conjunction with his view of the infantry in *Death's Men: Soldiers of the Great War* (London: Penguin Books, 1978).

19. On the development of grand strategic ideas, see note 10 above as well as *Makers of Modern Strategy: Military Thought From Machiavelli to Hitler*, ed. E. M. Earle (1941) and *Makers of Modern Strategy: Military Thought From Machiavelli to the Nuclear Age*, ed. by Peter Paret (1986), both (Princeton, N.J.: Princeton University Press); and Robin Higham, *The Military Intellectuals in Britain, 1918–1939* (New Brunswick, N.J.: Rutgers University Press, 1966). Theory must be seen against practice and here Allen R. Millett and Williamson Murray, eds., *Military Effectiveness*, vol. 1, *The First World War* (Boston: Unwin Hyman, 1988), which takes a country-by-country approach, is useful.

20. Very largely neglected, for instance, are studies of the weather, of actual operations and maintenance through squadron and unit operations record books, and aviation medicine within the context of medical knowledge then and now.

The True Believers:
Airpower between the Wars

Alan Stephens

It is the opinion of those most competent to judge that the aeroplane, as a weapon of attack, cannot be too highly estimated.

—Gen Hugh Trenchard, 1916

To conquer command of the air means victory; to be beaten in the air means defeat and acceptance of whatever terms the enemy may be pleased to impose.

—Gen Giulio Douhet, 1921

Air power, both from a military and economic standpoint, will not only dominate the land but the sea as well.

—Gen William Mitchell, 1925

Those are not the words of uncertain men. They are, rather, the words of true believers. During the years between the First and Second World Wars it was the *idea* of airpower, as much as any demonstrated capability, which played a dominant role in international affairs and predisposed statesmen and airmen in the United Kingdom and the United States in particular towards strategic bombing as a potentially war-winning force. More than that, the belief in a rapid "knockout blow" from the air appeared to offer an alternative to the squalid slaughter in the trenches, a perception which, in the peculiar logic of warfare at least, was comparatively humane.

The Classical Theorists

World War I had glamorized air war, a public perception which was enhanced by the exploits of the civilian aviation pioneers in the following years. The period from 1918 to 1939 was one of extraordinary achievement for aviation. Long-distance air travel, which had scarcely existed at the end of the Great

War, became sufficiently commonplace to change international relations irrevocably. A succession of record-breaking flights captured world attention. Hero worship of Charles Lindbergh reached astonishing proportions after he piloted the *Spirit of St Louis* across the Atlantic in May 1927. Amy Johnson was met by a crowd of 50,000 when she arrived at Mascot in June 1930 following her solo flight from England. Almost 60 years after his death, Sir Charles "Smithy" Kingsford-Smith remains an Australian icon, rivalled only by Bradman, Bondi, and Phar Lap. Newspapers and newsreels were filled with popular heroes: pilots like Jimmy Doolittle, Alan Cobham, Bert Hinkler, and Amelia Earhart. Aviation enjoyed a public profile and glamour which exerted a powerful psychological force.

Nor should the military implications of the feats of the aviation pioneers be overlooked. Achievements in long-distance, high-altitude, high-speed, endurance, and instrument flying demonstrated the rapidly improving efficiency and reliability of airframes and engines and their associated systems, developments with obvious military utility.

Popular perceptions of airpower were not based on epic flights alone. The interwar period was also the era of the "classical" theorists, the most important of whom were the Englishman Trenchard, the Italian Douhet, and the American Mitchell. The public profile of the airpower debate should not be underestimated. It is not overstating the case to draw an analogy between the fear of atomic warfare, which existed at the height of the Cold War, and the fear that the specter of aerial bombardment created in Europe in the 1930s. The psychological force of classical airpower theories—regardless of whether they are considered right or wrong—can be gauged by the fact that they remain the subject of intense debate in universities and military colleges.

Many important, complex, and contentious issues were raised by the three major theorists and their contemporaries. There was one, however, which was of overriding moment: the belief that offensive airpower through the form of bomber aircraft would dominate future wars, to the extent that it alone could decide the outcome. That proposition was in direct contradiction to the conventional Clausewitzian wisdom, dominant in strategic thinking for almost one hundred years, that defense was the stronger form of warfare and that an enemy's army was his center of gravity. Now, the imperative would be to take the war directly to the heart of the enemy homeland and population.

By definition, strategic bombing theory challenged the pre-eminence of armies and navies. Based as it was on limited experience, the belief of victory through airpower clearly was going to agitate many people, not least the admirals and generals. That was not a prospect which concerned Trenchard, Douhet, or Mitchell (the latter two were in fact court-martialled by their respective armies for their outspoken views, Douhet in 1916 and Mitchell in 1925).

As chief of staff of the world's first independent air force, Sir Hugh Trenchard dominated the Royal Air Force (RAF) in its formative years. Trenchard's inability to express himself fluently has occasionally been taken as an indication of a mediocre mind; suggestions have been made that his allegedly slender claims to intellectual distinction rested largely on the literary skills of his aide-de-camp, the Cambridge-educated man of letters, Maurice Baring. Nothing could be further from the truth. As Trenchard's biographer has written, "In the scores of official papers which stand out like milestones in the development of the RFC [Royal Flying Corps], the strain of prophecy . . . is Trenchard's, the clear measured prose Baring's."[1]

British airpower developed squarely from the base of Trenchard's vision and practical experience. Under his leadership the essential building blocks were put in place or consolidated: a central flying school to set and maintain standards; research and development establishments for the technological edge; a cadet college at Cranwell to produce the future leaders; a staff college at Andover to give those leaders the finishing touches; and an apprentice scheme to train the mechanics. The Trenchard model has been emulated by effective air forces ever since.

Doctrinally, Trenchard was committed uncompromisingly to the notion of the offensive. That commitment was in part related to his determination to preserve the RAF as a separate service, for it was offensive action, expressed through the relatively untested but already psychologically powerful notion of strategic bombing, which underpinned the RAF's claim to equal and independent status.[2] There was, however, much more to his position than mere parochialism. His directive of 1916, "Future Policy in the Air," written when Trenchard was a general and the RFC was a corps of the British army, remains to this day the classic expression of the intrinsically offensive nature of airpower.[3]

Trenchard's belief in an unremitting offensive did not initially extend to the notion of strategic bombing, but instead applied only to the use of tactical airpower over the battlefield. It was left to others to argue the case for the bomber. In a report on airpower prepared for the British government in mid-1917, the South African soldier and statesman Jan Smuts recognized that strategic air attack might be "the determining factor" in future conflicts.[4] Trenchard's rival for the leadership of the RAF, Sir Frederick Sykes, was another who promoted the idea of making war-winning strategic strikes from the air against vital targets. Three months before the end of World War I, Sykes advised the British War Cabinet that airpower, exercised by an independent force and directed against Germany's munitions industry, submarine force, and moral and political "heart and brain," would be the "most prominent determining factor for peace" at the Allies' disposal.[5] The influential newspaper commentator, Brig P. R. C. Groves, was another whose support for bombers was argued publicly and more coherently for some time before Trenchard took up the cause; while Capt B. H. Liddell Hart's writing was also important.[6]

None of that detracts from Trenchard's status as the preeminent British airpower strategist. It was Trenchard who adapted whatever he needed from the work of others, added his own forceful ideas and unique experience, and then provided the leadership which was necessary to turn beliefs firstly into policy and then into force structure. Trenchard gave the belief in strategic bombing form and official status.

In addition to popularizing the airman's belief in the offense, Trenchard was the driving force behind the novel concept of *substitution*, known also as *air control* and the *air method*. The idea was simple: in many circumstances air forces could be substituted for land or naval forces and do the job effectively at far less cost in terms of casualties and cash. With the support of Winston Churchill as minister for war and air, Trenchard applied the concept in British territories in the Middle East and on the Northwest Frontier throughout the 1920s, using the RAF instead of the army to police vast, remote areas. Basically, errant communities were given a warning, sometimes by notes dropped from the air. If they remained refractory, bombing attacks would be conducted, usually against a high-value target like crops or herds of animals, often at prewarned times. Attacks could be sustained if necessary, in effect "blockading" a village.[7]

Substitution was not always successful, particularly when rugged terrain and/or nomadic peoples made targets difficult to find and attack. However, when geography and demography were favorable, the concept could be highly effective. Iraq, for example, proved to be an ideal location for the innovative application of airpower in 1921 (just as it did 70 years later), when five RAF squadrons without any army forces in support were successfully substituted for 33 imperial battalions, reducing the annual cost of the garrison from £20,000,000 to less than £2,000,000.[8]

Part of the appeal of substitution for airmen was the fact that the concept best suited forces which could be rapidly deployed and change roles, and which placed few friendly lives at risk. In other words, the concept applied far more to the employment of airpower than it did to either sea or land power. Not surprisingly, the "substitution debate," as it came to be known, was perhaps the most contentious issue in British defense policy in the late 1920s and early 1930s, a reaction which did not deter Trenchard and his supporters as they sought to introduce the practice as widely as possible.[9]

Gen Giulio Douhet's book, *The Command of the Air,* was first published in 1921, at the same time as Trenchard was trying to turn ideas into reality in the United Kingdom, and then Wing Comdr Richard Williams was establishing the Royal Australian Air Force (RAAF) against the determined opposition of admirals and generals. Presenting ideas the Italian had been developing and publishing for over a decade, *The*

Command of the Air gave the concept of strategic bombing its most powerful and influential expression.[10] While Douhet couched some of his notions of air warfare specifically in the context of defending Italy against Austria during the First World War, not too much should be made of that setting. Regardless of Douhet's outlook, airpower scholars and practitioners have applied his central themes universally.

Douhet needed no Maurice Baring to translate his vision into compelling prose. His writing is fluent, forceful, and provocative. The question is, though, is it any good?

Douhet's central thesis was unequivocal, and was presented under the portentous heading "The Extreme Consequences": "To conquer command of the air means victory; to be beaten in the air means defeat and acceptance of whatever terms the enemy may be pleased to impose." In Douhet's opinion that was not an assertion but an axiom. From that axiom came two corollaries:

> In order to assure an adequate national defense it is necessary—and sufficient—to be in a position in case of war to conquer the command of the air, [and]

> All that a nation does to assure her own defense should have as its aim procuring for herself those means which, in case of war, are most effective for the conquest of the command of the air.[11]

Douhet accordingly concluded that air forces were destined to become the dominant arm of the military, to the extent that they should gradually be strengthened at the expense of the other services. Airpower had introduced a "new character to war," which emphasized the "advantages of the offensive" and would make for "swift, crushing decisions on the battlefield."

General Douhet took his argument even further in his definition of the *battlefield*. Because of the aircraft's range, speed, relative invulnerability, and unparalleled striking power, and its predicted ability to create fear and panic among the enemy's population, it was logical, he stated, for aerial bombardment to be directed primarily at population centers and the national infrastructure. The destruction of "governing bodies, banks and other public services in a day" would plunge an enemy into "terror and confusion," especially if, as proposed by Douhet, incendiary and chemical weapons were used in addition to high explosives.

A "battleplane" which combined the capabilities of bomber and fighter aircraft and which would ensure control of the air was proposed as the means to those ends.[12] Incidentally, Douhet's idea of the battleplane was one of the first proposals for a general purpose or multirole aircraft, a concept which has been something of an article of faith for airmen ever since and one which, like the belief in strategic bombardment, for many years never quite met the expectations of its advocates.

Staff college libraries are full of analyses of Douhet. Two of the better examinations, those by Edward Warner and David MacIsaac, acknowledge the correctness of several of Douhet's major propositions: Command of the air is vital; the primary targets of strategic air attack should be national institutions and infrastructure rather than armies; and it is preferable to attack an enemy's air forces on the ground rather than in the air.[13] Equally, they identify Douhet's "first and gravest error"; namely, his gross overestimation of the damage a given tonnage of bombs could cause, both physically and psychologically. But as Bernard Brodie has noted, time has rescued Douhet from that particular error through the development of the nuclear bomb.[14] Brodie's observation could be extended to include precision-guided munitions; indeed, in the wake of the 1991 Gulf War, a number of articles and papers appeared from Western military academies with titles like "What Will Douhet Think of Next?" and "Douhet was Right."[15]

The validity of those kinds of reexaminations of Douhet may promote discussion during later presentations in this conference. As far as this paper is concerned, the most intriguing questions are how influential was Douhet's work during the interwar years, and how fair is it to categorize the general concept of strategic bombing as "Douhetism"? Those questions will be addressed once brief comment has been made on the third classical theorist, Gen William "Billy" Mitchell.

The suggestion has been made that if Douhet wrote for the professional military audience, Mitchell addressed his convictions on airpower primarily to the public.[16] Unlike the more scholarly Italian, Mitchell was passionate and outspoken in his beliefs, particularly regarding the independence of air forces. Notwithstanding the difference in temperament, he shared with Douhet an overriding faith in the inevitable dominance of airpower through offensive action. Key factors in that belief were Mitchell's perception of the continually increasing technical superiority of the aircraft over other machines of war and the fragility of civilian morale. In a moment of the first magnitude in the history of combat, Mitchell's First Provisional Air Brigade provided a dramatic demonstration of his theories by sinking the captured German dreadnought *Ostfriesland* with 2,000-lb bombs during trials off Norfolk in 1921. From then on, surface ships operating without air cover had to be considered at risk.

Mitchell had been a combat pilot in World War I, but his projections for the future uses of airpower were, like those of Douhet, excessively speculative. He thus overestimated the extent to which the aircraft would achieve technical dominance and underestimated the capacity of the civilian population and industry to withstand the effects of strategic bombing.

Given the opprobrium area bombing subsequently attracted during World War II, it is noteworthy that, like many other air strategists, Mitchell saw airpower almost as a "civilizing" instrument, writing in 1930 that "[bombardment] is a distinct move for the betterment of civilisation because wars will be decided quickly and not drag on for years. . . . It is a quick way of deciding a war and really more humane."[17]

As mentioned above, one of the most intriguing questions from the period between the wars concerns the influence of the most enduring and important of the airpower theorists, Douhet. The debate is a controversial one.[18] Two of the architects of RAF bombing policy between the wars, Marshals of the Royal Air Force Sir John Slessor and Sir Arthur Harris, stated later in their lives that they had no knowledge of Douhet as they went about formulating that policy, with Slessor adding that as late as 1956 he had not read the Italian's work; while Sir Basil Liddell Hart claimed in his last essay, dated 1970, that Douhet had no influence in Europe generally during the interwar years.[19]

36

There is no reason to question the statement that British air policy in the first instance developed independently from the ideas and experiences of men like F. W. Lanchester, Smuts, Sykes, Groves, Liddell Hart, and Trenchard. *The Command of the Air* did not appear in translation until 1923, by which time ideas on strategic bombing in the RAF were well formulated. However, with due respect to Slessor, Harris, and Liddell Hart, the suggestion that Douhet had no influence at all in the following 15 years seems curious.

Throughout the 1930s, a series of articles on Douhet's work appeared in the preeminent publication for British airpower scholars, the *RAF Quarterly*. These included a four-page summary, titled "The Air Doctrine of General Douhet," in April 1933 and 17 pages of extracts from *The Command of the Air* in April 1936.[20] If Slessor and Harris (and the other officers responsible for RAF policy) were indifferent to their own service's professional journal, exposure to Douhet might still have come from the book, *Air Strategy*, published in London in 1936 by the noted expatriate Russian military scholar Lt Gen Nikolai Golovine.[21] Golovine's work was described in the *RAF Quarterly* as "the most complete treatise on the subject yet to be written . . . a classic on the subject . . . required by all students of air warfare."[22] Throughout *Air Strategy*, Golovine assumes some familiarity on the part of the reader with Douhet's main theses.

As regards to Liddell Hart's comment that Douhet had no influence in Europe generally, plainly that was not true for Italy.[23] Nor was it for Germany. Horst Boog, a prominent historian of the Luftwaffe, has referred to Douhet's "great influence" in the prewar German air force, a conclusion supported by the high regard in which Gen Walther Wever, one of the architects of German airpower, held the Italian's theories.[24] The extensive exposure Douhet was given in Britain through the *RAF Quarterly* has already been noted. Even Australians were familiar with his work. During his preparation for the entrance exam to the RAF Staff College in 1936, the RAAF's Flight Lt (later Air Marshal Sir) Valston Hancock studied Douhet, noting that the Italian's thesis that airpower could win wars had made him "prominent on the international scene."[25] According to Eugene Emme, Douhet's name became virtually a household word in France and England during the Munich crisis of September 1938.[26]

Turning to the United States, Mitchell's familiarity—or otherwise—with Douhet's work was, like Slessor's and Harris's, attended by some mystery. In 1922 the Italian air attaché in Washington, Lt Col A. Guidoni, sent a summary of *The Command of the Air* to the Air Service Headquarters and to the editor of *Aviation* magazine, Lester Gardner, who told Guidoni that he had discussed the summary with an impressed Billy Mitchell. Following a visit to Europe that same year, Mitchell wrote that he had met "more men of exceptional ability in Italy . . . than in any other country," but made no mention of Douhet.[27] It would take 10 years before Mitchell admitted that he had had "frequent discussions" with Douhet during his visit to Italy, although the precise circumstances are not fully clear.[28] Mitchell's best biographer, Alfred Hurley, found no evidence that his subject fully developed his concept of attacking "vital centers" until 1926,[29] that is, after he had had time to reflect on his discussions with Douhet.

Notwithstanding Mitchell's evasiveness on the subject, there is strong evidence of Douhet's influence in the United States. In March 1922 a five-page extract of *The Command of the Air* prepared by the United States War Department Military Intelligence Division was forwarded to the Air Services Plans Division. The Air Service Field Officers' School received a typewritten translation of the first one hundred pages of the book in May 1923.

It was, however, through that remarkable institution, the Air Corps Tactical School, that Douhet's theories primarily found their way into the thinking of American airmen. Established at Langley Field in 1922 before being relocated to Maxwell Field in July 1931, the Air Corps Tactical School was a vibrant, innovative environment, in which the evolving and often competing schools of airpower doctrine—fighter versus bomber, precision attack versus area attack, independence versus integration, escorted versus unescorted bomber fleets, and so on—were argued with a passion.[30] Many of the airmen who were to become the leaders of the United States Army Air

Forces (USAAF) during the Second World War were involved in the debates generated at Langley and Maxwell: men like Claire Chennault, Carl A. Spaatz, Ira C. Eaker, Hoyt S. Vandenberg, Curtis E. LeMay, John P. McConnell, and George C. Kenney.

An English translation of *The Command of the Air* was available at the Air Corps Tactical School in 1923.[31] Extracts of Douhet's work were circulated at the school and amongst members of Congress. In 1933 George Kenney had a summary of Douhet's ideas translated from French into English, and the chief of the Air Corps, Maj Gen Benjamin Foulois, formally endorsed Douhet's theories.[32] Gen Hap Arnold, commander of the United States Army Air Forces during World War II, wrote in his autobiography, "Douhet's theory came out in 1933, and was studied by airmen all over the world."[33] Arnold continued, "As regards strategic bombardment, the doctrines were still Douhet's ideas, modified by our own thinking in regard to pure defense."

According to Claire Chennault—an advocate of fighters and an instructor at the Air Corps Tactical School in the mid-1930s—Douhet's book "became the secret strategic bible of the Air Corps."[34] Courses taught at the school envisaged massed air attacks being driven home against an enemy's vital centers, while land and sea forces were ignored.[35]

Douhet's impact on the United States Army Air Corps (USAAC) should not be emphasized at the expense of immensely significant, original American thinkers. In addition to those already mentioned, two important contributors in the early years were Capt Robert Olds and Lt Kenneth N. Walker. As staff members at the tactical school, they promoted the concept of fast, heavily armed, unescorted bombers making war-winning knockout blows deep into enemy territory.[36] Their concept was rejected by other staff members led by Chennault, who argued that command of the air would only be achieved by the use of fighter aircraft, either defending vital points or escorting bombers. Chennault described the tactical school as a "crucible" of doctrinal debate, in which the dispute over the relative effectiveness of fighters and bombers reached "white-hot intensity."[37]

The Specter of Douhet

At the risk of oversimplification, the main point which statesmen, strategists, and military leaders drew from the air-power theorists was their belief that civilian morale would be fragile and national infrastructures vulnerable in the face of irresistible strikes from the sky, to the extent that offensive airpower would dominate future warfare.

The theorists' faith in offensive airpower was not based on any kind of operational analysis as we understand that science today; indeed, even to ascribe the use of the word *analysis* would be generous. Surveys conducted of the bombing attacks of the First World War were superficial at best.[38] But to leave the issue there would be unfair. Trenchard's famous dictum from 1919 that "the moral effect of bombing stands undoubtedly to the material effect in a proportion of 20 to 1" may have been more the perception of a true believer than the findings of a rigorous analyst, but it was nevertheless a perception arising from substantial, and apparently compelling, observation. The specter of "Terror Bombing" was in the first instance as much the product of popular belief as it was the pronouncements of airmen.

Any reading of the news reports of the bombing attacks against England and Germany during World War I conveys the sheer panic and fear which was created. The raids by Gotha bombers against London in June and July 1917 probably caused more alarm in the United Kingdom than any other event during the war, even though the material damage was slight. Similarly, accounts in German newspapers of the attacks by British bombers against Cologne in May 1918 spoke of the "terrible panic" and "deadly terror," of "nerves ruined for life"; while a captured letter pleaded, "It is really terrible. May God protect us from anything so awful."[39]

Throughout Europe statesmen were haunted by the specter of fleets of marauding bombers, against which it was thought defense would be powerless. The notorious claim that the bomber would always get through came not from an airman but a politician, former British Prime Minister Stanley Baldwin during a speech to the House of Commons in 1932. "I think it well . . . for the man in the street to realise," Baldwin informed

Parliament, "that there is no power on earth that can protect him from bombing, whatever people may tell him. The bomber will always get through."[40] Baldwin's despairing remarks, which envisaged the inconceivable horror of men watching helplessly as their wives and children were slaughtered from the air, were widely reported.

It was because of the perceived disturbing offensive potential of airpower that successive conferences on international law and disarmament considered proposals as extreme as completely banning aerial bombing.[41] The Hague declaration of 21 July 1899 had contained only a single clause relating to air warfare, prohibiting the release of shells and explosives from balloons. Within a decade, annexes to the Second Hague Convention of 1907 explicitly banned the bombing of towns, villages, houses, churches, hospitals, and the like. Momentum continued to gather after the First World War. The Washington Conference of 1921–22 is often recalled only in relation to naval disarmament. In fact its official title was the Conference on the Limitation of Armament, and one of its subcommittees (of which Billy Mitchell was a member) dealt with aircraft. The conference recommended that military objectives should be the only legitimate targets for aerial bombardment.[42]

A commission convened under the auspices of the League of Nations in 1925 to control armaments was urged by the United Kingdom to place severe limits on aerial warfare. British officials promoted measures as extreme as abolishing air bombardment; failing that, they recommended confining the maximum weight of aircraft to three tons. The proposals were never adopted, serving instead only to circumscribe the development of heavy bombers in Britain.

The specter of the Luftwaffe intimidated Europe during the 1930s. Because of the fear of air attack, plans were made for the mass evacuation of cities, the construction of shelters, and the issue of gas masks. In March 1935, Sir John Simon and Anthony Eden went to Berlin to discuss placing limits on air armaments with Hitler, and were told instead that Germany already claimed equality with Britain's first-line air strength and planned soon to match France, a revelation which caused panic in the British cabinet.[43] The RAF told the government to expect 20,000 casualties a day if the Luftwaffe attacked London.[44] During the Munich crisis of 1938, fears of the Luftwaffe's alleged bombing capability saw trenches dug in London parks, while nearly one-third of the population of Paris evacuated the city.[45]

Evidence of the assumed fearful effects of terror bombing was seen in a number of highly publicized attacks on civilians during the wars of the 1930s. The Italian air force flew hundreds of bombardment missions against Ethiopian towns and caravans, as well as military targets, between October 1935 and May 1936, killing many noncombatants. Japanese air forces similarly ranged throughout China during the Sino-Japanese war from 1937 to 1939, bombing major population centers including Beijing, Shanghai, Nanking, Hankow, and Chungking. Perhaps the most infamous attack on civilians came during the Spanish Civil War. The horror bombing of the Basque town of Guernica by the Luftwaffe on 26 April 1937 has achieved enduring international notoriety, partly through the callousness of the attack and partly through Pablo Picasso's painting of the event. Heinkel 111s and Junkers 52s attacked Guernica on market day, repeatedly bombing and strafing a defenseless crowd of about 7,000. It was alleged that some 1,700 were killed and another 900 wounded. The razing of Guernica was publicized by the world press, led by *The Times* in London, as the symbol of barbarity. In movie theaters around the world, people for the first time were able to watch similar air attacks against other Spanish cities.

According to one authority, the "very idea of bombing seemed, especially in the 1930s, to portend barbarism and anarchy."[46] General Arnold has noted how air bombardment came to be perceived as criminal; that in Anglo-Saxon countries in particular a prejudice developed that bombing was somehow, in some undefined way, "less humanitarian" than an attack by artillery shells or naval gunfire. The *idea* of airpower, typified in Stanley Baldwin's bleak prognosis, had become a powerful force.

Yet while horrific, the air attacks in Ethiopia, China, and Spain bore little resemblance to a fully developed version of strategic bombing. Most of the aircraft used were short-range, lightly armed fighter/bombers rather than long-range heavy bombers, and their objectives were tactical rather than strategic. Often there was little opposition: one historian has described airpower's success in those three wars as "victories won in battles that were never fought."[47] Nor were the results an unqualified success which drove populations to abject surrender. On the contrary, there was ample evidence of hardened resolve, of an increased determination to resist, prompting claims that the concept of "terrorism from the air" had been "tried and found wanting."[48]

That was a conclusion based on observation and experience. Notwithstanding that conclusion, the fact remained that most public reactions to the threat of air bombardment were still based on beliefs, and in Europe and the United States, those beliefs were shaped more by images from London in 1917 and Guernica in 1937 than through any rational analysis of ideas and realities.

Precision Is a Relative Term

As the menace of Hitler's Germany became increasingly apparent, thoughts of placing some kind of international prohibition on air striking forces were abandoned. In the United Kingdom in particular, politicians reversed their attitudes and thought instead about acquiring a knockout force of their own.

But the belief that the bomber would always get through was nothing more than that—a belief. An examination of that proposition must focus on the experiences of the Royal Air Force and the USAAC, the only two air arms which seriously tried to develop the doctrine and systems of strategic air attack before World War II.

With his powerful personality, authoritative wartime record, and great stature as the "main creator of the Air Force," Trenchard dominated the airpower debate in the United Kingdom. His prime objective was, simply, to give the RAF maximum offensive power by establishing as many bomber squadrons as possible. Under his influence the government began to channel large amounts of money into bombers, partly at the expense of fighters. It was Trenchard alone who decided that the RAF's fighters should be short range, as they would be employed only for home defense, and that long-range fighters would not be needed to protect bombers. As the RAF's official historians from World War II have noted, this was a decision of fundamental importance to the future development of British airpower.[49] It was also a decision which was opposed by some of Trenchard's staff officers, who believed unescorted day bombers would sustain heavy casualties. Trenchard would not be denied, insisting that the next war would be won by dropping the heaviest possible bomb load on the enemy's homeland to destroy the morale of its inhabitants.

But in applying Trenchard's doctrine the Royal Air Force made dangerous assumptions. If strategic bombing were to be a credible strategy, it followed that the bomber force had to be able to penetrate to its targets and accurately drop enough bombs to inflict worthwhile damage. Implicit in the strategy was a belief in "precision": precision in aircraft performance, aircrew skills, and weapons systems.

The claim to precision was superficially plausible. Aircraft had bombed targets with considerable accuracy in a number of peripheral conflicts during the 1920s and 1930s when operating under favorable conditions. Trials like Billy Mitchell's sinking of the *Ostfriesland*—described by General Arnold as the "beginning of precision bombardment"—had also made a strong impression, again notwithstanding the lack of opposition.[50] Despite those qualified successes, the fact remained that none of the qualities essential for precision bombing was present in sufficient quantity before the outbreak of the Second World War.

Characteristics which aircraft designers and air force leaders might build into their bombers included a mix of high speed, good maneuverability, long range, large weapons payload, high service ceiling, and heavy defensive armor and armament. For much of the 1920s and 1930s, the emphasis in the RAF was on the first two only. A development scheme proposed in 1934 envisaged expanding Bomber Command to 41 squadrons, 22 of which were to be equipped with light bombers, aircraft with performance reasonably equivalent to the fighters of the day, but with limited range and payload. Eventually larger aircraft like the Hampden and the Wellington entered production and, most significantly, design work began on four-engine aircraft. The construction of heavy bombers had not, however, developed sufficiently before the Wehrmacht rolled into Poland in September 1939.

In any case, the equation had changed. During the late 1930s fighters with dramatically improved capabilities had started to enter service. After two decades of fabric and wire biplanes, the emergence of low-wing, all-metal monoplanes, fitted with retractable landing gear, propelled by powerful, reliable engines, and armed with heavy caliber guns, was nothing less than revolutionary. The Supermarine Spitfire Mk I of 1938 flew twice as high and three times as fast, and had four times the armament of the Sopwith Camel F.1 of 1918. It is true that bombers were also improving: the Vickers Wellington Mk IC of 1938 carried a bomb load of 4,500 lbs at a speed of 230 miles per hour, compared to the 2,000-lb bomb load at 90 miles per hour of the Handley Page O/400 from 1918. But the Spitfire was still 120 miles per hour faster than the Wellington, flew 15,000 feet higher, and was immensely more maneuverable. The performance gap had widened dangerously in favor of the fighter.[51]

Improvements in fighter aircraft were complemented by the development of the first effective long-distance control and reporting system, as scientists on both sides of the English Channel produced a revolutionary warning device known as radio detection and ranging apparatus—radar. This was a system which transformed the possibilities of defense against bombers.[52]

That gap in the respective capabilities of the offense and the defense was not recognized in doctrine, as the Air Ministry held fast to its belief that the air weapon was essentially offensive, and that the way to beat the Nazis was for the RAF simply to drop more bombs on Germany than the Luftwaffe could drop on the United Kingdom. Following a series of development schemes and after prolonged debate, the British cabinet finally endorsed a proposal in April 1938 under which the RAF would reach a strength of 1,352 bombers and 608 first-line fighters within two years. Aircraft production favored bombers over fighters by a ratio of 2.3 to 1 between 1936 and 1939.[53]

The proponents of strategic bombing now placed their trust in unproven concepts and tactics: flight at high altitude, tight defensive formations, and the notion of the bomber as a "flying fortress." Untried practices were supplemented by technical innovations such as defensive armor and self-sealing fuel tanks (the latter a tacit admission of a problem if ever there was one).

High-quality navigation and target identification were the second component of the assumption that the bomber could reach and destroy its target. Neither of those precise skills received the attention it demanded. Too much credence was placed on the success of offensive operations in places like Iraq, Somaliland, and the Northwest Frontier, where primitive opponents and undefended targets provided neither any measure of how difficult it might be to attack an industrialized enemy, nor the incentive to address the technical and individual challenges which might arise in less favorable circumstances.[54] Thus, little thought was given to the challenge of how to find and hit targets by day and night in unfavorable weather and over unfamiliar territory. The RAF's 1937 manual of navigation advised that night navigation was to be conducted using the lights of towns. Clearly that was operationally naive. Equally clearly, navigation standards were poor: during a night exercise in 1937, two-thirds of a Bomber Command force was unable to find the fully illuminated city of Birmingham.[55] In the final two years before the war, 478 Bomber Command crews force-landed during exercises in the United Kingdom, having lost their way.[56]

Finally, the aiming systems simply were not good enough. In 1938 the standard system in the RAF was still the Course-Setting-Bomb-Sight which had been introduced during World War I.[57] The best-known system from the 1930s was the American Norden tachometric bombsight, whose manufacturers claimed it could "drop a bomb in a pickle barrel from 25,000 feet," a claim echoed by airmen from the USAAC who first used it in 1935.[58] With clear skies, consistent wind velocities, and no enemy opposition, the Norden was an excellent piece of equipment. However, the challenge was vastly more difficult under less favorable conditions. In northwest Europe, for example, cloud or industrial haze prevailed two days out of every three, and meteorological reports were unreliable.[59] Under those conditions, average bombing accuracies expressed as a circular error probable were more likely to be in the order of three quarters of a mile rather than the circumference of a pickle barrel.[60] Aiming problems were not confined to the Allies. In March 1939 the commander of the Luftwaffe's First Air Fleet, Field Marshal Albert Kesselring, doubted whether his average crew could hit a target with any degree of accuracy at night or in bad weather.[61]

Early performances in World War II justified the concerns of both sides. A statistical investigation into Bomber Command's results completed in August 1941 by Mr. D. M. B. Butt of the War Cabinet Secretariat concluded, among other things, that of those aircraft recorded as having attacked their target, only one in three had in fact been within five miles.[62] Worse still, that wretched statistic related only to those aircraft which claimed to have attacked the target: if all of those which took-off were counted, the figure was reduced by a further one-third. As Max Hastings has concluded, "For all the technology embodied in the bomber aircraft [by the end of the war], its load once released was an astonishingly crude and imprecise weapon."[63]

Why then, was the notion of precision bombing so enthusiastically endorsed, especially in the United States? Four contributing factors can be identified.

In the first instance, there was the pressure to substantiate theories in the face of persistent navy and army hostility. For example, in the early 1930s, the chief of staff of the United States Army, Gen Douglas MacArthur, had aligned himself with pacifists and proponents of disarmament by proposing the abolition of military aviation in the cynical hope of releasing funds for his ground forces.[64] Second, and related to the first factor, the claim to precision countered the accusations raised at the Hague and Washington Conventions that air bombardment was indiscriminate and barbarous. At the least, it implied that aerial bombing was not being directed against civilians; that a conscious attempt was being made to hit something else. The doctrine raised airmen's status and eased moral torment.

Third, intelligence from the Sino-Japanese war had indicated that, contrary to conventional wisdom, Japanese bombing of cities had strengthened rather than weakened the Chinese will to resist, a response also noted in Ethiopia in 1935–36. Strategists in the Air Corps Tactical School accordingly advocated attacks on an enemy's "National Economic Structure"—defined as food distribution, steel production, transportation and, above all, electrical power—which would generate guaranteed, cumulative, and lasting results. Similar target analysis of the German economy was conducted in Britain from 1937 onwards, with the objective of identifying the most vulnerable points.[65] Without precision, the strategy of striking at discrete vital centers could not work.[66]

Finally and most significantly, the objective of airmen on both sides of the Atlantic was to attain organizational and intellectual independence. Precision bombing was the doctrine which gave that objective military validity.[67]

In short, the concept of precision existed because it had to.

Air Forces and Wars

The approaching war with Germany was preceded in the mid-to-late 1930s by several limited but intense conflicts in which airpower was used extensively. Accepting that each of those conflicts was different, valuable general conclusions could nevertheless be drawn. Brief mention should also be made of other air arms whose development between 1918 and 1939 provided useful lessons.

The Spanish Civil War from July 1936 to April 1939 was the first occasion since 1918 in which the main protagonists fielded air forces of a reasonably comparable size and technical proficiency.[68] Franco's Nationalists were supported by air units from Germany and Italy, and the Republicans by the Soviet Union; while the Spaniards themselves both developed significant capabilities. The fighting therefore offered an opportunity to test some of the conceptual and technical developments of the past two decades.

Most of the airpower roles which were subsequently to be used in World War II, and many which had been evident during World War I, were employed, including airlift, reconnaissance, counterair, strategic bombing, and close air support. While all roles were significant, most attention was directed towards the last three.

A doctrine for strategic bombing quickly emerged. Within a month of the outbreak of fighting, the chief of the Nationalist air forces, Gen Alfredo Kindelan, had issued a directive on the employment of offensive airpower. Kindelan instructed his commanders to select targets which were at least 30 kilometers behind the front line, and which were of strategic importance, such as bridges, airfields, railways, factories, and munitions works. Later he specifically identified the gasoline depots in the Republican-held cities of Valencia and Barcelona as priority targets. Repeated attacks were called for, as was the systematic bombardment of key railway lines.

Kindelan appreciated from the outset that his objective would be placed at risk without control of the air. As early as September 1936, Nationalist strike aircraft were targeting the Republican's air defenses through attacks on fighter aircraft, fuel supplies, and airfields, as local air superiority was sought for specific operations.[69] General Kindelan also insisted that whenever enemy fighters were expected, his bombers were to have their own fighter escort, a practice which was to be at odds with the thinking of the RAF and the USAAF in the early years of World War II.

Other nations were learning important lessons. Luftwaffe commanders in Spain noted that while fast bombers were able to survive fighter attacks, slower machines, regardless of how well armed they might be, were a dubious proposition. Coincidentally, at the same time on the other side of the world, Japanese airmen were learning a similar lesson. Japanese naval air force crews on long-range strikes against China discovered with "devastating thoroughness" that unprotected bombers were no match for enemy fighters; conversely, they discovered that escorted bomber groups were far more likely to reach and return from their targets.[70]

Returning to Spain, the claim by Gen Karl Drum that the Luftwaffe's experience in northern Spain in 1937 was "the birthday of the principle of tactical employment of air forces within the framework of ground operations" has correctly been described as an overstatement;[71] on the other hand, another of Drum's claims that close air support provided "the most important and significant result of the German involvement in Spain" was closer to the mark, as evidenced by blitzkrieg two years later. Soviet airmen fighting for the other side drew the same conclusion. Red Army generals had come to appreciate the value of ground attack during the Russo-Polish War of 1920. Their positive experience in Spain strengthened their predilection to use air forces as tactical rather than strategic weapons.

A thoughtful analysis of the Spanish conflict was published in England by the French engineer, C. Rougeron, on the eve of the Second World War.[72] Rougeron noted that the extensive and effective use of the Nationalist air arm to attack ground forces was largely dependent on first establishing air superiority. As far as aircraft performance was concerned, he categorically dismissed the concept of the general purpose machine, arguing that in air combat, specialized performance was everything, with success depending on an aircraft's speed, ceiling, armament, and range. Finally, and in contradiction to much of the prevailing wisdom, Rougeron observed that the effect of air attacks on the morale of the population was "less than sometimes supposed."

Spain was an invaluable testing ground for the Luftwaffe. The Treaty of Versailles, which came into effect in January 1920, had prohibited Germany from possessing military aircraft (as well as submarines and tanks). German initiative had, however, countered one treaty with another. In 1922 the pariah states Russia and Germany had concluded the Treaty of Rapallo, ostensibly a trade and diplomatic agreement. Under the umbrella of that treaty, the Germans established secret military flying units in the Soviet Union. Germany's military leaders also made shrewd use of civil aviation. During the 1920s German airlines flew further with more passengers than their commercial competitors in France, Great Britain, and Italy combined.[73] Valuable long-distance and instrument flying skills—both of which are crucial for strategic bomber crews—were developed.

Public demands for a military air arm grew during the 1920s as Germans recovered and regrouped, with one such notable call coming from the floor of the Reichstag in 1929 from the newly elected Nazi Party representative, World War I fighter ace Hermann Goering. By the time Hitler formally denounced the Versailles Treaty in 1935, Goering—now the air minister and commander in chief—was able officially to reveal the existence of an independent Luftwaffe of 48 operational squadrons.

Two men who played a major role in shaping the Luftwaffe were the first chief of staff, Walther Wever, and his successor, Albert Kesselring. Some significance is often attached to the fact that Wever was an admirer of Douhet, the inference being that had Wever not died in an aircraft accident in 1936, Germany might have progressed further towards developing a genuine heavy bomber force. Like Douhet, Wever believed that the objective of any war was to destroy the morale of the enemy and that the bomber was the decisive weapon of air warfare, an outlook which made him a strong supporter of the proposed long-range, four-engine *Uralbomber*.[74] Nevertheless, it would be a mistake to categorize Wever's thinking on air strategy as doctrinaire. On the contrary, his outlook was broad and, as might be expected of a former member of the general staff, he believed that the air force's fundamental responsibility was to complement the other services in the prosecution of the overall strategy.[75]

General Wever was killed in June 1936 when a Heinkel 70 he was piloting crashed shortly after takeoff, reportedly because the flight control locks had not been removed. His death was a major blow for the Luftwaffe. While his successors were highly capable men, they perhaps lacked his commitment to the full development of airpower, being soldiers first and airmen second. Under the pressure of competition for insufficient resources, the Luftwaffe's leaders gambled on initially building a tactical air force, hoping to add a strategic heavy bomber force in the late 1930s or early 1940s. However, Germany simply did not have the labor, capital, raw materials, and productive capacity available when the time came, as other arms were given priority.[76]

At least German airpower was unified. Japan entered the Second World War with two separate air forces, which had been created, developed, and maintained to meet the separate needs of the army and navy. The functions of each air arm reflected its origins, with the Japanese army air force being committed to ground support; and the naval air force to surface fleet and convoy protection, coastal defense, and sea and antisubmarine patrols.[77] Both forces profited in their formative years from the generous assistance of countries which were to be their enemies in World War II. A French aviation mission was sent to help the development of the Japanese army air force in 1919; similarly, Japanese naval aviation owed a good deal to the expert training provided by France, the United States, and Britain. Herbert Smith, chief designer for the Sopwith Company, went to Japan in 1923 and passed on his invaluable expertise, while an RAF mission to Japan in 1930 provided instruction in air fighting tactics and gunnery, advice that was to prove particularly helpful against Commonwealth forces over Malaya and Singapore 11 years later.

Several years of fighting in China in the late 1930s meant that Japanese air forces, like much of the Luftwaffe but unlike the Allies, entered World War II as combat veterans. In addition to fulfilling their primary role of support for surface forces, Japanese aircrews had carried out long-distance transoceanic bombing raids, sometimes in extremely poor weather, from bases in Japan and Formosa against targets in and around Shanghai, Nanking, and Hanchow. The return distance of about 1,250 miles was by far the longest flown by any bombers from any country.[78]

Given the number of Western advisers who served in China and Japan between the wars (including an RAAF officer, Wing Comdr Garnet Malley, who was air adviser to Chiang Kai-shek in the late 1930s), there was no excuse for the disgraceful ignorance in some quarters regarding the capabilities of Japan's air forces. Technical information on the Zero was available to Western intelligence sources before the war; while Brig Gen H. H. Arnold had described Japan in 1937 as a "first rate air power."[79] Yet in the weeks prior to the attacks on Pearl Harbor, the Philippines, and Malaya, RAAF Hudson crews were told their aircraft were faster than any Japanese fighter and that the Orientals were inferior airmen.[80] Little wonder, then, that RAF and RAAF pilots were devastated by the "shock of the Zero" in 1941. The dismissive attitude of some senior Allied airmen towards the Japanese can perhaps only be explained in terms of racism.

The ridiculously titled Workers and Peasants Air Fleet, later renamed the Red Air Force, was established by Lenin after the 1917 revolution. Like the Luftwaffe, the Red Air Force found its development largely determined by the demands of a dominant army. A modest strategic bombing capability was acquired, but Soviet airpower existed primarily to support land forces. It excelled in that role, Joseph Stalin describing, for example, the remarkable Ilyushin Il-2 Sturmovik ground attack aircraft as being "as essential to the Red Army as air and bread."[81]

Given the constraints of time and space, little comment can be offered here on the two remaining major air forces of the interwar period, those of France and Italy. In any case, like the other armed forces of those countries, while ostensibly impressive in 1939, neither air arm played a particularly noteworthy role during the Second World War. The French air force possessed a large number of aircraft, but many were of dubious quality. Further, not only was it structured primarily to provide tactical support for ground forces, but also it was gripped by what one writer has called a combination of "parsimony, lethargy, and senility."[82] Douhet's countrymen in the *Reggia Aeronautica* had used the war against Ethiopia to test the concept of bombing civilian populations into submission, and had found that in those circumstances at least, it had not worked. They enjoyed more success when offensive airpower was applied against land forces in transit or over the battlefield, particularly when combined with a ground assault.[83]

The development of airpower was not confined to land-based platforms. Following the appearance of converted aircraft carriers during World War I, warships which for several centuries had been the centerpiece of global military power were now exposed far more to a potential enemy's striking forces. Admirals found themselves having to confront the distasteful question of whether or not a flimsy, relatively lightly armed aircraft could find and sink a battleship. Answers varied. Construction of purpose-built aircraft carriers began in the

United Kingdom in 1918. The United States's first specialized carrier, the USS *Langley*, was launched within a year of Billy Mitchell's sinking of the *Ostfriesland*. After trials in the North Sea in 1934, a Royal Navy report concluded that "aeroplanes are certain to find and locate a hostile fleet [and] would probably inflict heavy losses."[84] In general, though, the Royal Navy believed reconnaissance was the most valuable role for airpower at sea.[85] Britain's First Sea Lord suggested in 1936 that offensive air operations would be made unacceptably dangerous by intense shipborne antiaircraft fire. Vice-Adm Sir Tom Phillips, commander in chief of the British Eastern Fleet at the end of 1941, was contemptuous of the danger posed to battleships from the air (an attitude which regrettably contributed to the loss of *Prince of Wales* and *Repulse* under his flag off Malaya).[86] Consequently, Britain entered World War II with inferior naval aircraft and insufficient naval pilots.[87]

A more thoughtful appreciation was evident in Japan, which was at the forefront of countries committed to seaborne attack aircraft. Once again, the development of Japanese airpower was abetted by the Allies, although this time less deliberately so. The main discussion at the Washington Conference of 1921–22 had centered around the size and number of battleships various countries would be allowed.[88] British delegates, believing that capital ships were still the decisive factor in maritime operations, suggested to Japan and the United States that they should each convert two of their uncompleted battle cruisers into fast carriers. By endorsing the proposal, Japan not only complied with the demands of the conference but also satisfied its military objective of increasing fleet striking power. Carriers became central to Japan's Pacific strategy,[89] to the extent that all officers who aspired to flag rank had either to have qualified as an aviator or commanded a seaplane tender.[90]

Conclusion

Airpower played an important but by no means decisive role in a number of conflicts around the world during the interwar years, primarily in support of land operations. At the same time, the specter of strategic air bombardment against which defense would be futile and which would reduce nations in days, haunted statesmen and helped shape the course of international relations. Yet while the air weapon's potential was clear enough, the fact remained that its most potent expression— strategic attack against an enemy's vital centers—remained unproven. It was the *idea* of airpower—an idea sustained primarily by public perception and the advocacy of theorists— which was so compelling.

The relationship between theory and practice is delicate, and commentators enjoying the benefit of hindsight should think carefully before criticizing visionaries. That caution notwithstanding, in this instance, the relationship was out of balance. Twenty years after the end of World War II, the distinguished historian Noble Frankland suggested that people have perhaps preferred to "feel rather than know" about strategic bombing.[91] Dr. Frankland's observation could well be extended to attitudes about airpower in general during the period between the wars, when the doctrines which were developed for its employment owed too little to rigorous analysis and too much to the true believers.

Discussion

Air Vice-Marshal Tony Mason: Could I first of all thank Alan very much for that quite superb presentation and analysis? I'd also like to thank him for the credit he gave to Sir Hugh Trenchard, and it's on that, if I may, I would like to add a couple of comments.

There is still a tremendous need for a new biography of Trenchard because a lot of questions remain to be answered; a lot of papers still require comprehensive analysis. For example, when Trenchard took over the Independent Bomber Force within the new Royal Air Force in June of 1918, he kept meticulous personal diaries at headquarters in addition to his normal diary; he kept comprehensive squadron records of bombing sorties, of weather cancellations, and of overall achievements. And he notified the then minister of air, Weir, and his chief of air staff, Sykes, of those papers. Sykes suppressed them. When Sykes wrote his autobiography in 1941 titled *From Many Angles*, he omitted completely the highly critical period of July 1918 when Trenchard sent him several papers, all of them explaining quite clearly and fully why the expectations for the independent force were unrealistic. When the Independent Bomber Force was wrapped up, Trenchard wrote in his diary words to the effect, "Thank God that's finished, never was so much time and effort wasted in warfare with so little purpose." For reasons best known to himself, Boyle, his biographer, did not use that quotation. Sometime between November 1918 and 1922, Trenchard became a convert to strategic bombardment. I don't know the reason why, and I'd be very pleased to hear if anybody does.

I'd just like to mention one more thing. Simply because something was written in the *RAF Quarterly*, it doesn't necessarily mean that an air marshal has read it.

Professor Richard Overy: I thought you were rather hard on the French. You dismissed the French air force as reactionary and conservative. But French air historians have done a great deal of work in the last 10 years looking at the way in which they thought about airpower between the wars. What I think French airmen did was to produce a concept of airpower entirely different from that of the Anglo-Saxons. Their view was very much that bombing was likely to be a diversion of strategic effort and that bombing would involve a great deal of fighting to and from the target. They were perfectly right, of course, as the Second World War showed. In their view, if you were going to use bomber aircraft at all, they were best used in conjunction with ground forces to produce a kind of rolling power which combined tanks, infantry, and aircraft moving forward to attack enemy formations and supplies. They considered that would be a strategic use of airpower. In the 1930s they wrote a number of sophisticated operational studies about how you developed that battlefield aviation, and they spent a great deal of time exploring the whole question of what role might heavy bombers have in a future campaign. It was an honest difference of opinion that they arrived at, I think, not mere conservatism. So I think one ought to rescue the reputation of French theorists a bit from the characterization that Anglo-Saxons normally give them.

Dr. Stephens: Thank you. Those certainly were sophisticated theories. But I wonder if it wasn't the classic case of a disconnect between theory and practice. For example, when the French air force reorganized in 1931, Marshal Petain was appointed inspector-general of aerial defense, a position he held for the next three years. Petain was aged well over 70, was an advocate of defensive strategies and, I think, had no significant firsthand flying experience. His appointment seems to me indicative of a highly reactionary organization. Theories notwithstanding, little money was spent on the French air force, which at the outbreak of World War II was seriously obsolescent.

Group Capt Andrew Vallance: You said that the advocacy of the theorists had a remarkable prominence in the interwar years. Undoubtedly that was so, they were influential to an extent which I doubt theorists have been before or since. The question is, why was the ground so fertile for these theories to take root? Linked to that, you mentioned the reluctance to accept Douhet's dominant influence in the theories and doctrines of strategic bombing. In particular you mentioned that Harris and Slessor denied all knowledge of his work. In truth, it seems to me, that they must have known. Similarly with Mitchell, it's often said that there were two Mitchells; the early one who was from the "anything that flies" school of airpower, and the later one who was essentially a Douhetist. Here again there seems to be a reluctance to acknowledge Douhet. Do you think this was some form of racial prejudice or professional jealousy?

Dr. Stephens: I tried to stress in my paper the remarkable psychological power the notion of air bombardment developed between the wars. The Gotha raids against London in June and July 1917 created an extraordinary reaction in the UK; there were the continual disarmament conferences focusing world attention on the perceived horrors of bombing; and there were highly visible events like Guernica. There was a widespread belief that Stanley Baldwin was correct. I think that's the main reason why the theorists enjoyed such a high public profile.

The related question of why Douhet was denied by men who were his contemporaries is a fascinating one. I appreciate Tony Mason's comment that the fact something appears in a journal doesn't mean everyone's read it. But as far as Slessor is concerned, he's such a fine scholar that frankly I find it very hard to believe that he of all people wouldn't have been reading his service's preeminent professional publication. Liddell Hart's book from 1925, *Paris: or the Future of War*, is, in my opinion, somewhat overexcited speculation on the possibilities of air bombardment; as it happens, not unlike Douhet's overstated theories. So perhaps there was some professional rivalry and some cultural imperialism at work.

I should add that while I believe Douhet's prominence should be acknowledged, I'm no apologist for him. I think much of his work is facile, but he had two or three very powerful ideas and he expressed them very powerfully.

Mr. Carlo Kopp: Perhaps people have not been judging Douhet fairly, as one of the basic elements of his strategic bombardment doctrine was the use of chemical weapons. I think if we look at his doctrine in the context of large-scale bombing raids involving both conventional and chemical weapons, his work gains more impact.

Dr. Stephens: I'm skeptical about much of Douhet's so-called analysis. For example, he made some attempt to analyze Austrian bombing attacks against Italian towns during World War I, which gives his work a veneer of being scientific. But it's no more than a veneer. His use of such unrealistic tools as a "unit of bombardment" and a "unit of combat" really is rather facile stuff, as is his casual approach to in-flight tactics.

I think Douhet's value—and it's a legitimate and significant value—lies in the fact that he identified and articulated a very powerful concept, and he expressed it publicly and most forcefully. In that respect I would liken him to Karl Marx, who also presented two or three very powerful ideas to great effect. Marx, however, then padded those ideas out with 50 or so very large volumes of turgid nonsense. Happily for those of us who read airpower, Douhet's main work can be presented in one manageable volume. It's well-written, confident, and compelling reading. I would describe Douhet as an immensely important visionary and polemicist.

Air Marshal David Evans: You have very eloquently told us about the RAF's and Trenchard's commitment to the offensive use of air, and one might think that commitment permeated the whole Royal Air Force between the wars—it was a bomber air force. Yet during those years the Royal Air Force developed a highly efficient fighter force. Air Staff requirements for an eight-gun fighter, radar, and a good command and control system were developed. By contrast, the raison d'etre they saw for themselves was not developed. Where were the Air Staff requirements for a decent bombsight or better aircraft than the Fairey Battle?

Dr. Stephens: For much of the period between the wars the Royal Air Force struggled along like the other services on extremely low budgets. Further, in Britain in particular, the series of international conferences on peace and disarmament greatly circumscribed the development of an effective bomber force. And finally, a lot of the thinking simply didn't go past the most cursory acceptance of the doctrine that the offensive was the way to win wars. I think the Royal Air Force was extremely lucky that it had a number of dedicated and highly perceptive people who insisted on developing the air defense system.

Professor Robin Higham: I'd like to make a comment and then add a question. I think one of the reasons the airpower people had so much influence during the interwar years was that so many of those who had fought in World War I did not want to see that kind of war again. My father was an infantry officer in the First World War and was in the reserves right up to 1939. I remember in the 1930s he was afraid he would have to go back to the trenches again. Airpower was a nice solution to avoiding another trench war. I think also as Alan said earlier, airpower had a tremendous glamour like show business, which attracted attention.

The question I wanted to ask was, could you say a little more about the Soviet air force, which was the world's largest in 1934?

Dr. Stephens: Thank you for the comment on trench warfare, I agree that was an important factor.

I touched very briefly on the Soviet air force. In its early years the Red Air Force developed a strategic bombing capability. But it was essentially structured to support surface forces, an almost inevitable outcome given the size and dominance of the Red Army. That predisposition was strengthened by the experiences of the Russo-Polish War of 1920 and the Spanish Civil War. When you look at Russian geography—large shared borders which are easily crossed—and the fact that they've been invaded over the centuries, it's hard to dispute the argument that their priority should be with the army. But the air force was a vital component of land operations; for example, as you know, during World War II about 35,000 copies were built of the remarkable Il-2 Sturmovik, a ground attack aircraft described by Joseph Stalin as being essential to the Red Army as bread and as air.

Professor James Mowbray: You said that Douhet was known at the Air Corps Tactical School in 1923, do you possibly remember your source? I'll tell you why. I've talked with an officer who was there in 1931, now deceased, and I've looked at a lot of the records and have not found hard evidence that before Kenney's translation they had any great knowledge at all. Where did you get the 1923 information from?

Dr. Stephens: The main sources are Raymond Flugel's PhD thesis from the University of Oklahoma in 1965, and Kohn and Harahan's introduction to the USAF edition of *The Command of the Air.*

I should emphasize that I'm not disputing that a great deal of original thinking was done at the tactical school, and you'll find more details on that in the published version of my paper, which I simply didn't have time to cover in the oral presentation. What I would suggest though is that the thinking they were doing at the tactical school was strongly influenced by Billy Mitchell, especially after 1926 when Mitchell left the Air Service, and as Andy Vallance mentioned several minutes ago, there seems to have been "two" Billy Mitchells. The evidence suggests to me that the post-1926 Mitchell was strongly influenced by his meetings, discussions, and reading of Douhet.

Air Vice-Marshal Peter Squire: You've talked about the motivation of the theorists for propounding the independent use of airpower and the bomber force, and we've also heard that Trenchard himself changed his position on strategic bombing. Also I was very interested to hear what the French air force was thinking. Is not perhaps part of the motivation for advocating the bomber force so strongly a means of justifying an independent air force as opposed to it continuing as either a Royal Flying Corps or Royal Naval Air Service? And as a slightly cynical approach, in this day and age, Lord Trenchard as a 39-year-old passed-over major might well have been a prime candidate for redundancy.

Dr. Stephens: Part of the rationale for combining the RFC and the RNAS to become the RAF was to achieve economies by not duplicating effort. But yes, I'm sure that the support for strategic bombing was based in part on the fact that it alone justified the existence of a single, equal, independent air force. I would think, though, that there was a stronger element of conviction and objectivity in the theorists' beliefs.

Air Vice-Marshal Tony Mason: Excuse me for speaking twice, but I must elaborate on one comment. I personally interviewed John Slessor and Arthur Harris before they died, several hours with each man, and I pushed very hard on the subject of Douhet. Both were adamant: Slessor had heard of the work of Douhet, but he assured me he had never read any of it, or extracts from it. And Arthur Harris assured me, as only Arthur Harris could when a junior officer tried to push him on a subject, that he had certainly neither heard of nor read Douhet, and furthermore stated, "We didn't need him."

Dr. Stephens: As I stated in my presentation, there's no doubt that British bombing policy was developed independently within the RAF. The point I was making, which I think is important, related to Douhet's influence subsequently. I have the highest regard for Slessor. He's been one of the most important writers on airpower. Nevertheless, given the extent of the debate on Douhet's theories during the 1920s and 1930s in Europe, the United States and, indeed, in the professional journal of Slessor's own service, if Slessor had not read even an extract from Douhet, then his [Slessor's] standing as a scholar would be diminished.

Notes

1. Andrew Boyle, *Trenchard* (London: Collins, 1962), 146.

2. Sir Charles Webster and Noble Frankland, *The Strategic Air Offensive Against Germany 1939–1945*, vol. 1 (London: Her Majesty's Stationery Office [HMSO], 1961), 54.

3. Gen Hugh Trenchard, "Future Policy in the Air," in *The Decisive Factor: Air Power Doctrine by Air Vice-Marshal H. N. Wrigley*, ed. Alan Stephens and Brendan O'Loghlin (Canberra: Australian Government Publication Service [AGPS], 1990), 131–34.

4. "Extracts from a Report by General Smuts on Air Organisation and the Direction of Air Operations," in Stephens and O'Loghlin, 145–47. There were two members of the Smuts Committee which was formed to report on "Home Air Defence and the Direction of Aerial Operations": Smuts and the volatile Prime Minister Lloyd George. The Smuts Report led to the establishment of the RAF as an independent service in April 1918.

5. Frederick Hugh Sykes, *From Many Angles: An Autobiography* (London: G. G. Harrap and Co., 1942), 555–58; see also Robin Higham, *The Military Intellectuals in Britain, 1918–1939* (Westport, Conn.: Greenwood Press, 1966), 157–59.

6. B. H. Liddell Hart, *Paris: Or the Future of War* (London: Kegan Paul, 1925).

7. C. F. A. Portal, "British Air Control in Underdeveloped Areas," in Eugene M. Emme, *The Impact of Air Power: National Security and World Politics* (Princeton, N.J.: Van Nostrand, 1959), 351–62. See also Bruce Hoffman, *British Air Power in Peripheral Conflict, 1919–1976* (Santa Monica,

Calif.: RAND, 1989), 13–20; and Sir John Bagot Glubb, *War in the Desert: An RAF Frontier Campaign* (London: Hodder and Stoughton, 1960).

8. *Aircraft* (Australia) 7, no. 4 (October/November 1928). See also H. Montgomery Hyde, *British Air Policy Between the Wars, 1918–1939* (London: Heinemann, 1976), 167–74.

9. According to Sir John Slessor, intense army and navy opposition did not deter Trenchard at all. In 1929 Trenchard prepared a paper, "The Fuller Employment of Air Power in Imperial Defence," which according to Slessor "fairly took the gloves off" by declaring "unequivocally the belief of the Air Staff that real economies with at least no less efficacy could be secured by the substitution of Air Forces for other arms over a very wide field." See Marshal of the RAF Sir John Slessor, *The Central Blue: Recollections and Reflections* (London: Cassell, 1956), 45–75.

10. Giulio Douhet, *The Command of the Air*, trans. Dino Ferrari (Washington, D.C.: Office of Air Force History, 1983). For contrasting recent assessments of Douhet, see Claudio G. Segre, "Giulio Douhet: Strategist, Theorist, Prophet?" *Journal of Strategic Studies* 15, no. 3 (Frank Cass, London, September 1992); and Phillip S. Meilinger, "Giulio Douhet and Modern War" (Maxwell Air Force Base [AFB], Ala.: School of Advanced Airpower Studies, 1993).

11. Douhet, 28.

12. Ibid., 117–20.

13. Edward Warner, "Douhet, Mitchell, Seversky: Theories of Air Warfare," in *Makers of Modern Strategy: Military Thought from Machiavelli to Hitler*, ed. Edward Meade Earle (Princeton, N.J.: Princeton University Press, 1973), 489–91; and David MacIsaac, "Voices from the Central Blue: The Air Power Theorists," in *Makers of Modern Strategy: From Machiavelli to the Nuclear Age*, ed. Peter Paret (Princeton, N.J.: Princeton University Press, 1986), 624–47.

14. Bernard Brodie, *Strategy in the Missile Age* (Princeton, N.J.: Princeton University Press, 1971), 73.

15. See Segre; Meilinger; and Silvanus Taco Gilbert III, "What Will Douhet Think of Next?" (unpublished thesis, Maxwell AFB, Ala.: School of Advanced Airpower Studies, June 1992); published as *What Will Douhet Think of Next?: An Analysis of the Impact of Stealth Technology on the Evolution of Strategic Bombing Doctrine* (Maxwell AFB, Ala.: Air University Press, 1993).

16. Warner, 497–501. See also William Mitchell, *Winged Defense: The Development and Possibilities of Modern Air Power, Economic and Military* (New York: Dover Publications, 1988), x.

17. Quoted in Phillip S. Meilinger, "Global Air Power and Power Projection," *RUSI's* [Royal United Service Institute] *and Brassey's Defence Yearbook 1992* (London: Brassey's, 1992), 195. Douhet also expressed that view: "Future wars may yet prove to be more humane than wars in the past in spite of all, because they may in the long run shed less blood," 61.

18. See for example, Higham, 257–59.

19. Barry D. Powers, *Strategy Without Slide Rule, British Air Strategy, 1914–1939* (London: Croom Helm, 1976), 177–78; and M. J. Armitage and R. A. Mason, *Air Power in the Nuclear Age*, 2d ed. (Urbana, Ill.: University of Illinois Press, 1985), 5.

20. For articles in the *RAF Quarterly* between 1933 and 1939 which refer to Douhet's work, see "The Air Doctrine of General Douhet," April 1933, 164–67; "The Universal Arm," October 1934, 467–72; "Air Power and Security," July 1935, 251–57; "General Giulio Douhet—An Italian Apostle of Air Power," April 1936, 148–51; "Air Warfare—The Principles of Air Warfare. By General Giulio Douhet," April 1936, 152–68; "Air Strategy," April 1936, 169–213; "Views on Air Defence," January 1937, 1–13; "Air Operations," April 1937, 118–40; "Air Strategy," July 1937, 245–53; "Fighter versus Bomber," October 1937, 329–50; "Ashmore Modernized," July 1938, 233–73; "Rougerons 'Aviation de Bombardment,'" October 1938, 392–415, and January 1939, 34–44; "Italian Air Strategy," July 1939, 292; and "How to Learn from the Experiences of the War in Spain," October 1939, 401–16.

21. N. N. Golovine, *Air Strategy* (London: Gale and Polden, Ltd., 1936). Golovine was formerly a professor at the Russian Academy of the General Staff (1908–1913) and chief of staff of the 7th Russian Army in World War I. A supporter of the Whites during the Civil War, he moved to France after the Reds' victory. He was sentenced to death by French communist guerillas in 1944. *Air Strategy* was the fourth of his books published in English and was written in collaboration with "a technical expert."

22. *RAF Quarterly*, April 1936, 169–213. The entire book was serialized in subsequent editions of the *RAF Quarterly*.

23. See "Italian Air Strategy" ("which once again asserts Italy's belief in the Douhet theory"), *RAF Quarterly*, July 1939, 292; and R. J. Overy, *The Air War 1939–1945* (London: Papermac, 1980), 16.

24. Horst Boog, "Higher Command and Leadership in the German Luftwaffe, 1939–1945," in *Air Power and Warfare: The Proceedings of the 8th Military History Symposium, United States Air Force Academy, 18–20 October 1978*, eds. Alfred F. Hurley and Robert C. Ehrhart (Washington, D.C.: Office of Air Force History, 1979), 151; and Max Wever, "Doctrine of the German Air Force," in Emme, *The Impact of Air Power*, 181–85.

25. Air Marshal Sir Valston Hancock, interview, record no. TRC 2841, National Library of Australia. Hancock became CAS of the RAAF from 1961 to 1965.

26. Eugene M. Emme, "The American Dimension," in Hurley and Ehrhart, 67.

27. Frank P. Donnini, "Douhet, Caproni and Early Air Power," *Air Power History*, Summer 1990, 45–52. For an observation on Mitchell's thinking from those years, see Robert Frank Futrell, *Ideas, Concepts, Doctrine: Basic Thinking in the United States Air Force 1907–1960*, vol. 1 (Maxwell AFB, Ala.: Air University Press, 1989), 21–22.

28. Futrell, 38; Emme, "The American Dimension," 67. See also Donnini.

29. Alfred F. Hurley, *Billy Mitchell: Crusader for Air Power* (New York: Franklin Watts, 1964), 168–69.

30. The institution was originally known as the Air Service Tactical School and was renamed the Air Corps Tactical School in 1926. See Futrell, 62–82.

31. Raymond Richard Flugel, *United States Air Power Doctrine: A Study of the Influence of William Mitchell and Giulio Douhet at the Air Corps Tactical School, 1921–1935* (unpublished PhD thesis, University of Oklahoma, 1965), 200–201. See also Richard H. Kohn and Joseph P. Harahan (eds.) in the Introduction to Douhet, ix; and Hurley, 75–77.

32. Futrell, 69; and Douhet, ix.

33. Henry Harley Arnold, *Global Mission* (Blue Ridge Summit, Pa.: Tab Books, 1989), 131–32. Arnold presumably was referring to the Kenney translation.

34. Claire Lee Chennault, *Way of a Fighter: The Memoirs of Claire Lee Chennault* (New York: G. P. Putnam's Sons, 1949), 20.

35. Thomas H. Greer, *The Development of Air Doctrine in the Army Air Arm, 1917–1941*, USAF Historical Studies no. 89 (Manhattan, Kans.: *Aerospace Historian*, Department of History, Kansas State University, 1955), 48.

36. Futrell, 65. See also Donald Wilson, "Origin of a Theory for Air Strategy," *Aerospace Historian*, March 1971, 9–25.

37. Chennault, 27.

38. For example, the RAF did not scientifically examine the effectiveness of bombs until June 1938. See Malcolm Smith, *British Air Strategy Between the Wars* (Oxford: Clarendon Press, 1984), 280–81. See also Donald Cameron Watt, "Restraints on War in the Air," in *Restraints on War*, ed. Michael Howard (Oxford: Oxford University Press [OUP], 1979), 65; Robin Higham, "The Royal Air Force at the Crossroads, 1934," (unpublished paper, 1993), 5, especially footnote 12; and H. A. Jones, *The War in the Air; Being the Story of the Part Played in the Great War by the Royal Air Force: Appendices* (Oxford: Clarendon Press, 1937), appendix 23, "Methods of Bombing."

39. For examples of both the British and German reactions, see "Extracts from a Report by General Smuts on Air Organisation and the Direction of Air Operations," "Reports on the Attack on Cologne," and "Examples of Effect of Air Bombardment," Stephens and O'Loghlin, 22–25, 145–48, 158–62.

40. Stanley Baldwin, "The Bomber Will Always Get Through," in Emme, *The Impact of Air Power*, 51–52.

41. George H. Quester, *Deterrence Before Hiroshima: The Airpower Background of Modern Strategy* (New York: John Wiley, 1966), 77–89, 123; and Watt, 57–77.

42. "Aerial Bombardment in the Law of War," *RAF Quarterly*, October 1934, 462–64.

43. Webster and Frankland, 69–70. Simon was the foreign secretary, Eden his deputy.

44. R. J. Overy, "Air Power and the Origins of Deterrence Theory Before 1939," *Journal of Strategic Studies* 15, March 1992, 79.

45. Quester, 98. British war planners calculated in 1938 that the Luftwaffe could drop 600 tons of bombs a day on Britain compared to the 100 tons a day the RAF could drop on Germany. Watt, 74.

46. Noble Frankland, *The Bombing Offensive Against Germany; Outlines and Perspectives* (London: Faber and Faber, 1965), 42; see also Arnold, 159.

47. James L. Stokesbury, *A Short History of Air Power* (London: Robert Hale, 1986), 148.

48. Report from the *Saturday Evening Post* of 3 December 1938, quoted in Michael S. Sherry, *The Rise of American Air Power: The Creation of Armageddon* (New Haven: Yale University Press, 1987), 69–70.

49. Webster and Frankland, 54.

50. Arnold, 111.

51. Technical details are from John William Ransom Taylor and Jean Alexander, *Combat Aircraft of the World* (London: Ebury Press, 1969); H. F. King, *Armament of British Aircraft 1909–1939* (London: Putnam, 1971); and *Weapons* (New York: The Diagram Group, St. Martin's Press, 1990).

52. See Frankland, 53–54, 73; John Terraine, *The Right of the Line: The Royal Air Force in the European War, 1939–1945* (Sevenoaks: Sceptre, 1988), 21–23, 175–76; and Basil Collier, *The Defence of the United Kingdom* (London: HMSO, 1957), 36–40.

53. Max Hastings, *Bomber Command* (London: Michael Joseph, 1987), 49. The endorsed plan was known as "Scheme L." See also Overy, *The Air War*, 20. For a complete list of the RAF's prewar expansion schemes from "A" to "M," see Slessor, 184.

54. Webster and Frankland, 60–61.

55. "The Effects of Pre-War Theory and Doctrine," Group Discussion Period, in *Reaping the Whirlwind: A Symposium on the Strategic Bomber Offensive 1939–45: 26 March 1993*, Royal Air Force Historical Society, 1993, 43–44. For more detail on Bomber Command's shortcomings, see Smith, 270–81; and Slessor, 206, 208, 214, 223, 232–33, 239.

56. Hastings, 44.

57. Sir Michael Knight, *Strategic Offensive Air Operations* (London: Brassey's, 1989), 20; and Hastings, 75.

58. Arnold, 150.

59. Knight, 22.

60. Richard Hallion, "The USAAF Role," *Reaping the Whirlwind*, 17.

61. Williamson Murray, *Strategy for Defeat: The Luftwaffe, 1933–1945* (Secaucus, N.J.: Chartwell Books, 1986), 25.

62. Terraine, 292–93.

63. Hastings, 351.

64. D. Clayton James, *The Years of MacArthur*, vol. 1, *1880–1941* (London: Leo Cooper, 1970), 378–81. MacArthur's proposal was made against the background of the Geneva World Disarmament Conference of 1932–33.

65. Frankland, 40, 56; *Reaping the Whirlwind*, 45; and Overy, *The Air War*, 14.

66. It was as a direct consequence of the doctrine of "precision" that daylight bombing was officially adopted by the USAAC. Greer, 115.

67. Sherry, 50.

68. See R. Dan Richardson, "The Development of Airpower Concepts and Air Combat Techniques in the Spanish Civil War," *Air Power History*, Spring 1993.

69. Carl A. Spaatz, "Ethiopia, China, and the Spanish Civil War," in Emme, *The Impact of Air Power*, 363–67; and Richardson, 15.

70. Masatake Okumiya and Jiro Horikoshi, with Martin Caidin, *Zero! The Story of the Japanese Navy Air Force 1937–1945* (London: Cassell and Co., 1957), 5–6.

71. Quoted in Richardson, 20. Richardson has noted that Soviet airmen in Spain were also impressed by close air support, with one journal article describing it as the "decisive factor in modern combat"; see page 21.

72. C. Rougeron, "How to Learn from the Experiences of the War in Spain," *RAF Quarterly*, October 1939, 401–16.

73. Murray, 14.

74. Maj Gen Walter Wever, "Doctrine of the German Air Force," in Emme, *The Impact of Air Power*, 181–85.

75. Murray, 17.

76. Edward L. Homze, "The Luftwaffe's Failure to Develop a Heavy Bomber Before World War II," in *Aerospace Historian*, March 1977, 20–25; and Powers, 177–78.

77. *The Japanese Air Forces in World War II: The Organization of the Japanese Army and Naval Air Forces, 1945* (London: Arms and Armour Press, 1979), 1–4.

78. Okumiya and Horikoshi, 4–5.

79. Quoted in Richard P. Hallion, *Strike from the Sky: The History of Battlefield Air Attack 1911–1945* (Shrewsbury: Airlife Publishing, 1989), 116.

80. Group Capt H. C. Plenty, in Chris Coulthard-Clark, "The RAAF in the Southwest Pacific Area 1942–1945: An Overview," in *The RAAF in the Southwest Pacific Area 1942–1945: Proceedings of the 1993 RAAF History Conference* (Canberra: Air Power Studies Centre, 1993), 15–16.

81. Quoted in John W. R. Taylor, 572. About 35,000 Sturmoviks were built.

82. Telford Taylor, *Munich: The Price of Peace* (Garden City, N.J.: Doubleday, 1979), 490.

83. Hallion, *Strike from the Sky*, 83–88.

84. "Night Torpedo Attacks Made on the Fleet," *Aircraft*, 1 January 1935, 22.

85. Overy, *The Air War*, 6–7.

86. Martin Middlebrook and Patrick Mahoney have written that Phillips's views on the dangers of air attack against capital ships "were considerably more out of touch and mistaken than those of most of his contemporaries": see *Battleship: The Loss of the Prince of Wales and Repulse* (London: Allen Lane, 1977), 56–59. See also Wing Comdr A. J. Curr, "What a Hell of a Mine," *Defence Force Journal*, November/December 1991, 31–35; and Slessor, 277.

87. Overy, *The Air War*, 7.

88. Clark G. Reynolds, *The Fast Carriers: The Forging of an Air Navy* (New York: McGraw-Hill, 1968), 4; and Sir Arthur Richard Hezlet, *Aircraft and Sea Power* (New York: Stein and Day, 1970), 111.

89. Overy, *The Air War*, 6–7.

90. Reynolds, 4.

91. Frankland, 18.

Did the Bomber Always Get Through?: The Control of Strategic Airspace, 1939–1945

John McCarthy

Perceptions

The Lord demonstrated the power to control the air when the cities of Sodom and Gomorrah reportedly fell under a rain of fire and brimstone. No defense was possible against this overwhelming attack. It was the developing industrial and scientific revolution which for the first time, however, made it seem possible that such power might be fashioned to fulfill human purposes. From the midnineteenth century a future war conducted from the third dimension excited speculative fiction writers. Often a single air weapon, against which there was little or no defense, was sufficient for an unscrupulous will to be imposed upon an entire nation.[1]

Experience between 1914 and 1918 indicated though that the air weapon might be countered. The Royal Naval Air Service attacked Zeppelin bases. In flight such craft proved vulnerable to the new incendiary bullet. Altogether 10.4 percent of Zeppelin sorties flown against Britain were lost. From June 1917, day and night attacks by the Gotha and the Giant posed a more difficult problem. By November 1918, 469 guns backed by searchlights and primitive sound detectors together with 376 aircraft were deployed against them. A loss rate of 6.36 percent resulted.[2] In defeating attacks on Paris in 1918, the French claimed even greater success. They argued of the 483 sorties dispatched, only 37 reached the target and of these 35.1 percent were lost.[3] The British bomber force fared badly. Five months of operations in 1918 saw a monthly loss rate of just under 70 percent.[4]

In the First World War, all bomber forces suffered such casualties that a continuation of a sustained campaign by any side would have been impossible. It is one of the oddities of military aviation history that this conclusion was either ignored or heavily discounted in the interwar years. Service professionals at times sensed danger. In 1930 the American Air Corps Tactical School admitted, "Bombardment formations might be defeated"; yet concluded: "losses must be expected [but] these losses will be minimised by proper defensive tactics."[5] In November 1935 Maj Gen Walther Wever, the first chief of staff of the Luftwaffe, pointed to the error in believing that bombers could be dispatched and return without loss. Rather, he argued, it would be better to imagine "a difficult and costly attack against strong defence."[6] In October 1936 a joint planning subcommittee of the British Committee of Imperial Defence argued a properly organized air defense system would be likely to "take a considerable toll of attacking aircraft."[7] But it remains true that Germany had no night-fighter force until 1941 and that for most of the interwar years Britain's air defense system was allowed to decay.

Orthodoxy dictated only one strategic method of controlling the air: a counterstrike bombing force. Names are familiar: Smuts hinting this as early as 1917; Douhet utterly convinced in 1921; William Mitchell with a doctrine which became a reason for being to the Air Corps Tactical School; Liddell Hart in 1925; and Lord Trenchard in 1928. There were others but Stanley Baldwin was speaking received wisdom when he told the British House of Commons on 10 November 1932: "I think it well for the man in the street to realise there is no power on earth that can protect him from bombing. . . . The bomber will always get through. . . . The only defence is offence, which means you have to kill more women and children quicker than the enemy if you want to save yourselves."[8]

Imagination conjured horrors. Italian use of airpower against undefended Abyssinian targets, the bombing of Guernica, and Japanese air attacks on Chinese cities seemed to give them substance. The fate of the Sudetenland was partly decided by the supposed power of the Luftwaffe to deliver the feared "knockout blow."[9] Donald Davie caught the mood writing after the war, "The Anschluss, Guernica, all the names, at which those poets thrilled or were afraid."[10] Louis MacNeice expressed it in his moving *The Sunlight on the Garden:*

The sky was good for flying
Defying the church bells
And every evil iron
Siren and what it tells:
The earth compels,
We are dying, Egypt, dying.

And so it seemed. In the midthirties Sir John Hammerton edited the popular two-volume *Aerial Wonders of Our Time.* It contained seven articles with themes such as "Death from the Skies," "The Doom of Cities," and "New Horrors of Air Attack." In April 1939, Neville Shute's prophetic novel, *What Happened to the Corbetts,* was published. The publisher, William Heinemann, distributed a thousand free copies to Air Raid Precaution workers so accurate did the prediction of unhampered air attack appear. For Shute with his aviation background there was no defense apart from a counterbomber offensive.

Clausewitz notes with a famous axiom: in war everything is very simple but the simplest thing is very difficult. To launch an effective bombing campaign which would result in the control of the air did seem such a reasonably simple operation. Douhet had written, "An aerial fleet capable of dumping hundreds of bombs can be easily organised." Baldwin mentioned, "Any town in reach of an airfield can be bombed within the first five minutes of war." Was Clausewitz once again to be proven right? Could a bombing force control the air or was the experience of the First World War to be repeated? And what were the consequences of losing control of the air to a strategic bombing force?

Realities

The attempt to control the air by strategic air attack could be defeated provided early detection was made; the nature of the threat identified; interception achieved; and an unacceptable proportion of the attacking force either destroyed, deterred, or diverted from its task. The main initial problem was early detection. For Britain it was quite vital. The governmental, financial, and distribution center of London lies only some 90 miles from the French coast. Attacking aircraft at heights of 20,000 feet and travelling at 250 miles per hour

(MPH) with a short overland flight across hostile territory could avoid interception entirely before delivering an attack. Ground observation posts had an obvious limited utility, and the sound detectors were unreliable. Radar changed this.

Much might depend on the strategic significance given to the Battle of Britain, but it has been argued when Air Chief Marshal Sir Hugh Dowding took the decision to support fully the British work on radar early in 1935 it was perhaps "as decisive for his country as any event recorded in British history."[11] By the time the German air attacks did begin in August 1940, the British coast was ringed with radar units capable of detecting and determining the altitude of high-flying aircraft at a range of 120 miles and less successfully low-flying aircraft. Without radar the whole of Dowding's elaborate and brilliant system of integrated air defense would not have been possible. Ultra had little or no part in the battle; the British Y-Service monitoring Luftwaffe signal traffic was useful but could not have been decisive.

In September 1939 the Germans themselves had a slight lead in radar technology.[12] It was a Freya radar unit which located at a range of 70 miles the ill-fated Royal Air Force (RAF) raid of 18 December 1939 when 24 Wellingtons attacked naval units at Wilhelmshaven. The loss of 12 aircraft to the Messerschmitt Bf-109 determined that henceforth Bomber Command would operate only at night. General Kammhuber, charged with countering the night attacks, may be regarded as the German Hugh Dowding. Freya with its hundred-mile range was supplemented by the Werzburg which allowed Kammhuber from 1941 to erect a string of night-fighter control stations at 25-mile intervals extending from Denmark to the Swiss border. It was a remarkable detection achievement, and once his night fighters were equipped with airborne radar even more effective. Only the introduction of Window (or chaff) in August 1943 made the system briefly inoperable. Kammhuber, the system's architect, was replaced. So then had Dowding previously.

For two major European powers, radar provided early detection of strategic air attack. Without radar, the perceptions of the interwar years would have closer approached reality.

Minding the variables, the fate of Japan makes the point. The possibility of the homeland coming under air attack was discounted in 1941. Home defense radar had only a limited capacity. The position of an incoming aircraft could not be determined, and the Japanese air raid warning system was largely based on visual observation.[13] A mass production of a more sophisticated radar was planned after the Doolittle raid of April 1942, but even though the Japanese knew by April 1943 that the B-29 (designed specifically for attacks on the homeland) was in production, it was only by late November 1944 that the technology could identify the B-29 and hopefully predict speed and altitude, though not always the direction of attack.[14] Rightly it has been argued that Japanese radar could not cope.[15] That it failed in its very first task of early detection contributed to the fact that Japanese airspace was virtually controlled from mid-1945 by a hostile power. There was no Japanese Dowding or Kammhuber; there was no radar-directed and centralized fighter center.

Technology might detect. It could not interpret and decide on the most possible target and thus assess the nature of the threat. Only human intelligence and action was capable of that. The failure to apply both after attacking aircraft had been detected 132 miles away led to the Japanese controlling the air over Pearl Harbor on 8 December 1941 (7 December Hawaii time zone). Generally, however, it was the task of the attacking force to confuse the defenders, to confound the opposing mind. The Luftwaffe introduced the tactic of splitting defenses by diversion attacks on the night of 1–2 November 1940. The German targets were Birmingham and London. Sparse British night-fighter forces were drawn to London with the result that Birmingham suffered an unopposed heavy attack which came close to the type predicted by Neville Shute.[16] From 1943, Bomber Command's increasing strength together with the application of a refined bomber stream technique, deception raids involving small numbers of aircraft later provided with Window became an accepted tactical element for most major attacks.[17]

There were notable successes. Perhaps the most important was the ability of eight Mosquitoes to divert most of the German night-fighter defenses away from Peenemünde on

22–23 August 1943 while the main force of 596 aircraft badly damaged the experimental rocket center. On 3–4 December 1943 a third of Leipzig was destroyed when once again the night fighters were deceived by a handful of Mosquitoes. It says much, however, for the adaptability and flexibility of the human mind that the German night-fighter controllers (coping with clouds of Window, feint attacks, and British-based German speakers issuing false instructions) were far from being always confused. When mistakes were realized, response came quickly. The Peenemünde attack cost 40 bombers, that on Leipzig 24. By then, however, the objective had been achieved: control of the air over the target for albeit a limited period of time.

Detection and identification of the target should ideally have led to interception. Successful interception could lead to an attacking force sustaining heavy if not unacceptable losses. The fate awaiting *Luftflotte* 5 on 15 August 1940 is an example. A projected attack on Newcastle and Sunderland across the North Sea from bases in Denmark and Norway precluded Bf-109 escort. An early detection on Chain Home radar led an inspired, imaginative, and courageous 13 Group controller to vector all his available squadrons into the calculated path of the oncoming bombers and place them at a higher altitude. What followed has been termed "a memorable action."[18] More than this, it was inspired interception. None of the targets was hit, the raids were dispersed, 20 percent of the attacking force was lost, and *Luftflotte* 5 never attempted a similar attack again. In dispute for control of the air in the Second World War, the defenses would hardly have expected a better result. German defenses never did as well, but the American Eighth Air Force suffered grievously from the time it launched its first deep penetration of German airspace with its 17 August 1943 attack on Schweinfurt and 14 October 1943 when that ball-bearing manufacturing target was attacked a second time.

By August 1943 the Luftwaffe fighter force had been centralized, placed under one controller, and given access to one radio frequency. Such essential organization made it a potent weapon, and first Schweinfurt gave the Americans a demonstration of it. The attacking force was quickly radar detected, interception awaited the forced return of its short-ranged fighter escort, then for six hours the B-17s were savaged in German airspace. Sixty American bombers were destroyed, a 19 percent loss rate. Between 10 August and 6 September 1943, Eighth Air Force mounted four major attacks on German targets. All encountered similar interceptions, 133 B-17s were lost for an average rate of 11.5 percent. Final disaster came at second Schweinfurt. Sixty aircraft or 26 percent of the attacking force failed to return. The Americans had lost all pretence of controlling the air to or from the target; indeed, they had even lost the ability to compete for it. Only the belated introduction of long-range fighter escort saved the American strategic bomber offensive.[19] The whole of the Battle of Berlin, which extended from 18 November to March 1944, was a disaster for RAF Bomber Command. The Nuremberg attack of 30–31 March 1944 was final proof. Despite fake attacks, the main force was soon recognized and as the bomber stream left Britain, German night fighters drawn from all over Germany were moved into position. Bomber Command lost 107 of the aircraft dispatched. Overall, despite Window and all the countermeasures, the Battle of Berlin campaign cost 1,117 British aircraft or 3.8 percent of the attacking forces. Opinion will vary, but possibly it achieved little apart from demonstrating the efficiency of the defenses.

Without the ability to intercept, one again must turn to Japan to see Baldwin vindicated. The maximum range of the Japanese radar was some 300 kilometers, but Japanese geography precluded, in most instances, the location of a radar station further than 150 kilometers from a vital target area. Generally, the B-29 could thus be within 50 minutes of being over the target before detection. Poor organization, lack of centralization, and inefficient lines of communication meant that it took over an hour before Japanese fighters could reach interception height. Therefore, only the first aircraft off the ground had any chance of engagement. As one Japanese commander recorded after the war, the majority of interceptors "would have difficulty in becoming airborne in sufficient time to attack the enemy even on their return run."[20] But then the Japanese had never learnt, or given the intense interservice rivalry, could never implement, the basic principles of successful air defense necessary for contesting the control of the air. Even against these deficient Japanese defenses, however, the Twentieth Air Force lost 414 B-29s. And this was the most modern, powerful, and heavily armed aircraft of its time.[21]

A general statement becomes evident: attempts to control airspace worth defending were costly in lives and material. Bare figures further endorse the point. In three and one-half months in 1940, the Battle of Britain cost the Luftwaffe 1,733 aircraft of all types in daylight attacks.[22] The April–May 1942 Badeker raids, often carried out at low level against virtually undefended targets, cost 40 bombers in 14 operations.[23] In the last attacks against the United Kingdom made by manned aircraft, the Luftwaffe lost between 5 and 8 percent of sorties.[24] By the end of the war, 8,205 RAF Bomber Command aircraft were listed as missing on operations, while the command itself suffered two out of three deaths sustained by the Royal Air Force as a whole.[25] In its attempt to control the air directly over Germany and indirectly over the Normandy beaches for the forthcoming invasion, the USAAF Eighth Air Force lost 5,548 heavy bombers from August 1942. Operating from Italian bases, the Fifteenth Air Force lost 2,519 bombers in some 20 months of operations.[26] After detection was achieved, the nature of the threat identified, and interception obtained, what caused such destruction?

A point should be made: as a lethal weapon directed against its own aircrews, the bomber killed long before it entered enemy airspace. In 1942 nonoperational accidents were causing 250 Royal Air Force deaths each month.[27] In September 1943 an ex CINC Bomber Command, Air Chief Marshal Sir Edgar Ludlow-Hewitt, reported that aircraft accidents "possibly [accounted] for almost as many of our aircraft as the Luftwaffe itself."[28] Loaded with explosive, incendiary, oxygen, flares, ammunition, and volatile high-octane fuel and cruising at some 180 MPH, once the bomber came under attack all hazards were compounded and the chances of survival often slight.

First principles of destruction had been devised by General Ashmore for the defense of London in 1917–18. Guns, aided by searchlights, ringed the city. A fire-free fighter zone followed in front of which were placed anchored balloons. Far forward as a first line of defense were the coastal batteries. Above all, command was coordinated. Given all the technological refinements, the Kammhuber line possibly resembled Ashmore's model. In 1938 it had been argued, "Adequate protection can be achieved only by the combined action of fighter aircraft and AA defence."[29] It proved a reasonably accurate prediction.

Flak and fighters were the main killers. Even in the Battle of Britain, when the critical shortage of antiaircraft equipment virtually made all depend upon Fighter Command, 6th Anti-Aircraft Division, working with the heavily involved 11 Group, claimed the destruction of 203 aircraft on day operations.[30] German flak units were considered an elite, and the skill of combining with the night-fighter force after 1941 was quickly mastered. Between July 1942 and May 1945, it was considered that Bomber Command lost 2,278 aircraft to fighters and 1,375 to flak. The Operations Research Section could not even speculate why 2,075 bombers did not return.[31] The American daylight operations gave German flak a good chance of success. From August 1942 and the first tentative foray to Rouen, the Eighth Air Force lost 2,452 bombers to fighters and 2,439 to flak. It was the relative failure of an air defense system which led to Japanese desperation and the formation of Special Attack Units. Stripped fighter aircraft equipped with a nose bomb and flown by virtually untrained pilots rammed American bombers. As the Japanese argued, "The loss of one fighter aircraft and its pilot [was] a cheap price to pay for the elimination of a B-29 and its crew."[32]

Well-organized flak operating by itself, however, was capable of inflicting almost unacceptable losses on an attacking force. A classic Ashmore system was designed by the highly efficient Lt Gen Alfred Gerstenberg in 1942 for the defense of the huge oil-refining complex around the Rumanian city of Ploesti. More than 100 balloons covered the city area, and two belts of flak guns were sited from five to 30 miles from the target. This obstacle had to be crossed.[33] The target, attacked at low level by 178 B-24s of the Ninth Air Force flying from Libya in August 1943, extracted a toll of 54 aircraft or 30.3 percent. Ploesti, attacked at high level 19 times between April and

August 1944, saw Gerstenberg's flak destroy 58.7 percent of the 223 bombers lost.[34] British guns had an outstanding success when pitted against the V-1. Once the decision was made to move some 2,600 guns to form a coastal gun belt in July 1944, antiaircraft fire using the newly available radar-directed proximity fuse won the battle. Static defenses accounted for nearly 62 percent of these unmanned bombers destroyed, and of the 4,656 V-1s launched, only 1,070 penetrated to the London Civil Defence Region.[35]

Conclusion

Between 1939 and 1945 the bomber did get through, yet the cost was high. It is a comment on the level of economic resources, on the ruthlessness of bomber commanders, and on the collective store of raw courage among aircrews that the attempt to control airspace by the strategic bomber continued at all. Only 7.1 percent of Bomber Command aircrews operating between July 1943 and June 1944 had a statistical chance of completing the requirement of two tours when pitted against German targets.[36] Finesse had little part in the campaigns: attrition governed the actions of air commanders, and aircrews were used as a readily disposable commodity. Sir Arthur Harris, for example, in November 1942 was prepared to equate their life expectancy with that of a junior infantry officer on the First World War western front and to be undismayed at a casualty level which marked an unrelieved Second World War disaster. As he argued, "The infantry subaltern's expectation of life in 1917–18 was about 10 days in the front line and in this war our ground casualties at Dieppe were a very high proportion of the attacking force."[37]

An American counterpart may be found in Maj Gen Frederick Anderson. At 38 and an ex-director of bombardment at the Air Corps Tactical School, he was given charge of the Eighth Bomber Command in July 1943. A remorseless tunnel-visioned driver as totally committed to the strategic bomber as Harris, the heavy losses of autumn 1943 failed to affect him. In March 1944 he directed that B-24s should attack Berlin. Faced with a protest from his chief of operations that lack of ceiling meant that "aircrew would just get killed in them"

Anderson only replied, "Well?"[38] It might be only a blurred and idealistic hindsight which makes such attitudes seem worthy of comment, but it must be true that without such people the bomber would hardly have attempted to get through at all.

The control of the air in the Second World War was a fluid concept and remains so. If controlled at all, it could only be for limited periods. Aircraft cannot "hold ground." Staying power is limited, and what airspace was controlled at one time had to be refought for at another. The prototype Scud missiles of 1944–45, the V-1 and the V-2, also showed that although the Germans, in a conventional sense, had lost control of the air, they were still capable of striking. And against the V-2 there was, of course, no defense. It was a forerunner of future scenarios.

There remains a speculation. In March 1945 the director of bomber operations in RAF Bomber Command presented a paper which asked, "What is the highest percentage of losses the Royal Air Force could stand over a period of three months of intensive operations?" The conclusion was that a strategic bomber force would become "relatively ineffective" if it suffered a 7 percent loss rate over that period, while a loss rate of 5 percent would result in its operational effectiveness becoming "unacceptably low."[39] Might it then be argued that if the German defenses had been able to destroy three or four more bombers out of each 100 dispatched in 1943, then the British night offensive could not have continued? If so, then the British bomber would not have got through at all, and surely the Eighth Air Force attacks without the Mustang would have been halted after second Schweinfurt. The Luftwaffe, faced with such a consistent loss rate in January–February 1944, was forced to stop. The proposition that the bomber would always get through was more doubtful than Baldwin could ever have considered.

Discussion

Maj Todd Vercoe: I think perhaps the issue from your presentation is not so much to what extent did the bomber get through, but to what effect. A certain amount of what we now call operational analysis was carried out under the guidance of Professor Solly Zuckerman, and I know they had some fairly harsh things to say about the inaccuracy of bombing. What sorts of changes to the tactics of the bomber streams resulted, if any, from that analysis?

Associate Professor McCarthy: You're quite right on the bombing accuracy as the Butt Report of 1941 showed. But very significant improvements were made with the advent of things like H2S radar and Oboe for navigation, better training, better bombsights, and of course the Pathfinders. Also, as the German fighter force was gradually defeated, more day raids were possible.

Flight Lt Fred Anderson: I flew in Bomber Command as a member of the RAAF. You mentioned ground-based, German-speaking people who were used to confuse the Luftwaffe's radar control by giving false information to their fighters. How effective were those people?

Associate Professor McCarthy: Not very, from my reading. The countermeasures adopted by the Luftwaffe included speaking in provincial German accents and using special codes. Still, from a German night-fighter pilot's point of view, it must have been very frustrating to get contradictory instructions.

Air Commodore Alan Titheridge: John, in comparing the different approaches of the Royal Air Force and the US Army Air Forces to strategic bombing, I've heard it said that the Americans were so rigid with their doctrine after 10 years of development that it took them three and a half years to realize that the bomber wouldn't always get through; while conversely, the RAF had Bomber Harris and no doctrine, and they never did learn it. Would you care to comment on the two approaches?

Associate Professor McCarthy: I think, as was said in the previous presentation, the doctrine of precision bombing was more acceptable to humane-thinking people. It did seem to put limits on bombing raids, to harness them, whereas the area attacks didn't. The odd thing though is that a lot of the strategic air effort over Germany was directed at destroying the Luftwaffe's fighter force in the air. That surely was a bit of doctrine cobbled up from nowhere. The Air Corps Tactical School never argued that the purpose of its B-17s was to shoot down enemy fighters so that a landing force could get ashore unopposed somewhere else. But they were very effective at that, and they finally did win the air battle, albeit at tremendous cost.

Personally, I think the area attacks were a complete waste of energy, effort, and lives. That is not to say that the Eighth Air Force didn't engage in them either because they did; they had to at times. But I hold the view that the area attacks were a misuse of airpower, that there were better target systems available.

Group Capt Ian Madelin: The distinction which history draws between the precision bombing of the USAAF and the area bombing of the RAF is very largely an artificial one. Several years ago I heard Gen Ramsay Potts, who flew from Britain with the US Eighth Air Force during the war, summarize it thus: "You guys did area bombing of area targets and we did area bombing of precision targets."

Dr. Dan Keenan: Even given the inaccuracies of night bombing, do you think that if Air Marshal Harris had concentrated on vital targets like the synthetic oil plants and perhaps some of the larger electric power stations, that this would have produced a better result for Bomber Command?

Associate Professor McCarthy: Once again it's the problem of finding the targets at night and hitting them, that was the difficult part. The center of the city is a lot easier to find and hit. Certainly, if attacks on vital targets could have been concentrated and repeated heavily, it would have been more effective than bombing hospitals in the hope that you're going to hit a nearby factory. But Harris was a bit of a law unto himself; he wouldn't take a lot of direction even from Sir Charles Portal. He was certain that those so-called vital targets were panacea targets and that it was only by hitting the urban centers that you'd win.

Personally, I think hitting selected targets is infinitely better than just scattering bombs at random.

Air Vice-Marshal Tony Mason: I think many British observers of Bomber Harris would agree that he was rather inflexible late in the war when he had weapons systems which could have achieved greater precision. Nevertheless, the image of Harris, as a man who didn't care about his casualties and who was just scattering bombs across Germany because he thought that was a good thing to do, doesn't stand up when you look at the papers to which you yourself have just alluded, that is, the correspondence between Harris and Charles Portal between November 25th and January 18th, 1944–45. Those papers are now fully accessible.

In that long argument, Portal was trying to get Harris to drop his city list and go after targets Harris regarded as yet more panacea targets. Harris had considerable logic on his side, as recent raids against four or five similar panacea targets had just been conducted unsuccessfully. The economic survey used to justify attacking those targets had subsequently been shown to be incomplete, as it had failed to recognize that alternative supplies of the resources being targeted were available to the Germans. So Harris argued to Portal—and we don't have to agree with him, but at least we should do him the justice of listening to his argument—that the vagaries of weather, of target concealment, and of actually being certain that the panacea was what it was and where it was, was still, even in late-1944, very difficult to achieve. On the other hand, he knew that if, for example, there was a synthetic oil plant in a particular city, then if he blanketed that city, he was certainly going to get the synthetic plant as well as everything else. Therefore to portray Harris as a mindless, doctrinaire air marshal who hadn't read anything and didn't understand a great deal, is not, I think, an accurate picture of a man who retained the loyalty and affection of those who flew and fought for him.

Associate Professor McCarthy: I certainly didn't say what you suggested I did: in fact, you and I are very close together in our points of view. I've got many good things to say about Bomber Command's offensive, but I wasn't asked to talk on them.

Notes

1. Michael Paris, *Winged Warfare: The Literature and Theory of Aerial Warfare in Britain, 1859–1917* (Manchester: Manchester University Press, 1992), 16–29.

2. Figures from Kenneth P. Werrell, *Archie, Flak, AAA, and SAM: A Short Operational History of Ground-Based Air Defense* (Maxwell Air Force Base [AFB], Ala: Air University Press, 1988), 1–2.

3. Lt Gen N. N. Golovine, "Ashmore Modernized," in *Views on Air Defence* (London: Aldershot, Gale and Polden, 1939). Originally published in *The Royal Air Force Quarterly*, July 1938.

4. John H. Morrow Jr., *The Great War in the Air: Military Aviation from 1909 to 1921* (Washington, D.C.: Smithsonian Institution Press, 1993), 321.

5. Williamson Murray, *Luftwaffe, 1933–45: Strategy for Defeat* (London: Brassey's, 1983), appendix 1, 299.

6. Address given at the opening of the German Air Warfare Academy, 1 November 1935, in Eugene M. Emme, ed., *The Impact of Air Power: National Security and World Politics* (Princeton, N.J.: Van Nostrand, 1959), 185.

7. Sir Charles K. Webster and Noble Frankland, *The Strategic Air Offensive Against Germany 1939–45*, vol. 4, *Annexes and Appendices* (London: Her Majesty's Stationery Office [HMSO], 1961), appendix 4, 88.

8. Baldwin was speaking in the context of the Geneva Disarmament Conference. It became British policy to urge a complete abolition of bombing aircraft, which from the United Kingdom's point of view, possessed distinct naval and military advantages. As the CIGS argued, "An effective total abolition of all naval and military aircraft cannot but be advantageous to this country, as tending to restore to us the sea as our first line of defence and as removing the danger of air attack on London." Memorandum by the Chief of the Imperial General Staff, 30 May 1932, Public Record Office (PRO), Cab. 24-230, C. P. 176 (32). Finally, however, the Geneva debate ended without result when Germany withdrew in October 1933.

9. See Wesley K. Wark, "The Air Defence Gap: British Doctrine and Intelligence Warnings in the 1930s," in *The Conduct of the Air War in the Second World War: An International Comparison*, ed. Horst Boog (New York: Berg, 1991), 511–26. For a well-known exposition of the "knockout blow" point of view see, "Aide Memoire by Sir Thomas Inskip, Minister for Co-ordination of Defence," 9 December 1937, in Webster and Frankland, appendix 5, 96.

10. Donald Davie, "Remembering the Thirties," in *The Oxford Book of Twentieth-Century English Verse*, ed. Philip Larkin (Oxford: Clarendon Press, 1973), 532–33.

11. Basil Collier, *The Defence of the United Kingdom* (London: HMSO, 1957), 37.

12. Alfred Price, *Instruments of Darkness: The History of Electronic Warfare* (London: Macdonald and Jane's, 1977), 60–61.

13. Japanese monograph no. 17, "Homeland Operations Record," Headquarters United States Army Forces Far East (USAFFE) et al., circa 1946, 8.

14. Japanese monograph no. 157, "Homeland Air Defense Operations Record," Headquarters USAFFE et al., circa 1946, 114.

15. R. J. Overy, *The Air War 1939–1945* (London: Papermac, 1980), 202.

16. Refer to the narrative of night attacks made by the Luftwaffe from November through December 1940 in Francis K. Mason, *Battle Over Britain: A History of the German Air Assaults on Great Britain 1917–18 and July–December 1940 and the Development of Britain's Air Defences Between the Wars* (Bourne End: Aston, 1990), 383–90.

17. See Martin Middlebrook and Chris Everitt, *The Bomber Command War Diaries: An Operational Reference Book, 1939–1945* (New York: Viking, 1985), for details.

18. Collier, 193.

19. Stephen Lee McFarland and Wesley Phillips Newton, *To Command the Sky: The Battle for Air Superiority Over Germany, 1942–1944* (Washington, D.C.: Smithsonian Institution Press, 1991), 132, for this and the preceding opinion.

20. Japanese monograph 157, no. 111.

21. Roger Anthony Freeman, *The US Strategic Bomber* (London: Macdonald and Jane's, 1975), 9, Operational Statistics, 151–60.

22. Derek Wood, *Target England: The Illustrated History of the Battle of Britain* (London: Jane's Publishing, 1980), appendix 3. Night losses were much lower with the raids of November–December 1940 showing a rate of 1 percent of sorties flown. Mason, 383.

23. Collier, 308.

24. Ibid., 327.

25. Webster and Frankland, appendix 41; W. Franklin Mellor, ed., *History of the Second World War: UK Medical Series: Casualties and Statistics* (London: HMSO, 1972), table 7, 600.

26. Freeman, 9; and Operational Statistics, 161–66.

27. Lord Brabazon to Secretary of State for Air, 13 May 1942, PRO, Air 19/319.

28. "Organisation for the Prevention of Accidents," report by Inspector-General, 18 September 1943, PRO, Air 19/319.

29. Golovine, 100.

30. Collier, appendix 23, "Some Problems and Achievements of Anti-Aircraft Gunnery During the Battle of Britain," report, 2 August 1941.

31. Webster and Frankland, appendix 40, 429–30.

32. Japanese monograph no. 157, 14–16.

33. Leroy W. Newby, *Target Ploesti: View from a Bombsight* (Navato, Calif.: Presidio, 1983), appendix B, Air Objective Folder no. 69, 1, Rumania, 223.

34. Werrell, 29.

35. Collier, appendix 45, 523.

36. John McCarthy, *A Last Call of Empire: Australian Aircrew, Britain and the Empire Air Training Scheme* (Canberra: Australian War Memorial, 1988), 107.

37. "Note by C-in-C Bomber Command on Second Tour of Operations," 24 November 1942, PRO, Air 14/1846.

38. McFarland and Newton, 153, 197.

39. Webster and Frankland, appendix 42, 445–46.

World War II:
Air Support for Surface Forces

Vincent Orange

The current edition of Royal Air Force doctrine on airpower was prepared under the direction of the chief of the air staff in 1993. It begins with a quotation from Arthur Tedder, one of his greatest predecessors and one of the Second World War's greatest commanders—land, sea, or air. "Air warfare cannot be separated into little packets," wrote Tedder in 1947, "it knows no boundaries on land and sea other than those imposed by the radius of action of the aircraft; it is a unity and demands unity of command."[1] Let me, like a bishop or even an air marshal, preach upon that text (we academics easily succumb to delusions of grandeur when allowed out of our cozy nooks).

Successful air warfare in support of surface forces during the Second World War *depended* on fighter aircraft, but was best *provided* by fighter-bombers. Without the aerial superiority which fighters alone could achieve and maintain, no other aircraft type could function effectively by day or by night—because fighters would shoot them down or scatter them or turn them back to their bases or prevent them from taking off. Without that aerial superiority, operations could rarely be carried out safely because fighters were able to protect bombers while they destroyed infantry, motor transport, artillery positions, and even tanks—or scattered them, turned them back to their bases, or prevented them from setting out. The very bases themselves became vulnerable.

In 1945, as in 1918, the most effective day fighters were single-seat, single-engine machines. Until 1934, however, they had been aerodynamically primitive biplanes of frame and fabric construction with open cockpits, fixed undercarriages, light armament, and low-powered engines. Lacking radios, they could not be controlled, warned, or guided either from the ground or in the air. But after 1934, fighters appeared that were aerodynamically advanced monoplanes of all-metal construction with enclosed cockpits, retractable undercarriages, heavy armament, and high-powered engines. They were equipped with radios, and the development of radar would permit effective ground and air control. This worldwide revolution in fighter design and equipment came in response to the appearance of streamlined metal monoplane bombers that were much faster than biplanes, better armed, and capable of carrying what was believed to be a devastating load of bombs over an alarming distance and, with radio aids, arriving exactly over the designated target. Such bombers, it was widely believed, might win the next war on their own. Strong land forces might no longer be needed if bombers could destroy the cities supplying those forces with men and materials.

When these beliefs were put to the test, it was learned (quickly in Britain, more slowly elsewhere) that modern fighters coped easily in daylight with modern bombers—unless they were escorted by friendly fighters sweeping the skies clear around them by attacking enemy fighters in the air or on the ground. Twin-engine fighters (with a far longer range and unobstructed forward visibility for a pilot assisted by a radar operator sitting behind him) coped even more easily with bombers obliged to seek the cover of darkness—unless they, too, were escorted by friendly fighters able to sweep a clear path for them. Some fighters were equipped with bomb racks to produce a dual-purpose fighter-bomber that proved more useful on or near battlefields than either dive-bombers or light level-bombers because these types could only operate effectively under fighter protection. The fighter-bomber could look after itself, once it had got rid of its load. Until that moment, however, like all other aircraft, it needed fighter protection.

The Second World War, then, would not be won by unaided bombers, although some airmen believe it could have been. For instance, Rick Atkinson's account of the recent Gulf War (according to Max Hastings) examines arguments between American airmen, "some of them passionate to win the war single-handedly by strategic bombing rather than to carry out tactical operations in support of the army." When the ground offensive at last began, Gen H. Norman Schwarzkopf ruthlessly—and probably rightly—ordered the airmen to focus their sorties on tactical support, and denied them the chance they craved to continue the strategic missions against Iraq, designed to cause the collapse of its entire infrastructure.[2]

Like all earlier wars, the Second World War would be won by the stronger surface forces (on land, at sea, or in combination). At first, air support for German armies greatly helped those surface forces win decisive victories in western Europe. An equally decisive victory might have been achieved in North Africa and that victory might have led to the overthrow of Stalin by opening another route into the Soviet Union, one fuelled by Middle Eastern oil. Neither catastrophe happened, and this war, like the First World War, became a long war. Against an alliance of enemies with vastly superior military and industrial resources, the Germans could not indefinitely retain their conquests abroad, though their defeat at home was by no means certain.

Although the fighters employed by the major powers were comparable in performance, better rates of production, maintenance, and repair ultimately gave the Allies a massive advantage over the Germans.[3] The Allies were also readier to reject clever modifications and interesting designs that excited backroom boffins, rather than frontline ground or aircrews. Nevertheless, the bravery, aggression, and experience of the man in the cockpit often made the difference between victory and defeat. Pilots who lacked these personal qualities were killed or driven away whatever they flew and however carefully they had been trained. As Alfred Price wrote, "It isn't the size of the dog in the fight that counts, it's the size of the fight in the dog."[4]

Under fighter protection, other aircraft types caused ever-increasing harm on all German fronts: fighting, transporting, manufacturing, and farming. By 1944 the deaths, injuries, and damage caused by repeated aerial attacks upon such a wide range of targets were of vital assistance to Allied land forces advancing from the east, south, or west. Air warfare, as Tedder often emphasized, was a cooperative venture in which all types, unarmed as well as armed, played their parts in helping soldiers to occupy enemy territory and sailors to close enemy ports. From 1944 till the war's end, Allied forces rarely endured serious aerial attack. In addition, their efforts—and those of partisans among the subjugated peoples—were helped by transport aircraft dropping troops or supplies or carrying casualties to hospital.[5]

Tedder's tripartite plan for the employment of airpower was worked out in the North African desert by Arthur "Mary" Coningham, his great executant.[6] It was founded upon those three principles still singled out by the modern Royal Air Force for approval: no division into "little packets," "no boundaries on land and sea," and "unity of command." Incorporated into the plan, these principles would soon be enshrined in American doctrine, where they remain alive and well—modified, but never rejected, by generations of analysts. The doctrine made possible, in the opinion of John Fagg (an American official historian), "one of the most effective collaborations known to military history."[7] Geoffrey Perret has wisely observed, however, that Coningham, like all the best military commanders, "was an opportunist, not a dogmatist."[8] Never having studied at a staff (or any other) college, he was the least doctrinaire of men. For him, doctrine was a guide, not a rule; it might help in making hard choices, but local circumstances mattered more.

The Tedder-Coningham plan aimed first to achieve air superiority, second to isolate the battlefield, and third to provide surface forces with close support. That superiority, once achieved by fighters, could only be maintained by continuous effort; it could never be more than temporary or local, as long as an enemy fighter force remained in being; and all other uses of airpower must be limited or even abandoned whenever that superiority was in jeopardy. Battlefield isolation was seen to have two distinct advantages. One, to deny enemy reinforcements *immediate access* to it by using escorted medium bombers and fighter-bombers to attack roads, railways, cross-country movement, and supply dumps. And two, to impede *distant supply* to it by using escorted heavy and medium bombers to attack factories, railways, shipping, and ports providing those reinforcements with their weapons, ammunition, fuel, food, and men.

Close support was seen to have two distinct tasks. One, to attack the enemy *flanks or rear* by using escorted fighter-bombers in operations as frequent as the air commander's resources and judgment would allow, mounted while the ground commander was preparing (or recovering from) his own action. And two, to attack the enemy *front* in operations that must only be mounted for a very great purpose, either to prevent a rout (not merely a forced withdrawal) or to permit a major breakthrough (not merely a convenient advance). Here lies the nub of my paper: the root of angry, exasperated, or bewildered exchanges between soldiers and airmen through-out the Second World War. Direct attacks upon the enemy front, where soldiers most wanted or needed air support, was precisely what airmen were least able or willing to deliver. Least able, in the early war years, because they had neither suitable aircraft nor crews trained in such tasks. Least willing, because heavy casualties must be suffered in attacking targets that airmen believed artillery, mortar, or machine-gun fire could deal with more effectively as well as more safely.

By the end of 1944, Allied air superiority had become air *supremacy.* Numerous ground-attack aircraft were built, the best of them single-engine types with huge air-cooled radial engines (less vulnerable to flak than liquid-cooled engines), but all of them heavily armed, armored, and flown by thor-oughly trained, combat-experienced pilots. By long trial and error, practical methods of cooperation were devised between these ground attackers and forward troops, now themselves far better equipped and versed in combat.[9]

We must emphasize the fact that the young men who did the actual fighting on the ground or in the air on all fronts learned quickly how to survive, how to kill, and how best to help each other. Nothing compares with the certainty of combat—next month, if not tomorrow—for concentrating attention during lectures or training exercises. Those who fought in the second half of the war were professionals in comparison with their unlucky amateur predecessors. They were skilled in many tasks that had not even existed in 1939, and the weapons, instruments, or tools they used had been tested and proven in demanding service. Among the Allies, though less so among the Germans, systematic rotation of soldiers and airmen between front and rear ensured the vivid transmission of recent lessons to attentive newcomers. Their commanders also improved. The inept or unlucky were mostly gone by 1943, and those who arrived or survived to make famous names became surer of their own capacity, and that of their colleagues and subordinates, in the rarest of military arts: waging total war. Above all, the Allied commanders enjoyed the confidence and prestige of victory. They never suffered the despair of defeat, as opposed to the humiliation of setbacks, and were increasingly concerned with their postwar ambitions, as well as the most economical means of ending the current conflict.

Only in the last year of the war did close support, of a kind and impact that soldiers naturally preferred, become common. Until the end, however, fierce, cleverly directed ground fire made it perilous work. Pilots were asked to fly over hidden batteries until gunners revealed their positions by opening up; those who survived were then to dive-bomb the batteries and finally to strafe them. Such missions, wrote Bill Dunn, a Thunderbolt pilot with over 500 combat hours to his credit, "were nothing more than flying directly into the firing barrels of hundreds of antiaircraft cannon and machine-guns, with the chances about one in five you'd get hit, one in 10 you'd get shot down. As the German army was gradually compressed by our forces into small defense pockets, so their flak was also compressed, with many more guns now defending each target area." And yet it is a well-attested fact that some pilots were readier to press home very dangerous attacks in direct support of frontline soldiers than they were to attempt the destruction of such impersonal targets as bridges, although they clearly understood the overall military significance of wrecking these.[10]

A question often asked was: "Will close air support work best in *fluid* situations, against forces in movement—forward or back?" "Perhaps" was the answer because at such times opportunities for hits are fleeting and may easily be missed even by experienced pilots amid traffic dust, smoke screens, or light flak, even when clouds, rain, snow, adjacent hills, and enemy fighters are not additional hazards. Moreover, it is likely that friendly and enemy troops will be near each other, thus increasing the chances of hitting the wrong ones, especially if they are using captured vehicles. While fighting virtually hand to hand, it will be very difficult for soldiers to indicate precisely where they need help and just as difficult for airmen to deliver it accurately. We must also bear in mind the fact that the ground situation may change crucially during the time it takes, however short, for aircraft to arrive on the scene.

If all that is true, the question naturally followed: "Will close air support work best then in *static* situations, against forces virtually immobilized by prior action?" "Perhaps" was again the answer because at such times flak is likely to be carefully sited with all weapons providing mutual aid at optimum angles, ranges, and altitudes. Crews will be well protected with ample ammunition ready to hand, and the whole complex will have been lovingly camouflaged. On the other hand, just as the defenders—given time—will organize themselves efficiently, so will the attackers. It is in static situations that combat pilots serving a stint in radio-equipped tanks or light aircraft can best work with frontline troops to direct accurate strikes. Flak crews reveal their positions when they fire, and their supply lines should be identifiable (and therefore cuttable). Heavy equipment cannot be moved quickly and not at all without large transport vehicles and a deal of commotion. Regular aerial photo-reconnaissance may reveal when a move is imminent and also its destination—unless traffic dust, smoke screens, light flak, clouds, rain, snow, adjacent hills, and enemy fighters spoil a pilot's observations.

Effective aircraft operations in close support of land forces required reliable systems of communication between airmen at or beyond the front line, soldiers below them, and their respective commanders in the rear, who would take a long time to recognize the advantages of a joint headquarters. It also took a long time to design and produce in quantity such essential equipment as radios, radars, and cameras, as well as to train men and women to use them correctly and interpret their information accurately. In addition, the Second World War demonstrated yet again that systems of communication will always break down at unpredictable times and places because human beings of every rank and age are so unreliable. They make mistakes, slack off, get in a muddle, panic, tell lies, refuse to listen, act without thinking, fall sick, or drop dead at inconvenient moments. Even when the human element works adequately, the natural (or, if you prefer, the divine) element intervenes: floods, storms, and fires wreck communications and upset commanders' choices. Not least, the enemy element is never less than a nuisance, interfering with our most cunningly wrought systems and devising his own along lines unforeseen except by subsequent historians.

Unlike the French, the British were given time and space—thanks to the English Channel and their forethought in creating an effective air defense system—to consider and practice in North Africa methods of air support for surface forces in ideal conditions during 1941 and 1942. That is, against an enemy strong enough to punish their initial weakness and many subsequent mistakes, without being strong enough to sweep them out of Egypt and the entire Middle East. British methods worked and, during Operation Torch (the Allied landings in Northwest Africa in November 1942), were taught to Americans inclined to be receptive for three reasons. One, some of their fellow citizens, serving under British command in the Desert Campaign during 1942, voiced enthusiastic approval. Two, other American airmen in Tunisia, as well as back home, were already thinking along similar lines.[11] And three, the early conduct of Torch generated a shambles of such heroic proportions that any different methods must produce improvement. On the other hand, the Americans contributed in areas quite beyond British capability. On one December day, for example, 49 C-47 transports carried nearly 50,000 gallons of fuel forward in under two hours to assist the pursuit of Rommel; it would have taken 59 trucks three days to do that.[12] Like the Desert Campaign, that in Tunisia was also fought in ideal conditions. Long enough and bloody enough to concentrate everyone's attention wonderfully on interservice and international problems, it was a perfect training exercise in that it could not be lost whatever mistakes were made. The Allies had command of the sea and the air, plenty of well-equipped soldiers, and fuel. Not least, they enjoyed (as in Desert Campaign days) full information about enemy plans, strength, and supplies.

Rapidly growing numbers of aircraft better designed, equipped, and employed, gradually deprived German armies of tactical mobility. As a commander wryly remarked, "We could make one move to your three." The flow of reinforcements, fuel, and ammunition to the front lines was so reduced or delayed that by 1944 German chances of mounting a major offensive were gone. They defended with ferocious tenacity, but on the only occasion that such an offensive was attempted (through the Ardennes in December 1944), it failed to reach any of its objectives, even though it began with the rare advantage of complete surprise. In the same year, American long-range escort fighters, assisted by British long-range night fighters, ended the Luftwaffe's defensive capacity over the Third Reich in daylight or darkness, permitting heavy bombers to wreck transport systems, end oil production, and ruin urban areas.

Ultimately, the Allied call for "unconditional surrender" became irresistible. And yet that last resort had been avoidable. Even without air support, most Germans fought so stubbornly and skillfully, both in the field and in dispersed factories (assisted by ample slave labor), that an adroit leadership might well have managed a military stalemate in 1944, followed by a negotiated peace leaving intact the rule of that leadership over Germany. The rival surface forces were so nicely balanced (even on the eastern front, until Hitler's mistakes threw away German men and materials) that airpower probably made the difference. Tactical medium and fighter-bombers, strategic heavy bombers, and transports carrying troops or supplies, all protected by numerous fighter aircraft, ensured in 1945 a complete Allied victory and not merely a favorable armistice, as in 1918. "The old saw has it," wrote John Keegan, "that air power cannot hold ground." That dictum remains as valid today, when the question arises of creating an artillery-exclusion zone around Sarajevo which will be useless without as many as 30,000 troops to enforce it, as it was half a century ago: each campaign of the Second World War ended only when German soldiers were driven away, killed, wounded, or forced to surrender and were replaced by Allied soldiers.[13]

Unless they are permanently broken, nations learn more from defeat than from victory. Spectacular Luftwaffe successes against opponents either irredeemably weak or poorly organized and equipped disguised several grave weaknesses in command, equipment, and production that were never remedied. Consequently, the Luftwaffe failed to maximize or rationalize production between 1939 and 1941, during what Churchill would have called "the locust years."[14] Chief among the aircraft types not produced in quantity was a four-engine bomber, even though promising examples were flying as early as 1936. The lack of such a weapon, plus the failure to build fighters at an urgent rate to escort it, ensured that air support for surface forces intending to invade Britain in September 1940 would be insufficient for them even to attempt the task. Britain's air and flak defenses, focused on the southeast and sorely pressed in that small area, were not stretched beyond a breaking point by the wider-ranging and much heavier attacks that escorted heavy bombers could have delivered.[15]

A year later, when Hitler's attack upon the Soviet Union began, air support for surface forces would again prove inadequate in quantity and function. In order to provide effective support in a long campaign against a major power, a tactical air force needs soldiers to win, supply, and guard its bases; it also needs a *strategic* air force. Ultimately, the lack of a *Uralbomber*—a weapon that could reach factories in the region for which it was named but not built—exposed German armies to a weight of attack unrestricted either by destruction of those factories or diversion of aircraft, guns, and men to protect them. The Red Air Force was no better provided with heavy bombers than the Luftwaffe, but Soviet land forces benefited as much as their Western comrades from Anglo-American pounding of the Reich. Neither Stalin nor the British Joint Intelligence Committee had realized, wrote Alan Bullock, that Hitler "was such a fool as to think that Russia could be defeated by a blitzkrieg."[16] No one in his right mind would attempt to conquer an immense land without long and meticulous preparation. Hitler did. Those who knew better dared not gainsay their fuehrer and despite a string of impressive—though increasingly costly—successes, ruthless determination among soldiers and airmen could not make up for unrealistic planning.

Although the Luftwaffe destroyed numerous aircraft, many were obsolescent and caught on the ground, and their crews (ground and air) survived. Even though its bombers and fighters were still unable to communicate with each other and with their bases or ground forces on a common radio frequency, the Luftwaffe covered the rapid advance of armor and infantry more skillfully than in earlier campaigns, until the sheer breadth and depth of the advance dissipated its strength. For the first time, German surface forces failed to occupy the enemy capital. Stalin, though severely shaken, was not obliged to surrender because his essential tank and aircraft factories had been moved beyond the reach of medium bombers. These lacked the numbers, escorts, and handy, well-supplied bases necessary to deliver concentrated, repeated attacks. With a secure manufacturing base, large numbers of trained pilots and technicians still alive, a people steeled by Nazi atrocities to endure any hardships, a ruler temporarily persuaded that military efficiency mattered more than ideological conformity, and plentiful material support from Britain and the United States, the Soviet Union would survive, rally, and conquer. The escorted heavy-bomber fleet did not exist that might have clinched a final German victory before Russia's traditional resilience in adversity could make itself felt.[17]

In North Africa, meanwhile, Tedder needed *American* aircraft to give effective air support to surface forces. Neither Britain's aircraft industry nor her merchant fleet was able to supply enough machines. Good relations with Americans were therefore essential. These became, for Tedder, an imperative as vital during the rest of the war and beyond as any doctrine he expounded on the proper use of aircraft.[18] As for Coningham, his gradual mastery of the tactical battle was founded on personal experience. By the time of the armistice, he recalled in 1946, fighters and fighter-bombers were cooperating closely with tanks to make the German retreat "expensive and chaotic." The principles there thrashed out, he believed, remained valid, and much of Coningham's best effort in the Second World War was devoted to restoring "mutual appreciation" between soldiers and airmen.[19]

Tedder had told Coningham to "get together" with the army commander as his *first* task on going out to the desert in July 1941. Coningham's opinion that this was a decision of "fundamental importance and had a direct bearing on the combined fighting of the two services until the end of the war" is supported by Field Marshal Lord Carver who wrote, when evaluating airpower in the Second World War, that "by far the most significant contribution [to victory] was made by the tactical air forces in support of the army." They were greatly helped by a steady flow of reliable intelligence about enemy strength and intentions from photo-reconnaissance, prisoner interrogation, tapping radio messages, and—most famously—the decoding of signals traffic far away in deepest Buckinghamshire.[20]

The army responded to Coningham's initiative and agreed to set up a joint headquarters when the Eighth Army was formed in September 1941. In that same month, Prime Minister Churchill ruled (in response to Tedder's arguments, relayed to him by Charles Portal, chief of the air staff) that ground forces must not expect "as a matter of course" to be protected against aerial attack. "Above all, the idea of keeping standing patrols of aircraft over our moving columns should be abandoned." Hopes of winning and keeping air superiority would be undermined by this "mischievous practice." When a battle was in prospect, continued the prime minister, the army commander was to "specify" to the air commander the tasks he wanted performed, both before and during the battle, but it was the duty of the air commander to decide how best to carry them out. These fundamental rulings were widely publicized and vigorously enforced by Coningham, with Tedder's whole-hearted support, in all the Mediterranean and northwest European campaigns.[21]

"Whoever held the airfields on the shores of the Mediterranean," reflected Peter Drummond (Tedder's deputy) in October 1943, "could pass his own ships through that sea with reasonable safety and could forbid the route to the ships of the enemy."[22] For two years from mid-1940, the Axis Powers held most of those airfields but failed to seize Malta, the key to permanent retention. Their last chance came after the fall of Tobruk in June 1942. Rommel had still not grasped the need to protect his supply lines from Italy by taking Malta before pressing on to Cairo and the Suez Canal. Nor did he realize how greatly air support could aid his eastward advance, for he did not demand an urgent transfer of aircraft even to restore, let alone strengthen, the forces of his air commander (Otto Hoffman von Waldau). Rommel actually began his fatal invasion without informing Waldau and therefore gave him no time to move his airfields forward.[23]

These decisions deprived Waldau of the opportunity to turn retreat into rout. Only if British troops were panicked into fleeing *through* defensible positions at El Alamein would Rommel be able to follow them. A classic blitzkrieg situation arose for a fighter force strong enough to hold off Coningham's fighters while level and dive-bombers enjoyed themselves shooting up trucks and armor, killing and scattering men already demoralized—and poorly provided with light flak weapons. In fact, during the three days that it took the Eighth Army to retreat from Gazala to El Alamein, a distance of nearly 350 miles, only six soldiers were killed by air attack. This crisis showed British defensive air support at its strongest, German offensive air support at its weakest; Coningham's name was made, Waldau's wasn't.[24]

Neither Rommel nor Waldau would ever revel in Egypt's varied delights, nor would they sample Malta's more sober offerings. Correlli Barnett regards that island as "the Verdun of maritime war," a fortress not worth its cost. Many ships were indeed sunk or damaged by Axis aircraft and submarines while trying to supply Malta; many British aircraft were lost trying to protect those ships; and the actual weight of air-sea support mounted from there to assist desert campaigns by cutting Axis sea or land links with Italy was by no means decisive. But at least Rommel never *benefited* from that island's strategic value. Tedder and Coningham feared the prospect of a German Malta until August 1942. From then on, the growing prospect of a revitalized British Malta excited them. That is why they were so angered by Bernard Montgomery's tardy pursuit of Rommel after El Alamein. By October Malta was critically short of food and fuel. A convoy was to be run from Alexandria early in November to supply these. That "unsinkable aircraft carrier" would then be able to support the armies advancing eastward to Tunisia. In order to protect that convoy, the airmen needed bases in western Cyrenaica; bases which, as always, only soldiers could capture. They got them, with a day to spare; the convoy passed unscathed, and Malta played a key part in the Allied victory.[25]

Only after spurning all realistic Mediterranean options did Hitler send vast resources there. The men and materials wasted in Tunisia during the six months from November 1942 might well have taken both Malta and Egypt during the six months before that date. Thousands of troops were airlifted into Tunisia in response to Allied landings in Morocco and Algeria, sea ferries took across heavy weapons and supplies, while numerous aircraft flew in to all-weather bases.[26] Until mid-April, these troops were supported by over 300 German aircraft offering "a classic example" (in the RAF's official opinion) "of what may be accomplished, in the face of a superior enemy, by a small, compact force of high morale and efficiency, although outnumbered."[27] The Allies were held at bay and a refuge provided for Rommel's forces, retreating westward after their defeat at El Alamein. But those men arrived too late to do more than delay the collapse of Axis power in North Africa. By March 1943 at the latest, one-quarter of a million men were trapped there. These well-trained, experienced soldiers, supported by the crews of a thousand combat and transport aircraft lost in Tunisia, would have made the subsequent Allied landings in Sicily and Italy far bloodier.

Winston Churchill wrote that his first reaction to news of the Japanese attack upon Pearl Harbor was: "We had won the war. . . . All the rest was merely the proper application of overwhelming force. . . . Many disasters, immeasurable cost and tribulation lay ahead, but there was no more doubt about the end."[28] So might I write of air support for surface forces, from the Allied viewpoint, after the Tunisian Campaign. During the two years after May 1943, lessons learned during the two preceding years were refined and employed in Sicily, Italy, and northwest Europe. Effective air support became a matter of standardizing tested procedures and publicizing them widely among airmen and soldiers, a task made easier by the fact that many of the senior army and air commanders in May 1943 remained in office until the end of the European war.

Aircraft were now rarely used in "little packets" and the lack of "boundaries on land or sea" was exploited boldly through "unity of command." Just as immense Soviet production more than compensated for any doctrinal deficiencies on the eastern front, so also did American production on the southern and western fronts, supplemented by that of Britain.[29] Efficient maintenance and repair organizations maximized the value of that torrent of production. From Tunisia onwards, squadrons had their own transport and workshops; airfields were built, stocked, and guarded for them; and communications between units and with army units became faster and more accurate. Doctrine mattered less and less as it became easier for air commanders to accept more and more demands for assistance of all kinds.

It is well that this was so because on five occasions (in Sicily, twice in Italy, Normandy, and southern France) the Allies attempted the most hazardous of all military ventures: a seaborne landing upon a defended shore. A major addition to combined operations was the large-scale use of transport aircraft and gliders to drop paratroops behind enemy front lines. Although their value remains controversial, they could not have been employed at all without air superiority. Despite fierce resistance that threatened on three of these five occasions to sweep the invaders back into the sea, the Allies were not in fact repulsed. They were saved by the courage and skill of the soldiers ashore, the sailors who got them there, and the airmen fighting above and ahead of them. The initial landings therefore survived; massive reinforcements, covered by aircraft, arrived safely; and sooner or later a successful breakout from the bridgehead, assisted by aircraft, was achieved.[30]

Normandy, the ultimate examination in combined operations, could not have been passed without years of study and practice in the Mediterranean, nor without the help either of escorted strategic bombers over Germany or the victories of Soviet armies (ground and air) in the east. Once ashore in

Normandy, Allied artillery fired at will, without fearing to reveal its positions to enemy aircraft. Guns, trucks, armor, and infantry moved freely in daylight. Airfields were set up wherever convenient, and airmen did not long trouble about camouflage or dispersing aircraft because air superiority soon became complete. However, air support was limited throughout the war by bad weather and, less excusably, by the inability of tactical air forces to operate in darkness. German ground forces made good use of every minute of bad weather, every hour of darkness, and their flak gunners labored with a will to compensate for the Luftwaffe's weakness. During the nine-week campaign before D day, for example, nearly 2,000 Allied aircraft were shot down.[31] The triumph of air support for ground forces, in this as in all campaigns, was bitterly earned. But let me end on a happier note. As early as 24 June 1944, Lt John Eisenhower sat with his father in a car held up by heavy traffic in Normandy. "You'd never get away with this if you didn't have air superiority," observed John. Gen Dwight D. Eisenhower replied, "If I didn't have air superiority, I wouldn't be here."[32]

Discussion

Group Capt Andrew Vallance: You said that air forces cannot hold ground, that only ground troops can do that. While that has been the case as a general rule, I don't think it has always been true, and it's certainly not true now. I'll just offer you three examples from World War II when it wasn't true. One, with which you'll be very familiar, was at Pantelleria, where the islands were in effect taken by the air forces 20 minutes before the first land forces arrived. The second one was the use of the 19th Tactical Air Command south of Loire, which compelled German forces to surrender before they'd been engaged by ground forces. Later on in Burma, the fortified town of Gangaw was actually taken by the air forces. There's a classic quote in Slim's book, *Defeat into Victory,* where he says, "Gangaw was taken by the Air Forces and occupied by the Army, a most satisfactory affair."

I think it's important to make this distinction. While I acknowledge the complementary capabilities of air forces and ground forces, I don't think we should divide them with heavy pencil lines saying, "This can be done only by this force, and this one cannot do that."

Dr. Orange: I've spent the afternoon sitting beside an RAF Regiment officer, and that has helped to remind me that the RAF Regiment came into existence during the Desert Campaign, partly because the army wasn't able to do, or perhaps in some cases wasn't willing to do, what the air commanders wanted, and that was protect their airfields. Coningham on several occasions needed his uniformed ground personnel to hold land otherwise they would have been pushed back towards Cairo.

Air Commodore W. H. Garing: I don't agree with that previous question. I've always believed that the army held ground, and when we captured ships at sea, the navy boarded them.

On the morning of D day the weather was pretty foul, and we got ashore by a whisker, and it was made possible, I think, by the Halifax bombers which went in and attacked those nine heavy defense positions; heavy guns pointing seaward on the coast, near the area where the D day landings took place. I think that was a very vital operation.

Dr. Orange: I can only comment by repeating one sentence, a theme I tried to bring out in my paper. I do feel that as Tedder always argued, it has to be all hands to the pump depending on the time and the circumstances. Strategical, tactical, fighter, fighter-bomber, transport, everything has its part to play. Tedder was adamant about avoiding interfunctional rivalry—fighters against bombers, bombers against transports, and so on. Everybody had to pull together, and on the occasion you mentioned, the Halifax bombers certainly made a valuable contribution.

Air Commodore Gordon Steege: I had a P-40 squadron in the Western Desert under Air Marshal Coningham, and I saw quite a lot of him. He was a very good-looking man, a man of great personal charm and approachable at any time by squadron commanders. He was also a man with great flexibility of mind. The arrival of the Bf-109s in North Africa brought an airplane which was superior to anything we had at that time, the P-40 and the Hurricane. The 109s were in fact operating at will way behind British lines. Coningham arranged that South African bomber squadrons, which had some problems operating against the 109s, would be escorted by a large number of at least two or three squadrons of P-40s. When this was first introduced, we approached it with some trepidation, as you could see the 109s taking off from their airfields. But I don't think that we ever lost a day bomber on those operations, which went on for a very long time and certainly kept the Germans back where they belonged.

Dr. Orange: The Germans certainly had some superior aircraft in North Africa and Tunisia, the latest models of the Bf-109 and also the FW-190, but in fact, largely through the excellence of the British repair and maintenance organization, the Western Desert Air Force kept more of its aircraft flying more of each day than the Germans did. The man whose name who has always stood in mention here is Air Vice-Marshal Grahame Dawson.

Notes

1. Air Publication (AP) 3000, *Royal Air Force Air Power Doctrine*, 2d ed. ([United Kingdom]: Her Majesty's Stationery Office [HMSO], 1993), iii. The quotation (not there identified) is from the fourth of Marshal of the Royal Air Force Lord Tedder's four lectures given in February and March 1947 in Cambridge University, entitled "Air Power in War," issued by Directorate of Command and Staff Training, Air Ministry, London, September 1947, 40.

2. Rick Atkinson, *Crusade: The Untold Story of the Gulf War* (New York: HarperCollins, 1993), reviewed by Max Hastings in the *Weekly Telegraph*, London, 19–25 January 1994, 20.

3. R. J. Overy, *The Air War, 1939–1945* (London: Europa Publications, 1980), 149–84.

4. Vincent Orange, "The Fighter Aircraft, 1915 to 1945: A Vital Weapon in the World Wars" in *Historical News*, Department of History, University of Canterbury, no. 60, May 1990, 1–4; Williamson Murray, "The Influence of Pre-War Anglo-American Doctrine on the Air Campaigns of the Second World War" in *The Conduct of the Air War in the Second World War: An International*

Comparison, ed. Horst Boog (New York/Oxford: Berg, 1992), 237–39; and Alfred Price, *World War II Fighter Conflict* (London: Macdonald and Jane's, 1975), 158.

5. The contribution of transport aircraft, worth a paper on its own, is admirably outlined in AP 3231, *Airborne Forces* (London: Air Ministry, Air History Branch [AHB], 1951).

6. Arthur William Tedder, *With Prejudice: The War Memoirs of Marshal of the Royal Air Force Lord Tedder* (London: Cassell, 1966); and Vincent Orange, *Coningham: A Biography of Air Marshal Sir Arthur Coningham KCB, KBE, DSO, MC, DFC, AFC* (Washington, D.C.: Center for Air Force History, 1992).

7. John E. Fagg, "Mission Accomplished" in *The Army Air Forces in World War II*, vol. 3, *Europe: Argument to V-E Day, January 1944 to May 1945*, ed. Wesley Frank Craven and James Lea Cate (1948–1958; reprint, Washington, D.C.: Office of Air Force History, 1983), 807. See also Daniel R. Mortensen, *A Pattern for Joint Operations: World War II Close Air Support, North Africa* (Washington, D.C.: Office of Air Force History and US Army Center of Military History, 1987); Daniel R. Mortensen, "The Legend of Laurence Kuter: Agent for Airpower Doctrine" and David R. Mets, "A Glider in the Propwash of the Royal Air Force?: Gen Carl A. Spaatz, the RAF, and the Foundations of American Tactical Air Doctrine" in *Airpower and Ground Armies: Essays on the Evolution of Anglo-American Air Doctrine, 1940–43*, ed. Daniel R. Mortensen (Maxwell Air Force Base [AFB], Ala.: Air University Press, 1998); Richard H. Kohn and Joseph P. Harahan, eds., *Air Superiority in World War II and Korea, An Interview with Gen James Ferguson, Gen Robert M. Lee, Gen William W. Moyer, and Lt Gen Elwood R. Quesada* (Washington, D.C.: Office of Air Force History, 1983); and Maj John Patrick Owens, "The Evolution of FM 100-20, *Command and Employment of Air Power*, 21 July 1943, The Foundations of Modern Airpower Doctrine" (masters thesis, Fort Leavenworth, Kans., 1989).

8. Geoffrey Perret, *Winged Victory: The Army Air Forces in World War II* (New York: Random House, 1993), 193.

9. Procedures clearly described in AP 3235, *Air Support* (London: Air Ministry, AHB, 1955).

10. Perret, 352.

11. Richard P. Hallion, *Strike from the Sky: The History of Battlefield Air Attack, 1911–1945* (Shrewsbury: Airlife Publishing, 1989), 52–53, 150; Mortensen, "Laurence Kuter," and Mets, "A Glider in the Propwash," in Mortensen, *Airpower and Ground Armies*.

12. Lewis H. Brereton, *The Brereton Diaries: The War in the Air in the Pacific, Middle East, and Europe, 3 October 1941–8 May 1945* (New York: W. Morrow and Co., 1946), 172.

13. John Keegan in the *Weekly Telegraph*, London, 16–22 February 1994, vii.

14. Paul Deichman (Littleton B. Atkinson, Noel F. Parrish, and Albert F. Simpson, eds.), *German Air Force Operations in Support of the Army* (New York: Arno Press, 1962), original publication (Maxwell AFB, Ala.: Air

University, USAF Historical Division); David John Cawdell Irving, *The Rise and Fall of the Luftwaffe: The Life of Luftwaffe Marshal Erhard Milch* (London: Futura Publications, 1976); and Harold Faber, ed., *Luftwaffe: An Analysis by Former Luftwaffe Generals* (London: Sidgwick and Jackson, 1979).

15. The Dornier Do-19 and Junkers Ju-89 were cancelled in May 1937; the Heinkel He-177, first flown in November 1939, would have performed well had its four engines not been coupled in two nacelles and had a dive-bombing capability not been thought desirable. J. Richard Smith and Antony L. Kay, *German Aircraft of the Second World War* (London: Putnam, 1972), 279–89; see also Faber, 160–64.

16. Alan Bullock, *Hitler and Stalin: Parallel Lives* (London: Fontana Press, 1993), 776.

17. Kenneth R. Whiting, "Soviet Air-Ground Co-ordination, 1941–1945," in *Case Studies in the Development of Close Air Support*, ed. Benjamin Franklin Cooling (Washington, D.C.: Office of Air Force History, 1990), 115–51; Overy 47–60; Von Hardesty, "The Soviet Air Force: Doctrine, Organisation and Technology," in Boog, 208–22; and Hallion, 228–60.

18. Vincent Orange, "Getting Together: Tedder, Coningham, and Americans in the Desert and Tunisia, 1940–43," in Mortensen, *Airpower and Ground Armies.*

19. Air Marshal Sir Arthur Coningham, "The Development of Tactical Air Forces," *RUSI* (Royal United Service Institute) *Journal* 91, 1946, 32; see also Charles Carrington, *Soldier at Bomber Command* (London: Leo Cooper, 1987). As John Terraine points out in his introduction, Carrington's repeated assertion that the principles of close support were devised in England, not in North Africa, is mistaken. See also David Syrett, "The Tunisian Campaign, 1942–1943," in Cooling, 153–92.

20. Coningham, 213; and Michael Carver, *Twentieth Century Warriors: The Development of the Armed Forces of the Major Military Nations in the Twentieth Century* (London: Weidenfeld and Nicolson, 1987), 313.

21. Orange, *Coningham*, 79.

22. Air Marshal Sir Peter Drummond, "The Air Campaign in Libya and Tripolitania," *RUSI Journal* 88, 1943, 257.

23. David John Cawdell Irving, *The Trail of the Fox: The Life of Field-Marshal Erwin Rommel* (London: Futura Publications, 1978), 182–83, 189, 201.

24. Matthew Cooper, *The German Air Force, 1933–1945: An Anatomy of Failure* (London: Jane's, 1981), 209–10; and Orange, *Coningham*, 97–103.

25. Ronald Lewin, *Hitler's Mistakes* (London: Guild Publishing, 1984), 117–19, 144–45; Correlli Barnett, *Engage the Enemy More Closely: The Royal Navy in the Second World War* (New York and London: Norton, 1991), 491–94, 525–26; Maj Gen R. F. K. Goldsmith, "The Development of Air Power in Joint Operations: Lord Tedder's Contribution to World War II," two parts, *Army Quarterly and Defence Journal* 94, no. 2, July 1967, 192–201, and vol. 95, no. 1, October 1967, 59–69; and Vincent Orange, *A Biography of Air Chief Marshal Sir Keith Park GCG, KBE, MC, DFC, DCL* (London: Methuen, 1984), 172–76.

26. George F. Howe, *Northwest Africa: Seizing the Initiative in the West* (Washington, D.C.: Center of Military History, US Army, 1991), 682–83. From November 1942, 172,783 men (142,047 of them German) reached North Africa with 544 tanks, 8,173 vehicles, and 1,093 guns.

27. *The Rise and Fall of the German Air Force, 1933–1945* (London: Arms and Armour Press, 1983), 250–52.

28. Winston S. Churchill, *The Grand Alliance* (London: The Reprint Society, 1952), 477.

29. The Allies built 634,142 aircraft between 1939 and 1945; Germany built 117,881 and Italy 10,000. Overy, 150.

30. Alan F. Wilt, "Allied Co-operation in Sicily and Italy, 1943–1945," and Will A. Jacobs, "The Battle for France, 1944," in Cooling, 193–293.

31. John Terraine, "Theory and Practice of the Air War: The Royal Air Force," in Boog, 493.

32. Quoted in Hallion, 227.

World War II:
The Bombing of Germany

Richard J. Overy

Ever since the American economist John Galbraith as a matter of "intellectual honesty" revealed in 1945 that the bombing of Germany had accelerated rather than reduced production, the Anglo-American bomber offensive has been regarded as a flawed campaign. For not only was the central aim of the offensive, the progressive reduction of the economic capacity and war willingness of the German home front, not apparently achieved, but the bombing appeared to have had the opposite effect, actually to stimulate greater production and firmer morale.[1] The conclusion reached at the end of the war was that bombing cost the Allies more in economic resources than it did the enemy and that the great manufacturing effort in Britain and the United States would have been better devoted to tanks, guns, and ships. For it was the ground troops, according to Galbraith, who won the war. All bombing did was "to ease somewhat their path."[2]

These were provocative claims, but they have solidified since the war into historical orthodoxy. The bombing of Germany has generally been regarded as a waste of strategic effort. Yet much of the argument remains speculative; even where issues might be quantitatively verifiable, little effort has gone into their historical verification. Of course, without bombing the Western Allies would certainly have had more troops and weapons for a surface assault on Europe (though shortage of equipment was never a serious constraint even with the bombing), but they would almost certainly have faced a larger and more heavily armed force in France and far greater tactical airpower. How much stronger it is impossible to say, for considerations like these are the stuff of war gaming, not history. There is only one sure way to assess the effects of the Combined Bomber Offensive, and of the great strategic investment in Allied bombing, and that is to reconstruct as fully and carefully as possible the actual impact of bombing on German strategy, economic power, and morale.

Much of the groundwork for such an assessment was laid by the United States Strategic Bombing Survey, of which Galbraith was a senior member. But the survey has a number of drawbacks as a historical source. It was put together in great haste in the few weeks after victory, with many of its general conclusions based on interviews and statements from senior German officials. It was in no sense a historical record, nor was it intended to be. Its brief was to examine the damage to German industry, not to make wider judgments about German strategy or military effort. It was staffed by academic experts many of whom were skeptical of what airmen claimed for bombing and inclined by training and outlook to view the offensive critically.[3]

The survey took a narrowly economic view of the purposes and effects of bombing, and much of the critical postwar literature on bombing has followed suit. This has tended to distort assessment of the offensive in several ways. It ignores the other strategic considerations which drew the Western Allies to select bombing as a major element of Allied war making. Bombing was regarded, rightly or wrongly, as one of the few ways that first Britain, then her American ally, could get at Germany, while they cleared the seas of submarines, stabilized the Mediterranean theater, and built up the large, fully trained forces necessary to breach the Atlantic Wall. Bombing signalled Allied commitment to the fight with Germany. It also fitted with other Western preferences. The Allies expected that bombing would produce lower manpower losses than ground war. No doubt memories of the Somme played a part in this, as Lord Cherwell once remarked to Gen George C. Marshall, but the fact remains that reducing overall combat losses was an important consideration in preferring airpower to land power. The loss rates for both the Royal Air Force (RAF) and the United States Army Air Forces (USAAF) were high on bombing missions, but the absolute totals of approximately 50,000 per force over three or four years were tiny compared with the millions lost on the eastern front, or even with the 200,000 Western casualties suffered between June and August 1944 in the invasion of France.[4]

Finally, bombing was seen as a "Second Front," designed to absorb German manpower and weapons in order to ease conditions for the Red Army. Bombing forced dispersal on German forces that had proved so effective between 1939 and 1941 only when they were able to achieve unrestricted concentration of effort. After the combined offensive was sanctioned at the Casablanca Conference in January 1943, the assault on German airpower became an important intermediate priority before bombing could come fully into its own. The bombing campaign was in this sense a military conflict, not just an instrument of economic warfare. With the introduction of long-range strategic fighters in 1944, the bombing offensive became the means to blunt and then defeat German airpower, the most formidable element in German military success since 1939.[5] The military confrontation between Allied offensive airpower and German active and passive air defenses absorbed substantial resources on both sides. Albert Speer, the German minister of armaments during the period of the bombing offensive, doubted the effectiveness of many of the economic attacks, but he regarded the military conflict as "the greatest lost battle on the German side."[6]

Even on the narrower economic issues, the survey's assumptions should be cautiously approached. It is true that German war production expanded continuously during the period of bombing until the autumn of 1944. But this was not due, as the survey insisted, to a great deal of productive slack in the German civilian economy which was gradually absorbed into weapons production after 1942. The expansion was largely achieved by the rationalization of the armaments economy from 1941 onwards and a program of administrative centralization. The aggregate resources devoted to war production—labor, raw materials, factory space—were not much greater in 1944 than in 1941 (in some cases it was less), but the resources were used more efficiently. Labor engaged in war production increased by 149 percent between 1939 and 1941, but by only a further 11 percent between 1941 and 1944.[7] Allied intelligence assumptions that the German economy was already heavily committed to the war effort in 1941 were correct; what was underestimated was the extent to which increased efficiency and greater coordination and planning could transform German war industry, even in the face of heavy bombing.

The survey was chiefly concerned with assessing the effects of bombing on the industrial system. This was measured by looking at month-by-month production planning and gauging the monthly shortfall. The survey's *Overall Report* estimated that bombing reduced gross industrial production by 9 percent in 1943 and by 17 percent in 1944.[8] These were significant figures in their own right in an industrial economy the size of Germany's, the equivalent of a particularly acute downturn in the business cycle.[9] But the aggregate figures obscure the real impact of bombing, for there were obvious differences in the effect of bombing on the industries chosen as targets, and between war industry and the rest of the civilian industrial structure. Nor did the survey take account in these calculations of the redistribution of resources and productive capacity within the war economy from the output of battle-front weapons to equipment for air defense. The emphasis on industrial performance also disguised other economic costs: the distortion of the labor market, the demands of repair, rehabilitation, and evacuation, or the opportunity costs of dispersal and decentralization of production. The estimates of production loss were based on plans which already reflected these other constraints. In an economy without bombing, none of these other constraints would have existed, and the production threshold could have been pushed well beyond the plans that were actually drawn up. Bombing did not stop production from expanding, but it placed important limits on how far that expansion could go. Without bombing, German managers and officials would have worked without the inhibiting effects of high levels of absenteeism and slack working, or the redistribution or relocation of much of the workforce, or the constant and debilitating fracturing of the delicate network of distribution and fabrication produced by rationalization. The aggregate effect of bombing on German economic performance, or on that of Italy and Japan, was necessarily greater than the rough-and-ready estimates of overall percentage loss expressed by the survey.

The question of what effect bombing had on Germany's war effort has no simple statistical answer. The effect can be broken down into a number of distinct elements, though they are not necessarily mutually exclusive. There were in the first place what might be regarded as *intended effects*. These comprise the direct physical damage to German war industry, the indirect factors reducing economic capability, and the effects on labor morale and utilization. Second, there were *diversionary effects* on German strategy and military effort. These included the dislocation of Germany's air effort, the allocation of manpower and weapons to air defense, and the distorting effects on Germany's war effort of the search for weapons of revenge. Third, there were unintended or *subsidiary effects* which also undermined the production effort by taking resources away from the output of battlefield weapons and by injuring the administrative apparatus set up by Speer in 1942 to run the war economy. Most disruptive were the program of underground relocation, pursued at great expense in 1944, and the program of research and production for the V-weapons. Both invited the growing encroachment of the *Schutzstaffel* (SS) at the expense of the circle of industrial and engineering experts recruited by Speer in 1942. This political shift was a direct result of the bombing, which encouraged the search for radical economic solutions and increased the need to coerce the home population and the foreign workforce. Directly or indirectly, bombing had wide-ranging and diverse effects on the German war effort which went well beyond the material damage to factories and infrastructure. Indeed, by 1944 bombing was the central issue on the German home front.[10]

Intended Effects

In assessing the intended effects of the bombing offensive it is necessary to be clear from the outset about what those intentions were. There were senior airmen in Britain and the United States who subscribed to the view that bombing, given its head, could end the war on its own. It was to counter this exaggerated view of airpower that Galbraith and his team emphasized its limitations. But the directive agreed at Casablanca was more modest. The combined offensive was one of a number of strategic initiatives, not a war-winner on its own. The bomber forces were directed to undertake "the progressive destruction and dislocation of the German military, industrial and economic system and the undermining of the morale of the German people." To achieve this objective a number of specific targets were chosen—the aircraft industry, the submarine industry, oil, ball bearings, and military vehicles—to which transportation was later added in 1944. The RAF attacked the cities where these industries and facilities were located; the USAAF attacked the industrial targets directly with as much precision as was then technically feasible, which was not a great deal.[11]

The cumulative effect of these attacks in 1943 was relatively small, though it was higher in the cities and industries actually bombed. During 1944 and the first half of 1945, bombing played a major part in reducing production in the central cluster of industries and industrial regions chosen for attack. The loss of production in the armaments sector was calculated by the British Bombing Survey Unit at 14 percent in 1944 and 48 percent in 1945, though the latter figure also reflected circumstances other than bombing. However, the effects on the specific industries within the war economy subject to attack were considerably more substantial. The British survey noted that the loss in aircraft production in 1944 was one-fifth and in 1945 59 percent; tank production was down by 16.5 percent on plan in 1944 and 42 percent in 1945.[12] Figures produced by the Speer ministry in January 1945 showed an even higher shortfall in 1944: a loss of 35 percent in armored vehicles, 31 percent in aircraft of all types, and 42 percent in the output of military trucks.[13] On the basis of these estimates, Germany could have had between 7,800 and 17,000 more aircraft in 1944. Additional numbers would have reduced the high levels of attrition, allowed a better rate of survival for German aircrew, and more protection for the oil production on which the Luftwaffe depended. These estimates relate, however, only to the gulf between plan and fulfillment. Speer calculated that the shortfall between potential capacity and actual production was much higher, in the case of fighter aircraft as much as 50 percent. The plans for aircraft production were scaled down during 1944 to match the economic reality imposed by bombing. The effect of bombing on these key sectors—tanks, aircraft, and trucks—was markedly higher than the effect on armament production as a whole, and it was the failure to supply more of this equipment that contributed to the decline in German fighting capability in 1944 and the progressive "demodernization" of its forces.

The physical destruction of selected raw material industries also produced rates of loss well above the aggregate for German industry as a whole. The oil industry was hit heavily in 1944, forcing the use of scarce oil stocks and reducing the fighting power of all German forces. From September 1944 the Luftwaffe received only 30,000 tons of fuel a month instead of the 160,000 to 180,000 tons it needed, so that the large increases in fighter aircraft produced could not be used effectively nor pilots properly trained.[14] Oil production declined from the early spring of 1944, to reach by September 27 percent of the level in March. Aviation fuel was reduced to 5 percent of its spring level (see table 1).[15] Attacks against the basic chemical industry produced similar results in 1944, severely reducing explosives production and forcing the use of accumulated stocks. The production of nitrogen for explosives was reduced by three-quarters during 1944, of methanol by four-fifths, soda by 60 percent, chlorine by 40 percent, sulfuric acid by 55 percent, and so on.[16] Unlike the armaments industry where production increased for most of 1944, though well below plan, the losses in oil and chemicals represented an absolute decline in output which proved irreversible. The shortfall from planned production was even higher. Output of nitrogen was scheduled to reach 87,000 tons in December 1944; actual output was 19,000 tons. The effect of the loss of chemical production was a serious decline in explosives, from a peak of 51,000 tons in June 1944 to 30,000 tons in December, a shortfall of 42 percent.[17] Attacks against the synthetic rubber industry were carried out simultaneously. Production here fell from 12,000 tons in March, the wartime peak, to 2,000 tons in November. The shortfall between planned and actual output was 11 percent in March but 88 percent in November.[18]

Table 1

The Loss in Oil Production, 1944 (thousands of tons)

	Synthetic Fuel	Total Home Production*	Aviation Fuel
Jan	336	673	159.5
Feb	306	638	163.7
Mar	341	733	180.4
Apr	348	658	175.4
May	285	606	156.1
Jun	145	427	53.8
Jul	86	344	34.7
Aug	47	318	17.1
Sep	26	265	10.0
Oct	38	279	21.0
Nov	78	290	39.0
Dec	56	272	24.5

*Total Home Production includes domestically produced natural oil and other low-grade synthetics.

Source: Charles K. Webster and Noble Frankland, *The Strategic Air Offensive Against Germany, 1939–1945*, vol. 4, *Annexes and Appendices* (London: Her Majesty's Stationery Office [HMSO], 1961), appendix 37, 516.

The success against oil and chemicals reflected the capital-intensive nature of the industry and the large body of detailed target intelligence on both sectors collected since the beginning of the war, when oil had been regarded as the critical German bottleneck. These were industries difficult to relocate quickly and highly susceptible to bomb damage. Their progressive destruction compelled German manufacturers to use up stocks. By the last nine months of war, much of the new output was based on what had been saved from earlier production rather than on new supplies. The long-term provision of basic materials and oil for the war economy and the armed forces was eroded during the course of 1944 to a point where the cycle of decline could not easily be reversed.

Not all of this decline was due to the direct attack on industrial targets. At least some of the production loss from 1943 onwards was the result of more indirect pressures exerted by bomb attack. In the first place, the sophisticated central system for the control of flows of raw materials and components established in 1942 was particularly vulnerable to arbitrary interruption and dislocation. To increase production Speer discouraged the holding of large stocks of parts and materials which had been common practice in the early years of the war. Under the rationalization drive arms production was concentrated as far as possible in larger, more technically efficient plants, which were nourished by a flow of components and subassemblies from smaller subcontractors. Such a system placed a premium on the smooth flow of supplies feeding into the final assembly plants.[19] It was designed to make possible mass production and long production runs, with special-purpose machinery and a higher ratio of less skilled workers.

Bombing distorted this production system in a number of ways. It interrupted the structure of distribution of both materials and components through damage to rail links, roads, and waterways. City attacks destroyed small businesses or storehouses where stocks of components awaited delivery. The supply of energy—gas and electricity—was routinely cut. None of these interruptions on their own held up production for very long, but their effect was cumulative. German managers and officials were forced to devote organizational effort and resources to repair the damage. Labor had to be detailed to antiaircraft precautions, particularly the building of dummy targets and the camouflaging of operational plant.[20] Some effort was made by the bombing survey to calculate the quantitative impact of the indirect attacks. In Berlin, where 45 percent of all industrial and commercial buildings were destroyed and 30 percent damaged, it was found that in 1942, 4,000 local workers were engaged in repair work on average over the year. In 1943 the figure was 10,000, in 1944 9,000, or the equivalent of 2.7 million working days. Attacks on gas supplies in January 1944 reduced Berlin's gas by half for two weeks, but constant fracture in the pipe work produced a long attrition of gas pumped into the capital throughout 1943 and 1944. Stocks in gasometers were reduced from 2.25 million cubic meters in early 1943 to 900,000 by December of that year and 480,000 by March 1944. Random destruction of electrical power supply had the same effect: in 1943 Berlin received 2,297 million kilowatt-hours, in 1944 only 1,946 million.[21] The burden on industry was eased where possible by imposing cuts in energy use by ordinary civilians and by the establishment of mobile emergency repair teams, but even the limited statistical evidence available suggests a margin of resource loss that rose steadily over the war and left many businesses in the unhappy position of having to run simply to keep still.

The most conspicuous indirect effect was the forced decentralization and dispersal of production. The German authorities from 1942 insisted on establishing new production facilities in areas more remote from the air threat in southern Germany, Austria, and occupied central Europe. While dispersal did allow production of key armaments to continue, it proved very disruptive in the short term and brought with it a whole host of new problems.[22] Firms found that the premises to which they were dispersed lacked equipment or amenities; local support services were often deficient. In one case, the transfer of Daimler-Benz aero-engine production to a new purpose-built plant in Austria, shortages of construction materials and labor held up completion of the project for months, while production at the main plant was run down. When Daimler-Benz finally made the transfer, American bombers damaged the works so severely three weeks later that the new production had to be dispersed again into the surrounding region.[23] The program of decentralization also ran counter to the rationalization drive. The move to new production sites reduced the opportunities for mass production with less skilled labor. Instead a higher number of skilled workers, using general-purpose machine tools and increased handwork, were once again necessary. In many cases the skilled labor could not be found, and the quality of production declined, together with prospects for effective inspection. Even where the main assembly plant was retained, much of the subassembly work was dispersed to more secure sites. The effect was to lengthen the distance considerably between the central plant and its main subsidiaries. The average distance of the main dispersal sites from the Junkers central aircraft assembly at Dessau was 92 kilometers; from Junkers at Magdeburg the distance was 160 kilometers.[24]

Whatever advantage dispersal brought in protecting production was compromised as the war went on by the problems of communication. Once the two Allied air forces agreed to coordinate the attack on transport in the autumn of 1944, the prospects for maintaining a decentralized system of production declined sharply. Almost all the senior German officials interrogated at the end of the war agreed that the systematic disruption of traffic by bombing was the critical factor in the collapse of the industrial economy from September 1944. The number of freight-car placings by the German railways declined by just over one-third between April 1943 and April 1944; by the end of 1944 total placings were down two-thirds.[25] Raw materials and finished armaments piled up at the railheads. Unable to move the coal and steel from the Ruhr, production progressively declined. Output of steel fell by three-quarters at the *Vereinigte Stahlwerke* during 1944, while stocks of coke and iron ore were rapidly run down. The collapse of the rail network split Germany into smaller economic regions which were unable to support armaments production once remaining inventories were used up. From January 1945 bombing made it impossible to support a serious economic war effort. Its effects were, according to one senior German official, "catastrophic."[26]

The effects on German morale were equally debilitating. Although bombing did not produce a popular uprising against the German government, nor the complete collapse of war-willingness, all the evidence suggests that the experience of bombing was uniquely demoralizing. Of course only a fraction of the population, concentrated in the major industrial regions, was subjected to the regular threat of bombing, but it was a fraction vital to the war effort. The progressive destruction of the urban environment and the major consumer services, far from stiffening resolve and encouraging greater productive efforts, made the workforce listless, nervous, and prone to illness and absenteeism. The head of the Labor Section in the German Armaments Ministry described the deteriorating social conditions to Allied interrogators: "The burdens were: accommodation in mass and emergency quarters, difficulties of going to and from work, loss of personnel and personal property on account of bombing, disturbed rest at night on account of air-raids, difficulties of supply, change of place of work when the firms were evacuated, working in factories without a roof or working underground."[27] When German civilians returned American questionnaires on wartime morale, 91 percent said that bombing was the hardest thing for them to bear.[28]

The social dislocation and psychological crisis induced by bombing were reflected in problems of work discipline. In 1944 the average level of absenteeism was 23.5 days, or almost four full working weeks. At the Ford works in Essen the average rate of absence throughout 1944 was 25 percent among the native German workforce (though only 4 percent among foreign workers who could more easily be coerced). Even in areas more remote from bombing, the fear of attack could still be effective. At the BMW works in Munich, absenteeism averaged 10 percent in 1943, but reached a peak of 19 percent by August 1944.[29] Populations in the big cities beneath the bomber flight paths were forced to spend long hours in shelters as the aircraft passed overhead and back again. In a recent study of the air defense of Mainz, it has been shown that between January and November 1944 a state of alarm existed for a total of 540 hours, reaching a peak of 117 in October.[30] Much of the population reacted by evacuating to safer areas. Estimates of the numbers evacuated vary between eight million and four million. The population of Berlin declined from four million in January 1943 to 2.7 million in May 1944.[31] The effect of large-scale evacuation was to create social strains in the main reception areas, in the countryside or the small towns of the south, and to increase the mobility and turnover rates of the industrial workforce. This is part of the explanation for the great increase in the employment of forced foreign labor and prisoners of war from 1943; forced labor was easier to discipline and was decidedly less mobile, even if its average productive performance was below that of the native German workforce. But with less effective provision for air-raid precautions, the forced laborers also experienced higher rates of casualty from bomb attack.

There can be little doubt that without bombing the German workforce would have been much more productive, and the German economy and welfare services would have been relieved of the obligation to rehouse bomb victims, evacuate a large fraction of the population, and cope with the costs of medical care and rehabilitation. The effects of widespread fear, apathy, and despondency on a population from whom the regime expected great sacrifices in living standards and political freedoms can hardly be exaggerated. Bombing persuaded a great many Germans that the war was lost, but it scarcely produced the political will or physical desperation necessary to confront and overthrow the Nazi state. People continued to work, but they did so less frequently, less attentively, and less willingly than hitherto.

Diversionary Effects

The impression is often given that the bombing offensive was a battle between aircraft and enemy civilians when in reality it was a campaign fought against the antiaircraft defenses of the enemy, guns and planes. The ultimate objectives were German economic power and domestic morale, but these were increasingly shielded as the war went on by a substantial military shell. The consequences of this military confrontation for the German war effort were disastrous, for the bombing not only diverted very large resources away from the main battlefronts where it was needed, but it created the circumstances for the defeat of German airpower in 1944 as the Allies sought for ways to break through the Third Reich's defenses. The bombing distorted German strategy in such a way that German military capability was weakened, not only in defense of the German economy but on the main fronts in eastern and western Europe.

From the early years of war the German military leadership saw little need for extensive aerial defenses. Great reliance was placed on antiaircraft fire and effective observation. But by 1942 the scale of attack forced the gradual establishment of fighter and night-fighter forces in the Reich and the creation of an elaborate network of static defenses—antiaircraft guns, radar stations, and searchlights. By 1943 the balance between frontline and Reich air forces changed sharply. On 1 January 1943 there were 59 percent of German single- and twin-engine fighters in the west facing the bombers, and 25 percent were on the eastern front. By 1 January 1944 there were 68 percent in the west, 17 percent in the east. By October 1944, 81 per- cent of an enlarged fighter force faced the combined offen- sive.[32] Many of these fighters were effectively immobilized for long periods waiting for the bomber streams and could not easily be redeployed to the fighting fronts.

The emphasis on fighter defense also produced a forced restructuring of German airpower. Up to the beginning of 1943, the bomber force and fighter force were of roughly equal size, and bomber production was higher. In 1942 fighter production was just over three-quarters the level of bomber output. But in 1943 one-third more fighters were produced than bombers, and in 1944 bombers made up just 22 percent of the number of fighters (see table 2).[33] By the summer of 1944 the German air force had on hand over 2,200 fighter aircraft but only 1,000 bombers, of which almost one-half were out of service. The bomber commanders urged Goering to restore a balanced force in 1944, but the desperate need to protect the rest of German war production against bomb attack gave fighters an irre- sistible priority.[34] The effect was to reduce the bomber compo- nent on all fronts, in the Soviet Union, in Italy, and in France, at a time when the German armies needed tactical bombing more than ever to slow up the movement of enemy reserves and attack enemy air installations. By the summer of 1944 the German air force faced an unbridgeable disparity of force. The Allies mustered 12,000 aircraft for the invasion of France and were faced by 170 serviceable German fighters and bombers. By the end of 1944 Soviet aircraft outnumbered German by 10 to one. Levels of force attrition were as a result overwhelming.

The diversion of resources was felt not only in aircraft. During 1943, in anticipation of an escalation in the bombing,

Table 2

Production, Strength, and Serviceability of the German Bomber and Fighter Forces, 1943–44

A: Production

1943	Fighters	Bombers	1944	Fighters	Bombers
Jan	512	674	Jan	1,555	522
Feb	858	781	Feb	1,104	567
Mar	962	757	Mar	1,638	605
Apr	936	735	Apr	2,021	680
May	1,013	718	May	2,212	648
Jun	1,134	710	Jun	2,449	703
Jul	1,263	743	Jul	2,934	767
Aug	1,135	710	Aug	3,020	548
Sep	1,072	678	Sep	3,375	428
Oct	1,181	738	Oct	2,973	326
Nov	985	702	Nov	2,995	412
Dec	687	643	Dec	2,630	262

B: Strength (Serviceability Rate in brackets)

1943	Single-engine Fighters		Night Fighters		Bombers	
Mar	1,535	(66%)	493	(73%)	1,522	(55%)
Jun	1,849	(74%)	554	(67%)	1,663	(64%)
Sep	1,646	(66%)	574	(60%)	1,080	(59%)
Dec	1,561	(70%)	611	(66%)	1,604	(67%)
1944						
Mar	1,696	(70%)	565	(64%)	1,331	(62%)
Jun	1,523	(59%)	778	(68%)	1,089	(64%)
Sep	1,984	(71%)	1,018	(84%)	929	(69%)
Dec	2,260	(67%)	1,256	(73%)	528	(68%)

Source: Charles K. Webster and Noble Frankland, *The Strategic Air Offensive Against Germany, 1939–1945*, vol. 4, *Annexes and Appendices* (London: HMSO, 1961), appendices 22 and 27, 494–95 and 501–2.

Germany's static defenses were much enlarged. Three-quarters of all heavy antiaircraft guns were positioned in the Reich, manned by 900,000 antiaircraft personnel. The total number of guns reached a peak of 14,489 heavy and 41,937 light antiaircraft artillery, and production ran at well over 4,000 a month. Speer later calculated that this represented about one-third of all gun production, while the antiaircraft effort absorbed 20 percent of all ammunition in 1944, one-half the production of the electro-technical industry, and one-third of optical equipment.[35] This represented a formidable diversion of manpower, fighting equipment, and industrial resources. There were as many guns defending Germany as there were on the entire eastern front in the summer of 1943. The total personnel engaged in antiaircraft work, in ancillary air defense services, and in the repair teams and the reconstruction of damaged buildings and communications has never been fully calculated, but was almost certainly in excess of two million men.[36]

Of course none of this expenditure of effort would have mattered if the bombing offensive had been defeated, and indeed in the winter of 1943–44 and the early spring, both the RAF and the USAAF faced loss rates so high that regular attacks were temporarily suspended. The critical factor was the introduction of the strategic fighter, principally the P-51 Mustang, which, with enhanced fuel capacity, could fly with the bomber streams deep into Germany and engage the defense forces directly. These attacks permitted a high level of attrition against fighters whose principal task was to attack bombers rather than engage in fighter-to-fighter combat. From the early spring the Allied air forces attacked aircraft production on the ground and fought German fighters in the skies at the same time. Loss rates were exceptionally high. As Allied air superiority came to bear, it proved possible to attack airfields and air depots, where thousands of the new fighter force were destroyed in ground attacks before they had reached the squadrons or even left the factory.[37] Although some 43,000 aircraft were allocated to the German air force in 1944 (33,864 newly produced, 9,448 repaired), most were destroyed or damaged within days of release. By 1 July 1944 there were 306 operationally ready fighter aircraft in the Reich. With the effective defeat of German airpower, it became possible to inflict much heavier levels of damage on German industry and communications.[38]

The military conflict between Allied bombers and fighters and German air defense forced a critical division on German resources. There were never enough German aircraft to perform both the attack and defense functions effectively. By the time German fighter production achieved the high levels of output necessary in 1944, the bombing offensive was sufficiently advanced both to cripple aircraft output and to attack the force in being with devastating effect. The diversion of effort starved the German armies of air protection, of adequate radio equipment and very large numbers of guns, and a further two or three million men and women who might otherwise have been engaged in armaments work or fighting at the front line. Added to the physical destruction of plant and the dislocation of the wider economic fabric, the diversion of resources to fighting the bombing offensive undermined German military strategy and weakened the tactical capability of Germany's formidable ground army.

Subsidiary Effects

The progressive reduction in German frontline fighting power, and the growing destruction and diversion of resources inside Germany, prompted responses from the German authorities that the Allies could not have predicted. Though unintended in effect, the wider initiatives not only failed to reduce the impact of bombing but contributed in significant ways to further undermining the German arms economy. The onset of heavier bombing in the spring of 1943 prompted Hitler to counter the threat with a two-fold strategy. First, the movement of all essential military production into underground factories, where it would be safe from the bombs; and, second, to adopt a more offensive posture by retaliating against England with bombers and the new weapons of revenge, rockets and flying bombs, in the hope of deterring the Allies from further attacks.

The program of underground construction was a radical solution. It made sense only if a large part of essential production could be transferred, but the costs in manpower and resources in constructing and equipping new plant on this scale carried the risk that they would undermine the very economic fabric the program was designed to protect. Not until the autumn of 1943 did Hitler finally sanction the underground dispersal. Speer did what he could to slow the program down for fear that it would disrupt the system of centralized production set up since 1942. But in the spring of 1944, Hitler insisted on pushing it through so that aircraft, rocket, and oil production in particular could be safeguarded against heavier air attacks.[39]

The whole construction program was, as Speer feared, planned on the largest scale. By December 1944 the program absorbed almost half the labor force engaged in industrial construction, over 200,000 workers, and took 75 percent of the steel allocated to construction. The total planned floor space of the underground plants was 93 million square feet. By November work was under way on 71 million, and 13 million were already completed. The distribution of the program between different industrial sectors is set out in table 3.[40]

Table 3

Germany's Underground Factory Program
(square feet of floor space)

	Planned	In Progress	Completed
Aircraft Industry	48,150,900	21,933,971	8,371,320
Tanks	2,109,000	1,818,400	290,500
Vehicles	2,808,360	2,711,500	96,800
V-Weapons	1,538,700	387,400	1,151,300
Ships	1,775,400	1,248,200	527,200
Weapons	2,173,500	2,119,720	53,800
Machine Tools	7,101,600	6,079,400	1,022,200
Other Supplies	16,839,400	10,512,500	None
SS Projects	11,298,000	8,651,100	1,883,000
Grand Total	93,794,900	71,318,000	13,396,200

Source: Public Record Office (PRO), Kew, London, AIR 10/3873, British Bombing Survey Unit, "German Experience in the Underground Transfer of War Industries," n. d., 12. The table is taken from a Rustungsamt report for the Armaments Ministry, 11 November 1944.

Some of the underground plant came into operation during 1944 and early 1945, though conditions were generally poor, but most of the projects had little hope of completion because of the scarcity of labor and materials and the gradual running down of the transport network. Much of the building and operation of the plants were undertaken by foreign labor and prisoners who were forced to work in unsanitary, poorly ventilated, and ill-lit facilities, where labor productivity was inevitably much reduced. The competition for scarce resources produced by the underground program, and the increasingly arrogant and wayward behavior of SS officials as they tried to compel firms to move underground, disrupted what efforts were still being made to maintain production through dispersal on the surface. Both the scale and disruptiveness of the program vitiated what gains might have been made by a more modest and coordinated effort or by more effective programs of surface repair. But, instead, almost one-half the construction workforce found itself, in the words of the British Bombing Survey Unit, "burrowing away from reality."[41]

Nor was the offensive effort to halt the bombing any more successful. The renewed bombing of England begun in the winter of 1943, the so-called Baby Blitz (Operation Steinbock), lacked the necessary equipment and manpower, and dropped only 1 percent of the tonnage dropped on Germany in 1943. Hitler placed his faith instead in new weapons developed to take the air war to British cities, the "weapons of revenge" (vergeltungswaffen). There were two weapons involved, the small flying bomb (V-1) and the much larger A-4 rocket (V-2). The weapons, first launched successfully in October 1942, carried only one ton of explosive and could not be targeted with any accuracy. The first flying bombs were launched in the middle of June 1944, and the first rockets reached England in September. Their firepower was extraordinarily small in relation to the costs of producing and launching them. Only 14,000 tons (9,521 flying bombs, 5,000 rockets) were fired, and most of these either failed or missed London altogether. Total tonnage dropped on Britain in 1944 was a mere 0.77 percent of the quantity dropped by the Allies on Europe.[42] The object of the V-weapons campaign was to cause sufficient levels of civilian casualty to persuade the Allies to halt the bombing of German cities. The quantity of missiles dispatched was far too small to produce this effect, and the equipment was in its infancy, technically unreliable and relatively easy to destroy in the air. The V-weapons failed entirely to halt the conduct of the Allied air war.

Instead the effort to research, develop, and manufacture the V-weapons had serious repercussions for the German scientific and industrial system. Research on the German antiaircraft rocket (*Wasserfall*), which might well have produced more significant strategic results, was held up so that technicians could concentrate on the A-4 rocket. The production plans were to build 60,000 V-1s a year and 36,000 V-2s. In practice, output of V-ls reached 30,000 altogether and of V-2s, 6,000. Even these more modest sums made very large demands on German materials and manpower, equivalent, according to the bombing survey, of 24,000 fighter aircraft. The explosives allocated to the program equalled one-half of all military consumption in July to September 1944.[43] And all this for a campaign that delivered no more than the tonnage from a single large-scale Allied raid. The only strategic gain was the diversion during 1944 of about 13 percent of Allied bombing capacity directed against the V-weapon sites which might otherwise have been used against German industry.[44]

The V-weapons program, like the underground dispersal, was the product of an understandable desire on Hitler's part to find an antidote to bombing before it eroded war capability fatally. Yet the means chosen were improvised and irrational, serving only to distort still further the structure of the war economy and to reduce the prospect of producing large numbers of conventional aircraft which could have inflicted a more effective rate of loss on Allied airpower. There certainly were German leaders—Albert Speer, Erhard Milch at the Air Ministry—who argued the case for concentration on fighter output. But their attempts to resist Hitler's priorities were treated as political disobedience, while those who flattered his search for wonder-weapons and emergency programs improved their political stock. In the summer and autumn of 1944, the bombing served to undermine the existing wartime apparatus of control and evaluation. It was replaced by a system of commissars and plenipotentiaries, drawn predominantly from radical party circles more willing to follow Hitler's flights of fancy and to use coercion to achieve them.[45]

In the final months of the war, bombing contributed a great deal towards the creation of a more ideologically charged technological and economic system, run by extremists anxious to extract the final ounce of sacrifice from an exhausted and dispirited population. Both employers and workers found themselves the victims of accusations of defeatism and slack working, and of arbitrary punishment. To keep the underground and emergency factories going the SS mobilized the concentration camp population in a final drive for production, brutally compelled. The system of economic control broke down in confusion, which compounded the problems already experienced by industry as a result of bomb attack and the transport crisis. Hitler and the party radicals grasped at any straw. In September 1944 aircraft designers were ordered to produce a "people's fighter" made of cheap substitute materials and wood, which could be used for suicide attacks on Allied bombers. They were to be piloted by boys from the Hitler Youth imbued with the National Socialist "spirit," German kamikaze. Within 69 days of the order, designers at Heinkel finished the first prototype of the chosen model, the He-162. Hitler ordered one thousand a month. The project achieved nothing, except to divert more resources away from the manufacture of standard fighter aircraft.[46] In this case, too, the production was driven by the SS, under the leadership of Kurt May, who commandeered the factory capacity and labor to fuel the new projects.

All the expedients pursued by Hitler from 1943 to avert the bombing failed in their purpose; all of them made heavy claims on German industrial and labor resources at the expense of the system of concentrated, rational production set up in 1942. In the desperate search for relief from air attack, the domestic political and administrative structure was subject to a progressive radicalization, as experts and officials were displaced by party fanatics. The effect was to reduce the prospects for the serious evaluation of ends and means, and to politicize production in ways that made an effective technical and tactical response to bombing less likely. By the spring of 1945 the effort was no longer possible. "The air war," complained Goebbels in his diary on 1 March, "has now turned into a crazy orgy. We are totally defenseless against it. The Reich will gradually be turned into a complete desert."[47]

Conclusions

Was strategic bombing a wasted effort? The balance of evidence suggests that it was not. Of course the bombing offensive had limitations. Bombing accuracy was poor, even for the American forces practicing "precision" bombing. The destruction of German oil production was achieved with only 2.2 percent of bombs dropping within the productive area and 84 percent of bombs falling outside the target altogether.[48] Nor was all Allied bombing equally effective. The impact changed over time; it was influenced by the nature of the target and by differences in night and daytime bombing. Bombing was most effective in the last 18 months of the war, least effective in its first two years. It is often argued that the wrong target systems were chosen or that targets were not hit regularly or accurately enough. This may well be so, though beyond historical proof. The test for judging bombing is the effect it actually had, rather than the effect it might have had with different priorities and different tactics.

On this criterion the impact of bombing was wide-ranging and ultimately devastating for the German war effort. The initial attacks on industrial cities and industrial target systems produced a chain reaction that affected the military structure, social life, and the political system. Its effects were cumulative, prompting a variety of strategic and organizational responses as the ramifications of bomb attack became clearer. Some of those responses produced positive results. The system of formal dispersal and the concentration and simplification of production that accompanied it allowed more weapons to be produced by 1944 than would otherwise have been the case. Bombing compelled the German authorities to improvise and maneuver, to anticipate the bombing rather than merely react to it.

Yet, after all allowance is made for the limitations of Allied bombing and the countermeasures bombing provoked, the catalogue of debilitating effects is a long and complex one. Bombing physically destroyed or limited the productive capacity of a key cluster of major armaments industries. The indirect effects of attacks on oil, raw materials, and transport, and the demoralizing impact of bombing on the workforce, placed a clear ceiling on German war production in 1944 and undermined it fatally in 1945. The diversion of resources to halt the bombing removed three-quarters of the fighter force, 56,000 guns, and a million men and women. The battle for air superiority broke the back of German airpower in the spring and summer of 1944 over the Reich. Damage to the urban environment, the decline of amenity, and the programs of evacuation and rehabilitation were major social and economic disasters. Six million households were destroyed or badly damaged; 4.8 million people were rehoused.[49] To try to save the economic fabric and to avert social collapse, the regime resorted to ever more desperate remedies, which served only to squander additional resources for little strategic gain, while the increased coercion that accompanied it alienated and terrorized wide sections of the population. Taken together the effects of bombing reduced potential German war production by perhaps as much as a half in 1944–45. It inflicted terminal decline on German forces by interrupting supplies and destroying German airpower. And bombing hastened the demoralization and social impoverishment of Germany's urban population.

There is a striking contrast here with the role of bombing in the Korean War and in Vietnam, where the effect of very large-scale campaigns was small in relation to the effort expended. The German case was very different. Germany was a predominantly urban and industrial society. Its industries and cities were conspicuous targets, and much of the productive system was concentrated and highly visible. The economic system was sophisticated, reliant on structures of production and distribution that were closely integrated and interdependent. The urban workforce had, by the standards of east Asian societies, high levels of amenity and socioeconomic expectations, and found it difficult to adjust to exceptional rates of casualty and physical damage. Much of this was anticipated by Allied air forces when they began to think about the probable effects of bomb attack in the 1930s, and it colored the development of the force structure and the technology. By 1945 the effect of Allied airpower against a modern industrial state with a highly trained workforce and a sophisticated technological and scientific establishment was qualitatively distinct from the effects of the same technology used against developing states. Bombing may well have been the most strategically cost-effective way of reducing the economic and technical advantages Germany enjoyed and of stifling German fighting power to a point where the Allies could be confident of complete victory.

Discussion

Mr. Brian Hayes: As a veteran of Bomber Command I'd like to thank Professor Overy for a very concise paper on the command's operations. There are one or two things I would like to clear up. Firstly, almost nothing favorable was said about Air Marshal Harris yesterday. I was on my third term of operations when I was shot down over Germany and became a prisoner of war. In both those environments I never heard a single derogatory remark about our great commander in chief.

I'd like to read a message sent to Air Marshal Harris by Winston Churchill at the end of the war:

Now that Nazi Germany is defeated, I wish to express to you on behalf of His Majesty's Government the sense of gratitude which is felt by all the nation for the glorious part Bomber Command played in forging the victory. For over two years (and this is a very significant point) Bomber Command alone carried the war to the heart of Germany, bringing hope to the peoples of occupied France and the other occupied territories; and to the enemy a taste of the mighty power which was rising against his. As the Command expanded, the weight of attacks was increased, dealing destruction on an unparalleled scale on the German military, industrial and economic system. Your Command also gave powerful support to the Allied armies in Europe and made the most vital contribution to the war at sea, things quite often overlooked. You destroyed or damaged many of their ships of war. You sank or damaged much of his merchant shipping. All of your operations were planned with great care and skill, they were executed in the face of desperate opposition and appalling hazards. They made a decisive contribution to Germany's final defeat. The conduct of these operations demonstrated the fiery gallant spirit that animated your aircrews, and the high sense of duty under your command. I believe that the massive achievements of Bomber Command will long be remembered as an example of duty notably done.

Flight Lt Fred Anderson: I am also a veteran of Bomber Command who wants to set the record straight. After the war many trendy academics tended to write Bomber Command off so I was pleased to hear your argument today. My question is: would you like to comment on the changing role of Bomber Command in the period from April to December 1944 when we changed from strictly night operations to more and more daylight precision attacks?

Professor Overy: I ought to make clear from the outset that even if I'm not a trendy academic, I don't think I'm a reactionary one either. Your question does allow us to look in more detail at the critical period of the war from the summer of 1944 onwards. I didn't touch on what Bomber Command was doing in support of D day or, indeed, in support of the antisubmarine campaign or naval warfare. I was concentrating particularly on the bomber offensive against the German economy and German morale. If one looks at the whole range of heavy bomber operations, the contribution was even more substantial. Nobody can doubt that the successful interdiction campaign that backed up D day was a very important factor in holding up the movement of German reserves. But once the German air force had largely been crippled by attacks on the aircraft industry and attacks on aircraft on the ground and their airfields, and subjected to high rates of attrition over the Reich itself, daylight bombing over western Germany was possible almost at will. In the last nine or 10 months of the war, both Allied air forces were able to achieve a much higher level of precision and were able to join forces in accurate attacks against transportation and oil targets, for example.

What I wanted to argue this morning was that the distortion and disruption of German strategy was something which had begun earlier than 1943 and characterized the whole of the last two and one-half years of the war.

One should add, I think, something which was touched on yesterday in the discussion on "area" bombing and "precision" bombing. During 1943 and 1944 there wasn't a great deal to distinguish one from the other. An increasing proportion of British bombs fell within a mile of the markers in the cities, but when American airmen attacked precision targets a great number of bombs fell outside a mile from their targets. So in tactical terms the big difference was fighting during the day or at night, which required rather different flying and navigational skills. But by late 1944 it was possible for both air forces to attack with a much higher level of precision. The technology was much better and was complemented by improved navigational skills and the development of the Pathfinder force. By the end of the war bombing was a very much more sophisticated animal.

Dr. Dan Keenan: Two questions. You mentioned the distortion of the Germany economy caused by the bomber offensive, but one must not forget the possible distortion of the British economy. As I recall, 30 to 40 percent of British production in the United Kingdom went into supporting heavy bomber production and training crews. Secondly, while the heavy bombers made many attacks against the U-boat pens in France and Germany, they were largely ineffective because of the concrete bunkers that were protecting those pens. Further, Air Marshal Harris was reluctant to support the Battle of the Atlantic, when heavy long-range aircraft were desperately needed to suppress the U-boats. So there was a lot of distortion on the Western side as well, particularly with Britain.

Professor Overy: I certainly wouldn't argue that mistakes were not made. I concluded my paper by saying that the bombing

offensive was a blunt instrument. The antisubmarine campaign and the use of heavy aircraft over the Atlantic in support
of naval operations was not something I addressed because I
was discussing the Combined Bombing Offensive. I would certainly take the view that if larger numbers of heavy aircraft
had been detailed sooner to the Battle of the Atlantic, it might
well have made a difference of a number of months. But I
should add that both air forces, British and American, had
doubts about how effective very long-range aircraft would be
and had to be persuaded of that as a priority. We know after
the event that it made a substantial difference. But the difference was also made by a wide range of other changes which
were brought about by the navies themselves in addition to
the use of a long-range aircraft.

Submarine pens? Well, Harris was not really surprised by this;
he did not support bombing submarine pens. It was entirely
ineffective, a complete waste of bombing effort. In his view
you'd gain a lot more by bombing the production facilities in
the Reich, which both air forces then did in 1944.

The other question was: did it distort British and American
production? The issue here is that the American and British
leaders had made a positive choice. This was their strategic
objective, and they planned their economies and devoted their
resources accordingly. When the Americans came into the
war, they balanced their effort. Britain produced more heavy
bombers, and America produced a lot more fighter and transport aircraft, and so on. From the American point of view the
distortion was really not that great. America mobilized its
industrial economy to a lower proportion than any of the other
combatant powers. Another 5 or 10 percentage points of
industrial production devoted to the war in the United States
would have provided enormous numbers of additional fighter
aircraft and tanks and so on. The shortage of materiel was not
much of a problem for the Allies in 1943 and 1944, except of
course for landing craft. The necessary level of industrial production was built into their expectations and planning. The
problem with the Germans was that it wasn't built into their
planning. Their planning was predicated on producing large

quantities of high-quality battlefront weapons to defeat the Allies in the Mediterranean and in the Soviet Union, and to defeat the coming invasion, which they expected from 1943 onwards. What the bombing offensive did was essentially to deny German battlefront forces a very large proportion of what an unbombed German economy would have been capable of producing. I think it is misleading to talk about it as a distortion in the Allied case, for it was a deliberate strategic option. In the German case it was not; it was something to which German leaders were then forced to react and against which they had to maneuver and shift their own strategy.

Group Capt Andrew Vallance: First to reiterate the views of previous speakers. Congratulations on what I thought was an absolutely first class analysis. We heard the price of the bomber offensive yesterday; we have now learnt the value of it, and I think both need to be said. Second, critics of the bomber offensive sometimes say German industry in the early part of the war was underutilized, and that one of the effects of the bomber offensive was to act as a trigger to the Germans to get their act together and produce more. How much credence do you put on that view?

Professor Overy: I don't put much credence on it at all. Much of that view rests on assumptions based on the bombing survey which has now been found to have given a very misleading picture of the German war economy. In fact the German war economy was very heavily mobilized from quite early on. Indeed, by the summer of 1941, war production made a larger claim on the German workforce, on German industry, than was the case in Britain, and it remained higher throughout the war.

The real problem for the German war economy was the ineffective way in which the mobilization of resources was translated into the production of finished weapons. Under pressure from Hitler, in 1941 to early 1942, the military and the administration began a thoroughgoing rationalization of the German war economy which enormously increased the quantity of weapons produced from the resources that were already there. Even by 1944 the aggregate resources in Germany devoted to war production were not much larger than they'd been in 1941, but the level of weapons output was three to four times higher. So there was an enormous improvement in the efficiency of the German economy over that period. But it was precisely because of the growing dependence on a system that was increasingly rationalized and streamlined that the bombing was actually more disruptive than it might otherwise have been. Albert Speer developed in Germany an extremely sophisticated system of allocation and distribution of components, materials, and labor, centralized on Berlin where all the planning took place. What bombing did was to interrupt that web all the time so that it could not operate as effectively.

The other point I should make is that the decision to kick-start the German economy, to make it more effective, actually predated bombing. It was in the spring of 1941 that Hitler discovered how ineffective German war production was. He knew he would need large quantities of materiel to defeat the Soviet Union and then to turn and defeat the Anglo-Saxon powers. So Germany's enormous increases in production were in the pipeline before Allied bombing became very effective. Once bombing had started seriously in 1943, the German authorities began to plan even higher levels of production. What Speer and the Air Ministry really wanted in 1944–45, for example, was to reach a production figure of 80–90,000 aircraft a year; more or less what the Soviet Union and the United States were capable of producing. That target was well within the production capabilities of a vast continental economy, but in practice they were only able to produce 39,000. And many of those 39,000 were destroyed in the factories or in the depots or in transit. The German fighter force was not much larger by the end of 1944 than it was at the beginning. I think we need to be aware that the expansion of the German economy was fuelled by things other than the bombing offensive, though the bombing eventually did encourage a much higher concentration on fighter production.

Air Chief Marshal Sir Patrick Hine: Two questions if I may. First of all, one focusing on the effectiveness of night bombing. You were right, Professor Overy, to remind us that it was a blunt instrument, something of which Harris was well aware and which he tried to do something about. You mentioned yourself the Pathfinder force, which in a sense was the 1940s equivalent of today's laser designation. Could you give us any measurement of the increased effectiveness of night bombing as a result of the introduction of the Pathfinder force?

My second question is on the issue of morale and whether or not the bombing offensive could have cracked German morale. If I recall correctly, in 1943 there was one attack on Hamburg where incendiaries caused a firestorm and a loss of something approaching 50,000 lives. Some commentators have said that if we could have repeated that attack against another 10 or 12 cities within the next two or three months, German morale may have cracked. I wonder if you could tell us whether there was any evidence from interrogating Germans after the war if that might have indeed been the case?

Professor Overy: The answer to your first question is yes, the Pathfinder force made a huge difference. Refinements were introduced with new navigational aids and better bomb aiming. Much higher standards of pilot and navigator training were also developed during 1942–43 at Harris's insistence. Those changes made the bomber force more effective tactically. Oddly enough, the best single report on the improvement in the RAF was produced by the Americans at the end of the war. That report demonstrated clearly that by 1944 the ability of night bombing aircraft to get within a mile of the target had improved beyond all recognition from the dismal performance of 1940 to early 1942.

To the second question about morale. I still think that in some ways people are asking the wrong question. It's hard to envisage quite how an apathetic, miserable, dispirited population, subject to high levels of bombing, is going to be in a position to overturn a regime in the middle of a war, especially when that regime is committed to maintaining fighting power to the end and is willing to impose terror on its own population. It's a little bit like Iraq, where everybody thought once the Coalition attacked, Saddam Hussein would be overturned by palace revolution or a popular uprising. But I'm not sure that politics really works that way. If the attack on Hamburg had been repeated in other cities, I think all you would have had would have been a very much larger level of German casualties and social dislocation and misery. The Hamburg raid was one of those interesting cases where the consequences were so horrific that there was something of a backlash against area bombing inside the British leadership. I don't think Harris would have been allowed to conduct 10 more firestorm raids, even if he'd argued it was strategically necessary. There's little evidence to suggest—and the whole thing is speculative of course—that it would have brought the regime down through popular revolt. I think that the expectation held in Britain since the late 1930s that Hitler would be overthrown once he was faced with firm resistance was always a misreading of the nature of the Third Reich, just as it was a misreading of the nature of Saddam's rule in Iraq in 1991. I think we should always be wary of the idea that by a mere show of force it might be possible to produce a political revolution in the enemy state.

Group Capt Mike Rawlinson: Professor Overy, in Albert Speer's book, *Inside the Third Reich*, he comments that if the attacks on the ball-bearing factories had been sustained, it would have crippled aircraft production in Germany. Could you comment on the issue of panacea targets?

Professor Overy: A list of targets was drawn up in 1943 for the combined offensive. Ball bearings was one of the targets. It was attacked at great cost, and one should add that the ball-bearing industry was subsequently attacked again in 1944. I think we tend to forget that it continued to be attacked. The ball-bearing industry was quite effectively dispersed, which made it very difficult for Allied intelligence to pick up in detail where the main locus of production was. I think Speer was being a little bit mischievous in arguing that the Allies should just have kept attacking it, because it was Speer's job to ensure ball-bearing production was continued and to prevent the Allies from finding out where the factories were.

When Allied intelligence staffs actually sat down to determine the industries and infrastructure they needed to attack in order seriously to undermine levels of armaments production, I think they recognized that it would really be impossible to attack a single target, that they would have to attack a cluster of targets. Bomber Command from 1938–39 onwards had stuck to the panacea target of oil. Oil was the issue, they said; if you could find ways of undermining Germany's oil supply, that was Germany's weak link. When the American Air Intelligence staff came to think about the bombing campaign, they were initially influenced by the British preoccupation with oil. But they then decided to look at their own industry: what would interrupt the American war industry if it were attacked? They then projected that analysis onto German industry and decided in fact a cluster of industries would have to be attacked. The top priority ones I have talked about. But there was also a series of lower priority industries—machine tools and various other forms of capital production which were systematically attacked from 1944.

Notes

1. John Kenneth Galbraith, *A Life in Our Times: Memoirs* (London: n. p., 1981), 219, 239–40.

2. Ibid., 240. These views have been recently endorsed in Stephen A. Garrett, *Ethics and Airpower in World War II: The British Bombing of German Cities* (New York: St. Martin's Press, 1993), 158–64.

3. These included the economists Burton H. Klein and Nicholas Kaldor, whose postwar publications elaborated the survey's conclusions that the German war economy reached its peak only when the bombing was at its most intense. See Klein, *Germany's Economic Preparations for War* (Cambridge: Harvard University Press, 1959); and Kaldor, "The German War Economy," *Review of Economic Statistics,* 13, 1946.

4. Estimates on loss rates differ. It is virtually impossible to break down the figures for losses to show how many died in the strategic assaults on Germany. Casualties for the Eighth Air Force and Bomber Command include losses in the war at sea, tactical bombing, accidents, and training. The number of Bomber Command aircrew lost totalled 47,268 operational crew, 8,090 nonoperational (accidents, enemy bombing attacks, ground battle). The Eighth Air Force lost 43,742, but an estimated 46 percent of sorties were in support or defensive operations, so that the figure of those who died in the skies over Germany is considerably lower than this. Aggregate figures on the losses of bombing personnel are not the same as losses sustained in bombing operations against strategic targets in Germany and central Europe, though they are often cited as if they were. On Bomber Command

casualties see Charles K. Webster and Noble Frankland, *The Strategic Air Offensive Against Germany, 1939–1945*, vol. 4, *Annexes and Appendices* (London: Her Majesty's Stationery Office, 1961), appendix 41, 440. For American casualties, Alan J. Levine, *The Strategic Bombing of Germany 1940–1945*, (London: n. p., 1992), 189.

5. Stephen L. McFarland, "The Evolution of the American Strategic Fighter in Europe 1942–1944," *Journal of Contemporary History*, 10, June 1987, 198–208.

6. Albert Speer, *Spandau: The Secret Diaries*, trans. Richard and Clara Winston (London: Collins, 1976). See too, Albert Speer, *Inside the Third Reich* (London: n. p., 1970), 278–91, for his general views on bombing. Also, Roger Beaumont, "The Bomber Offensive as a Second Front," *Journal of Contemporary History*, 22, January 1987, 3–17.

7. R. J. Overy, *War and Economy in the Third Reich* (Oxford: Clarendon Press, 1994), 294.

8. *The United States Strategic Bombing Survey: Over-all Report (European War)* (Washington, D.C.: Government Printing Office, 30 September 1945), 3. Hereafter *USSBS* for the series of publications.

9. The decline in industrial output in the slump in Germany between 1929 and 1932 averaged 10.5 percent a year.

10. The best study on the home front is Earl R. Beck, *Under the Bombs: The German Home Front, 1942–1945* (Lexington, Ky.: University Press of Kentucky, 1986).

11. Maurice Matloff, *Strategic Planning for Coalition Warfare, 1943–1944*, United States Army in World War II Series (Washington, D.C.: Office of the Chief of Military History, Department of the Army, 1959), 27–30.

12. Public Record Office (PRO), Kew, London, Air 10/3871 British Bombing Survey Unit, "Potential and Actual Output of German Armaments in Relation to the Combined Bombing Offensive," n. d., 7, 11, 13.

13. Imperial War Museum (IWM), London, Albert Speer Collection, box S368, Report 67, 14. See too, Report 65, 18, for details on tank production.

14. Wladyslaw Anders, *Hitler's Defeat in Russia* (Chicago: H. Regnery Co., 1953), 227–28.

15. *USSBS*, Report 109, *Oil Division Final Report*, 25 August 1945, 17–26.

16. Ibid., figure 49.

17. Ibid., figures 49, 60.

18. Ibid., figure 52.

19. Overy, *War and Economy*, 358–62.

20. IWM, box S368, Report 67, "Economic Branch Interrogations," 13 December 1945. Most of those interviewed claimed that bombing undermined the attempt to rationalize and centralize the production and distribution of weapons and components, particularly the supply of *vormaterial*, the equipment, parts, and subassemblies necessary to sustain the final assembly plants. See in particular interrogations I, II, III, VIII.

21. *USSBS*, Report 39, *A Brief Study of the Effects of Area Bombing on Berlin, Augsburg, Bochum, Leipzig, Hagen, Dortmund, Oberhausen, Schweinfurt and Bremen*, 26 October 1945, 8, 10–11, 15. See too, IWM, box S368, Report 67, Interrogation II, Dietrich Stahl (head of ammunition production): "All kinds of air attack were effective, whether directed against transport, towns, gas and electricity installations or factories"; and Interrogation III, Wilhelm Schaaf (head of main committee vehicle production), who estimated

that area bombing produced a 20 percent loss of output due to absenteeism, damage to transport, and destruction of industrial services.

22. On aircraft production see R. J. Overy, "The Luftwaffe and the European Economy," *Militargeschichtliche Mitteilungen*, 21, 1979, 55–76. The dispersal program began in late 1942, well before bombing became a serious threat. See IWM, Milch Documents, vol. 56, 2648–55, Minutes of a meeting in the German Air Ministry, 11 November 1942, on dispersal to areas outside the Reich; vol. 56, 2662–66, German Air Ministry memorandum on dispersal, 14 October 1942. By November 211 out of 290 major firms working exclusively on aircraft contracts had produced detailed dispersal plans.

23. Details in IWM, Speer Collection, Privafirmen, FD 778/46, records of the meetings of the Beirat of Flugmotorenwerke Ostmark, 9 May 1941 to 18 August 1944.

24. IWM, Privafirmen, FD 5665/45, Junkers Interrogation Reports, no. 5, Production Statistics, section F.

25. Alfred C. Mierzejewski, *The Collapse of the German War Economy, 1944–1945: Allied Air Power and the German National Railway* (Chapel Hill, N.C.: University of North Carolina Press, 1988), 191, 198.

26. IWM, box S368, Report 67, II Stahl Interrogation, 3; and Mierzejewski, 147.

27. IWM, box S368, Report 85, Interrogation of Dr. Theodor Hupfauer (Labour Section, Armaments Ministry), 10 September 1945, 1.

28. *USSBS*, Report 64B, *The Effects of Strategic Bombing on German Morale*, vol. 1, May 1947, 14.

29. On Ford, see IWM, box S126, FD 4396/45, BBSU "Manuscript Notes on Ford Cologne"; on BMW, *USSBS*, Report 18, Aero-Engine Plant Report no. 4, *Bayerische Motorenwerke AG*, 22 October 1945, 5 and exhibit E.

30. D. Busch, *Der Luftkrieg im Raum Mainz wahrend des zweiten Weltkreiges* (Mainz: n. p., 1988), 363.

31. *USSBS*, Report 64B, *German Morale*, vol. 1, 17–10; and *USSBS*, Report 39, *Effects of Area Bombing*, 11. By March 1944 1.5 million people in Berlin were homeless.

32. British Air Ministry, *The Rise and Fall of the German Air Force* (London: published in-house as Air Ministry Pamphlet no. 248, 1948; reissued London: n. p., 1983), 274.

33. Ibid., 273–75, 307–9.

34. National Archives, Microcopy T321, Luftwaffenfuhrungsstab papers, frames 6754–69, "Studies uber die Flugzeuglage der Kampfverbande," 5 May 1944.

35. Figures from *Rise and Fall*, 274, 298; and Anders, 229. On flak defenses, see Friedhelm Golucke, *Schweinfurt und der strategische Luftkreig 1943: Der Angriff US Air Force vom 14 Oktober 1943 gegen die Schweinfurter Kugellagerindustrie* (Paderborn: Schoningh, 1980), 153–59. On flak output, IWM, Milch Documents, vol. 53, 877, letter to Milch from Flak Office, German Air Ministry, 12 August 1943.

36. Speer calculated that by 1944 one million men were engaged in repairing bomb damage, clearing rubble, and restoring services, in addition to some 803,000 in the air defense system (manning search lights, radar stations, observation posts, etc.). See Anders, 229; Webster and Frankland,

Interrogation of Albert Speer, 6th sess., 30 May 1945, 377–78; and Interrogation of Albert Speer, 18 July 1945, 383–84.

37. Wesley Frank Craven and James Lea Cate, eds., *The Army Air Forces in World War II*, 7 vols. (Chicago: University of Chicago Press, 1948–1958), 56–64; *Rise and Fall*, 306–10, 314–16.

38. Williamson Murray, *Luftwaffe: Strategy for Defeat* (London: n. p., 1985), 248; Webster and Frankland, vol. 4, appendix 27, 500.

39. PRO, Air/3873, BBSU "German Experience in the Underground Transfer of War Industries," n. d., 7–9. For a general discussion, see Albert Speer, *The Slave State: Heinrich Himmler's Masterplan for SS Supremacy* (London: Weidenfeld and Nicolson, 1981), especially chaps. 16 and 17.

40. PRO, Air/3873, 6–7.

41. Ibid., 5. On the conditions in underground plant, see for example, Combined Intelligence Objectives Sub-Committee, Report xxx-80, *Bavarian Motor Works: A Production Survey*, sec. 8, "Salt Mines as Factories."

42. On the V-weapons program, see D. Holsken, "Die V-Waffen: Entwicklung und Einsatzgrundsatze," *Militargeschichtliche Mitteilugen* 27, 1985, 95–119; Michael J. Neufeld, "The Guided Missile and the Third Reich: Peenemunde and the Forging of a Technological Revolution" in *Science, Technology, and National Socialism*, ed. Monika Renneberg and Mark Walker (Cambridge: Cambridge University Press, 1994), especially 61–67.

43. USSBS, Report 60, *V-Weapons (Crossbow) Campaign*, 24 September 1945, 33–36.

44. Ibid., 3. From August 1943 to August 1944 Crossbow absorbed 13.7 percent of joint USAAF/RAF bombing sorties and 15.5 percent of their joint bomb load.

45. Speer, *Slave State*, 363–76; on Milch see David John Cawdell Irving, *The Rise and Fall of the Luftwaffe: The Life of Luftwaffe Marshall Erhard Milch* (London: n. p., 1973), 274–88; R. J. Overy, *Goering: The "Iron Man"* (London; Boston: Routledge; Kegan Paul, 1984), 225–28.

46. Ulrich Albrecht, "Military Technology and National Socialist Ideology," in Renneberg and Walker, 101–13.

47. H. R. Trevor-Rope, ed., *The Goebbels Diaries, The Last Days*, trans. Richard Barry (London: Secker and Warburg, 1978), 18.

48. USSBS, Report 109, *Oil Division*, figure 7. The estimated distribution of bombs was as follows:

In target area:	Productive area	2.2 percent
	Pipelines	1.2 percent
	Open terrain	7.6 percent
	Unexploded	1.9 percent
Outside target:	Decoy plants	3.0 percent
	Remainder	84.1 percent

49. USSBS, Report 64B, *German Morale*, vol. 1, 7. For the effects on German communities in the last year of the war, see Beck, chaps. 7 and 8; Marie-Luise Recker, *Nationalsozialistische Sozialpolitik im Zweiten Weltkrieg* (Munich: R. Oldenbourg, 1985).

Definite Limitations:
The Air War in Korea 1950–1953

Jeffrey Grey

> *There were those who felt, at the time of the Korean War,*
> *that air power might accomplish miracles of interdiction, by*
> *cutting the flow of reinforcement and supply to the embat-*
> *tled enemy. The fact that it could not accomplish these mir-*
> *acles has not yet been accepted as widely as it should. . . .*
> *Air power does have its definite limitations, and even some*
> *in high position still fail to acknowledge them.*
>
> —Matthew B. Ridgway

The Korean War marked one of the two or three most dangerous periods in the history of the Cold War. It was dangerous not merely because it represented the first open conflict
between the two emergent blocs, both equipped with atomic
weapons, but because it was fought in large part with the
assumptions of the preatomic era. Coming so closely after the
end of the Second World War, which had been waged on a total
basis and to complete victory (unconditional surrender), the
Korean War was fought with mostly Second World War technology and doctrine, and under the leadership of men who had
held senior commands in the war against Germany and
Japan. The Korean War for a long time enjoyed the reputation
of the "forgotten" or even the "unknown" conflict. The regular
appearance of books and articles on Korea in recent years
belies that notion now, but it remains true that this, one of the
most important examples of modern conventional conflict to
have faced Western armies, is still imperfectly understood in a
number of key respects. Our understanding of the higher command relations, key decision making at the strategic and
national policy levels, and the internal political dynamic in
Korea itself has been shaped by a number of excellent scholarly studies appearing throughout the 1980s; analysis of the
operational and tactical problems of the war, in all three
dimensions, remains much less developed. It should go almost
without saying that these remarks apply to the United Nations

(UN) side only; our knowledge of the communist side is seriously deficient in almost every respect.

It might be thought that the literature of the air war in Korea formed an exception to my stricture above. The United States Air Force (USAF) published a massive and scholarly official history within less than 10 years of the war's end,[1] and the command and control arrangements, air interdiction campaigns, and thorny issues of close air support have all attracted considerable analysis over time. The air efforts of other contributory UN members, whilst far smaller in scale than that of the US Far East Air Forces (FEAF), have also received some attention.[2] But I suggest that the American writing on the subject—and the great majority of it is American—reflects many of the doctrinal and operational disputes that have characterized the airpower debate within the United States armed forces from the Second World War onwards and that it must be read with this in mind. In this paper then, I want to examine some of the issues and arguments thrown up by the literature and then reinforce some of these points through an examination of the experience of the small Commonwealth air contingents which flew as part of the UN effort.

Korea was a fortunate conflict for the US armed forces. It demonstrated the continuing utility of conventional forces at a time when the secretary of defense, Louis A. Johnson, had started reducing the forces' capabilities because they did not, in his view, match the projected combat needs of the United States in a climate in which the possession of atomic weapons rendered traditional armed forces "obsolete." It also helped to end the internecine bickering over roles and missions which had characterized interservice relations in the late 1940s on issues such as the future of naval aviation or the cancellation of the B-36. It achieved this by ensuring that all the armed forces would expand considerably to meet the Cold War challenge posed by hot war in a peripheral region.

But the US forces, and especially the Army and the Air Force, went into the Korean War with a set of attitudes governing the correct use of the air weapon in their particular environment, and with grievances and prejudices concerning each other, which were firmly grounded in recent historical experience. The Second World War had seen major advances in the technologies of close air support, air interdiction, logistic support, and naval aviation, and these were to provide the major features of the air war in Korea as well. The arguments over their correct application during the war spill over into the literature produced after the war, to which must be added disagreement over air command and control doctrines. The establishment of the Air Force as a separate service in the immediate postwar period provided an additional context into which to place the disagreements that ensued.

There were three air forces in Korea: the Fifth Air Force, commanded by Far East Air Forces, the 1st Marine Air Wing, and the air groups on board the carriers, both under the command of Naval Forces Far East (NavFE). Their principal client, and principal critic, was the Eighth US Army in Korea (EUSAK), commanded by Army Forces Far East (AFFE). The command of all three was united in the person of the commander in chief, Far East (CINCFE), who was also the commander in chief, United Nations Command (CINCUNC) and the supreme commander Allied Powers (SCAP) with responsibilities in occupied Japan. This was the first problem; for most of the war there was no joint staff at Far East Command headquarters, nor any unity of command when it came to the control of joint air operations.[3] "In the absence of the joint headquarters staff," wrote Dr. Robert Futrell, the USAF historian, "the full force of United Nations air power was seldom effectively applied against hostile target systems in Korea."[4] This overstates the case, but it is certainly true that unity of command in the air was rarely attained, in part, because MacArthur's staff neither understood joint air operations, nor had made staff provision for their conduct, and because on occasions MacArthur made command arrangements which further divided the control of air assets; the creation of X Corps under Maj Gen Edward M. Almond in northeast Korea in the latter part of 1950 not only divided command of the ground forces available to Gen Walton Walker, but by assigning the 1st Marine Air Wing to Almond's command, it further split command of air assets.

Command of air force and naval air components only came together at the level of the commander in chief, and this clearly posed problems since the successive theater commanders, MacArthur, Ridgway, and Clark, all had their own ideas concerning the proper applications of airpower which did not necessarily coincide with United States Air Force doctrine. Air Force thinking on the conduct of air operations was set out in Field Manual (FM) 100-20, *The Command and Employment of Air Power*, issued in July 1943. Undoubtedly influenced by the postwar debates over future roles and missions, in Korea the USAF attempted to enforce Navy and Marine compliance with Air Force procedures and assumptions, a move which prompted the Navy to carve out an independent role based on geographic demarcation lines and to avoid coordination of effort except in the face of severe operational necessity on the ground. Marine aviation, of course, was dedicated primarily to close air support of ground forces, which was why Marine aviators found such favor with the Army. Army thinking on the subject was encapsulated in FM 31-35, *Air-Ground Operations*, issued in 1946 but which in 1950 was undergoing a review that had not been completed when war broke out.

In the postwar period the Army had attempted to cultivate a continuing interest in ground support operations within the Air Force, but the results of joint tactical exercises between 1947 and 1950 were not happy ones, and one student of the subject has suggested that by 1949 most senior Army commanders "appear to have regarded close air support as a lost cause after the Air Force became a separate service."[5] A British observer made the same point: "In the US Air Force, as in the RAF, far greater importance and priority was given to 'strategic' air than to 'tactical' air."[6] The problem here lay in the definition of support, coupled with the fact that at the outbreak of war the USAF was "quite unprepared to participate in joint air-ground operations," as Gen George Stratemeyer's staff admitted.[7] The Air Force view was that "the capabilities of tactical aviation in Korea have not been fully exploited due to disregard of basic principles: e.g., by the Army ruling that all available aircraft must be employed on close support to the detriment of an interdiction program."[8] Where the Air Force would argue that 80 percent of sorties were in support of ground forces, divided into close support and interdiction, the tendency on the part of ground commanders was to count only those missions flown in direct support of units engaged with the enemy, which reduced the figure for the war overall to between 10 and 15 percent (although it must be noted that in the dangerous early weeks of the war up to 74 percent of combat sorties were close support).[9]

In the first months of the fighting, air support gave ground forces a considerable edge over the North Koreans, and this advantage was extended against the Communist Chinese during the fluid phase of the war, which ended in late 1951. Thereafter, the enemy had to pay extra attention to concealment and dispersion, with which the United Nations Command (UNC) did not need to bother because of the absence of an enemy air threat to its forward positions or rear areas. The absence of enemy air operations over UN lines permitted the allocation of a substantial proportion of the available combat aircraft to support missions, but tensions persisted in the system nonetheless. The Air Force insisted on centralization of control of air support through the joint operations center, and initially at least declined to provide either additional forward air controllers (FAC) or ground FACs as the Army requested. The request itself was a consequence of the Army's inability to provide a ground-air liaison signals capability, despite the fact that FM 31-35 specified that the Army was responsible for providing its own request net, and secondly of observation of the 1st Marine Air Wing's support of the 1st Marine Division and the detached X Corps in late 1950.

Invidious comparisons were drawn which were to fuel the debate over control of close air support for the rest of the war. The Marine system, one advocated by Almond among others, provided a FAC to every battalion, but the reasons for this need to be understood. Marine doctrine had evolved during the amphibious campaigns of the Pacific war; Marine formations were much lighter than Army equivalents, especially in terms of organic supporting arms. The Marine air wing was intended to compensate for the lack of Marine artillery. The Army, on the other hand, usually preferred to engage enemy targets within the first thousand yards of its own front with artillery fire, since a divisional fire was to be equated with 1,800 sorties with 500-pound bombs.[10] Air support within that range was generally only requested when artillery could not be brought to bear. The Marines, on the other hand, insisted on routine close air support within that range.

Futrell argues that adoption of such a system on an Army-wide basis would have been hugely expensive and unjustified.[11] In any case, he argued, "the USAF-Army system proved able to meet requirements laid upon it in Korea," which would seem an overly sanguine reading of the experience. In the early, critical months of the war, ground forces were badly short of artillery as a result of the run down of capabilities during the occupation of Japan, while later attempts to keep down the costs of the war through reducing the availability of ammunition stocks hindered ground operations in much the same way. "The routine use of air power as flying artillery" may have constituted "a severe expense to American taxpayers,"[12] but in the desperate fighting of August–September 1950, there is little evidence that the Air Force stinted in its provision of close air support. Overall in the period to 30 November 1950, 52 percent of the combat sortie effort was devoted to close support (and 46 percent to interdiction); from 1 to 15 August the figure was 74 percent, from 1 to 15 September 62 percent, and for the second half of that month 61 percent.[13]

The heart of the argument was less over the fact of close support than its control, and this issue was not resolved during the war because the Army seems not to have pushed the issue. In exercises in the United States between 1951 and 1954, however, many of the same problems reasserted themselves. The air-ground operations system, which the Air Force agreed to, was usually undermanned because the Air Force would not supply sufficient personnel of the appropriate rank and experience even when the Army agreed to furnish the equipment and enlisted personnel for the tactical air control parties; the Air Force nonetheless insisted that all traffic be handled in this highly centralized manner. Futrell argued that the Army's preferred option would have required the Air Force to find an additional 364 pilots for forward air control duties in Korea alone and that such a requirement would have been extremely expensive. This formed the basis perhaps of the Air Force evaluation that the Army's use of air support "was so wasteful that the Air Force should make no special concessions until ground commanders became more competent in planning air support."[14] In 1955 the Air Force took the logical step and abolished all joint boards charged with writing doctrine. The Air Force Manual 1-2, *United States Air Force Basic Doctrine*, which had appeared in 1953, had reasserted the primacy of centralized air war, while the supporting manual on theater air war, which was published the following year, made the joint operations center an all Air Force organization to which the Army would attach liaison officers. Small wonder, perhaps, that Gen Mark Clark declared before taking up his post as commander in chief in Korea that "all elements of the ground forces must make a firm bid for the control of close support operations and until such time as this control is assigned to ground force commanders, close support operations can never achieve maximum effectiveness."[15]

The primary missions from the Air Force point of view were air superiority and interdiction. Korea demonstrated, to Futrell's satisfaction at least, "one more historical justification for the overriding priority which USAF doctrine accords to the air superiority mission"; the air pressure strategy, he further concluded, "made the war too expensive for the Communists to continue."[16] The air superiority mission had two phases, and two features, not necessarily parallel. In the opening weeks of the war, UNC aircraft destroyed the relatively small North Korean air force with ease, in the air and in large part on the ground. UN ground forces thus operated, as we have noted, without fear of air attack, which given their manifold other problems was probably just as well. After November 1950 when the Chinese entered the war, and did so equipped with MiG-15 jet aircraft, the nature of the struggle changed. In general, the enemy operated aircraft from bases in Manchuria, which meant that these were inviolate because of strict orders not to enter Chinese or Soviet airspace. On occasions the

Chinese attempted to rebuild airfields inside North Korea, but the airfield neutralization program employed to counter it proved highly effective. It should be added, however, that towards the end of the war the Chinese created a sophisticated ground-controlled air defense system over northwestern Korea which had a significant impact on American bombing raids, and had they been willing to use, or the Soviets to supply, electronics-equipped all-weather fighter aircraft, there seems little doubt that the older B-29 aircraft, which provided the "heavy punch" in terms of bomb loads, would have found it difficult to continue operations, especially at night (which was when the airfield neutralization missions were flown).

Although the Chinese, Soviet, and North Korean pilots who flew against the UNC lost 810 aircraft against 139, their planes were good and some of the pilots skillful; aerial combat in "MiG Alley" had its hazards.[17] As the first example of air war in the jet age, combat in Korea held considerable interest for Western air forces, a point to which I wish to return shortly. But it is important to recognize that the enemy did not employ their full resources in the contest for control of the air, and the absence of enemy aircraft over the UNC's lines was a conscious imposition of limitations on the part of the Chinese, just as the decision not to attack UNC ships prevented the war from getting dangerously out of hand. In the view of some in the United States Air Force, this was not an unmixed blessing. Gen William Momyer, one of the fathers of American tactical airpower and later commanding general of the US Seventh Air Force in Vietnam, observed much later that "we would be in a much stronger position today with regard to the importance of air superiority if the enemy had been able to penetrate and bomb some of our airfields and had been able to bomb the front lines periodically. It would have brought home to our ground forces and other people the importance of air superiority."[18] Futrell likewise believed that the absence of a significant enemy air threat distorted aspects of the US air war in Korea.[19]

There was little opportunity for strategic application of airpower until relatively late in the Korean War, but heavy bombers—specifically the B-29—were used in a tactical application in the interdiction role and against industrial and infrastructure targets within North Korea. Of the interdiction campaign, two American analysts have suggested:

> One of the most important conclusions to be drawn from an unbiased examination of interdiction experience is that the outcomes seldom come close to the expectations of the interdiction planners. Even when an interdiction effort has been judged successful, the achievement has not infrequently been quite different from the original objective. Misperceptions as to what was feasible, misunderstandings about the appropriate payoffs to be sought, differences of opinion as to the most suitable targets, and misevaluations about what was actually being accomplished were common.[20]

Interdiction was one area at least where the failure to create a joint headquarters staff showed itself clearly in the early days of the war, and it was only after heated arguments between Gen O. P. Weyland and MacArthur's staff that FEAF was permitted to mount an interdiction campaign, beginning in August 1950. Even then, general headquarters staff frequently interfered in target selection and allotment of effort against individual targets, to the considerable dissatisfaction of Air Force commanders.

North Korean industrial targets posed little problem, although the destruction of the North Korean industrial base made virtually no difference to the enemy's ability to maintain his military effort. There were two reasons for this: the enemy demonstrated consistently an ability to operate on a much slimmer logistic tail than the UNC, and hence the assumptions of air planning staff concerning the necessary minimum supply rates were usually wrong; secondly, North Korea's industrial heartland lay not inside its own borders, not even in Manchuria, but in the Soviet Union and Eastern Europe. By dint of an aerial logistic support effort, the dimensions of which we are only just beginning to appreciate, a Soviet air corps provided a vital link between the Chinese and North Korean armies in the field and their principal sources of resupply in the rear, all the while protected by the sanctuary status which operating out of Manchurian bases provided. This measure of Stalin's support had been given hesitantly; it was not until a month after Chinese intervention that the Soviet air force began its major supply lift effort. Once it began, it proved crucial.

The interdiction effort lacked nothing in intensity, totaling some 320,000 sorties for the whole of the war, approximately 9,000 per month on average or 48 percent of combat sorties overall. As in the Second World War, although damage claimed was probably in excess of damage inflicted, the level of destruction was real enough. FEAF aircraft expended nearly 220,000 tons of bombs and 3,800 tons of napalm on interdiction missions alone, and these figures do not include Navy and Marine Corps sorties. The major target of interdiction missions was the enemy's supply system and transportation infrastructure. Enormous damage was done to bridges, rail lines, roadways, locomotives, rail cars, and road transport. The effort, like the close support role, was at its most effective in the crisis period leading up to the UNC breakout from the Pusan perimeter in September 1950, but thereafter its overall effectiveness declined. Operation Strangle I, the air interdiction effort aimed at roadways and trucks in the spring and summer of 1951, was a disappointment, and although high expectations were maintained for Strangle II, a rail interdiction program beginning in August 1951, these expectations remained unfulfilled. Operation Saturate, mounted in early 1952 against rail lines, likewise failed to justify the optimistic evaluations made of it. Communist countermeasures proved sufficient to break the railway blockade of Pyongyang, for example, by the end of 1951. The objective of Saturate in 1952 became the much more modest intention to "interfere with and disrupt" enemy efforts, but even this fell some way short of realization. In July 1951 the Chinese and North Korean forces were firing about 8,000 artillery and mortar rounds a month; in May 1952, after 10 months of transport interdiction, they fired over 100,000 rounds. Not only that, but their capacity to mount and sustain an offensive actually increased, demonstrated by the ferocity of attacks against Republic of Korea (ROK) positions in April and July 1953.

Part of the problem, and the cause of much of the frustration, lay in the assumptions made about the level of destruction achieved. In the air attacks mounted against North Korean targets in October–November 1950, very precise claims were made for the effectiveness of the interdiction effort. The report on a raid against the Sonjin dock and port area and neighboring marshalling yards in mid-October 1950, for example, claimed: "destroyed 36 vehicles, 106 supply carts, 3 gun positions, 6 locomotives, 3 railway cars, 11 buildings housing enemy troops; damaged 27 vehicles, 33 supply carts, 7 gun positions, 3 locomotives, 63 railcars, 9 small villages, 390 troop casualties," prefaced by the observation "results unobserved."[21] Throughout this period, while attacks on large targets like marshalling yards were consistently claimed as excellent, assessments of the results against communications targets varied much more widely, from poor to excellent.[22] The confident assertion, reported by the British representative on MacArthur's headquarters to the UK chiefs of staff, that "our air forces will . . . turn North Korea into a veritable hell for the enemy,"[23] may have been true as far as it went, but apparently did little to dent the enemy's capacity to continue the war, as other RAF observers noted.[24]

Nor did the "Air Pressure" strategy, embarked on in the spring of 1952 and intended to give the Air Force an independent role after a period of being "tied down" to support of the ground forces, deliver all that was hoped for it. Intended to put pressure on the negotiations at Panmunjom, it involved the bombing first of the North Korean hydroelectric power system and the capital, Pyongyang, and then, when the talks apparently reached a further impasse in April–May 1953, the targeting of the dams system which controlled irrigation for the North Korean rice crop. The first phase exhausted the target list with little obvious impact on the communist negotiating position, and the signing of the cease-fire in July 1953 owed as much, probably more, to political factors, although some in Air Force circles claimed it as a victory for the Air Pressure strategy. The interdiction campaign was at its most effective when it was most closely tied to the situation on the ground, as in the early months. On such occasions, as the testimony of prisoners of war made clear, "unremitting daylight air attacks on enemy ground targets and troop concentrations acted as a disorganising and disrupting factor on N[orth] K[orean] tactics,"[25] lowering morale, blunting combat effectiveness, and forcing the enemy to confine much of his movement to the hours of darkness. As the British naval staff study concluded, however, the continuation of the interdiction effort "throughout the procrastinated armistice negotiations savoured dangerously of trying to win the war by air power alone, while the army and navy were relegated to comparatively static and defensive roles."[26]

As noted earlier, Korea was the first air war of the jet age, and thus a subject of considerable interest and study to Western air forces. I want to conclude this paper by considering some of the problems of operational flying in Korea as experienced by squadrons of the Commonwealth air forces and fleet air arms which took part. Full accounts of their daily activities may be followed elsewhere, and I do not intend to provide one here.[27]

The Commonwealth air effort in Korea was small, and Commonwealth forces were not represented in all areas of activity in the war in the air. The initial response of the RAF to American requests for air units was that nothing could be spared from existing commitments in Hong Kong and Malaya. A Sunderland flying boat squadron (No. 88) was authorized to be sent from Hong Kong in July 1950 for use on antisubmarine tasks in the Yellow Sea, with a second (No. 209) joining it in September. Ultimately three squadrons (the third was No. 205) rotated on duty through the Japanese port of Iwakuni, joining American naval patrol aircraft in watching for Soviet submarines and maintaining the 24-hour blockade of North Korean waters and the monitoring of shipping in the area. The only other RAF contributions took the form of aeromedical evacuation flights and the provision of No. 1903 Independent Air Observation Flight and No. 1913 Light Liaison Flight, both of which worked with Commonwealth ground forces.

In order to benefit from the opportunities which flying against the MiG-15 presented, the RAF attached small groups of pilots to American Sabre and Thunderjet squadrons and, after it converted to the Meteor-8 in February 1951, to the Australian No. 77 Squadron as well. The experience gained and the reports on American activities submitted by the first group of RAF officers so attached persuaded the chief of the air staff, Air Chief Marshal Sir John Slessor, to ask the Americans to accept British pilots on a regular rotation, and from December 1951 four at a time were posted to the Fifth Air Force. So successful did this prove that by 1953 there were 17 British pilots attached to squadrons in Korea.

The major Commonwealth air contributions were made by the Australian No. 77 Squadron, the South African No. 2 Squadron, and the fleet air arms of the Royal Navy and Royal Australian Navy operating from carriers off the Korean coast. They flew in all the tactical air roles on offer in Korea, but three in particular are worth looking at for what they illustrate about the broader issues of the air war: ground support (both close support and interdiction), aerial combat, and the deployment of naval aviation.

The first carrier, HMS *Triumph*, arrived in Korean waters only in September 1950, having been dispatched from Hong Kong. Carrier-based aircraft proved particularly valuable early in the war because of the lack of secure airfields in South Korea and, in consequence, the very short endurance over targets of American jet aircraft operating from bases in Japan. Although the overall numbers of British and Australian naval aircraft committed were not large, their presence enabled the UNC to maintain carrier-borne forces off both sea coasts and to conduct a more or less continuous air offensive against the North Koreans.

The biggest problem that faced the Royal Navy was the need to relieve carriers every six months, deemed by the Admiralty the maximum period which aircrews in particular could be expected to operate without relief. Britain's carrier assets, like all its other defense resources, were stretched thinly in this period, and the refit schedule for carriers in Korean waters necessitated the deployment of ships from the Mediterranean and home waters as well as from the Far East station, and the relief of HMS *Glory* by HMAS *Sydney* in October 1951 to enable the former to refit in Australia. Because only part of the navy was at war, the commitment to Korea distorted training cycles and interrupted normal posting and planning. This was felt the more keenly because of what the Admiralty saw as the relegation of naval aircraft to "what is normally a secondary role," an outcome ascribed to "political (and US interservice) reasons."[28] What this meant was the use of naval aircraft in the ground support role, for which Royal Navy aircrews generally were not trained. The emphasis in NATO planning for British carriers was on the antisubmarine and trade protection roles. "I think it correct to say that we have never considered it a primary task of our carriers to support the Army on the flanks," noted the Air Branch of the Admiralty.[29] The training of aircrews had been based on the assumption, drawing heavily on experience in the Second World War, that in a major war the first phase of operations would last two or more years and require every effort to be lent to trade protection, with support of the army on the offensive coming only in phase II.

"As a result of this assumption Army Support training was given a low priority but nevertheless kept alive. Accordingly when Korea started our aircrews knew the subject but were not in practice. They had to be given a short working up period before going into action."[30] The implied lack of versatility of their carriers concerned the Admiralty, but at "an awkward moment in both aircraft and carrier development," any long-term change seemed unlikely. The fleet air arm, like the US Air Force, found itself initially fighting a war other than that for which it had armed and trained.

In any case, naval aviators soon overcame the problems of lack of familiarity with the ground support mission, and the Royal Navy took considerable interest in their performance. Particular attention was paid to sortie rates, which were generally felt to be more favorable than on American carriers, accident rates, and difficulties experienced through adverse flying conditions. During its deployment between October 1950 and April 1951, crews from HMS *Theseus* managed nearly 30 sorties per 30-day operational cycle, averaging 45 flying hours per month. American carrier air groups in an overlapping two month period (November–December 1950) managed only 11 sorties and 31-32 flying hours per month, although the figures for escort carriers were generally higher.[31] (In an earlier period on station, HMS *Glory* had been mounting over 50 operational sorties per day.)[32] Accidents and other wastage were of particular concern, since 50 percent of UN aircraft losses overall were from causes other than enemy action, with just 7 percent owed to combat with enemy fighter aircraft.[33] Increasingly, and in line with the diversion of aircraft from the close support mission on the part of Fifth Air Force, naval aircraft found themselves tasked to the interdiction campaign. During its tour between May and October 1952, HMS *Ocean* launched 4,143 sorties in prebriefed and ship-controlled strikes from a total of 5,877; close air support accounted for just 211 sorties in the same period.[34] As part of the plan to target road and rail infrastructure, over 65 percent of their bomb load was dropped against bridges, as opposed to about 25 percent against troops positions and stores.[35]

At least initially, close support was the primary mission of both the Australian and South African air force squadrons, equipped at the beginning of the war with the Mustang (P-51/F-51). Unlike American squadrons on occupation duty in Japan, No. 77 Squadron had undergone some training in ground support, and this preparation paid off handsomely in the early days of the war in concerted strikes against North Korean troops. The Mustang was particularly suited to these sorts of missions and, flown by experienced pilots (which both the Australians and South Africans were), was highly regarded by the American command. As a later British report noted, "attacks with conventional weapons against most types of targets can be made more economically by ground attack aircraft than by high-level bombers,"[36] a point confirmed by a US Air Force report which, in assessing the use of B-29 aircraft in the close-support mission, concluded that while it had made a valuable contribution to the interdiction campaign, "any evaluation of the close support effort must remain wholly inconclusive."[37]

The importance of Korea as a test for new, specifically jet, technology has been noted already. The appearance of MiG-15s in the skies of North Korea in November 1950 affected the balance of the air war immediately, with serious consequences for the Australian squadron whose Mustangs were now obsolete and whose pilots were thus felt to be at considerably greater risk from enemy interceptors. The Americans had deployed six Mustang squadrons to Korea, and these were now replaced with more modern jet aircraft, the F-84—which lasted only a few months on operational deployment against

MiGs—and the much more suitable F-86 Sabre. The South African squadron retained its Mustangs and its close-support mission until reequipped with Sabres in January 1953. The Australian squadron was withdrawn to Japan in April 1951 for conversion to the British Meteor-8.

Nothing exemplifies better the problems which adapting to the new technology posed than the fortunes of the Australian squadron during the remainder of the Korean War. The Meteor was obsolescent; it had first flown in 1943 and was outclassed by the newer, swept-wing aircraft with which both the Americans and Chinese were equipped. The commanding general Far East Air Forces, Lt Gen George E. Stratemeyer, urged the Australians to reequip with jet aircraft quickly, but added that the aircraft of choice, the Sabre, could not be supplied due to shortages in the United States inventory. The selection was bedeviled further by the requirement in Australia that the new aircraft must fly in an air superiority role, since that was No. 77 Squadron's assigned task in the air defense of Australia. Even then the Meteor was not the preferred aircraft. Nor was the RAF altogether happy about providing them, since to do so in the time frame requested would mean delaying the reequipping of at least one squadron in Germany. Australian representations prevailed, however, and the RAAF acquired the Meteor, at an overall cost of £5 million, with the first aircraft delivered to go straight into frontline service in Korea.[38]

The Australian squadron returned to operational flying on 29 July 1951. In the words of its commanding officer, Wing Comdr Gordon Steege, "It required little appreciation to reach the conclusion that the Meteor [was] vastly inferior in performance . . . borne out by actual experience on the 29th [August]. . . . Unless the MiGs are operated unintelligently Meteors are not going to account for many."[39] He foreshadowed that the squadron might have to consider redeployment to a "more economical role," which duly followed in September. Henceforth, they were to be utilized in "middle cover" as escorts for bombers and fighter-bombers, but south of the Chongchon River. This did not remove the MiG threat by any means, as Chinese air patrols became more aggressive, and after further losses to enemy fighters in early December, the decision was made to take them off fighter sweep operations altogether. Henceforth, the Meteor was to be utilized largely in the air defense and ground attack roles.

The Meteor's inadequacies were not simply nor solely a matter of concern to the RAAF, of course.[40] Steege's pessimistic analysis earned him no points with the RAF, especially not with its roving representative in Korea, Air Vice-Marshal Bouchier. The United Kingdom chiefs of staff, when informed of Weyland's decision to alter 77 Squadron's role, reported themselves "deeply disturbed . . . and concerned over the effect [these events] may have on the morale of Meteor pilots in all the allied air forces which have, or plan to have, this type in their front line for some years to come."[41] They promptly raised questions about the experience of the Australian pilots and the qualities of the squadron commander. Bouchier replied with a damning and unfair portrait of Steege and an almost equally damning description of the Australian squadron. The Meteor "has not had a fair chance yet to show what it can do," he reported, "largely because the pilots in this Australian squadron have not been hand picked."[42] This latter he thought was an essential requirement in circumstances where the Meteor was "called upon to face up to a very high performance fighter." Perhaps he missed the point that an aircraft which required above average pilots to survive in relatively normal combat conditions was unlikely to be of much use on frontline service. Weyland likewise expressed concern at "the undesirable implications of changing the Meteor operations since a number of NATO nations are depending upon the aircraft for air defense purposes and the implication of a 'bad name' . . . could be serious," but he decided not to interfere.[43]

The concern expressed over Australian criticisms of the Meteor soon blew over, not least because in essence they told the Air Ministry nothing it did not know already. The deputy chief of the air staff minuted that in spite of the fact:

> that it has now been proved by experience (as we already knew from comparative data) that the Meteor is no match in performance for the much more recently designed MiG-15, I do not think we need be unduly despondent on that account. The Meteor is a robust and well-tried aircraft from the flying point of view and has shown itself in Korea to be a good gun and rocket firing platform. It still has an adequate

159

performance to intercept and destroy the Soviet long-range bombers at present in use—its primary role in air defence operations, and is certainly a very useful ground attack aircraft. It is inevitable that it should be outclassed in fighter v. fighter work.[44]

The change in role eventually convinced even Bouchier, who wrote six months later that "everyone in this squadron is enthusiastically convinced that the Meteor is a really first class aircraft in the ground attack role," that morale in the squadron "is excellent," and that the aircraft was "a wonderfully steady gun and rocket platform and great accuracy is being obtained with rockets."[45]

The relative failure of the Meteor had its most serious implications for the RAAF, of course. As one analysis of the problem has suggested, the Australian squadron in Korea became increasingly specialized not through doctrinal necessity but as a consequence of aircraft inadequacy.[46] The RAAF felt this sufficiently keenly to approach the British again in April 1953 with a view to reequipping No. 77 Squadron, this time with the new Swift Mk 2, at an estimated cost of £4.5 million. Whilst the RAF thought that combat testing of the Swift had its attractions, it was unhappy about the prospect of again delaying the deployment of aircraft to frontline RAF squadrons in order to meet the Australians' needs. This time, however, the Australians themselves killed the proposal.[47]

The decision to buy the Meteor seems an ill-considered one. Not only did the aircraft not meet Australia's frontline requirements, as was more than amply demonstrated on operations in Korea, but it is not self-evident that the changeover from Mustangs to jet aircraft was as pressing as was presented in Canberra at the time. The South African squadron continued to fly Mustangs in the ground support role until January 1953, at which time it was converted to Sabres, which by then were in more plentiful supply. Nor was the MiG threat as great perhaps as suggested. In the course of the war the South Africans lost to enemy action or accident 74 Mustangs and five Sabres; of the 34 pilots killed (all in Mustangs), only one was lost to air-to-air combat, the rest falling victim to ground fire. To have followed suit would have necessitated reverting to a less high-profile role for the RAAF squadron, but then this eventuated in any case and, given the known inadequacies of the Meteor, might have been predicted.

The Korean War marked a transitional rather than transformational period in the development of airpower. Jet aircraft proved themselves, and the tactics and techniques of jet combat were further developed and refined. Helicopters made their first significant appearance, giving an indication of the potential which was to be realized in the following decade. The US Air Force benefited organizationally, undergoing considerable peacetime expansion which it was largely to retain following the cease-fire. The rivalry with the Army was intensified (although that with the Navy was resolved legislatively by the war's end), with the consequent growth in Army aviation which was to reach its apogee in the 1960s. Closer to home, the Korean War demonstrated the penalties to be paid in failing to keep abreast of technological and operational developments.

Operationally, as opposed to organizationally, however, the Korean War presents a less reassuring picture. The interdiction campaign was in most respects an expensive failure; the air superiority campaign was a success but a limited one given the constraints which the enemy chose to apply to the conduct of his own operations. Close air support seemed to go begging by the war's end, with consequences discussed already. And yet, the war must be broken into two phases. In the critical early period—say, June to September 1950—airpower was almost certainly the margin of survival, if not necessarily of victory.[48] Ironically, the very success of airpower in destroying the North Koreans' capacity to wage mechanized armored war forced the enemy back into fighting the sort of war which he was best equipped to wage in a prolonged fashion, one moreover against which high-technology solutions would prove least effective. As two British analysts have noted then, Korea emphasized once again "the unsurprising fact that aircraft alone are not enough."[49] As Air Chief Marshal Sir John Slessor, who initially had had to be convinced of the desirability of involving RAF personnel at all, further observed, "The idea that superior air power can in some way be a substitute for hard slogging and professional skill on the ground in this sort of war is beguiling but illusory . . . all this is cold comfort for

161

anyone who hopes that air power will provide some kind of short cut to victory." The lessons of American military policy in the 1950s, however, suggest that many American military planners believed exactly that.

Discussion

Air Commodore Gordon Steege: I think the lecturer has covered the period accurately and well. The Meteor was purchased as a replacement for the P-51 Mustangs of No. 77 Squadron which had been operated with great distinction by Wing Comdr Dick Cresswell, who is here today. The Meteor was purchased by the RAAF for the air-to-air role, but you didn't have to be a Rhodes scholar to know that it just wasn't going to cope with the MiG-15. I was quite convinced of the aircraft's inadequacies even before it went into operations, but of course my opinion wasn't well received by either Air Force Headquarters in Melbourne or the Royal Air Force representatives who naturally had their own ideas about the value of a British airplane. But the critical difference was that the RAF intended using it as a bomber interceptor, not for air combat, and it was suitable for the air defense of the UK in those days. But to put it into air-to-air operations against the MiG in Korea was just asking for an entire squadron to get knocked off. Having had some experience with fighters during the Second World War, that was not my way of doing things.

Dr. Richard Hallion: A couple of points for consideration. First on the P-51 versus Meteor issue. The P-51 was extraordinarily vulnerable to ground fire. In fact, in April 1951, the United States Air Force lost 30 P-51s to ground fire during close support operations. I think that has to be factored into the Meteor versus Mustang issue, because if you look at battlefield air attack in Korea, you find that the jets had a higher survivability on ground attack operations. Also, North Korean and Chinese prisoner interrogations indicated that they were far more often surprised by the relatively quiet approach of a jet as opposed to the noisy approach of something like a Corsair or a Mustang.

The interesting point you made on interdiction is well taken. In January 1951 there was an Air Force intelligence report which stated that the North Koreans were better equipped than they had been at any previous time in the war. Nevertheless, I would like your thoughts on the following comparison with Operation Strangle in Italy in 1944. The front in Korea was fairly stable and very long, but in 1953 the UN Command combined air attacks with ground action. Again using information based largely on prisoner interrogation reports, this forced a high consumption of supplies by the communist army. In other words, the Air Pressure campaign, particularly the Cherokee strikes that were undertaken in the fall of 1952, did seem to have some effect once high consumption fighting resumed.

I would like to offer a couple of other thoughts. First of all, there were occasions when communist air forces did come out and attempt to attack UN ground forces. For example, there was one particular raid by Tupolev Tu-2s that was decimated by intercepting F-86s, and then in another case some Russian MiGs came out in November 1952 and attacked the combat air patrol of Task Force 77 in the Sea of Japan and several of them were shot down.

Finally one tiny quibble. The F-84 actually served throughout the war, but primarily as a strike aircraft and not as a bomber escort aircraft.

Dr. Grey: I guess the comment that calls for response is your point about the interdiction campaign. I suppose the problem here—and this follows on from what Richard Overy was saying this morning—is that without that campaign you don't know what else the Chinese and North Koreans might have been able to do. That's speculative.

I think the real criticism that can be made about the conduct of the interdiction campaign is the rosy optimism with which the US Air Force planners in particular continued to regard it. There are a couple of very good examples of the way the high-technology Western mind-set simply didn't see what was in front of it. My favorite is from the period when interdiction strikes were being targeted against bridges in North Korea. They dropped every span in the country, really marvelous. But it was high summer and the water levels were low, so the North Koreans simply forded the rivers wherever they pleased. In other words, the antibridge campaign didn't matter then or for some months after, yet the Air Force planners congratulated themselves for knocking all those spans down. The actual effect on what the North Koreans and Chinese were able to accomplish at that time was probably negligible. It was a classic example of thinking entirely in terms of what would hurt your own side and then projecting it on to your opponent, even though his circumstances, values, and so on, might be entirely different. It was an attitude which I think provided an ominous premonition of what was to come in the following decade. I think that the Korean War provided the genesis of many of the bad habits of the American forces in Vietnam 10 years later.

Dr. Alan Stephens: A comment followed by a question. The comment is that you placed caveats on the success of the control of the air campaign, which I think's a little unfair. You can only fight a war as you find it. If the Communists chose to put restrictions on how they applied their airpower then that was their business. The fact of the matter was the United Nations surface forces fought completely free from enemy air attack.

My question relates to the air-land command relationship. The relationship between Douglas MacArthur and George Kenney in the Southwest Pacific area during World War II was one of the most successful between a soldier and an airman. The same general principles and working arrangements which made that partnership function so well were still relevant in Korea. In view of the joint command problems you outlined, it would seem that MacArthur did not understand those principles.

Dr. Grey: I accept your caveat entirely. My point would be not about the success of the air campaign, but rather about the extrapolations which were taken for future use. You find that happening repeatedly in the US Air Force official history of the Korean War, which incidentally is at times very self-congratulatory and I think unduly optimistic about some of the outcomes.

But to come back to your other point. I think you've got to see the command relationships and the interservice relationships in Korea very much in the context of the poisonous feuding that had gone on, particularly at the chiefs of staff level, after the Second World War and up to 1950. Let's remember, in 1947 the Army lost its air force, and it didn't like it. One of the fascinating things about the service dynamics in the US, I think, is that by 1967 it had gained it back again. The principal student of this has made the point that by the end of the Vietnam era the US Army was the world's fourth largest air force, which is bizarre. This "new" Army air force was a very different sort of air force, a consequence in part of the Army's dissatisfaction with the USAF during the Korean War. I think you've got to see the relationship in Korea in those terms. There was a great deal of bad blood on both sides. Having achieved independent service status, the USAF clearly was now ready to forge ahead and prove that it could do all the things that it said it could; that it could fulfill the air force mission which had been boldly asserted in the USAAF manual produced in 1943. On the subject of the 1943 manual, it's interesting that although the US Army Air Forces were still, theoretically at least, under the command of the US Army, no one outside the USAAF was consulted before the manual was issued. That perhaps gave a presentiment of future intention.

Mr. Peter Skinner: You made a couple of references in your most interesting paper to target damage assessment. Was this tackled in any particular way during the Korean War, especially by photographic reconnaissance?

Dr. Grey: Yes, photographic reconnaissance aircraft were available and were quite widely used. The problem though was in viewing the results and then extrapolating something meaningful from them. Reconnaissance and useful intelligence are not necessarily the same thing.

Notes

1. Robert F. Futrell, *The United States Air Force in Korea 1950–1953*, rev. ed. (Washington, D. C.: Office of Air Force History, 1983).

2. For example, Robert John O'Neill, *Australia in the Korean War 1950–53*, vol. 2, *Combat Operations* (Canberra: Australian War Memorial and Australian Government Publishing Service [AGPS], 1985), 293–409; Dermot Michael Moore and Peter Bagshawe, *South Africa's Flying Cheetahs in Korea* (Johannesburg: Ashanti Pub., 1991), which is more solidly researched than its deliberately populist title might suggest.

3. James A. Winnefeld and Dana J. Johnson, *Command and Control of Joint Air Operations: Some Lessons Learned and Four Case Studies of an Enduring Issue,* R-4045-RC (Santa Monica, Calif.: RAND, 1991), 24–40.

4. Futrell, 693.

5. Allan R. Millett, "Korea, 1950–1953," in *Case Studies in the Development of Close Air Support,* ed. Benjamin Franklin Cooling (Washington, D.C.: Office of Air Force History, 1990), 349.

6. Naval Staff History, *British Commonwealth Naval Operations, Korea, 1950–53,* London, 1967, 30.

7. Wing Comdr J. E. Johnson, "Five Reports on Tactical Aviation in Korea," Report no. 1 - general, 11, Public Record Office (PRO), Air 20/7796.

8. Squadron Leader C. N. Clements, memorandum to Director of Weapons, 23 January 1951, PRO, Air 20/7313.

9. "Close Support Operations," USAF Operational Report, 9 March 1951, PRO, WO 216/838. See also "Fighter Operations in Korea," USAF briefing paper, 10 March 1952, PRO, Air 20/7798. "80 percent of air action in Korea is in direct or indirect support of ground forces."

10. Futrell, 705.

11. Ibid., 706.

12. Ibid., 707.

13. "Close Support Operations," PRO, WO 216/838.

14. Millett, 397–98.

15. Johnson, 1, PRO, Air 20/7796.

16. Futrell, 694, 703.

17. These figures represent losses in air combat only. Total aircraft losses were Chinese/North Korean: 976, FEAF: 1466, Navy/USMC: 420. The great majority of UNC losses were to ground fire. Callum A. MacDonald, *Korea: The War before Vietnam* (New York: Free Press, 1987), 277.

18. Richard H. Kohn and Joseph P. Harahan, eds., *Air Superiority in World War II and Korea: An interview with Gen James Ferguson, Gen Robert M. Lee, Gen William W. Momyer, and Lt Gen Elwood R. Quesada* (Washington, D.C.: Office of Air Force History, 1983), 74.

19. Futrell, 699.

20. Edmund Dews and Felix Kozaczka, *Air Interdiction: Lessons from Past Campaigns*, N-1743-PA&E (Santa Monica, Calif.: RAND, 1981), v.

21. UK Liaison Mission, cable, Tokyo to Air Ministry, London, 18 October 1950, PRO, Air 20/6672.

22. Ibid., 13 October 1950.

23. Air Vice-Marshal C. A. Bouchier to Chiefs of Staff, London, 16 November 1950, PRO, Air 20/8007.

24. Loose minute, n. d. [1952], commenting on Wing Comdr J. E. Johnson's final report from Korea, PRO, Air 20/7313. "The effect of the interdiction campaign was over-estimated against the non-mechanised and living off the land enemy."

25. "Close Support Operations," 23, PRO, WO 216/838. The report cites prisoner of war statements collected and analyzed in US Army operational research reports.

26. *British Commonwealth Naval Operations*, 292.

27. In addition to O'Neill and Moore and Bagshawe, already cited, see George Odgers, *Across the Parallel: The Australian 77th Squadron with the United States Air Force in the Korean War* (Melbourne: n. p., 1952); and Anthony Farrar-Hockley, *The British Part in the Korean War*, 2 vols. (London: Her Majesty's Stationery Office, 1990 and 1995).

28. Director of Operations Division, minute, 24 November 1951, PRO, Adm 1/22667.

29. Ibid., minute, 1 May 1952.

30. Director, Naval Air Organisation and Training, note, January 1952, PRO, Adm 1/22667.

31. Report on operations of HMS *Theseus*, April 1951, PRO, Adm 1/22364.

32. *British Commonwealth Naval Operations*, 155.

33. "Fighter Operations in Korea," PRO, Air 20/7798.

34. "HMS *Ocean* in Korea," Operational Research Memorandum no. 167, April 1955, PRO, Adm 219/526.

35. Vice Adm A. D. Struble, commanding the US 7th Fleet, was of the view that the carrier aircraft would have been better deployed exclusively in close support of the ground forces, but he was overruled by Ridgway, acting on the advice of Far East Air Forces. *British Commonwealth Naval Operations*, 292.

36. "Carrier operations in support of *Operation Musketeer*," Directorate of Operational Research report 34, 1959, PRO, Adm 219/610.

37. "Close Support Operations," PRO, WO 216/838. Of two carpet bombing attacks in support of ground offensives in September 1950, the report noted that "there is no evidence that any significant results were obtained."

38. Robert John O'Neill, *Australia in the Korean War 1950–53*, vol. 1, *Strategy and Diplomacy* (Canberra: Australian War Memorial and AGPS, 1981), 149–51.

39. 77 Squadron monthly tactical report 3/51, PRO, Air 8/1709.

40. It should be understood that the Meteor was not a defective design, merely an outdated one. The biggest limitation on the aircraft was its maximum speed of Mach .82, while both the MiG and the Sabre managed in excess of Mach .90. In early combats the MiG enjoyed advantages in both speed and height, and while at lower altitudes the Meteor had an advantage in handling and maneuverability, this did not make up for the relative lack of speed. As one combat evaluation of the Meteor in Korea noted, "The Mach of .82 imposes a handicap of such magnitude that only fleeting shots can be hoped for while ever the MiG continues to use its superior speed to advantage." "Combat Evaluation of the Meteor VIII," n. d. [late 1951], PRO, Air 20/7798.

41. Chiefs of Staff to Bouchier, cable TOK69, 12 September 1951, PRO, Air 8/1709.

42. Bouchier to Chiefs of Staff, cable TRAIN34, 19 September 1951, PRO, Air 8/1709.

43. Lt Gen O. P. Weyland, to Maj Gen L. W. Johnson, commanding general, Third Air Force, letter, 30 September 1951, PRO, Air 8/1709.

44. DCAS to Secretary of State, minutes, 26 September 1951, PRO, Air 8/1709.

45. Bouchier to Chief of Air Staff, 7 April 1952, PRO, Air 20/7611.

46. Bruce Lyman, *The Significance of Australian Air Operations in Korea*, Air Power Studies Centre Paper no. 2 (Canberra: Air Power Studies Centre, 1992), 46. See also Alan Stephens, *Power Plus Attitude: Ideas, Strategy and Doctrine in the Royal Australian Air Force 1921–1991* (Canberra: AGPS, 1992), 122–23.

47. DCAS to Air Marshal Sir Donald Hardman, cable A1140, 8 April 1953, and reply, cable A601, 22 April 1953, PRO, Air 8/1626.

48. A point acknowledged explicitly by Ridgway: "No one who fought on the ground in Korea would ever be tempted to belittle the accomplishments of our air force there. Not only did air power save us from disaster, but without it the mission of the United Nations Forces could not have been accomplished." Matthew B. Ridgway, *The Korean War: How we met the challenge: How all-out Asian war was averted: Why MacArthur was dismissed: Why today's war objectives must be limited* (New York: Doubleday, 1967), 244.

49. M. J. Armitage and R. A. Mason, *Air Power in the Nuclear Age 1945–82: Theory and Practice* (London: Macmillan, 1983), 43.

The Air War in Vietnam:
Reevaluating Failure

C. D. Coulthard-Clark

Immediately after the end of the Persian Gulf War in 1991, the chairman of the US Joint Chiefs of Staff, Gen Colin Powell, made a point of thanking the American and Coalition forces involved in the decisive defeat of Iraq. "Operation Desert Storm" had been, he said, "a textbook joint operation, each service doing what it does best to ensure victory." General Powell went on to claim that, with the "thunder and lightning" of Desert Storm, the commander of US forces in the gulf, Gen Norman Schwarzkopf, had "laid to rest the phantoms of Vietnam."[1]

Powell's comment is revealing and provides a useful point at which to begin this review of the use of airpower as demonstrated in Vietnam. He was, we can be sure, expressing relief that the Gulf War had not led to the same sort of protracted and militarily frustrating conflict endured in Vietnam from 1961 to 1973 by the United States and its allies. He was apparently also referring to the widespread view of that earlier war as a somewhat shameful episode in the history of the American armed forces, one which had finally been redressed. While it might be reading too much into his meaning to seize on his use of the word *phantoms*, this could be taken to suggest that Powell considered that there has been something essentially unreal about much of what has been made of the Vietnam experience. If this was his intent, then let me say at the outset that I think he is right.

Earlier this year I read with interest an article written by the previous speaker this morning, regarding the popular tendency—certainly in this country—to forget or distort the facts regarding Vietnam. I am sure Jeff Grey will not mind me quoting his observation: "Because the war ended in defeat for the United States it has been easier to present its origins and course as the product of folly, its conduct fundamentally immoral. The focus of the criticism has moved. . . . But the fundamental elements of the anti-Vietnam War case—immoral war, incompetently handled—remain seemingly immutable."[2]

Jeff's objection was with the accepted wisdom that the war was little more than "a criminal undertaking which benefited no-one, a vast tragedy whose outcome was pre-ordained," and the way that "myopia, mythology and hindsight" has come to debase and overshadow a more objective look at the facts. Here again, I have to say that I agree.

Some of the most pervasive and enduring images of Vietnam concern aspects of the air war conducted there. Masses of Iroquois helicopters carrying troops in an awesome display of the new measure of battlefield mobility achieved in the conflict. Horrific pictures of children burned in the accidental napalm bombing of villages which became an icon for the antiwar movement. Also firmly part of the public memory is the opposition to the bombing campaign against North Vietnam, with captured American airmen put on public display in Hanoi much as Saddam Hussein's regime did during the gulf conflict. "Stop the Bombing" became the catch cry which effectively destroyed the presidency of Lyndon Baines Johnson (LBJ). It seems appropriate, then, to reconsider the proposition that the outcome in Vietnam represented a colossal failure, not just of American force of arms in general but of airpower in particular.

Lest some of you think it strange for an Australian to be undertaking this session, it is perhaps necessary to point out that Australia was the only one of America's allies to join it in making a major aerial contribution in this conflict. Thailand provided air assistance between 1964 and 1971 in the form of pilots who flew in the United States (US) and South Vietnamese transport units, while the South Koreans deployed a few transport aircraft in 1971 for administrative support of their large ground contingent. New Zealand also sent pilots, some serving in a Royal Australian Air Force (RAAF) squadron while others flew as forward air controllers (FAC) with the US Air Force (USAF).

Australia alone, however, sent operational units—the first in 1964—which served alongside or as part of the broader allied structure. By the time of our withdrawal in 1971–72, the RAAF had deployed three squadrons, comprising Caribou transports, Canberra bombers, and Iroquois helicopters. The RAAF also provided some 35 pilots who served as FACs, and others flew in USAF fighter squadrons. In addition, the Royal Australian Navy sent a helicopter flight which was integrated into a US Army assault helicopter company. My point is simply that Australia played a part in this air war, and although its contribution was dwarfed by the American effort, this involvement at least provided many of our airmen an opportunity to form perspectives on how the war was conducted.

As you have heard, my knowledge of this conflict stems from having been involved in researching and writing about Australia's part in the air war in Vietnam. In the course of talking to many of our veterans, I have been privileged to learn of their experiences and to gain an understanding of their perceptions, as professional airmen, of this conflict. I make no pretence of having a detailed grasp of all the technical aspects of air operations as these were carried out, a disclaimer I hasten to make in recognition of the wealth of experience present in this hall. What I would like to offer are some broader thoughts, derived from historical analysis, on what the Vietnam conflict can tell us about airpower and its application. These observations may not be particularly profound and original, but they will fill a gap in the chain of campaigns considered in this forum and put into context matters discussed here.

Before narrowing in to this particular theme, it is worth considering for a moment the changing way in which historians and other commentators are beginning to regard what happened in Vietnam, in particular the extent to which the outcome of that conflict should be judged to have been the abject defeat it is commonly held to be. That the United States and its allies were obliged to withdraw their forces from the southern Republic of Vietnam (RVN) by 1973, without achieving a decisive military victory after more than a decade of expensive effort, is undeniable. That this then left the gate wide open for a communist offensive, mounted and directed by the northern Democratic Republic of Vietnam (DRV), which toppled the southern regime in 1975, is also an inescapable fact of history. The passage of the last 20 years and the subsequent course of world events have, however, given different significance to all of this, although whether that filters through into the popular canon of the generation which lived through the conflict remains to be seen.

According to the new line of argument, when judged in terms of the motivations and objectives which inspired external involvement in Vietnam, America and her allies achieved far more than is commonly perceived. In the world order of the early 1960s, dominated by East-West confrontation in Europe, what we saw was an extension of Cold War concerns to prevent the expansion of communism. Specifically, the American aim in Southeast Asia was to contain the spreading of infection from Vietnam, Laos, and Cambodia to Thailand and into the new states of Southeast Asia emerging from colonial origins. Not just Malaysia and Singapore seemed vulnerable then but also Indonesia and the Philippines. The image conjured up by the "domino theory" of a sequential collapse of these states into the communist camp may belong to a crude and unfashionable political theory today, but it cannot be discounted as shorthand for a genuinely held concern at the time.

The situation accompanying the eventual triumph attained by Hanoi in 1975 was a far cry from the worst fears earlier held by the United States and its allies. The stability of Southeast Asia was nowhere near so fragile and at risk as in the early 1960s, with most of the fledgling states of that time having consolidated and matured enormously in the ensuing period. Moreover, a decade of direct American interest had helped the wider Asian region, bringing great benefits to the economies of South Korea, Japan, and Hong Kong in particular. Reunified Vietnam was no longer the threat it earlier was expected to represent either, since although heavy with military power, it was economically impoverished and faced with a massive task of reconstruction, particularly in the north as a result of the war damage inflicted by US bombing.

The policy of economic isolation pursued against Vietnam in the years since the communist victory, only abandoned in the last month or so with the ending of the embargo on American companies doing trade there, made the new regime even more dependent on its communist backers, the People's Republic of China and the Soviet Union. This source of aid, as we have seen, proved unsustained. Vietnam fell out with its Chinese ally and even fought a border war against it in 1979, while communism itself collapsed in the Soviet Union and across Eastern Europe in what will surely come to be seen as a bizarre twist to the domino theory.

In short, the northern Vietnamese regime that so doggedly pursued its war aims against the south paid a heavy and continuing price, one which might have left it wondering at times what it was precisely that had been won—although this is quite possibly a Western reservation no Vietnamese would share. And in the clear evidence that there were some positive long-term strategic consequences to the allied participation in the war, how then can we continue to characterize the outcome as a total defeat? It might not be exactly true to say that the lives and national treasure expended in Vietnam, Laos, and Cambodia had ever or fully justified the result, but it also would not be true to say these had been completely wasted.

The point in approaching my subject from this angle is not to reignite a debate over the moral issues of the Vietnam War. Indeed, to ensure that we are not diverted from the issues of proper concern here today, I must say now that I see little point to getting into any sort of discussion of that area at all. My purpose is really to draw a distinction between the short-term and long-term connotations behind such terms as *defeat* and *victory*. Making such a distinction seems to me necessary, if only to reconcile the ambiguity between notions of defeat with so many unmistakable signs of success.

But if not defeat, then what was it? Perhaps we are on safest ground if we accept that the outcome of the Vietnam War represented a failure to attain the expected result that such a large-scale application of military force ought to have brought. It is here that we find the basis for the belief that American might of arms had been humbled in Vietnam. How could the massive forces deployed have failed to prevail unless they pursued a false doctrine, were incompetently handled, or showed inferior mettle?

On the surface, the logic of such an argument seems compelling. At the height of the war the United States had committed to the contest in Vietnam one-half its tactical airpower, along with two-fifths of its combat-ready divisions and one-third of its Navy. That is, over one-half a million American ground troops deployed, in addition to the RVN's own sizeable forces, equipped with the best that the world's leading superpower could provide. On the air side, over 3,000 aircraft were available to the allies from within the RVN's borders alone by 1968, and many more were operating from bases in Thailand, the Philippines, and Guam.[3] How could force of this magnitude fail to gain the required result?

For purposes of comparison, it should be noted that the stunningly successful six-week air campaign against Iraq was carried out with less than 2,800 aircraft on the Coalition side and involved the dropping of only some 85,000 tons of bombs.[4] This tonnage was barely two-thirds of that dropped by Allied aircraft on Germany during March 1945 alone.[5] Adding weight to the point is the fact that the United States dropped eight million tons of bombs in Indochina between 1962 and 1973, compared with four million dropped by all the warring nations throughout the Second World War![6]

Apart from this, rarely could any side entering into a conflict hope to experience an air environment so much in its own favor, in terms of the three basic components or campaigns recognized by our air doctrine: that is, the battle for control of the air, the air bombardment effort, and air support for combat forces. Air superiority over the RVN was a given, since the Vietcong insurgents and People's Army of Vietnam (PAVN) forces up to 1973 lacked any air support of their own. Only in the late stage of the war did allied aircraft face any sort of challenge over South Vietnam, aside from ground fire, in the form of surface-to-air missiles (SAM). In such a benign environment, allied forces were able to concentrate on building effective cooperation with surface forces.

The battle for control of the air which the allies faced was, therefore, primarily associated with their attempts to bring the DRV's homeland interests, resources, and war-making capacity under attack by bombing. Here the opposition presented by DRV air defenses was formidable, principally in the form of Soviet-supplied SAM batteries. The threat posed to raiding allied aircraft by MiGs of the DRV air force was spasmodic, though nonetheless serious. In the period August 1967 to February 1968, for example, the USAF accounted for 31 enemy aircraft in combat but lost 24 of its own; even as late as 1972 the threat posed by DRV MiGs was considerable, with 18 US aircraft lost between February and July for the cost of 24 MiGs.[7]

So, to frame the question in the terms used by General Powell: Precisely which phantoms were laid to rest by the Gulf War? What was wrong with the way airpower was applied in Vietnam, or could it be that airpower inherently lacks the ability to consistently produce the promised results? Interestingly, we are told that Powell himself held doubts on such questions prior to the gulf, having "an Army officer's natural distrust of air power," dating from his own experience in Vietnam.[8]

In talking to many airmen who fought in Vietnam, or in reading the growing number of accounts which have been published or exist in the records, one never comes across individuals willing to declare that their units failed to do a useful or effective job of work. Many will admit to shortcomings in particular areas which might have been experienced from time to time—for example, in the levels of pilot training or experience—but in nearly all cases one finds that the problem was addressed and corrective measures implemented. It was interesting to find my experience mirrored by one US researcher, who commented, "Gradually, the accumulation of testimonies to the efficiency of various units in Vietnam defied the outcome of the war as a whole."[9] Basically, if everyone in the Air Force was doing their job, how come success still proved elusive?

On a wider scale, one occasionally encounters suggestions that the same phenomenon existed across the services: the sort of argument that goes, "Well, we in the Army did everything asked of us, but we were let down by the Air Force." Airmen, of course, can turn that line on its head by pointing to the oft-heard claim that Vietnam was primarily a ground war and that was where the conflict was going to be won or lost. This finger-pointing relates to the observation I made earlier: there is so much evidence that each of the services in Vietnam was operating successfully and effectively, at least much of the time, that it becomes hard to accept the notion that the "Free World Forces" did not, in fact, ultimately prevail.

There can be little doubt that in many areas there was scope for improving on what was done or aspects which specifically defied the superficial appearance of invincible might. The raw numbers of aircraft available are, for example, no clear guide to the operational capability or suitability of individual types. Several airmen I have spoken to have remarked on the number of older propeller-driven aircraft which they saw operating. Certainly many of these types, like the T-28 and A-1, were bottom of the range and carried quite small armament loads, but many jet aircraft that saw service in Vietnam also had limitations in close air support (such as the F-100 Super Sabre tactical fighter), setting up a "prop versus jet" controversy which raged throughout the war.[10]

In any event, old was not necessarily useless, as the RAAF came to appreciate in the case of its Canberra bombers. These aircraft were held to have already seen their best days when sent to Vietnam in 1967. As was quickly discovered, however, this obsolescent type—though in the planning process of being replaced by the F-111s which Australia had on order—proved remarkably effective in the level-bombing mode and achieved sometimes extraordinary accuracy in preplanned strikes. Although the USAF also operated its version of the Canberra, the B-57, these were effectively an entirely separate type, being designed and configured for use in a dive-bombing role.

In the same vein, technology in many areas was not always equal to the challenges presented by the operational environment encountered in Vietnam. Today we are used to and accepting of many of the developments pioneered in Vietnam, particularly in precision-guided munitions (PGM) which played such a conspicuous part in the gulf success, without recognizing that much of the vast amount of ordnance dropped in Vietnam was of the dumb or iron variety. The effectiveness of such weaponry in the Vietnam environment, where accuracy had to be within 10 meters to have any effect against some of the bunkers constructed by the opposition, was an acknowledged problem. As General Schwarzkopf remarked after the Gulf War, in answer to critics of the performance of PGMs, "I would have given my left arm if our Air Force could have had half the capability in Vietnam that it demonstrated in the Gulf."[11]

Having suggested that many of the statistics which can be used as yardsticks of performance or achievement must be regarded as misleading or worse, let me develop this theme for a moment. If the aircraft type flying a particular mission and the type of weaponry it carried were often important qualifiers in judging effort, other factors need to be taken into account too. The loss of effectiveness which went with the appalling weather during the middle months of each year also points up the fact that large numbers of aircraft flying often tell us very little about what was actually being achieved.

I recall one interview subject telling me, during my research of the practice adopted late in the war, of US sorties being sent off with less than full armament load but twice as many aircraft being used on each mission. This was, apparently, a deliberate device to keep up the figures for the number of hours and missions being flown, at a time when the number of targets was reducing. Without this practice being adopted, the fear was that political pressures would have built for a cutback in the number of squadrons deployed. Hearing evidence of this nature, it is hard not to wonder whether the allies might not have gotten by in Vietnam with even less airpower than they actually had.

Other complaints heard relate to the choice of targets (hitting small jungle camps on the basis of three-day-old intelligence), and the US reliance on bomb damage assessment (BDA) as a measure of operational effectiveness. Since this system relied on an individual FAC making a best estimate of the damage caused by any one strike, it was usually based on little more than guesswork. As such, it was a system open to serious abuse, becoming the Air Force equivalent of the Army's "body count" syndrome in creating an appearance of progress essentially for political purposes. I recall being told by an Australian FAC who, on one of the few occasions where he controlled a strike by a RAAF Canberra, rejoiced in giving his countrymen a "big fat zero" as their BDA—"just to keep them honest," as he put it. Perhaps if there had been a good many more like him, the operational statistics for Vietnam may have retained a good deal more credibility.

In the area of Army-Air Force cooperation, so vital to the main game being pursued within the southern republic's borders, there is similar evidence—a lot of it anecdotal—which points to periodic shortcomings. Individual instances can be found where air strikes summoned in support of ground forces in contact were late in arriving, failed to hit the intended target, or—worse—sometimes inflicted casualties among the troops being supported. Undoubtedly such things happened, just as they did during the Gulf War if we recall the losses through friendly fire.

In this area we need to beware of a number of dangerous myths which have been propagated regarding the Vietnam experience. For instance, the professed fear of some infantry commanders about using air strikes too close to their own positions, because of the lack of skill exhibited by Air Force pilots, is contradicted by other accounts from FACs. These tell you of instances where ground commanders deliberately misstated the safety distance of their troops from the intended target of an air strike, relying on the accuracy of ordnance delivery.

Other complaints about the response times entailed in obtaining air support for ground troops do not withstand scrutiny. The location of air bases throughout the RVN and the system used of holding pairs of fighter-bombers on standby at these bases meant that the occasions were very rare when air support could not be provided within 20 minutes anywhere within the RVN's borders. Added to this was the practice employed of diverting aircraft from preplanned missions to undertake more urgent tasks, which ensured that this time frame was frequently bettered. Indeed, where a planned target could not be hit because of weather or some other reason, aircraft could be left looking for a worthwhile alternative target and effectively "hawking" their armament load. In such cases, the response time involved could sometimes be almost instantaneous.

Of course, the very effectiveness of such a system brings its own problems. When 20 minutes becomes the norm for an air strike to become available, there is a natural tendency for a ground commander in difficulty to ask why the same support could not be provided in five, with little consideration of the numbers of assets needed to achieve that level of coverage. Using aircraft which had been armed in anticipation of a particular mission, or for stand-by against a range of contingencies, also did not guarantee a ground commander that the aircraft arriving to lend him support would be optimally loaded for the actual task required.

Whatever the distorting effects of the factors mentioned, or the deficiencies which might be held to have been revealed, none of these seems to stand out so clearly as to suggest that there was a widespread, endemic or systemic failure of the air capability available in Vietnam. There was, I conclude, plenty of airpower—indeed, it can even be argued that its levels were extravagant—and it was generally capable of doing the job required of it. What we are left with in the case of Vietnam is a failure to have properly or effectively applied airpower, or to have misdirected this effort.

Constraints on the use of airpower are undoubtedly observable at several levels of the structure which ran the war in Vietnam. At a purely local level, the requirement to obtain clearance from Vietnamese province chiefs before engaging targets in many areas was a frustrating limitation which allied airmen could do little about. Suggestions also can be found that there was, perhaps, an inadequate appreciation in the US Military Assistance Command, Vietnam (MACV) headquarters of how to get the best use of air resources in a counterrevolutionary warfare setting. Several Air Force accounts, for example, have pointed to the unwillingness of the Army generals who headed the MACV organization to achieve effective representation from the USAF on their staff.[12] This is pointed to as typifying a short-sighted attitude to achieving the centralized control of the total air effort which was seen as a desirable objective.

That the US military was obliged to fight in Vietnam "with one hand tied behind its back" is a charge which has been made often over the years. In essence, this line of argument points to there having been a political failure to win in Vietnam rather than a purely military one. As one popular account of recent years put matters, none of the presidents from Truman to Johnson who presided over the progressive US entry into the conflict had a plan behind their actions. "They were trapped between their fear of being blamed for the fall of Vietnam and widening the war so much it might bring in China or the Soviet Union. So each did only the minimum necessary not to lose it during his tenure in the White House. They nibbled the bullet rather than bit it."[13]

There is a considerable body of evidence to support the contention that misunderstanding and lack of resolve at the political level did much to squander the military effort devoted to Vietnam. That there was a degree of political control exercised over the detailed conduct of operations also seems unquestionable. On the air side this was manifested even in the selection of bombing targets in the DRV being made in Washington by President Johnson or the secretary of defense, Robert McNamara, rather than the military commanders responsible at the front.[14]

The fear that Vietnam would cease to be a limited war and bring about a direct confrontation between the United States and either or both of the Soviet Union and China stemmed, of course, from the experience of Korea. The entry of Chinese forces into that earlier conflict, precipitated by General MacArthur's UN offensive deep into North Korea, had convinced a later generation of American politicians to distrust the judgment of their military advisers and keep them on a short leash.

In the literature of the war, we find efforts to excuse Johnson's miscalculations in respect to the bombing of North Vietnam, arguing that the president was "misled by stupid or self-serving military advisers and ill-founded intelligence reports."[15] Not so, suggest other accounts, which make the point that Johnson and his advisers were skeptical about the field reports received from Vietnam, routinely discounting the accuracy of body counts and claimed successes of the pacification program and Air Force bombing estimates.[16] At the very least, we can be sure, the process of policy decision was much more complex than apologists for LBJ would have us believe.

However, while it may be convenient to adopt the line that the politicians got things hopelessly wrong, and did so despite the professionals' best efforts, there is a body of analysis which argues that the services, including the Air Force, do not stand absolved from blame. As one recent study has pointed out, the USAF was mentally ill-prepared for a conflict like Vietnam:

> Since its doctrinal departure point was that small wars could be won easily as long as it was ready to win big wars, the Air Force had to believe that once air power was properly employed, this war could be

won quickly. The Air Force, winging its way into Southeast Asia on a doctrine devised for bombing Nazi Germany, was not alone in its nostalgia for fighting World War II nor in its determination to envisage the enemy's capabilities as mirroring its own.[17]

In this writer's view, the USAF in the period of the early 1960s showed inferior intellectual caliber, tending more and more to abdicate strategic thinking to civilian think tanks like RAND: "Consequently, when Presidents John F. Kennedy and Lyndon B. Johnson turned to their military leaders for a strategy to follow in Vietnam, the generals could not devise one appropriate to the war as perceived by the civilian leaders. . . . In Vietnam, the Air Force along with the other services was rarely outfought, but like the other services it was often *outthought*."[18]

The advice the service was capable of giving to civilian policy makers was hardly of a kind to inspire confidence, therefore, appearing to be out of touch and heavy handed and giving rise to unfortunate comparisons between military dreamers and civilian pragmatists.[19]

However arrived at, the mistake which lay at the core of the strategic misdirection of the war came directly from Washington. Perhaps McNamara and Johnson were claiming superior knowledge over their military chiefs in taking matters such as target selection into their own hands, but the parameters they set for the conduct of the air war were, at least arguably, the wrong ones. In late 1964, for example, the US Joint Chiefs of Staff presented proposals for a hard-hitting 16-day air campaign against 94 strategic targets considered critical to the DRV's ability to wage war. This program was rejected by Johnson and McNamara, who decided that the option of bombing should only supplement pacification efforts focused within the RVN. Thus the Rolling Thunder program initially implemented by the United States amounted to a tactical rather than strategic air offensive, one aimed more at sending signals of political will rather than achieving decisive military objectives.

Both the political and military advocates in this debate were exhibiting mistaken ideas here. The latter had missed the point that Vietnam was a preindustrial, largely agrarian nation which was never likely to be subdued in the same way that Germany and Japan had been. At the same time, the wisdom of using a blunt and brutal instrument such as airpower to send diplomatic signals was open to question.

That the United States proceeded to forfeit the true impact of airpower through such a choice seems confirmed by subsequent events. Certainly the benefits of shock and surprise espoused in the RAAF's current air doctrine had been lost through the process of gradual escalation which subsequently characterized the US air campaign. The DRV was enabled to undertake major improvement of its air defense network which would cost the USAF dear in later operations over the north. More than this, however, it was fundamentally wasteful to devote air resources to knocking out enemy assets when these eventually appeared in the RVN, or to intercept them along the length of the Ho Chi Minh Trail, the major southern infiltration route for men and materiel running through eastern Laos.

The principle of economy of effort argued that the best effect would be achieved through attacking the enemy's war effort at its source, chiefly at the points where stocks of supplies destined for the south were concentrated on arrival in the DRV. Prime targets in such a campaign were the rail links to China and the port of Haiphong which serviced Hanoi. The validity of this was clearly demonstrated with the Freedom Train and Linebacker I bombing programs from April to October 1972, involving fewer target restrictions than Rolling Thunder, and more especially Linebacker II during December 1972 when there was unrestricted bombing of the north.

The sheer destructiveness of the Linebacker operations brought a resumption and eventual conclusion of peace negotiations, which by this stage was all that was intended of them. Interestingly, these have since been represented in much of the literature as one of the few demonstrations in the war of the effective and cost-effective use of airpower. Many writers have been tempted to ponder what might have been the effect of adopting this course much earlier in the war, preferably at the outset of the air campaign in 1965—a line of thought which has given rise to some disturbing mythology about the real value and achievement of these operations.

As previously indicated, the fear of provoking the major communist powers acting in support of the DRV was the principal constraint on engaging in unrestricted bombing earlier in the war. This raises a question, though, as to whether Vietnam was a war which the United States felt it could even afford to win in a conventional sense. Pulverizing the DRV into an acceptance of US will (even if achievable, and that is debatable) would have damaged the US's global standing by apparently confirming all the worse rhetoric of US opponents regarding its imperialist nature and ambitions. The problem from the outset was that the United States had no basis for intervening in Vietnam which was internationally recognized as legitimate.

Reverting once more to General Powell's comments in connection with the Desert Storm victory, it was probably the avoidance of political overcontrol which represented the most important "phantom of Vietnam" laid to rest. In Woodward's book, *The Commanders*, we are told that President George Bush took a key lesson from Vietnam into his handling of the gulf situation. This was that he should "send enough force to do the job and don't tie the hands of the commanders."[20] To further avoid "the military's Vietnam nightmare," typified by Johnson leaning over maps in the White House circling specific targets, Powell also reportedly determined to keep as much air targeting information as possible away from Washington,[21] thereby allowing Schwarzkopf and his commanders the maximum freedom to work within the guidelines set for them by the political leadership.

So, what do we take away from consideration of the Vietnam experience? It might be the proposition that the conduct of air operations in that theater cannot be taken as a fair test of airpower, any more than it provided the opportunity to usefully measure the strength and ability of ground combat or naval power. This was, surely, the implied conclusion offered by General Powell regarding the difference between Vietnam and the Gulf War: in the latter case, each service had been allowed to do what it does best to ensure victory, which was more than could be said of Vietnam.

To ignore the experience of Vietnam and to discount it as some sort of aberration to a golden rule of airpower which remains inviolate seems to me, however, a dangerous alternative. Airpower failed to deliver the goods in Vietnam, perhaps not in the way that we expect to have defeat presented, but through an inability of its practitioners and advocates to be realistic in their arguments of what could be achieved and might be expected from it. Here was a case where an out-dated doctrine, rigidly applied, proved unresponsive to the demands of a conflict demanding a more creative approach. Vietnam was a reminder that war frequently produces situations which defy rules which quantify or expectations which seem straightforward.

Discussion

Air Commodore C. H. Spurgeon: I was the commander of RAAF Vietnam in 1970–71. I don't think any commander has ever been sent on an RAAF mission with his duty statement written on half a piece of A4 paper, as I was. I don't think any air force commander should ever be sent anywhere with a directive on half a piece of paper. The two items on that paper gave me command of all RAAF forces in Vietnam and told me to keep them half a mile away from the Cambodian border. On that premise, I suppose the border was neatly marked by a white painted picket fence. As a result of that directive, such limitations as I could impose on the use of our Caribou and Canberras were made extremely difficult. Also, when I arrived I found that the targeting and mission responsibility for those aircraft was totally in the hands of a USAF operations room run by a lieutenant colonel. Our Canberras were listed on the mission board as B-57s, when in fact in some critical aspects they were quite different. When we came to withdraw from Vietnam, our air staff in Australia were too hasty in removing the helicopters, which were still needed to support the army. So I found my job up there very frustrating.

Dr. Coulthard-Clark: Perhaps I could make a few points about the RAAF commitment. I was critical in my talk about the doctrine pursued by the USAF. We have to be equally critical of the guidance provided to our RAAF commanders. A number of people who were interviewed as part of the Australian War Memorial's oral history program commented on the inadequate briefing they were given before taking up command and on the lack of debriefing on their return home. We seemed singularly determined neither to provide guidance nor to learn from the experience of Vietnam. So the malaise I was talking about certainly wasn't confined to the USAF. The inviolability of borders was a legitimate political constraint to set on our forces, but in some circumstances it was quite impractical. We had a number of fighter pilots flying with USAF squadrons which regularly operated over North Vietnam and Laos, and the simple fact is, our people flew with them. At least two RAAF pilots flew 10 missions over North Vietnam.

The point about tasking the Canberras is worth elaboration. One RAAF Canberra in Vietnam was definitely shot down by a SAM. That situation, as I understand it, probably arose because the tasking authority at Tan Son Nhut Airport in Saigon had no idea that our aircraft, not being the same as B-57s, lacked the necessary equipment to detect SAMs and consequently sent it into an area where SAM batteries were possibly operating.

Air Vice-Marshal Gary Beck: You say that the out-dated doctrine was rigidly applied. From my perspective as a squadron pilot, we measured our effectiveness by bomb damage assessment. This has all been discounted in the years since, but I can tell you then we thought we were doing a great job. I'd be interested to know how you're going to write about the RAAF's contribution in Vietnam. It seems you could write glowingly about what we think we did, but in the broader context you could be very critical.

Dr. Coulthard-Clark: Using American statistics, the RAAF's Canberra bombers had the best BDA record of any of the allied squadrons in South Vietnam. But one of the odd experiences I've had is going through the squadron's monthly reports which contain extensive data on BDA. When you look at the amount of damage claimed—the number of enemy personnel killed and injured, the yardage of trenches uncovered, bunkers destroyed, weapon positions knocked out, sampans sunk, and so on—you're left with a curious feeling. If we were doing so "well," why were so many of the enemy still so active? I think that's a real contradiction we face and that's what I was trying to highlight in my presentation. I'm not sure it necessarily answers your question.

Air Vice-Marshal Beck: I think the missing ingredient was clearly stated strategic objectives. The objectives for the air campaign weren't clearly enunciated, and neither was an air campaign plan. But at the tactical level we thought we were doing a great job.

Dr. Coulthard-Clark: I think we're dealing here with one of the odd aspects of Australia's commitment. We never believed we were making the kind of contribution which would significantly affect the overall outcome. We were engaged in an exercise of tokenism. The units we sent were those elements of our force structure which were most readily released. They were selected not by the RAAF but after discussion by the Chiefs of Staff Committee, and the decisions were made by the Defence Committee, not the Air Board. There's perhaps nothing strange about that. But you never find in the records of our higher defense organization debate over what we were specifically required to do in Vietnam and how best to do it. I think that typifies the Australian participation.

Air Marshal David Evans: You said that you found it odd that almost everyone you'd spoken to had claimed that they were operating effectively, and yet we didn't win the war. Well, you know as well as I do, the constraints placed on our forces prevented them from winning the war. The army, for instance, couldn't pursue people into Cambodia; generals couldn't decide to do an amphibious landing in North Vietnam. The circumstances were not conducive to winning the war. But that doesn't mean that the American and Australian units weren't operating as efficiently as they were allowed to in their specific tasks each day.

Dr. Coulthard-Clark: My point entirely.

Air Marshal Evans: The people who should learn from Vietnam are not the military but the politicians. Military power is only as effective as the guts of the politicians to use it, and I suggest that if we'd had LBJ and McNamara at the time of the Gulf War, we'd still be there and the casualties would be mounting.

Dr. Coulthard-Clark: I'll agree with you but with one qualification. The obligation is still on the practitioners of airpower to provide advice, and unless that advice is credible and realistic, we are always going to be ignored by the politicians.

Air Vice-Marshal Peter Squire: In the previous presentation Dr. Grey referred to inadequacies in the joint command and control arrangements in Korea, and suggested that perhaps lessons were not learnt from that conflict and translated to Vietnam. What are your thoughts on that?

Dr. Coulthard-Clark: I mention in my paper that the USAF was inclined to complain about their underrepresentation on what was supposedly a joint staff in MACV headquarters. It does seem as though there wasn't a strong Air Force voice and that, in turn, did affect the planning and conduct of operations.

Air Vice-Marshal Beck: Could I add that we've come a long way since Vietnam in terms of Australia and other countries being involved in a coalition force with the United States. While our contribution in a combined operation may still look like tokenism, it's certainly not the way the Americans view it from the command perspective. The command and control of operations in the Gulf War showed how much things have improved since Vietnam.

Dr. Coulthard-Clark: General Horner has made the point that in the gulf a conscious effort was made to decentralize command. In Vietnam the emphasis was entirely the other way, with, in effect, a number of separate air forces operating independently. The Marine Corps, for example, retained their aircraft specifically to support the Marines. Only if there was no requirement from the Marines would they be released to the broader air effort.

Professor Robin Higham: I'd like to make a couple of observations. It seems to me that one of the things that hasn't been talked about here is topography. The Gulf War was fought as the Western Desert was fought in the Second World War. Topographically, it was very suitable for military operations; there were very few places you could set an ambush and things of that sort. Secondly, it seems to me there's a parallel between what happened in Britain between the First World War and the Second World War. In the First World War the military were very poor at giving advice, and they determined by the Second World War that they were never going to allow the politicians to override them again.

Group Capt Gary Waters: Chris, you've brought us to the brink twice now, once in the presentation and once in the discussion. If the political parameters were askew or just plain wrong as you've suggested, what should or even could the military commanders have done?

Dr. Coulthard-Clark: Good question, Gary. In fact when I was preparing this paper I contemplated that question several times. It brings you face to face with one of the central dilemmas of Vietnam. The options confronting America's political leaders were limited and all unpleasant. They wanted to support the southern republic but not to the extent of bringing in the Soviet Union and China; but the very fact of an American military presence in Southeast Asia ensured that the Soviets and Chinese would be involved to some extent. It was that sort of war; it didn't allow simple solutions.

One point regarding the military I raise in my paper is that in the absence of any obvious answers, airpower practitioners were not sufficiently creative or flexible in their thinking.

Air Vice-Marshal Beck: If I can add another observation, air interdiction campaigns in counterrevolutionary warfare suffer from considerable constraints, and we have to recognise that there's a limit to what can be achieved.

Notes

1. *Canberra Times*, 6 March 1991.

2. *Bulletin*, 28 December 1993–4 January 1994, 47.

3. J. Schlight, *The War in South Vietnam: The Years of the Offensive, 1965–1968* (Washington, D.C.: Office of Air Force History, 1988), 129.

4. Gary Waters, *Gulf Lesson One—The Value of Air Power: Doctrinal Lessons for Australia* (Canberra: Air Power Studies Centre, 1992), 101.

5. Ibid., 8.

6. Earl H. Tilford Jr., *Setup: What the Air Force Did in Vietnam and Why* (Maxwell Air Force Base [AFB], Ala.: Air University Press, 1991), 293.

7. Robert Frank Futrell et al., *Aces & Aerial Victories: The United States Air Force in Southeast Asia, 1965–1973* (Maxwell AFB, Ala.: Albert F. Simpson Historical Research Center; Washington, D.C.: Government Printing Office, 1976), 2, 16.

8. Bob Woodward, *The Commanders* (New York: Simon & Schuster, 1991), 148.

9. Donald J. Mrozek, *The US Air Force After Vietnam: Postwar Challenges and Potential for Responses* (Maxwell AFB, Ala.: Air University Press, 1988), 10.

10. Schlight, 19.

11. H. Norman Schwarzkopf, *It Doesn't Take a Hero: General H. Norman Schwarzkopf, The Autobiography*, written with Peter Petre (New York: Bantam Books, 1992), 583.

12. See, for example, Schlight, 76–77, and William W. Momyer, *Air Power in Three Wars* (Washington, D.C.: Office of Air Force History, 1978), 73–77.

13. Fox Butterfield's introduction to John S. Bowman, ed., *The Vietnam War Day by Day* (London: n. p., 1989), 7.

14. Brian VanDeMark, *Into the Quagmire: Lyndon Johnson and the Escalation of the Vietnam War* (New York: Oxford University Press, 1991), 107–8, has Johnson acknowledging that he personally selected targets in the DRV for bombing attacks.

15. Booth Mooney, *LBJ: An Irreverent Chronicle* (New York: Crowell, 1976), 180.

16. Paul Y. Hammond, *LBJ and the Presidential Management of Foreign Relations* (Austin, Tex.: University of Texas Press, 1992), 198–200.

17. Tilford, 78.

18. Ibid., 287.

19. Ibid., 93.

20. Woodward, 306–7.

21. Ibid., 368.

Airpower as a National Instrument: The Arab-Israeli Wars

R. A. Mason

Origins

When Israel became independent in May 1948, the infant state was only nine miles wide to the east of Tel Aviv, 70 from the coast to the Dead Sea, and 400 miles long from the Lebanon border to Eilat on the Gulf of Aqaba. Its population was two and one-half million. It was surrounded by hostile states: Egypt, Jordan, Lebanon, and Syria with a total population of approximately 50 million. Beyond them were several other states which either opposed the establishment of the State of Israel from the outset or joined the opposition during the next 45 years. For the greater part of the next 45 years, Israel was either involved in open war with her neighbors or in hostile confrontation. The state was the product of armed struggle and has depended on military strength for its subsequent evolution. For 40 years the cornerstone of that military strength has been the Israeli Air Force (IAF). This paper seeks to analyze the sources of that strength, concentrating on peacetime preparation, and the occasional mistake, on which such an outstanding combat record was based, rather than on the conflicts which have been so assiduously documented.

The chronology of the modern state of Israel is punctuated by significant events in the history of airpower: the June War of 1967, the War of Attrition, the October War, the Entebbe raid, the Osirak raid, Bekáa Valley, Tunis, and finally, part of "The Patriot War" of 1991. Israel's strategic environment is unusual and therefore "lessons" read across to airpower elsewhere need to be drawn with particular caution. Moreover, until Israel regards her political position as secure and no longer feels dependent on her armed forces, any military information released "officially" is unlikely to be neutral, and a similar caveat is required for Arab sources. Very seldom, for example, do accounts of success and failure written by either side correspond with each other.

Most other air forces originated in peacetime and entered combat in either World War I or World War II with at least an embryonic structure, concepts of operations, and combat force. In 1937 the Jewish underground military organization, the Haganah, organized its first clandestine flying course, followed a year later by Irgun Zvai Leumi. By May 1948 Israel possessed a handful of unarmed aircraft and 22 registered pilots. Its combat strength was increased during the War of Independence by four Messerschmitt Me-109s, three B-17s, and then by a trickle of assorted relics from World War II.

The Egyptian Air Force (EAF) was established in 1932 and until 1945 had been effectively under British control. During the Second World War an Egyptian squadron of Hurricanes was formed primarily to provide air cover for shipping off the Egyptian coast. At the end of the war Britain handed over the squadron and one Spitfire squadron to the EAF. By 1948 the EAF was suffering from poor maintenance and lack of spares, and only 12 Hurricanes and 18 Spitfires were serviceable. Nevertheless, in the early months of war, the EAF enjoyed air superiority. It bombed Tel Aviv and other civilian/industrial targets and haphazardly attacked Israeli airfields. It had no intelligence on the infant but rapidly expanding IAF and, more seriously, it was not aware that a detachment of Royal Air Force (RAF) Spitfires remained at Ramat David. On 22 May five EAF Spitfires were shot down by their RAF counterparts and the Egyptian government apologized to London for attacking British forces. This event was not mentioned in any Israeli account of the war. Subsequently, when the IAF had increased to about 100 aircraft, it moved over to the offensive, taking its opponents completely by surprise. Cairo, Damascus, and Amman were all attacked and the remnants of the EAF neutralized by a heavy offensive counter air (OCA) attack on El Arish airfield.

One other incident, of no military significance at the time, foreshadowed events 25 years later. On 29 May 1948, under pressure from the ground forces and against IAF opposition, the general staff instructed the air force to launch all their four

Messerschmitts against an Egyptian column advancing on Tel Aviv, rather than attack airfields in the Gaza Strip and Sinai. One aircraft was destroyed and its pilot killed, another damaged and pilot wounded, for a 50 percent attrition rate. The episode was typical in scale of the efforts in the air on both sides at this stage: too small, too uncoordinated and inadequate weaponry to exercise any influence on the outcome of the struggle.

Establishment

After the war, cameos of struggles played out in Whitehall and the Pentagon were repeated in Israel before the "independence" or otherwise of the IAF was determined. There does not appear to have been any appeal to theorists by either side. The first leaders of the IAF had served in one or other of the Allied air forces, all in junior ranks, and none had any experience of bureaucratic infighting. Their common sense was based on experience and perception. So was that of the common sense high command, personified by Ygael Yadin, ex Haganah commander who subsequently commented, "When I took on the post of IDF Chief of Staff (in October 1949) I knew that our problem of problems [was] this: were we going to make the same mistake as other nations that established independent air, sea and land forces? Or were we going to establish one general staff for all the forces . . . as befitted a small country, a small force, and short, internal communication routes. It was clear to me that the second way was correct, and that if I could not solve the problem that way I had better resign my post."[1] The issue at stake, however, was not the independence or otherwise of the IAF, but the nature of its contribution to Israeli security and its subordination not to the Israeli Defense Force (IDF) but to the Israeli Army.

There was a curious reprise in Israel in 1948 of circumstances in Britain in 1917. David Ben-Gurion, like David Lloyd George before him, called upon a South African to advise him about his air force. In less than a week Wing Comdr Cecil Margo constructed the blueprint for the IAF. He observed that the IDF command had failed to include senior IAF officers in operational planning, dissipated already minuscule assets,

193

and failed to provide adequate support. The IAF's primary role, said Margo, was to defend Israel and its ground forces from enemy aircraft: that required air superiority. Because Israel was outnumbered by its opponents, victory in the air war had to be given resource priority. Once the air war was won, the IAF could help the ground forces. At present, army demands were draining the IAF's limited resources and weakening Israeli security rather than enhancing it. Margo fleshed out his comments with recommendations for new mission planning, control, and targeting procedures and finally urged Ben-Gurion to place the IAF supreme commander on equal footing with the heads of the other armed services, answerable to the IDF chief of staff.[2] Ben-Gurion listened, and on 26 July 1948 declared the air force to be an independent branch answerable only to the IDF chief of staff and appointed Aharon Remez to be its commander. But there was still a long way to go before Margo's recommendations were to be completely carried out.

David Ben-Gurion wished to base the nation's defense on a small regular army expanded in crisis by reserves. Remez argued that such a mobilization would be threatened by air attack, and therefore air superiority was essential from the out-set. Consequently, the air force had to be the exact opposite of the army. He repeated Margo's position: It had to be a power-ful full-time force capable of seizing an initiative and establish-ing air superiority. It had to have control of its own supplies, training, manpower, intelligence, and operations. It also had to take priority in defense resource allocation.[3] In December 1950 Remez resigned after failing to persuade Ben-Gurion or Yadin, and a large number of IAF officers followed him.

The debate rumbled on into 1953 until changes in leader-ship slowly began to modify entrenched positions. Dan Tolkowsky, air force commander in 1953, subsequently and astutely reflected that part of the problem had been that the airmen had translated their experience from World War II into an Israeli environment where the air force simply lacked the capacity to apply any kind of doctrine.[4] No wonder the indige-nous IDF leadership had no grasp of operations. Ezer Weizman recalled that in the War of Independence the ground forces lost 6,000 killed, while the air force lost 10 pilots, and some of these by accident. "None of the battles [was] decided by the Air Force."[5]

Instead of perpetuating the debate, Tolkowsky took two practical initiatives: First, he preached and practiced combat readiness so that commando and other army operations could be supported without notice; and second, he began to train his crews to attack the opposition on the ground. He also crystallized the significance of airpower to Israel. "From the ground forces point of view, we were unfortunate. We were surrounded by enemies on all sides. But from the Air Force point of view it was a terrific advantage. We could offer 360 degrees of protection, and Cairo, Amman, Damascus were only minutes away." And since to attack Israel the Egyptians or the Iraqis had first to move their forces across large expanses of open desert, it should have been "obvious [to] any fool that this was an ideal situation for the use of air power."[6]

This evaluation came to dominate Israeli defense policy, but the translation of the concept into combat success took time. In the nine days of the Sinai conflict in 1956, more usually referred to in the West as the Suez confrontation, Tolkowsky's air force made a significant contribution—fighting for air superiority and providing close air support—in a short and militarily inconclusive war.

By October 1956 both air forces had increased considerably in size. The EAF contained 80 MiG-15s, 45 Il-28s, 25 Meteors, 57 Vampires, and 200 trainer, transport, and others. They were faced by five fighter squadrons of 37 Meteors and 75 Ouragons plus a mixed bag of piston-engine Mustangs, Mosquitoes, and one or two B-17s. The battle, however, was joined and dominated by the British and French air forces. Engagements between the EAF and IAF were largely confined to the first two days of the war when the IAF shot down eight EAF aircraft but themselves lost 10 aircraft, all to ground fire.

The subsequent political debacle for France and Britain, plus some well-founded criticism of the British bombing campaign, were allowed by President Abdel Gamel Nasser to outweigh the obvious weaknesses disclosed in the EAF. Promotion was based on political affiliations, and combat readiness was actually relaxed. Along with one-third of the Egyptian armed forces, the EAF was diverted to the intervention in Yemen with further deterioration in combat training and neglect of the Sinai front. Consequently further purchases of Soviet bombers and air defense radars in the early 1960s were not accompanied by adequate modernized combat training.

Meanwhile, in Israel, almost the exact opposite was taking place. Political leaders were displeased by what they perceived to be unreliable support from their "allies" and began to provide for operational self-sufficiency in the next stages of what had come to be perceived as a war for the nation's survival. Military commanders constructed a concept of operations which was virtually an adaptation of blitzkrieg. IDF commanders had studied the theories of Basil Liddell Hart and his advocacy of fluid mobile warfare in conjunction with heavy air attack. They added to them the ingredient of preemptive attack.[7]

Superiority

In the 11 years between Suez and the Six Day War of June 1967, the concepts identified by Remez, Margo, and Tolkowsky were related to the ground strategy and given substance by reequipment, expansion, and above all, by training. In 1957 only 17 cadets applied for flying training, and the primary ambition of a young Israeli was still to be a commando in the Palmach tradition. The IAF Flight School had been a low priority both for resources and instruction, suffering in part from the exclusively elitist image of the fighter pilot inherited from the first generation of IAF aircrew and from anachronistic British methods. The problems were solved within 12 months by a barbary fighter pilot, Yeshayaho Gazit who at first resigned when assigned to the position of commander of the flight school in July 1957. In 12 months Gazit increased the intake to 80. He organized a personal letter from Tolkowsky to every qualified high school graduate; he insisted on all new instructors being fighter pilots and on two of his instructors going into a newly formed Super Mystere squadron. Subsequently, he reorganized the flying training syllabus to accelerate conversion to jet aircraft. It was a combination of strong leadership, personal example, personal contact, removing the chasm between training and operations, and above all, insistence on unalloyed standards of excellence. After several frank exchanges of view with the IAF commander, Ezer Weizman, Gazit became head of Training Command where he imposed his standards on frontline as well as training squadrons, using computerized records to monitor both unit and individual performance.

The allocation of frontline aircrew to flying training posts can be a source of additional turbulence and it can increase costs. If, however, frontline experience is not considered necessary or if flying instructing comes to be perceived as a dead end, one has to ask why does it remain a uniformed commitment at all. The cheapest approach of all is a civilian flying school, and the hope that "operational conversion" will produce both the military officer and the combat pilot. The interaction in the IAF between training and operational flying had been further developed by 1994 when flying instructors continued to "belong" and train with their frontline squadrons during their training tour.

The preparation of the pilot for combat received an increasingly sharp focus from 1963. Commander in Chief Weizman instructed his chief of operations, Yak Nevo to prepare a plan for "achieving air superiority through massive deployment of the IAF," a euphemism for OCA. The plan was to become the blueprint for the annihilation of the Arab air forces in the June War of 1967.[8]

Never was the aphorism "train as you intend to fight" so comprehensively addressed. Nevo and Col Raphael Sivron, later to be air attaché in London, requested and received detailed intelligence on almost every Arab airfield in the region, collating runway data, aircraft, and associated personnel. From that data, minutely detailed over-the-target requirements of bomb weight and aircraft were compiled to close runways long enough for the trapped aircraft around them to be destroyed. All the IAF aircraft types likely to be involved in such an attack, which was virtually the whole of the air force, carried weapon loads within Israeli airspace at the heights, speeds, and distances necessary to ensure that mission performance data was exact. Precision bombing and ground attack gunnery became a squadron's first priority, concentrating on low-level navigation, precise timing, and complete radio silence from start-up to touchdown. Finally, the entire plan, known as Moked for "focus," or "sacrificial fire"[9] was drawn up in outline and completed with operational appendices which would be kept up to date by the appropriate staffs. It would be kept until a threat to Israel was perceived to require a preemptive response. The plan took four years to construct, refine, and practice. It was to be executed in four hours on 5 June 1967.

By 1967 the EAF had expanded still further, to include 30 Tu-16s, 40 Il-28s, 130 MiG-21s, 80 MiG-19s, 15 Su-7s, and 150 MiG-15/17s. Of those, only 200 were serviceable, and there were only 150 combat pilots, according to a subsequent observation by the war minister, General Fawzi.

Pilot availability was in fact irrelevant as the first wave of IAF aircraft, with complete radio silence, hit the first EAF airfields at 8:45 A.M. Cairo time on 6 June. Within one hour 200 EAF aircraft had been destroyed. A second sortie followed in midmorning when air bases in the west and south of Egypt were attacked. Some aircraft, including the Mirage squadrons, made a third sortie before being switched at 12:45 P.M. to Syrian and Jordanian targets. By the end of the day some of the Vautour and Super Mystere squadrons had flown six sorties. For the rest of the week the IAF swept the Sinai desert annihilating Egyptian ground forces in support of the IDF advancing armored columns. A classic air superiority battle was followed by its maximum exploitation.

Subsequent analysis of the June War has naturally concentrated on the factors which produced the devastating IAF victory, its impact on the ground campaign in Sinai, and the subsequent revision worldwide of airfield protection and defenses. It is therefore worth noting that the outcome was by no means a foregone conclusion.

Nasser, like Saddam Hussein a generation later, pursued a provocative political and military policy without the detailed strategic planning and military preparation to support it. Nonetheless, at a meeting on 2 June with his senior commanders, he warned them that Israel might attack between 3 and 5 June.[10] The air force commander, General Sodki, argued for a preemptive strike against Israeli airfields, radars, and troop concentrations, even though no detailed EAF plans for such an offensive existed. He was refused by Nasser who explained that for political reasons Egypt must absorb a first blow before retaliating. In those circumstances the EAF was expecting to lose less than 20 percent of its strength. Despite that meeting and those assumptions, no action was taken to raise alert states or disperse aircraft, to the extent that Sodki did not cancel a proposed inspection of air bases in Sinai on 5 June. As a result, most air defense guns in the region were at "guns tight" when the IAF attacks began at 8:45 A.M.

Meanwhile, a prewar IAF internal analysis of the Moked plan had concluded that to achieve a 90 percent probability of closing the runways required many more planes than the 200 which the IAF possessed.[11] Rapid turnarounds and repeated attacks were therefore essential. Even if Sodki had only managed to launch a small number of preemptive attacks, he would have hit an IAF that had considerably reduced its air superiority training and would have undoubtedly disrupted a very complex plan which depended on absolute synchronization for its success. Thereafter, the sanctuary which the IAF enjoyed to turn round its aircraft for repeated waves of attack would have been jeopardized. The perennial lesson is that even a modest OCA effort can disturb an opponent's offensive equilibrium, and the more detailed the plan the more sensitive to disruption it becomes.

The opportunity was comprehensively missed later in the day by Syrian and Jordanian aircraft which, faced by only 12 Mirages retained by the IAF to protect the homeland, attacked scattered targets across Israel at noon. There was no apparent coordination or concentration even though Iraqi Hunters did reach the Mirage base at Ramat David. After the EAF had been eliminated, the Syrian and Jordanian air forces, together with a number of Iraqi aircraft, received similar treatment. It is generally agreed that the Arab air forces lost approximately 400 aircraft, the great majority on the ground, to almost 1,000 IAF sorties which cost the lives of 20 pilots. Thereafter, the Egyptian Army was decimated by ground attack in the Sinai desert.

The War of Attrition

After 1956 Nasser had been preoccupied by the attacks from the British and the French, and had consequently underrated the potential of the IAF. In the aftermath of the June War, the Egyptian government moved 180 degrees the other way, ultimately basing its military strategy and deployments on the assumption that the IAF was invincible. The war of Yom Kippur in 1973 was to spark a great deal of controversy about the impact of surface-to-air defenses (SAD) on tactical air operations. Just as the outcome of the June War was greatly influenced by the prewar attitudes and preparations of the two main combatants, so the events of the October War had their roots in the War of Attrition after 1967.

This phase of the Arab-Israeli conflict began on 8 September 1968 with an announcement in an Egyptian military communiqué in *Al-Ahram Weekly* on that date. It declared the start of "The Policy of Preventive Deterrence," an active defense policy aimed at forcing Israel to pay a high price for staying in Sinai, through inflicting heavy losses on its forces. On the same date an Egyptian artillery barrage along 65 miles of the Suez Canal caused 28 Israeli casualties. Retaliation by Israeli commandos 300 miles south of Cairo prompted an Egyptian pause until March 1969 when further artillery barrages were accompanied by President Nasser's announcement of the beginning of the "liberation" phase of the War of Attrition.

It was to continue incessantly until a cease-fire in August 1970 and was marked by Egyptian artillery and sniper fire, with occasional short-range air attacks on the static Israeli positions across the canal. It was punctuated by Israeli commando raids and dogfights in which invariably the EAF lost heavily.

The decision by Egypt to rely heavily on SAD rather than aircraft originated in the ignominy of the EAF as a result of its annihilation in 1967, but there were other factors which will continue to reoccur elsewhere.[12] At the time the EAF also commanded the SAD, but its equally inept performance was overlooked. In the subsequent reorganization of the Egyptian armed forces, the surface-to-air defenses were taken away from the EAF and a new Air Defense Command was subordinated to the army. Nonetheless, plans in 1967 to rebuild the Egyptian armed forces included an 800-strong EAF by 1971.

The target was not achieved. It was estimated that only one in a thousand candidates could pass medical and aptitude tests. Another estimate was that only one candidate in a million could become a fighter pilot. Egypt's population at the time was 35 million and already in 1967 was producing 50 pilots a year. There were insufficient flying instructors, even with infusion from India and the USSR, while language difficulties slowed down the process still further. Maintenance could not keep pace with the increased flying load and flight safety suffered. Between 1967 and 1970 more pilots were lost in training accidents—83—than in combat with the IAF. It was subsequently asserted that these generic problems were not unique to Egypt. Not only did the EAF fail to reach a 1:1 pilot to aircraft ratio, but the problem was common to most of the Arab world.

Meanwhile, the commander in chief of the Egyptian forces, General Fawzi, and the Soviet advisers imported immediately after the June disaster, strongly argued for giving resource priority to surface-to-air defenses. SAD offered many advantages. While Soviet systems were manpower intensive—an SA-2 battalion for example required 280 people—the required skill levels, even for the comparatively advanced SA-3, were far less than for combat aircraft, and there was no shortage of Egyptian conscripts. Training to operational level took only 12–15 weeks compared with three years for aircrew. Medical standards also were lower. Egyptian estimates of the cost of an SA-2 battalion were $8,000 in 1969, compared to $250,000 for a MiG-21.[13] The final factor in the Egyptian defensive decision was the influence of the USSR. It was quick to rearm the EAF after 1967 but was loath to supply offensive aircraft and actively encouraged both the separation of the air defense system from the EAF and the former's expansion.

The war presented the IAF with several problems. Egyptian policy was to maintain pressure on the Bar-Lev defensive line on the east bank of the Suez Canal by artillery and nuisance raids until international pressure could be brought to bear on Israel to withdraw from Sinai. The accumulative impact on the

IAF of the spasmodic air combat began to impose a strain. The IAF had lost 10 percent of its aircrews in the June War. Peacetime aircrew strength of the Israeli combat squadrons was roughly one-third active and two-thirds reserve in an establishment of 30. Of those, six would be squadron executives and senior pilots, the other three or four would be "ab initios" from flying training. Consequently the bulk of the fighting was borne by a small number of veterans. Ironically, their consistent superiority over the EAF contributed to the EAF's sense of inferiority as Egyptian intelligence failed to distinguish between the limited number of veterans and the rest of the reservist/ab initio IAF.

A longer term problem was disclosed: a cadre-reserve combat force designed for a national emergency was not best suited to continuous smaller scale engagements. It was this potential weakness in an otherwise impressive IAF that prompted the Israeli government to escalate the war in an attempt to stop Nasser's corrosive campaign. In July 1969 the SA-2 batteries in the northern area of the Suez Canal were destroyed. Six months later the IAF began a bombing campaign against military and industrial targets in Egypt which began to threaten Nasser's political survival. In January he turned to the USSR for help, arguing that his fight was not really with Israel, but the United States. The Soviet government responded by dispatching 32 battalions of SA-3 missiles, two squadrons of Su-15s, and six squadrons of MiG-21 interceptors, together with aircrew, ground crew, maintenance, and electronic workshops. By late 1970 there were between 15,000 and 20,000 Soviet military in Egypt.[14]

In the same period two bombing errors by the IAF killed a large number of civilians, including school children, and prompted a temporary suspension of US shipment of Phantoms and Skyhawks, reinforcing a neutral viewpoint that by 1970 Israeli airpower was no longer quite the dominant factor it had been previously. Indeed, IAF operations had been counterproductive: stimulating a massive enhancement of Egyptian air defenses and the public commitment of Soviet forces to Egyptian defense at a time when Israel's patron was heavily tied down in Vietnam and in no mood to risk further direct confrontations with the USSR.

On 7 August 1970 a cease-fire was agreed, but it failed to stop the completion of the SAD belt along the west bank of the canal. Israeli airpower had been stymied in the War of Attrition by a combination of political and military factors, and some at least of the IAF crews were pleased to be out of it. Squadron attrition exchange ratios had changed from 1:40 in the air to 2:4 against missiles. One very professional and very gallant Mirage squadron commander subsequently observed, "When the cease-fire was declared we thanked God." One night at the forward base of Bir Gafgafa he had actually declined a directive to scramble, saying, "We have no strength left." Another reflected: "We were fighting a centipede—you hit it here and two more legs grow in its place. You hit it there and it keeps growing. We were fighting an enemy that seemed not only irrational but with unlimited resources. It was like trying to empty an ocean with a bucket."[15] One Arab military scholar summarized the cause and effect of the War of Attrition in terms which could have been applied equally accurately to the Intifada on the West Bank and Gaza 20 years later: "The War of Attrition aimed both at imposing a higher price on Israel for keeping the occupied territories and bringing the Middle East crisis to the attention of world opinion."[16] It also marked the change of Egypt's political objective from the total "liberation" of Palestine to one of confining Israel to her pre-1967 borders.

In October 1970 Anwar Sadat succeeded Nasser, and in May 1971 his general staff began to prepare a new plan to liberate Sinai and the Gaza Strip. For the next 18 months two alternatives were debated. One proposed a longer preparatory period in which Egyptian forces, including the air force, would be strengthened to the point that with coordination with Syria and Jordan an attack across Sinai and into Gaza would have a good chance of success. Initially, Sadat supported this plan, specifying an increase in the EAF to 1,000 pilots and seeking Soviet supplies of modern bombers and fighters.

By July 1972, however, Sadat had become disillusioned with his Soviet sponsors. The USSR had failed to deliver promised aircraft, had diverted others away from Egypt to India, and in May 1972 in a summit meeting with the USA, appeared to have reduced superpower priorities in the Middle East. As a result he asked the Soviet military to leave Egypt while at the same time instructing his armed forces to begin preparations for offensive action.

The October War

In October Sadat chose the alternative plan for a limited offensive of up to eight kilometers across the Suez Canal in a shorter timescale and dismissed his commander in chief, Sadek, who had been the proponent of the sweep across Sinai. Egyptian perception that it would not be possible to challenge IAF superiority for some time appears to have been a strong influence on Sadat. Pilot shortages continued and were aggravated by the expulsion of more than one hundred Soviet aircrew. About 20 pilots were recruited from Korea, but by October 1973 the EAF's pilot to aircraft ratio was still less than 1:1. Moreover, the hoped for modernization had not taken place because Sadat was unable to replace his Soviet supplier by any Western alternative. Egyptian aircraft were considered inferior to their counterparts in range, payload, electronics, and missiles.

On the ground, only some 20 SA-6 batteries were mobile; 70 SA-2, 65 SA-3, and most of the 2,500 antiaircraft artillery (AAA) batteries could not be moved forward to cover an advance into Sinai. Three thousand handheld SA-7s could provide additional low-level protection, but they were obsolescent by 1973. Of the Egyptian Army's 800,000 troops, less than one-half were in combat units and of these two-thirds were infantry. In sum neither army nor air force was equipped to launch a mechanized, armored offensive across the open Sinai desert in the face of the IAF, regardless of any assistance forthcoming from Syria or Jordan. Consequently Sadat deliberately chose a limited operational plan dependent on ground-based air defense to provide air cover for a canal crossing.

On 6 October the offensive was launched, code named Badr, after a battle won by the Prophet Mohammed in the holy month of Ramadan in A.D. 624. On this occasion the Egyptian and Syrian attacks were well synchronized.[17] Both allies achieved tactical surprise even though the IAF had been on fully mobilized alert for several hours. The problem was that the IAF had prepared to repeat the 1967 preempt, this time against Syrian and Egyptian missiles. Defense Minister Moshe Dayan, however, persuaded Prime Minister Golda Meir to let the IDF accept a first blow for international political reasons. As a result the IAF's first task was to deal with the EAF strike across Sinai which accompanied the ground force crossing of the canal. There was therefore an immediate mismatch between the political objective, the IAF's operational posture, and in the event, weapons fit as IAF aircraft which had been bombed up for the antimissile strike were scrambled for air interception sorties.

Further confusion followed. The IAF established air-to-air superiority over Sinai and began its delayed attack on the canal missile batteries early the following morning. Then that attack was abruptly checked when the Syrian attack over the Golan Heights began to threaten northern Galilee, and the IAF squadrons were switched to the northern frontier.

At this point, in retrospect, the priority allocation of resources to the IAF probably saved Israel from extinction. Certainly the IAF checked the Syrian armored advance for long enough to allow the ground force reservists to reach the front line and incidentally ensure that their arrival was not interrupted by hostile air attack. In due course the Syrian armor was turned and thrown back onto Damascus. In the subsequent postwar analysis, however, IAF satisfaction was tempered by a great deal of critical reappraisal.

There had been only one plan for the IAF in the north, a variation of the preemptive antimissile attack across Sinai, itself very similar in concept to Moked of 1967. In the war game Eil Barzel played in 1972, IDF chiefs of staff concluded that air superiority was a precondition for a successful ground campaign. From this it was understood that the air force would join in the ground battle with support operations only after air superiority in the theater was achieved. This meant that the air force had first to destroy enemy missile batteries to secure that freedom of action.[18] But in October 1973 the Syrian missiles were on the move; they also included SA-6s on which initially the IAF had no intelligence. In the first antimissile attack, only two Syrian batteries were destroyed. There was no system for forward air control to focus close air support; initially all requests from ground force commanders had to go up to the general staff for approval. This was the penalty for the centralized control which had facilitated the strategic switch from south to north but had failed to incorporate any tactical flexibility into the structure. Ironically, the same Raphael Sivron who had been one of the architects of Moked now appeared on the northern front coordinating swiftly delegated tactical air control. His problems were aggravated by Syrian missiles inhibiting battlefield reconnaissance. Even the hardened professionalism of the IAF pilots was frayed by what appeared to be inconsistent orders, inaccurate target intelligence, and mounting losses with not a lot to show for them.

These factors are of longer term significance than the straightforward statistics of the SAD versus aircraft argument. The IAF plan was inflexible and based on assumptions which had been appropriate for 1967 but not for the political and technological circumstances of 1973. Initiative, aggression, and bravery by individual pilots were an inadequate substitute for a carefully coordinated attack on the layered, in-depth air defense lines either on the Suez Canal or over the Golan Heights.

Meanwhile heavy fighting continued in Sinai as the Egyptians consolidated their positions on the east bank of the canal under the umbrella of the SAD. IAF frustrations increased as lack of intelligence concealed the exact location of Egyptian bridges over the canal. Any time spent looking for targets, as opposed to their swift acquisition during a preplanned tactical-defensive approach, was very difficult over the missile protected area. In 1971 the IAF had abandoned high-level reconnaissance over Egypt and had subsequently lost a Globemaster over Sinai to slant range SA-2 while on a photo-reconnaissance sortie. Only after Yom Kippur was it discovered that there had been photographs of the canal bridges, but they were not considered relevant to the IAF because they were not airfields or SAD sites. The IDF still controlled all intelligence sources, including IAF photographic interpreters.[19] Between 8:00 A.M. and 3:00 P.M. on 8 October, the IAF flew only 62 sorties over the Sinai front, of which 20 were directed at the bridges. Below them an unsuccessful Israeli counterattack was taking place. A divisional commander, Major General Adan, called for urgent air support to Headquarters Southern Command. He was told by General Gonen that "I was already getting it. I told him that I didn't notice any."[20] The air commander in the theater was not aware that any counteroffensive was taking place, so General Adan's frustration was well founded.

Not surprisingly after this episode and the Golan experiences, among several reforms introduced after the war, air-ground coordination was taken out of the hands of the artillery, and the IAF was given responsibility for a structure based on that of NATO. A weakness had lain undetected for 25 years waiting for adverse battle conditions to disclose it.

The tide was turned in the south by the Egyptians themselves, when on 14 October they made the fateful decisions to move out into Sinai beyond their SAD umbrella and to move their strategic reserve across the canal. Whether the moves were made in response to Syrian requests to divert Israeli pressure from the north, or whether in ignorance of the real Israeli ground force strength is uncertain. There are however no doubts about the resulting impact of unrestricted IAF ground attack. Air-ground synergy was restored, and Israeli troops crossed the Suez Canal, fanned out, and overran or destroyed a significant number of surface-to-air missile (SAM) batteries. The exact number remains in dispute because of the widespread use of dummies and decoys by the Egyptians. Egyptian sources stated that most of the damage to SAM batteries came from ground fire, including five out of nine moved across onto the east bank. Such a loss would certainly account for the Egyptian failure to coordinate the movement of offensive ground forces and their air defenses.

The significant feature in this phase which ought to reoccur in the future application of airpower is the suppression of SAD by ground forces in their own interest. If airpower can deliver more firepower in support of either offense or defense, and if that contribution is being constrained by enemy SAD, then AAA and SAM batteries become a high-priority target for counterbattery fire. A soldier will need a lot of persuasion to give hostile SAD target precedence over hostile artillery, but to achieve the greatest air-ground synergism it will frequently be necessary.

Dominance

In the next major encounter between the Syrian and Israeli air forces, in the Bekáa region in 1982, the synergism worked again even though IDF ground forces did not enter the Bekáa Valley. The annihilation of the Syrian Air Force took place while the British and Argentinean forces were contesting the Falkland Islands. In terms of the evolution of airpower, the battle in the Middle East was a generation ahead.

On 6 June 1982 the IDF launched Operation Peace for Galilee, designed to destroy the Palestine Liberation Organization (PLO) in southern Lebanon. The contribution of the IAF was constrained by the presence of the SAM batteries to the east in the Bekáa Valley. Syria had deployed SA-6 units there in April 1981. By 1982 the position of every one was known, as were the missile acquisition and guidance frequencies. On this occasion there were no diversions from a carefully coordinated strike plan. On 9 October the 19 missile batteries were engaged first by long-range artillery and surface-to-surface missiles which were to destroy the majority of them.[21] Subsequent attacks were delivered by a variety of IAF aircraft with free-fall bombs and antiradiation missiles. In a peculiar operational sequence, the Syrian Air Force then rose to defend the air defense batteries and massacre ensued.

This was indeed a copybook air operation. Target intelligence was comprehensive and precise and, with battle damage assessment, was provided by battlefield drones. The mini remotely piloted vehicles *Scout* and *Mastiff* were controlled from the ground by soldiers who took three months to learn and six months to become expert in their craft. Photographic data was relayed 60 miles to ground stations by data link. Ground and air fire were completely coordinated. Thorough signals and electronic intelligence enabled electronic victory also as ground control, fire control, acquisition, and every other ground-based and airborne Syrian radar was either jammed or destroyed. On the Golan Heights in 1973, the electronic support aircraft had become separated from the Phantoms and Skyhawks seeking to engage the SA-6s. In 1982 they were in position and contributed greatly to the F-15s' and F-16s' one-sided victory. This was a combined arms victory on the ground and in the air.

It marked a complete recovery by the IAF to the levels of effectiveness traditionally associated with it after the two single spectacular operations: the hostage rescue from Entebbe in 1976 and the attack on the Osirak nuclear installation in 1981.

On 27 June 1976 Air France Flight 139 was hijacked between Athens and Paris and diverted to Entebbe in Uganda. Seventy-seven Israeli citizens and many other Jews were among the 256 passengers. They were rescued on 3 July in a brilliantly executed commando raid in which four C-130s flew in radio silence for 2,000 miles at low and medium level, through violent African storms, arriving 30 seconds behind schedule and prepared to land on a blacked-out runway, with command and control executed from an accompanying Boeing 707 with a second 707 carrying medical staff. Exercise Thunderball was conceived, planned, and executed in four days. Its success denied the terrorists victims, the freedom of their colleagues, and a propaganda coup. Instead the world was reminded that IAF professionalism extended well beyond fighter cockpits, and its reach extended far beyond Israel's own frontiers.

The extent and potency of that reach was reemphasized in the IAF attack on the Iraqi Osirak nuclear installation at Al Tuwaitha, 12 miles southeast of Baghdad in June 1981. Eight F-16s escorted by six F-15s flew 635 miles through Saudi Arabian and Jordanian airspace 100 feet above the desert. They achieved such complete surprise in their destruction of the installation that Iraq was unaware who was responsible until the Israeli government announced the success. The Al Tuwaitha raid checked Iraqi nuclear weapons development long enough for it to be still nonoperational in 1991, when first the United Nations (UN) Coalition air forces, and then the UN inspection teams, completed the task.

Although very different in kind, the Entebbe and Osirak operations, together with the attack on PLO headquarters in Tunisia in October 1985, demonstrated that the IAF had a flexible strategic capability which could be used either independently or with other arms. It was in every sense a national instrument of power and diplomacy.

In 1975 IAF Commander in Chief Benjamin Peled had laid out IAF mission priorities as:

- air superiority,
- strategic,
- deep interdiction, and
- close support.[22]

In Yom Kippur the IAF retaliated heavily against Syrian military, industrial, and economic targets after Scud attacks against Galilee. As already noted, one response to Nasser's War of Attrition comprised free ranging attacks deep into Egypt. If the original meaning of *strategic* and *tactical* are adhered to, where the former relates to the war as a whole and the latter to a specific combat area, General Peled's priorities are not only very logical, they illustrate the fact that to a country the size of Israel they are very often one and the same.

In 1991 there was an oblique postscript to the Arab-Israeli conflict. The overt action was the launching by Iraq of Scud missiles against Israel in an attempt to provoke retaliation which would have jeopardized the anti-Iraq coalition by making the position of its Arab members well nigh impossible.

Of longer term significance, however, was the strategic posture adopted by Iraq. It made no sense in pursuit of the retention of Kuwait in the face of the UN Coalition. It would have been well suited to a further round in the Arab-Israeli conflict.

The massive Iraqi airfields, with redundant runways and taxiways and dispersed hardened shelters, would have been impossible to close for any length of time by the comparatively small IAF. The hardened and duplicated command, control, and communications structure would have been difficult to disrupt. The carefully rehearsed Scud deployment and deception plans were laid well before the attack on Kuwait in July 1990. The multiple layers of thousands of SAMs and AAA were far more than required to cope with the Iranian air force. The subterranean location, camouflage, and dispersal of mass destruction weapon installations were designed to reduce vulnerability to air attack and effect concealment from airborne reconnaissance. This was a strategic infrastructure designed to sustain a war with a state dependent upon airpower. The link between the Gulf War and Israel was explicit in Saddam Hussein's appeal to his fellow Arabs in early 1990 to turn the oil weapon against Israel and her Western allies. His mistake was to go to war against the United States with an infrastructure designed to reduce the effectiveness of the IAF.

Sometime perhaps the Iraqi air force generals who survive may write their memoirs, and Iraq's attempt to cope with the IAF may be compared with that of Egypt's. It will be interesting to see if Syria, at much closer range, begins to prepare its own counter airpower structure and strategy after enduring so many air-to-air humiliations.

The Blueprint

In 1994 the IAF is still superior to the neighboring air forces, and to most of those in the rest of the world, for that matter. Its continued success over 45 years can be traced to a number of specific ingredients. No single one is unique to the IAF, but the combination is, and therefore when the IAF is held up as a role model to emulate, the interaction between the ingredients should also be noted. There are several.

Not only is there conscription in Israel for everyone over 18, there is ample motivation for it. One distinguished retired IAF officer observed, "Our success, our high motivation and quality are based on the special situation of our nation, the Zionist movement and the high priorities that the government has given us for a long time."[23] The IAF recruits from among the best of the conscripts. Recent waves of Soviet immigrants have widened the pool for maintenance engineers. Promotion depends solely on merit, with competence in the air a primary requirement, although "somebody who is just a good 'stick and throttle' jockey will not get too high."[24] Character, leadership, and intellect have consistently been distinguishing features of IAF commanders. Perhaps significantly, IAF promotion is based on a "mutual valuation" system in which every

211

officer has to answer questions not just about his subordinates but also about his commanders.

Many air forces extol the importance of the human factor in their operations, but somehow it gets overlooked in funding priorities and the subordination of personnel management to operational necessity. The IAF represents a nation in arms, both male and female. Females are not called upon for reserve duty, and if they enlist for regular service, marry, and have families, they will not be called for night maintenance shifts. In crisis and conflict, the ground crews are amplified by reservists.

Aircrews are selected for technical skills and the ability to make difficult decisions quickly in high-stress situations. They complete an initial eight-year engagement, followed by periods of three years with apparently an unlimited reserve commitment thereafter. It is difficult to imagine any other air force dispatching a previous commander in chief as a reservist to a regional subordinate position, as happened to General Hod in 1973. In the event, his presence and ability to implement delegated tasking authority on the Golan Heights proved critical. Nevertheless, in recent years the fighter squadrons have been fully manned by regulars,[25] while all reservists fly once a week and in crisis no distinction is made, in theory at least.

The product has obviously succeeded in blending strong individuality with corporate responsibility, reinforced by habits of constructive self-criticism. Doctrinal guidelines, for example, are reevaluated annually, and after the major conflicts special research studies were undertaken.

For the greater part of its history, the IAF has been better equipped than its opponents. The Super Mystere, Mirage, Phantom, F-15, and F-16 have all been superior to their Soviet produced contemporaries. In later years aircraft superiority has been matched by missiles and electronic warfare systems. As a consequence, the IAF has not yet flown against an enemy similarly equipped.

Such superiority is not bought cheaply. Ezer Weizman's request for 100 Mirages in 1959 was costed at $200 million.[26] In 1973 the 130-aircraft F-4 force had cost approximately $600 million.[27] Israel is not economically self-sufficient and relies on foreign assistance and borrowing to maintain its economy. Fifteen percent of the total population (46,500) was employed in defense industries in 1988, compared with 10 percent in the UK, 11 percent in the USA, 3 percent in West Germany, and 6 percent in France.[28]

Israel has been fortunate in receiving financial assistance from the US government since its formation in 1949. In 1974, when the armed forces' losses in the October War were made good, military assistance jumped from $307.5 million the previous year to $2.482 billion after President Nixon had asked Congress for emergency aid, including loans for which payment would be waived. Coincidentally, a modest military loan program began in 1959, the year of Weizman's search for Mirages. From 1971 to 1994 US aid to Israel averaged $2 billion per year, of which two-thirds has been military assistance. After 1987 military assistance leveled off at $1.8 billion per year.[29]

In the Arab-Israeli conflict, Israeli airpower dominated because it was in complete harmony with the strategic environment. For 45 years airpower was Israel's chosen security instrument. It was suited to the topography and climate. It capitalized on a literate and technologically advanced population. It offered defense and attack around 360 degrees against all manner of external threats. It derived the maximum effectiveness from superior technology wielded by highly motivated professionals, who remained professionals when they became reservists. Funding was not unlimited, as the cancelled Lavi project illustrated, but in Israel's case, without provision for security, there could be no provision for anything else.

But even for Israel, airpower could not provide complete security, especially against enemies within her own frontiers. In airpower's second century, the IAF will face three emerging challenges, none of them in the air. They will be the new generations of mobile SAMs, mobile surface-to-surface missiles, and targets concealed in a civilian population. If any air force has the skill, determination, and imagination to meet such challenges, it will be the IAF.

Discussion

Mr. Ben Cowen: To what extent will the dimensions of the Arab-Israeli conflict be affected by the acquisition of state-of-the-art

Western aircraft by so-called moderate Arab states, and if the dimensions are changed, will they permit the return of strategic ground such as the Golan Heights and the West Bank?

Air Vice-Marshal Mason: As I understand the question, you are referring to the purchase by countries like Saudi Arabia of equipment such as Tornado, the F-15, and AWACS.

For quite some time the Israelis have kept a very uneasy eye on developments in Saudi Arabia, and they have relied heavily on the Jewish lobby in the United States to constrain sales of that kind of kit. I'm not quite sure of the current state of the F-15 deal. I don't think it's gone through yet, but I know it was causing some concern. I also know from my conversations with officers from both sides that one of the reasons which has led Israel into talking peace has been the awareness that in the longer term, in an open market, their technological advantage will be eroded. Right now it is Egypt and Saudi Arabia who are buying advanced systems. But there's no reason why somebody shouldn't start selling kit to Syria. For example, France will not be the slightest bit inhibited about selling Rafale wherever it can.

So I think the point you make is a very important one. There is no immediate threat to Israel from Western arms sales, but there is a clear perception that if they continue, as seems likely, then ultimately the Israeli Air Force would have far more serious problems than it's had in the past.

Wing Comdr John Benjamin: One of the factors which contributed to the IAF's success in the Yom Kippur War was their ability to keep their aircraft flying, while their opponents were less successful in dealing with attrition and unserviceabilities. Do you think that with improving technology, the ability to keep aircraft serviceable, to improvise fixes, will become less important?

Air Vice-Marshal Mason: I tried very hard to get accurate statistics on Yom Kippur. I still don't know exactly how many Israeli aircraft were lost in the first two days or how many replacement F-4s and A-4s were flown in by the United States in the first four or five days. The evidence suggests that there were no maintenance problems per se.

I mentioned at the end of my summary that one of the great advantages Israel enjoys is the technological quality of the population, which extends to IAF ground crew. The question mark I would flag—and it's been a question mark now for at least 10 years—is how effective Israeli maintenance would be if it were ever attacked. And I think if I were an Arab and I was preparing for round four, I'd be looking long and hard at logistics support in the Israeli Air Force because no air force in this world could sustain the turn-around rates, the intensity of operations achieved by the IAF, with interruptions.

But to return to your question. First, there is no evidence of any maintenance slow down, in fact, just the opposite. The modification work associated with the electronic warfare kit during the Yom Kippur War was quite astonishing. The Israeli Air Force takes new aircraft in its stride, just as you would, we would, or the United States would. On the other hand, new technology presents tremendous problems for the Arab air forces who still do not have the necessary depth of technological base in their population to sustain both their military and their economic and industrial development.

Dr. Ben Lambeth: Could I add one comment regarding the introduction of Western systems to moderate Arab states? It has been declared US government policy from the beginning to maintain Israel's technological advantage. If you look at the history, there was about 10 years difference between the introduction of advanced systems in Israel and the Arab states. The F-4 went to Israel in the early 1970s, it was the early 1980s when it went to Egypt; the F-15 went to Israel in 1976, it was about a decade later before it went to Saudi Arabia. Of course that's narrowing now with a down-rated F-15E going to Saudi Arabia. The F-15I, which Israel has very recently agreed to buy, will include some Israeli add-ons which will contribute substantially to the capability of that system in the region.

Secondly, the Israeli Air Force has recently declined the opportunity to acquire the AMRAAM missile, in order to keep it out of the hands of other players in the region. That also stems partly from their self-confidence. They think they can get by well enough without it as long as no one else has it.

Squadron Leader Despina Tramoundanis: We heard from a previous speaker about the dysfunctional relationship which existed during the Vietnam War between the US military and political leaderships. Could you comment on the Israeli relationship?

Air Vice-Marshal Mason: It's not my specialist field, so my comments will be very much eclectic. Usually there has been complete harmony in terms of political, strategic, and operational thinking since 1948. To the best of my memory, the only time there has been a mismatch was the occasion in 1973 that I mentioned. There was great debate about Operation Galilee in 1982. Not all the military were keen on going north, and there have been occasional signs of strain since then over government policy on the West Bank and the Intifada. I've talked on a few occasions with current conscripts, reserves of various kinds, and the average Israeli soldier does not like doing counterinsurgency duties. In the later days of Menachim Begin's regime, when Ariel Sharon was exercising considerable influence, there were signs of strain there between the Israeli high command and the government. But as I said right at the start, the country regards itself as a state still at war or at armed truce, and even with a trusted friendly foreign face they are loath to pass comments on that kind of relationship. So I do say, my answer is very tentative.

Air Chief Marshal Sir Patrick Hine: Tony, you said you didn't have any accurate figures for the attrition rates during the Yom Kippur War. I got involved with that in a study a few years ago, and there's no doubt that in the first 24 to 48 hours on the Golan Heights, in particular, but also on the Suez front, the Israelis' loss rates were quite alarming. They were in the order of 3 to 4 percent. By the third day they had sorted out their electronic warfare countermeasures and had also got assistance from the

United States to counter the SA-6, which appeared for the first time in that war. From then on there was a real downturn in the loss rate, and by the end of the fighting—which went on if I remember rightly about 24 days—they had flown something like 11,000 sorties for an overall loss rate of about 1 percent. The research that we did showed that their loss rate during Yom Kippur was in fact very slightly lower than for the Six Day War.

I have a question to follow from that, and that is, what lessons did the Israelis draw from the bad fright Yom Kippur gave them? And in particular, have they now got, other than through smart bombs, a hard-kill capability against modern SAM systems?

Air Vice-Marshal Mason: First of all those attrition figures. I hadn't heard that source before, and it's very interesting because my figures from different sources are almost exactly the same. My best guess is that the IAF lost about 40 aircrew on the first day and about 100 overall, which coincides almost exactly with your statistics. [Dr. Lambeth indicated his concurrence from the audience.]

As far as the lessons are concerned, the first problem was that they hadn't had a chance to exercise their plan. They thought they knew how to take the defenses in the Sinai. They grossly underestimated SAM-6, and they grossly underestimated the ZSU-23/4. As you correctly say, those faults were largely remedied by American assistance within the first few days. But their subsequent analysis was complicated by the fact that they couldn't identify which particular SAM had done the damage. Interestingly enough, neither could the Egyptians when they did their analysis. Indeed, the best guess I've had from Egyptian sources is that in fact it was the old SAM-2 that was doing the bulk of the damage. That conclusion was based on the supposition that the SAM-2 crews were older and more experienced; they were steadier and handled their weapons better under Israeli pressure. There has tended to be a fixation with the new equipment—the SAM-6s, the ZSUs—people have tended to forget about the SAM-2s. The second problem was that although the attack aircraft were quickly switched to the

Golan Heights, backup EW kit was not switched. Why not? I don't know, but it wasn't. The Skyhawks carrying the jammers, and one or two other aircraft carrying other kit were not coordinated. This was a tremendous lesson which was not forgotten for the Bekáa Valley. So bringing those points together, they realized that you must combine strike and electronic warfare tactics when you take on this kind of defense.

But the lesson above all was the need for ground and air synergy, which is why the first attacks in the Bekáa Valley were launched by the ground forces and surface-to-surface short-range missiles. The second lesson was that you must go after the enemy tactically as well with EW. The third lesson was the introduction of different kinds of forward air control. And, of course, the most important one of all was revising air intelligence and making sure you had your asset in the right place at the right time.

Dr. Ben Lambeth: The SA-2 was a player because the F-4s had gotten, I think, the ALQ109 ECM pod. They were flying medium-altitude fighter formations, greatly suspicious about how tactically reliable that was. As I recall, the threat information was not what it should have been, and some of those F-4s with the pod were shot down at medium altitude. This quickly resulted in a tactical change where they would carry the pod but fly the mission as though they didn't have it. A chief of intelligence in the air force told me about 10 years ago that you never know whether it's ECM or luck that keeps you alive in a situation like that.

Notes

1. Interview in *Ma'ariv*, 23 October 1970, cited in Ehud Yonay, *No Margin for Error* (New York: Pantheon Books, 1993), 104.

2. Yonay, 45–46.

3. Ibid., 103.

4. Ibid., 118.

5. Ezer Weizman, *On Eagles Wings: The Personal Story of the Leading Commander of the Israeli Air Force* (London: Wiedenfeld and Nicolson, 1976), 103.

6. Yonay, 118.

7. Liddell Hart received several testimonies from IDF commanders after the 1967 war attributing the adoption of Israeli strategy to his concepts. Excerpts were received by the present writer.

8. Yonay, 208–13.

9. Ibid., 212.

10. Marouf Bakhit Nader, *The Evolution of Egyptian Air Defence Strategy 1967–1973*, DSS, King's College London, 1990, 45, citing several Egyptian sources.

11. Yonay, 212.

12. See Nader for a comprehensive analysis of the Egyptian debate over the position of air defense in the nation's overall security posture and the rationale for the selection of the strategy for the October War. His account is based primarily on interviews with Egyptian decision makers in this period and on Arab sources.

13. Ibid., 139.

14. Ibid., 226.

15. Even-Nir and Oded Marom, Mirage squadron commanders, interviewed by Ehud Yonay, 305.

16. Nader, 257.

17. For a detailed description and analysis of the air war and superpower involvement, see M. J. Armitage and R. A. Mason, *Air Power in the Nuclear Age*, 2d ed. (Urbana: University of Illinois Press, 1985), chap. 5, "Air Power in the Middle East."

18. Ze'ev Schiff, *The Israeli Air Force* (Tel Aviv: Rivivim, 1981), quoted by Uri Dromi in "Where Was the Air Force," *IDF Journal*, no. 17, 1989, 22.

19. Yonay, 341.

20. Schiff in Dromi, 21.

21. See Benjamin Lambeth, "Moscow's Lessons from the 1982 Lebanon Air War," in *War in the Third Dimension: Essays in Contemporary Air Power*, ed. R. A. Mason (London: Brassey's Defence Publishers, 1986).

22. Benjamin Peled at International Symposium, Jerusalem, October 1975, in Lon O. Nordeen, *Fighters over Israel* (Guild, 1991), 150–01.

23. Brig (Res) Giora Furman, correspondence with author, January 1994.

24. Brig (Res) Oded Erez, correspondence with author, January 1994.

25. Furman.

26. Weizman, 179.

27. Murray Rubenstein and Richard Martin Goldman, *Shield of David; An Illustrated History of the Israeli Air Force* (Englewood Cliffs, N.J.: Prentice-Hall, 1978), 107.

28. Statistical Abstract, Combat Bureau of Statistics, *IDF Journal*, no. 21, 1990, 26.

29. Clyde R. Mark, *Israel: US Foreign Assistance Facts*, Congressional Research Service Issue Brief Series (Washington, D.C.: Congressional Research Service, 1990, updated 27 January 1994).

It Was a Bit of a Close Call:
Some Thoughts on the
South Atlantic War

R. G. Funnell

Warfare is almost as old as man himself, and reaches into
the most secret places of the human heart, places where self
dissolves rational purpose, where pride reigns, where emo-
tion is paramount, where instinct is king.

—John Keegan

The events in the South Atlantic in the period April to June
1982 were of consuming interest to most of the world at the
time. This was especially so for students of military and political affairs. In the 12 to 24 months thereafter, the literature
was full of description and analysis, and many "lessons
learned" were developed and displayed both for experts and
lay people. I had the good fortune to head a group within the
Australian Department of Defence which, in that period, conducted a study of the war. It was a demanding task but it was
also professionally very satisfying. The world has, however,
changed considerably since then. Consequently, when I was
asked to reflect for this conference on the events of 1982 in the
South Atlantic and their implications for the use of airpower, I
wondered aloud to the organizers how many of the lessons
learned have stood the test of changing times and whether my
reflections on the use of airpower in that conflict would be relevant to the conference.

My difficulties were the outcome of my feeling that the diplomatic, political, and strategic aspects of the conflict had more of
enduring value to analysts and practitioners than did the airpower aspects. This is not to say that the airpower aspects were
either unimportant or insignificant. I felt, however, that there
was little that had not been previously and very thoroughly analyzed and commented upon. Certainly, I could review that body
of thought for the conference. That can be useful for we all tend
to forget even important ideas and concepts under the impact of

what is new and what is urgent. Still, given all that had happened with airpower since that conflict, I wondered if my review might not seem somewhat "old hat." As my work on the presentation developed and I reviewed what has been studied and what has been written on this conflict in the 10 years since I last looked closely at it, I saw that the topic still offers areas in which further thought can be beneficial for both the student and the practitioner of the application of airpower. I will set out to prove that point for you.

In this presentation, I will review the events which preceded and led to the conflict. I will similarly review and remind you of what occurred, and I will offer some views of how airpower was used and of its effectiveness or otherwise. Then, I hope to spur some thinking about airpower and its application by sketching an exercise for your consideration on how airpower might have been applied better.

Let us now move back to 1982. The events in the South Atlantic in the first six months of that year were so dramatic and so totally unexpected that they took our collective breath away. Who would have or could have predicted at the beginning of 1982 that the world would soon witness a major conflict between two nations who had never previously been at war with each other and whose capital cities were more than 6,000 miles apart? Even more outlandish would have been a prediction that the world was soon to see, for the first time since the Second World War, a major naval vessel sunk by a submarine, in fact the first time that a nuclear-powered attack submarine would be used in combat, the first naval vessel to be lost to a helicopter, and the first major conflict involving sustained use of such weapon systems as vertical short take-off and landing (VSTOL) aircraft and antiship missiles. Coupled with this were the extraordinary political and diplomatic events which saw the resignation of the British foreign secretary and the involvement of the United Nations (UN) Security Council, the secretary-general of the UN, and the US secretary of state. Reality seemed to defy the imagination of the novel writers, daring them to come up with some series of events as wildly unpredictable.

When you looked carefully at the conflict after the smoke of the various battles (military, political, and diplomatic) had cleared, you saw that few changes of significance had occurred. Please do not get me wrong. I am not saying that military conflict between two developed nations is insignificant; even less am I saying that the loss of hundreds of lives is insignificant. Military conflict is to be deplored, and the loss of so many lives is something which we all must regret. However, little that was new or startling about military operations was revealed. It was more a case of old ideas being recalled and some newer ones revised, and one of my aims this afternoon will be to review those ideas. Before we do so, however, let me remind you of the geographic, historic, diplomatic, strategic, and military context in which all of this occurred.

The Falkland Islands or as the Argentines describe them, *Las Islas Malvinas*, are predominantly two largish islands separated by a narrow strait in the South Atlantic Ocean at roughly 52° south latitude, 60° west longitude. They are some 400 nautical miles off the coast of Argentina, which is the nation closest to them. The total area of the islands is 13,000 square kilometers, which is about five times that of the Australian Capital Territory. The climate is unpleasant being characterized by cloud, cold, and wind. Conditions are usually that of wet underfoot, low-cloud overhead, and 30 knots blowing from the west. The land is undulating and low-lying, and populated mainly by millions of penguins, seals, and sea birds. Until 1982 the economy of the islands depended almost entirely on the production of wool for export. In 1982 the sheep population was estimated to be 650,000 and the human population 1,800. Almost all Falklanders were of British background, and most had been born on the islands. About a thousand of them lived in Stanley, the only settlement of any size, and the remainder on outlying properties and in small settlements. The infrastructure was rudimentary. Most settlements could be reached only by boat or air or along dirt tracks. The islands had 30 airfields that were usable by light aircraft and about five that were usable by C-130 aircraft. Only the airfield at Stanley was sealed and it was just 4,100 feet long.

The islands were uninhabited until the mid-eighteenth century when the French established a small colony on East Falkland. This was followed soon thereafter by the establishment of a British colony on West Falkland. Neither was successful. In the following years, other attempts at settlement were made. The Argentine flag was first raised on the islands in 1820, and the first Argentine settlement occurred in 1826. It was accompanied by British protests. The Argentines were forcibly evicted by the US corvette *Lexington* in 1831, and their attempt to reestablish the settlement in 1833 was bloodlessly but forcefully denied by the British, whose continuous occupation of the islands dates from then. The islands were accorded the status of a colony by the British government in 1840.

The islands have been a matter of dispute between the Argentine and British governments for a long time. Until recent times, however, it had been mainly a low-level diplomatic irritant rather than a matter of serious concern. This changed in the mid-1960s with a resurgence of Argentine interest in the islands with a matching increase in diplomatic activity in support of its claim to them. In 1964 the Argentine government raised the matter in the United Nations with the Special Committee of 24, which deals with the granting of independence to colonial countries and people. That led to a resolution of the General Assembly (No. 2065) which referred to the ending of colonialism in the islands. However, finding an acceptable solution to the dispute between two of the founding members of the UN has proved beyond the capabilities of the organization or anyone else.

The dispute has many facets, and the legal issues it raises are quite complex. Diplomatically, the difficulties have been summarized neatly by G. M. Dillon: "The United Nations was in favour of 'decolonisation' and the Falkland Islands, of course, were a Crown Colony. But, equally, the UN was in favour of 'self-determination,' and there seemed little doubt about the Falkland Islanders' determination to remain under British rule. Not surprisingly, therefore, the two parties were left to find their own reconciliation of the political principles involved."[1] This they have been unable to do.

Strategically, the islands, while once of some value, were by 1982 of little importance. In the nineteenth century the islands functioned as a naval base where ships traveling to and from the Pacific Ocean could obtain provisions and repairs. With the advent of the steamship, they became a coaling station. Long before 1965, however, these functions were of no consequence. Moreover, the economy was small, narrowly based, and had little or no potential. In addition, as Britain contracted its overseas military involvement and focused its strategic and military attention much closer to home, its capability to defend the islands also contracted. That capability depended primarily on the Royal Navy (RN). In the 1981 Strategic Defence Review, the defence secretary, John Nott, announced a number of major cuts in defense, the majority of which fell on the RN and especially on the RN's capabilities for amphibious operations. The aircraft carriers HMS *Hermes* and HMS *Invincible* were to be sold, the amphibious support ships *Fearless* and *Intrepid* were to be scrapped, and numerous other ships were to be paid off or scrapped. Of significance to the dispute in the South Atlantic, the Antarctic patrol vessel HMS *Endurance* was to be withdrawn without replacement in March 1982.

In Argentina in December 1981, the three-man military junta of Gen Leopoldo Galtieri, Adm Jorge Anaya, and Brig Gen Basilio Lami Dozo ousted the president, Gen Roberto Viola, and installed General Galtieri as president. Significantly, Galtieri retained command of the Argentine army. Soon thereafter the heat being applied by Argentina to the Falklands/Malvinas dispute, already at one of its cyclical high points, was increased. In March 1982 a party of Argentine scrap-metal workers and some military personnel landed at Leith Harbour on South Georgia Island to fulfill a contract with a British company.[2] They raised the Argentine flag which was subsequently sighted by a member of the British Antarctic Survey team on the island and reported to London and Stanley. That set in train a series of diplomatic and military events which culminated in the Argentine seizure of the Falklands/Malvinas on 2 April 1982 and South Georgia on 3 April, and the dispatch from Portsmouth on 5 April of the main body of an RN task force to reclaim the islands.

In summary, the major events of the rest of the conflict were as follows: The British, through their task force, recaptured South Georgia on 25 April. On 1 May the action to recapture the Falklands commenced with air attacks on Stanley airfield, first by a Vulcan flown from Ascension island and then by Harriers from the task force. On 2 May the Argentine cruiser, *General Belgrano*, was sunk by the British nuclear-powered attack submarine (SSN), HMS *Conqueror*. Two days later the HMS *Sheffield*, a Type 42 destroyer, was severely damaged by an Exocet AM-39 antiship missile fired from an Argentine navy Super Étendard aircraft.[3] Sporadic air, sea, and special forces operations occurred over the next three weeks. On 21 May the task force landed more than 5,000 troops who established a beachhead at San Carlos Water. The landings were unopposed at sea and only lightly opposed on land. Air attacks were intensive, a total of 54 sorties being flown by the Argentines with considerable success but with high losses. Incredibly, the SS *Canberra*, which sat in the middle of San Carlos Water throughout the day, was not attacked. Also incredibly, the attacks of 21 May were not followed up. The subsequent 36-hour respite allowed the beachhead to be swiftly and success-fully consolidated.

From 23 to 25 May the task force was subjected to renewed Argentine air attacks resulting in the loss of or damage to a number of ships and many Argentine aircraft. The British land forces suffered few attacks from the air. On 27 May the British land forces started to move out of the beachhead and, in a series of successful actions, conducted mostly at night, moved from San Carlos Water across East Falkland and isolated the major-ity of the Argentine land forces within the Stanley area. On 14 June the Argentine commander in the islands surrendered.

I believe that few people would doubt that the war which occurred in the South Atlantic in 1982 was totally unneces-sary. Neither side in that conflict can look back on the prelude to the war with satisfaction. Even more unsatisfactory for both sides is the position in which they now find themselves. The Argentines are further than they have been in decades from achieving their aim of incorporating Las Islas Malvinas into their republic. For their part the British now have a degree of commitment to the islands and the islanders beyond any which they have previously had, needed, or wanted. The costs of maintaining that commitment are great and lead to distortions in British military structures and activities. Meanwhile, the dispute remains.

The British failed to conduct and connect their diplomacy and politics with an eye to the long term, and no British government was willing to bear the political costs of a negotiated settlement with the Argentines on the highly emotional issue of sovereignty. As part of this, the wishes of the Falkland Islanders were given primacy of place over their interests and, by giving the Falkland Islands Legislative Council virtual power of veto over any action, the interests of the British people at large were discounted.

For their part, the Argentines failed to see the virtue of patience. Even if they wished to conduct a coup de main operation before the 150th anniversary of their forcible removal from the islands, the timing they had apparently established before or soon after achieving power in December 1981 was undoubtedly correct. That called for an operation in the southern winter, at sometime between July and October. In the words of the British task force commander, Adm John "Sandy" Woodward:

> They intended to execute this military coup de main sometime between July and October of the year, for reasons still unknown to me in detail. It was likely, however, that they had surmised that certain factors would be in their favour by July: Britain's Fleet would be seriously weakened by then; our lone patrol ship down south, HMS Endurance would have finally gone home at the onset of winter, to scrap; and anyway, the Royal Navy would be most unlikely to tackle the worst of the winter in the South Atlantic with a force large enough to remove Argentina from her "rightful territories." Above all, there was every indication that, by then, we would probably have no operational aircraft carriers, with Hermes and Invincible both victims of Mr. John Nott's Defence cuts. As far as Galtieri and Anaya were concerned the situation was now simple: no British carriers means no air cover, no air cover means no British surface ships, no surface ships means no British landing force, no landing force means "No Contest." Their reasoning was perfect. Their timing? That was the make or break factor.[4]

As it occurred, however, the junta first allowed events to carry them away. Then they embarked on two courses, one self-delusory and the other militarily inept. Firstly, they did not believe that the British would respond militarily. Perhaps they were influenced by their embassy in London which reported that "the British were militarily weak" and that its navy is "virtually non-existent,"[5] and further that "the English public will not fight for the Malvinas. The English will never again go to war for a colony."[6] The Argentine foreign minister, Dr. Nicanor Costa Méndez, an ardent Anglophile, stated in a British Broadcasting Corporation (BBC) TV interview on the day of the Argentine seizure of the islands that the British were "too civilized" to use force.[7] The mismatch of perceptions between Buenos Aires and London could not have been more stark. The Argentine view throughout April was that they were engaged in diplomatic crisis management; the British view was that they were at war. The language of the two leaders is instructive. In the House of Commons debate in the emergency session of Saturday, 3 April 1982, Mrs. Margaret Thatcher stated, "It is the Government's objective to see that the Islands are freed from occupation and are returned to British administration at the earliest possible moment."[8] General Galtieri believed that "English reaction was scarcely possible and totally improbable."[9]

Militarily, Britain quickly assembled and sailed a naval task force with the aim of supporting the prime minister's determinations. British planning for the conduct, the support, and the sustainment of operations in a difficult area of operations was intense and thoroughly professional. The Argentines, failing to comprehend in any serious way the depth of British resolve, did little other than pile men and materiel onto the Malvinas in the hope that the British would see that the mathematics of combat would preclude a successful landing. It had no such effect. In warfare, numbers are not enough; it is how you deploy and use your numbers that determines the outcome.

The use of airpower by both sides also offers a contrast in military professionalism. The *Fuerza Aerea Argentina* and the *Comando Aviacion Naval Argentina*, which I will hereafter refer to as the Argentine air force and naval air arm respectively, while decidedly more active in preparing for combat than the Argentine army, were nevertheless underprepared for what was to follow. On the other hand, the British quickly saw both the need for and the major difficulties in achieving control of the air when and where they would need it and swiftly actioned numerous initiatives to satisfy their needs. The result was that the Argentines failed to capitalize on the major advantages available to them while the British were able to work around or compensate for the major disadvantages of their position.

The British planners appreciated from the very beginning—in fact from before the task force was assembled—that to achieve the aims of the government might well require the landing of a substantial land force on the Falklands. This would be a difficult and hazardous task the success of which would depend critically on control of the sea and airspace at the time of the amphibious force's approach, landing, and consolidation. Airpower would be the key, for ships alone could not provide the control required. Surface ships and submarines could defend against a surface or submarine threat, but they could not reduce sufficiently the vulnerability of the amphibious force to air attack. This vulnerability would be particularly stark at the time of the landings. To achieve control of the air would require airpower, and this could only be effectively achieved organically. The aircraft carriers and the Sea Harriers were, therefore, the sine qua non for the success of the amphibious operation. Once ashore and consolidated, the land force would need to be supported and sustained. Here again airpower would be crucial, and planning had to ensure it was available to the land force in the quantity and of the quality required.

British planning was both broad and comprehensive. The land, sea, and air forces, which might be needed if conflict occurred, immediately began intensive training for the roles and missions they might have to conduct. Industrial, scientific, and logistic support agencies were similarly brought into the planning and preparatory phases. On the diplomatic front, major efforts were made—and very successfully so—to obtain the supplies and the support needed. At the same time, diplomatic effort was directed—and again successfully so—to denying the Argentines the supplies and support they needed. Two dramatic examples will illustrate this point. US logistics support of the British forces was crucial to the outcome. Mainly due to the personal efforts of the US secretary of defense, Caspar Weinberger, this was obtained. In fact it was given effect at Weinberger's insistence well before congressional approval to do so was obtained. The commander of the task force, Adm Sandy Woodward, believes that this support was so crucial that, without the Sidewinder AIM-9L air intercept missile and access to Ascension and its facilities, the result would have been reversed.[10] On the other side of diplomatic activity, British efforts largely isolated the Argentines. One result was the withdrawal of French support to the Super Étendard aircraft of the Argentine naval air arm and to the Exocet AM-39 missile.[11]

With airpower, the RN concentrated on the preparation of the carriers, Harriers, and helicopters. This preparation and training were conducted within the United Kingdom (UK) and in the task force on its passage to the area of operations. The Royal Air Force (RAF) prepared a wide range of its aircraft and personnel for possible conflict. The aircrews and support crews for Harriers, Vulcans, Victors, VC-10s, C-130s, Nimrods, and a variety of helicopters were those most heavily involved.

The Argentines were also determinedly active but less successful. The realization that the British might be serious about the recapture of the islands seems to have hit the Argentine forces well before it sunk in with the junta and such senior officials as Costa Méndez. A massive airlift of personnel and materiel to the islands was quickly planned and conducted throughout the month of April 1982. The Argentine Air Force and Naval Air Arm separately concluded that no airfield on the islands, including Stanley, was suitable for operations by fast jets. This ruled out the Mirage III, Dagger, A-4, and the Super Étendard, in effect almost all the Argentine combat airpower. These aircraft operated only from the mainland throughout the war, not even using Stanley in an emergency. The only aircraft which tried, a Mirage III that had been badly damaged in a confrontation with the very effective Sea Harrier/AIM-9L combination on 1 May, was shot down and its pilot killed by

Argentine antiaircraft artillery (AAA).[12] The only Argentine aircraft of any combat capability to operate from the islands during the war were 24 Pucaras, six Aermacchi 339s, and four Beechcraft Mentors, a very modest capability indeed.

During April the Argentine Air Force developed a retaliation plan to use in a major operation in the event that the British attempted a landing. It involved an attack force of 28 A-4s flying as seven flights of four, six Canberras in two flights of three, and 12 Daggers and 10 Mirage IIIs flying in pairs as escorts. In the event, the plan was never actioned. If it had been—and that would almost certainly have required better intelligence than the Argentines ever possessed—the British defenses would have been sorely tested.

I do not intend to work through the 50 days of combat operations from 25 April, when South Georgia was retaken, until 14 June when the Argentines on the Falklands surrendered. That is covered in detail in a number of excellent works on the subject. Instead, I will concentrate on just a few significant days and events, for they bring out most of what this conflict can tell us about the use of airpower. Also worth pointing out is that, although the conflict in the air was frequently intense, it was also sporadic, never being sustained by the Argentines for more than a few days at a time.

The first day of significant use of combat airpower was 1 May 1982. The British targets were—for eminently sound military reasons—the airfields at Stanley and Goose Green. In a predawn attack a single Vulcan dropped 21 1,000-pound bombs on Stanley. The mission took 15 hours and required the support of a back-up Vulcan and 11 Victors. The immediate results were not overly impressive. The first bomb in the stick had impacted and cratered the runway. The runway was quickly repaired to a standard sufficient for operations by Aermacchi 339, Pucara, and C-130 aircraft. Other than that, damage was minor. This attack was followed soon thereafter by attacks on Stanley and Goose Green by Sea Harriers from the task force, specifically, HMS *Hermes*, which had been brought within 70 miles of the islands. Three Pucaras were destroyed on the ground at Goose Green. All the British aircraft recovered successfully to the carrier which immediately headed further out. The Sea Harriers were quickly turned around, now equipped with AIM-9Ls for fleet air defense. Meanwhile a bombardment group of a destroyer and two frigates moved to within 12 miles of the East Falkland coast and shelled Stanley from the sea. As they withdrew they were attacked by three Daggers of the Argentine air force. All three ships were damaged, none substantially so. The three Daggers recovered successfully to their base on the mainland.

As that day progressed, other Argentine aircraft and their pilots were not so fortunate. The higher command in Argentina was all but totally confused. As the reports flowed in, and anticipating a British landing, the command considered that this must be the planned-for landing. Its response, however, was disjointed and ultimately disastrous. Instead of the 56-sortie, coordinated attack it had planned, a series of disjointed responses was initiated. No A-4 mission found a target; a flight of three Canberras did, only to lose one of their number to an AIM-9L fired by a Sea Harrier. A similar combination accounted for one of a pair of Daggers engaged on an escort mission. Late in the day a pair of Mirage IIIs was engaged by a similar number of Sea Harriers. One Mirage was destroyed and the other badly damaged. It was the latter aircraft that was mentioned previously as the victim of its own forces while attempting to land at Stanley.

The Argentine navy's carrier, *Veinticinco de Mayo*, had put to sea in mid-April with eight A-4s, six S-2 Trackers, and three Sea King helicopters. The next two weeks were spent in operational training to have the ship and its complement combat ready by 30 April. In the event, the carrier and its aircraft contributed little to the actions of 1 May. The Sea Kings were airborne throughout the day on antisubmarine warfare (ASW) missions, and the A-4s flew nine air defense sorties. The Trackers found and then lost the British task force. The loss of contact was mainly the result of confusion caused by the presence of 30 to 40 Soviet fishing vessels which were operating between the Argentine and British carrier groups![13]

At the end of that day, the events were both shattering and confusing to those planning the use of Argentine airpower. The British had shown their ability to bomb targets accurately at extreme range; the Canberra had shown that it was extremely vulnerable; and neither the Mirage III nor the Dagger was the equal of the Sea Harrier/AIM-9L combination, and neither had the range to operate with any true effectiveness in the area of the islands. The inability of these aircraft to be refueled in flight had exposed a major operational limitation on the very first day of operations. The wins and losses scoreboard also did not look good: one Dagger, two Mirage IIIs, one Canberra, and three Pucaras for, at best, some minor damage to three ships. Even more devastating for aircrew morale was the loss of three senior pilots and a navigator.

The outcome of what had been a confusing day for both sides was significant. The British were buoyed by their successes, the Argentines devastated by their failures and especially by their inability to seize the initiative and dictate the terms of the tactical contests. Their reactions demonstrated clearly the psychological blows they had suffered. Noting the Vulcan's capabilities and the Mirage III's ineffectiveness in the area of the islands, the Argentines withdrew the Mirages north to protect the national capital and heartland. The Canberras were thereafter confined to night operations, and the Daggers were not subsequently used as escorts.

On 2 May the results were, if anything, worse, and airpower played no part in the most significant event of that day, the sinking of the Argentine cruiser, *General Belgrano*, by the SSN, HMS *Conqueror*. Airpower was, however, affected by that event. The warships of the Argentine navy, including its only carrier, were immediately withdrawn to the mainland and never again ventured beyond the 12-mile limit imposed by the British. The aircraft and crews of the naval air arm were the only elements of the Argentine navy to play a part in further combat.

The sinking of the *General Belgrano* was a defining event in this conflict. It established that the RN through its SSNs commanded the seas. The Argentine navy, which had always assumed the major part in the planning of Malvinas operations and whose commander, Admiral Anaya, was undoubtedly the strongest advocate within the military and the junta of direct military action in support of Argentine claims, was pushed to the sidelines. The broader effect of the sinking of the

General Belgrano was that on world opinion. Any notion that this was some minor post-imperial scuffle that would eventually be acted out with few casualties and no great losses had to be discarded. I remember well my own feelings as I first learned of the sinking of the *General Belgrano* by car radio on my way to work in Headquarters Australian Defence Force. I had this sickness in the pit of my stomach as I listened to the account of the action and thought of the hundreds of young sailors dead or dying in the ice-cold waters of the South Atlantic. This was bitter, bloody conflict from which there was no smooth and simple way to work back.

The second defining event of the war came just two days later. It had a similar effect on world opinion and a major effect on both British opinion at home and British combat planning in the war zone. In the early afternoon of 4 May, in conditions of low cloud and poor visibility 85 nautical miles south of Port Stanley, the Type 42 British destroyer, HMS *Sheffield*, was struck by a single AM-39 Exocet fired from a range of 25 miles by one of a pair of Argentine navy Super Étendard aircraft operating from Rio Grande air base on the Argentine mainland. Although the warhead did not explode, the fire created within the ship spread very swiftly and could not be controlled. The ship was abandoned five hours later with a loss of 20 of its 268-man crew. Twenty-four others were injured.

This was a stunning blow to the British. To date, all had gone so well. Public opinion had been rallied and now stood firmly behind a government which, up until this time, was Britain's most unpopular of the twentieth century. International opinion had also been effectively mobilized in Britain's and against Argentina's favor. The task force had planned and trained well with the result that morale and confidence were high. The events of 25 April at South Georgia, of 1 May on and around the Falklands, and of 2 May with the sinking of the *General Belgrano* confirmed the validity of that confidence. However, 4 May showed that this was not to be a one-sided conflict. The vulnerability of the task force to modern weapons systems had been dramatically exposed.

From 4 to 20 May the conflict went into a lull. The British were waiting for the rest of the land force to join the task force.

The Argentines were reviewing what had occurred, regrouping their forces, and planning a maximum air effort in opposition to the British landings. The significant event of that period for the air forces was the loss to the Argentines of six Pucaras, four Beechcraft Mentors, and a Shorts Skyvan on the ground at Pebble Island in a raid mounted by British special forces.

During this lull the Argentine planners developed a 75-sortie effort to launch against the British as they landed, reasoning that maximum confusion in the British defenses would be created if they were flooded with aircraft. Sixty-three of the sorties were to be mounted in A-4s and Daggers of the Argentine air force and 12 in A-4s of the Argentine naval air arm. On the day of the landings, 21 May, an estimated 60 sorties reached the Malvinas in pursuit of the tactical aim, but the confusion that was planned was only partially realized. Journalists' accounts of the day's actions talk of unending waves of Argentine aircraft sweeping through San Carlos Water throughout the day. The truth is otherwise. No Argentine aircraft appeared until the morning was well advanced and then, having had to work their way through the outer defenses and having little tactical freedom due to lack of fuel endurance, they appeared a few at a time at widely separated intervals of time. Ten Argentine aircraft were lost, nine to the Sea Harrier defenses and one to a surface-to-air missile. The British forces lost HMS *Ardent,* HMS *Argonaut* was seriously damaged, and HMSs *Antrim, Brilliant,* and *Broadsword* were damaged to a lesser extent.

The greatest frustration to the Argentine airmen was that the damage should have been much greater. Many bombs hit their targets but failed to detonate due to delayed-action fuses that failed to operate.[14] Some bombs bounced off the water and over their targets. One bounced off the water, passed upward through the flight deck of HMS *Broadsword,* and demolished all in its path, including the nose of *Broadsword's* Lynx helicopter, before falling into the sea without exploding.[15]

An important statistic from that day of turmoil in San Carlos Water illustrates well the importance of airpower in the support and sustainment of operations. A detachment of Sea Kings ferried 520 troops and 912,000 pounds of stores from ship to shore.[16] Another important statistic was the Argentine loss rate. The Argentine forces had achieved much, but they had suffered greatly. Five Daggers, five A-4s, two Pucaras, one Chinook, and one Puma were their losses for the day. That rate of attrition could not be sustained.

Then came the seemingly inexplicable respite granted by the Argentines to the British, which allowed them to complete and consolidate their landings. One explanation for this is that so many Argentine aircraft had been damaged on 21 May that the mounting of a substantial effort the next day was beyond their capabilities. Lawrence Freedman and Virginia Gamba-Stonehouse offer a different explanation:

> The delay was the result of an argument that morning between the Air Force and the naval aviators over how air power should be properly deployed in these circumstances. . . . The Air Force wanted to make a decisive strike of their own, by attacking large targets, such as the carriers and major warships, with the hope of success having a commensurate political impact in London. . . . As a result, and to immense British relief, the supply ships were left alone.[17]

The Argentine air attacks resumed on 23 May. That and the next two days saw intense Argentine air activity resulting in British losses of HMS *Antelope* and HMS *Coventry* and substantial damage to HMS *Sir Galahad*. The latter's sister ship, HMS *Sir Lancelot,* was also damaged. The most significant British loss of the period was not, however, a naval vessel but a merchant vessel supporting the operations. On 25 May, by flying at very low level and using deceptive routing, two Super Étendards equipped with Exocet AM-39 missiles closed on the British task force undetected. The task force appears to have received about six minutes warning. This was not enough to deflect the attack, and the Super Étendards each fired one Exocet from a range of 31 miles. Subsequent analysis suggests that both missiles were effectively deflected by electronic countermeasures and chaff from their aimed targets. However, the container ship, MV *Atlantic Conveyor,* which had no such defenses was hit and caught fire. Twelve lives were lost. Fortunately for the British, all the Harriers and Sea Harriers the ship had brought south plus one Chinook and one Wessex had already been flown off. Nevertheless, the materiel losses were severe: 10 helicopters (six Wessex 5s, three Chinooks, one

Lynx), aircraft parts, ammunition and bombs, tentage for 4,000 men, aluminum planking for airstrips, a water desalinization plant, and many vehicles. Salvage of some of this was contemplated, but before it could be attempted the ship foundered.

Twenty-seven May, the last day of intensive Argentine air attacks in San Carlos Water, saw the most successful Argentine strike against a land target in the war. Argentine A-4s hit the British main logistics area and medical dressing station at Ajax Bay, which was on the other side of San Carlos Water from the beachhead. Guns, mortars, and ammunition being loaded into helicopter nets were destroyed, as were all of 45 Commando Battalion's antitank missiles and launchers. Several men were killed and wounded. The dressing station was rendered unusable for the rest of the war through two unexploded bombs having lodged there.[18]

These were not the only problems confronting the commander, 3 Brigade, Brig Julian Thompson, during this period. He was under great pressure from the heights of both political and military command to move out of the beachhead. High command seemed to have little appreciation of the operational and logistical circumstances on the islands. To quote Freedman and Gamba-Stonehouse: "Thompson was beginning to doubt that anybody in London had any conception of the logistical task he faced or the real risks his men were already running. From the standpoint of those facing daily air raids the opposition did not seem so weak as it appeared in London."[19] Although the British commander on the Falklands did not know it at the time, his plight was soon to be shared with his opposite number, Brig Gen Mario Benjamin Menendez, who was also unable to convey to his high command the true circumstances he faced.[20]

With the move out of the beachhead and a major lull in the Argentine antishipping campaign, the emphasis of air operations shifted to British support, both combat and logistic, of their land forces. I will use two illustrations, one descriptive and the other statistical, to emphasize the importance of both types of support. The first concerns the use of close air support in the battle for Goose Green. The paratroops' advance on that settlement had ground to a halt. They were moving against a

considerably larger force, and one that was being very effectively supported by artillery. In addition, Argentine Pucaras
were creating havoc among the British support helicopters. The
attack had stalled and ammunition was running low. The commander, Maj Chris Keeble, called for air support. It was provided by two GR-3 Harriers of the RAF. In Keeble's words, "The
attack gave a great boost to the morale of our troops. I think
some of them thought the Harriers had come in a bit too close
for comfort, but that is war."[21] To quote Ethell and Price: "[The]
attack was a textbook example of a close air-support mission:
a hard-hitting surprise attack against a target of great importance to the enemy, launched at a crucial time in the land battle, whose results were clearly seen by the ground troops—thus
strengthening the resolve of those on one side and demoralising those on the other."[22] The Argentine attacks slackened
markedly and, after dark, ceased. The next morning Keeble
opened negotiations for a surrender which duly followed. The
Argentine force was more than twice the size of the British and
was amply supplied with weapons and ammunition.

The statistical illustration can be expressed more succinctly
but it is no less telling. More than 80 percent of all sorties
flown by the British were those of their helicopters and, of
those, more than 80 percent were moving people and stores.
The RN helicopters flew 10,381 sorties for a total of 21,049 flying hours.[23] The RAF's lone helicopter performed splendidly. In
a single month that one Chinook—the only one to be flown off
the MV *Atlantic Conveyor*—lifted 1,530 troops, 650 Argentine
prisoners, and 600 tons of cargo, and it did so in often
appalling weather conditions and frequently when under fire.[24]

The last instance in the war which I wish to highlight is that
of the amphibious landings at Fitzroy-Bluff Cove late in the
war. The plan was to move 1,200 troops of the Scots and Welsh
Guards to the east coast of East Falkland rather than having
them walk there. Doing so would save time and effort. It was
also, however, hazardous. Admiral Woodward did not like the
plan, but he considered that they would probably get away
with it "as long as they were swift, spent as little time as possible in unloading the LSL [landing ship, logistic] and the
weather stayed favourable."[25] In the event, none of these

applied. The landing was detected by the Argentines who moved swiftly to mount an air attack utilizing Daggers and A-4s. The A-4s found *Sir Galahad* and *Sir Tristram* unloading in Pleasant Bay. *Sir Tristram* had disembarked many of its troops but, unfortunately, *Sir Galahad* had not. Both ships were bombed and strafed, suffering serious damage and loss of life. The most damage and carnage resulted from the detonation of a bomb deep within *Sir Galahad*. In total, 50 men were killed and another 57 wounded.

The Argentine Daggers did not even reach Pleasant Bay. En route they came upon HMS *Plymouth* leaving San Carlos Water alone and without air cover. They attacked and badly damaged the ship before returning safely home. In fact, all of the Daggers and A-4s involved in these missions recovered safely. Such was not the case for the follow-up missions now mounted by the Argentines. The defenses had been alerted and Harriers were deployed on combat air patrol (CAP) over-head. The result was no further damage inflicted on the ships and three A-4s lost.

Admiral Woodward speaks strongly of this whole incident in his book. One particular passage is worth quoting at length because it raises an issue of great importance in modern warfare:

> One of my deep regrets about the "Bluff Cove Disaster" is that it will always remain some people's abiding memory of the Falklands War—because television was there, filming horrific live pictures of burnt and badly injured soldiers. As a military disaster it was not, in context, so earth-shakingly dreadful. . . . I suspect we all have to learn to live with the fact that television magnifies drastically what is already awful and somehow diminishes in importance that which it does not see.[26]

At 9:00 P.M. local time on 14 June 1982, the Argentine commander and governor of the Malvinas, Brigadier General Menendez, surrendered all Argentine forces on the islands to the commander land forces Falkland Islands, Maj Gen Jeremy Moore. At the loss of 1,002 lives (256 British, 746 Argentine) and more than 2,000 wounded,[27] British administration of and sovereignty over the Falkland Islands had been restored.

Was it worth it? Who can say? It depends on the values you hold and the weight you allot to the criteria you use. As Michael Howard has pointed out, "That is the kind of hypothetical question which laymen put and historians cannot answer."[28] He also points out, however, that we can ask another and less impossible question; namely, what did the respective governments think would happen to them if they did not go to war.[29] I leave that for you to contemplate.

What can be said without question is that, in retaking the islands, Britain acquired a commitment to them that she did not previously have. In military terms, having previously been unwilling to place a deterrent force of moderate size on the islands, she has now had to spend hundreds of millions of pounds and distort her military structure to deter future Argentine aggression. For its part, Argentina had been beaten, perhaps to the point of humiliation, but her determination to incorporate the Malvinas into her republic had not been diminished. The status quo antebellum has not been restored; the status is much different. Even if one accepts the Clausewitzian dictum that war is the continuation of politics with the addition of other means, one must acknowledge that war is more than just another policy option. Once military action has been taken and blood spilled, a discontinuity has been introduced which makes it impossible to move back smoothly to previously possible positions. Argentine military power was used to seize the islands; British military power was used to retake and secure them; what military power has been unable to do is solve the problem of the Falklands/Malvinas.

What can be said about military power in this conflict is that the outcome was an affirmation of the value of military professionalism. The military task the British set themselves was daunting: transport a land force 8,000 miles to the South Atlantic, land on a bleak and unfamiliar group of islands defended by more than 10,000 troops, and reestablish British administration. Many factors, including good fortune, combined to bring the British victory. In a summary comment on the conflict, Adm Harry Train stated, "Mass, firepower, and logistics support are still the essentials in a military campaign,"[30] but he also remarked that "in the end it was British military professionalism that pulled the fat out of the fire."[31] One factor quoted by many observers as the key to victory was the British capability in joint operations. On that point Admiral Woodward and General Moore have been quite specific, stating that: "The ability to operate central joint command of our national force was war winning."[32] And further that: "We won because we were unified, the enemy was not."[33] I well recall, however, that when visiting Whitehall soon after the end of the war, the strong feeling was that, while joint operations had been conducted reasonably well, many weaknesses had been exposed, and there was much that needed to be improved.

If one accepts the adage that defeat is a better teacher than victory, the lessons which the Argentines learned have special significance. Brig Gen Ernesto Crespo, who became the Argentine air force's chief of staff, conducted a study of the war. His report was published in various editions of the *Buenos Aires Herald* in 1985. His report concludes with a series of recommendations that, in the words of Anthony Cordesman and Abraham Wagner, "are virtually the mirror image of the reasons for Britain's success"; namely:

- The responsibilities of each service must be clearly defined.
- Intensive permanent joint planning and training must be fully institutionalised.
- Joint planning at all levels must be implemented in the form of an integrated command, control, and training organisation.
- Operations must be commanded on the basis of a joint command for a specific theatre of operations.[34]

In all of this, however, the quality of the British forces stood out. They were determined, adaptable, physically fit, well trained, and well led. The mobility and the expertise of their ground forces in night operations are especially noteworthy. In contrast, the Argentine forces tried hard—and in some areas with considerable success—but they were outclassed. Nevertheless, as Admiral Woodward points out, echoing the Duke of Wellington after Waterloo, "It was a bit of a close call."[35]

The conflict has been a treasure trove for students and analysts.[36] It was the first conflict of its type for decades. Many of the weapons and systems involved were either in or being contemplated for the inventories of other nations, and many of them were being used in combat for the first time. "Lessons learned" became a growth industry of which I was a part. However, as I remarked, in the equivalent conference to this in 1991 on the subject of extracting lessons from military conflicts, "A common tendency is to extract data and form conclusions which accord with one's preconceptions."[37] I reiterate that. In doing so, I have the full support of no less an authority than Michael Howard who, in referring to the Russo-Japanese War of 1904–05, states: "As usual, the experts tended to read into the experiences of the war very much what they wanted to find."[38]

With those statements standing guard over us all, let me chance my arm with some summary remarks on the use of airpower in the South Atlantic in 1982.

In basic terms the air war in the South Atlantic was one in which land-based air forces attempted to prevent a naval task force from firstly putting a land force ashore and then supporting it. Consequently, the areas which stand out in any study of this war are maritime strike and fleet air defense. With the first, the vulnerability of surface vessels to air attack was again demonstrated in the South Atlantic. Ships are easy to find—if not always easy to identify—and, if undefended, easy to hit. Once hit, they are easily damaged and the damage is difficult to control. These factors worked in favor of both Argentine and British air attackers in this conflict.[39] Working against the Argentine forces were the facts that their attacks were ill conceived and tactically inept. This in no way detracts from the extreme courage shown by many of the Argentine aircrews. It does show, however, that the combination of personal bravery and professional ineptitude is frequently fatal.

Argentine targeting, as remarked above, was inexcusably bad. They targeted the pickets and not the ships they were protecting. The real prizes, apart from the carriers, were the two amphibious support ships, the support ships such as the MV *Atlantic Conveyor*, and most particularly the SS *Canberra*. I remember well being told in London in 1983 that, if the *Canberra* had been lost or badly damaged on the way into the Falklands, the British would not have continued the campaign.

Even when the Argentines targeted the carriers, they lost sight of their aim in the heat of combat. Postwar analysis indicates that the Argentine pilots in general attacked the first ship or ships they saw—and they were, by the very nature of naval combat dispositions, the pickets.

The Argentine planning was equally poor in not attempting to swamp the British defenses and confuse their tactical command and control. Despite operating toward the limits of their radii of action, the Argentine air forces still had the capacity to run a large number of maritime strike aircraft, plus escorts and other airborne support, against the British task force. A combination of spoof raids, feint attacks, escorted raids, and multidirectional attacks by 30 plus Daggers and A-4s against a high-value target—and that was well within the physical capabilities of the Argentines until the very end of the war— would have been very difficult to defend against. Yet nothing like that was ever attempted. Although up to eight Argentine aircraft would be in the area of operations at any one time, never more than five were used in a single attack. Even then they usually all attacked from the same general direction; to quote Cordesman and Wagner: "This normally allowed the British to focus all of their anti-aircraft defences on a comparatively few intruders."[40]

The most successful maritime strike unit was No. 2 Squadron of the Argentine naval air arm. It was equipped with five Super Étendard aircraft (one of which was used exclusively for spares) and five AM-39 Exocet missiles. The squadron had 10 qualified Super Étendard pilots. In the war they destroyed the HMS *Sheffield* and the MV *Atlantic Conveyor* with no damage whatsoever to any aircraft. Operating at extreme range (the mission which accounted for the MV *Atlantic Conveyor* was a round trip of 1,650 nautical miles) and often in poor weather, they showed themselves to be a highly professional outfit.[41] If more aircraft, crews, and missiles had been available, the Super Étendard/AM-39 Exocet combination might have been as effective for the Argentine in attack as the Sea Harrier/AIM-9L was for the British in defense.

243

The significance of the availability of the AIM-9L Sidewinder has already been commented upon. The missile proved to be both reliable and effective. Without it, the air-to-air contest would have been played to different rules. Equally, if the combat power represented by the Sea Harriers had not been available, the whole contest would have been played to different rules. Dispatching a task force would have been an act of futility and, instead, a diplomatic solution would have been sought. As it was, the Sea Harrier/AIM-9L overwhelmed the Argentines in the air. The exchange rate supports this statement: Sea Harriers 24, Argentines 0.[42] After that first day, 1 May, the Argentines never again attempted to oppose the Harriers in air-to-air combat.

Impressive as the figures are, as mentioned above, the task force was vulnerable to a properly planned and executed maritime strike. The reason was that the British did not have the wherewithal to defend the task force effectively against such an attack and that, in turn, was because the necessary measures had not been taken to provide defense in depth. What the British required was the capability for early warning of attack and continuous tracking thereafter of the attackers. That needed to be coupled with a layered series of antiair weapons systems to protect the high-value assets of the task force. The British had neither the early warning system nor true defense in depth. That they were able to compensate for those deficiencies shows both their skill and their ability to improvise, but it also shows a lack of operational insight on the part of their opponents. The summary conclusion, which is as pertinent today as it was in the South Atlantic in 1982, is that, if you have to operate your ships where they might be subject to air attack, you must provide them with all the elements of the system described above or your losses could be severe.

A major factor within the operational calculus of both sides was the range and endurance of their aircraft. The South Atlantic war showed yet again that aircraft of low fuel endurance are operationally inefficient. Unless an aircraft has a fuel endurance which is appropriate for its role and its tasks, extraordinary measures have to be taken to compensate. Endurance can be traded as circumstances dictate for range, speed, load, loiter time, or turning radius. Air-to-air refueling (AAR) can help to overcome the disadvantages of low fuel endurance, but it is only a partial corrective.

AAR presents planners with complex problems to ensure that the AAR aircraft are where they are needed when they are needed. Refueling aircraft are not only valuable air assets but also highly vulnerable ones, a fact which adds to the planners' problems. Nevertheless, the reactions of both sides in the aftermath of the war are instructive. The British white paper of 1983 highlights AAR as being vital in supporting operations at long range, stating that "large capacity strategic tanker aircraft are needed to provide greater operational flexibility in the future."[43] For its part, the Argentine actions speak as loud as words; after the war they retrofitted their Mirage IIIs and Daggers with AAR capability.[44]

Support operations were vital to British success and, with airpower, the role of support helicopters is worth special attention. Their significance to British operations has been commented on above. Despite the British success with helicopters, there is still much to learn about their use. In combat a Parkinsonian imperative applies with support helicopters: the tasks for which they are needed always exceed the capacity of those available. This makes the availability and the tasking of support helicopters critical to success. The British had the support helicopters, and they used them well; neither comment applies to the Argentines. Despite the British success, their tasking of helicopters could have and should have been much better. When I visited the RN Naval Air Station at Yeovilton in 1983, helicopter pilots told me of their extreme frustration as they waited for tasking which never came while, throughout the day, they were hearing radio requests from ground forces desperately in need of their services. As with all other forms of air assets, allocation and tasking are keys to their successful application.

The comments on support helicopters are part of another old lesson reemphasized, namely, the vital importance of logistics. The logistical chain which ran from the Falklands through the critical support base of Ascension island to the United Kingdom was a vital element of British combat power. The chain, in fact, went even further, namely, to the United States for many vital items, especially fuel, bombs and precision-guided munitions such as Sidewinders, Stingers, and Shrikes.[45]

A vital link in the British logistics chain was airlift. The British support base of Ascension had an airfield, Wideawake, but no port. Airlift of personnel and stores to Ascension was an important task throughout the conflict. During the campaign more than 5,500 personnel, 7,000 tons of supplies, almost 100 vehicles, and more than 20 helicopters were airlifted into Ascension island in operations that absorbed 17,000 flying hours.[46] A smaller but no less vital part of the total airlift effort was the airdrop from C-130 aircraft of critical spares and stores to the task force throughout the operation.[47] Air Chief Marshal Sir Michael Armitage considers that the transport force was vital to the success of the whole operation for the reconquest of the Falklands.[48]

The Argentines also used strategic airlift very effectively in difficult conditions. After the war, many people, myself included, were surprised to find that the Argentines were able with relative impunity to operate C-130s into Stanley right up until the night before the surrender.[49] The aircraft brought in personnel and stores and carried out wounded personnel. No aircraft were lost on these missions. The one Argentine C-130 that was lost was engaged in an unfortunate attempt by the Argentine air force to use the aircraft for maritime reconnaissance and raid direction. On 1 June the third such mission was flown. When the aircraft popped up from low level north of Pebble Island to make a radar sweep, it was detected by radar and a pair of Sea Harriers was directed onto it. The C-130 was destroyed with an AIM-9L. No further missions of this type were flown.[50]

Now I come to the exercise of which I spoke in the introduction. I consider that the South Atlantic war offers the airpower student or analyst an ideal opportunity to learn about campaign planning and the operational art. The trick is to place yourself not in Sandy Woodward's shoes but in Lami Dozo's. If what he had was yours, how would you have used it to thwart the British and achieve the national aim?[51]

For me, this is both an interesting and a relevant exercise, especially for Australians. In our nation's defense, we are most unlikely to be required to attempt what the British did. For as far ahead as we can see, however, we will be required to control an air/sea gap and defend a coastline. So let us look at the problem.

The British are coming, and we have a good idea of what their combat air assets are. In a nutshell, they have 28 Sea Harriers, gun and missile equipped, supported by shipborne radars and little else. The ships are well equipped for defense, but the only power the British can project until they land the amphibious force is that possessed by the Harriers. For our part, if I can put it in those terms without offense, we have 20 Mirage IIIs, 25 Daggers, 70 A-4s, five Super Étendards, 55 Pucaras, six Aermacchi 339s, seven Canberras, and four Beechcraft Mentors.[52] The A-4s and the Super Étendards are air refuelable. We have two KC-130s, and the A-4s can also buddy-refuel. We have numerous support aircraft and two mobile control and reporting radars, a TPS-43 and a TPS-44. We also have an aircraft carrier and a number of mainland bases. Having seized the Malvinas, we now have a 4,100-foot, sealed runway and numerous grass fields available to us there.

I have played this game many times and I am convinced that, properly used, airpower could have achieved the Argentine national aim. I leave it to you to contemplate how you would do so, but I will offer a few tips.

Your first task will be to devise a campaign plan and, within that, an air campaign plan to achieve your strategic aim. In doing so you will need to determine the operational and logistics concepts that you will employ. The tip I offer on planning your campaign is to seek out the Air Power Studies Centre's paper on the subject.[53] It gives an excellent framework within which to work.

The key to success is the airfield at Stanley. Lami Dozo has said that he contemplated using it but concluded that it was not possible.[54] On 17 October 1982, F-4 Phantoms of the RAF flew into Stanley, which had been lengthened with 2,000 feet of AM2 matting![55] F-4s operated continuously from Stanley until the new airfield at Mount Pleasant was built. The Argentines had AM2 matting, and the equipment needed to prepare the ground and lay the matting. With Argentine fast jets operating from Stanley, the operational calculus is transformed. Who now is forced to operate at the limit of range in conducting offensive operations? Adm Harry Train considers that "had the Argentines achieved the capability of flying A-4s, Super Étendards and Mirages out of Port Stanley, the course of the war would probably have been quite different."[56] Cordesman and Wagner draw a conclusion which they consider is of wide applicability in stating that, in any remote-area conflict, it is important to base as far ahead as possible.[57]

Another tip: fuel, bombs, and ammunition are a problem for operations from Stanley; you will have to determine a solution. In like fashion, maintenance for your fast jets, other than relatively simple on-aircraft maintenance, is a problem. The British submarine force is an insurmountable barrier for your surface navy and a major problem for your merchant shipping. The navy's own submarine force, however, can—as it did in the actual war—cause the British sailors great concern.

If you play the exercise seriously, I believe that you will gain much from it. The Australians among you will find that it offers insights that will assist your thinking on how we should use our airpower in similar circumstances.

The short but intense war in the South Atlantic in those 73 days in 1982 deserves serious consideration from a number of points of view. How two mature nation-states allowed a seemingly minor issue to escalate to war is a question that needs to be addressed. G. M. Dillon has summarized this aspect of the dispute quite neatly:

> The dispute was an apparently uncomplicated international disagreement between two otherwise friendly states, which historically have shared some mutual regard, transformed by military gamble and political misjudgment into crisis and war. It ought to have been resolvable, and yet it proved intractable. One might reasonably have thought also that even if no solution was immediately negotiable or foreseeable, a sense of proportion ought to have been sufficient to contain the disagreement below the threshold of violence.[58]

In the cold, harsh spotlight of hindsight, this unnecessary war shows once again that military action is truly the option of last resort. Both sides were too swift to resort to it; the Argentines in seizing the islands and the British in retaking them. Both sides allowed events to sweep them along without sufficient consideration being given to policy alternatives. A capacity for and a willingness to think in strategic terms, to take the long view and consider Michael Howard's question of what is likely to be the result—in broad and not narrowly political terms—of not taking military action would have served both sides well.

The British failed to deter the Argentinians from invading because they did not, and ultimately could not, demonstrate clearly that they were serious in retaining sovereignty over the islands and, to that end, were willing to commit major resources. They believed that, if the Argentines escalated the conflict beyond diplomacy, they would do so at the low end of the conflict spectrum. This is brought out in many sections of the Franks Report.[59] The line of thought was that, if diplomacy failed, extra-diplomatic action would be of a minor nature, such as severing postal and communications links or harassing aircraft and shipping. Moreover, a parallel line of thought was that any forthright British action would be provocative, would complicate diplomacy, and might lead to Argentine military action. There is no evidence of the contrary line of thought that not to take forthright action might encourage the Argentines to take action at the high end of the conflict spectrum, a line of thought with as much historical support as any.

This is not to say that the Argentine invasion was predictable. Although modern wars are almost always predictable, they are notoriously difficult to predict. The key to coping with this fact is not to seek to achieve an impossibly high level of predictability, but to act in such a way that, if the unpredictable should occur, you are prepared for it. That requires acting with circumspection and prudence before the event and swiftly and appropriately after it.

With airpower, we see once again its fundamental importance in modern military conflict. Control of the air was seen by both sides as one of the keys to success. The British started with few assets, but their thinking on how to use them to obtain control of the air was excellent; the Argentines began with most of the advantages and failed to capitalize on that fortunate circumstance. Airmen of both sides fought determinedly, frequently displaying courage of the very highest order. Unfortunately, in doing so, many fine young men lost their lives. That the war was fought at all was the fault of no airman, but the fact that many airmen and others lost their lives needlessly can be traced to air commanders, planners, and operators who did not know their basic business well enough. Let us hope that through studies of these conflicts and through convening conferences such as this, criticisms of that type can never be made of us.

Discussion

Air Commodore Bob Richardson: I think the Falklands showed that you don't fight the war you prepare for and that the ability to modify, to adapt, to meet the changing circumstances of any individual conflict is very important. I'm thinking of the mounting of Searchwater radars on naval helicopters, of air refueling modifications to transport aircraft, and most particularly, of the electronic warfare modifications that were introduced at very short notice. They all showed an ability to adapt to circumstances which is most important for us also. I wonder if you would agree with that.

Air Marshal Funnell: Yes, I do, Bob. I address those issues in my paper, but I didn't have the time to mention them. Just a point of clarification: although the British did have Searchwater radar adapted to fit on a Sea King, it wasn't used in the conflict. That occurred afterwards.

At the end of my paper I speak of reacting swiftly and appropriately to an event which you haven't predicted. You have to have that sort of capacity within your defense structure if you're going to react in effective and appropriate ways to the unexpected.

Dr. Ben Lambeth: Harking back to your title, "It Was a Bit of a Close Call," the war seemed to demonstrate how random luck can be a factor governing the outcome of war. I'd ask you to speculate first on what the operational consequences would have been had the *Atlantic Conveyor* gone down before the Harrier GR-3s went off rather than afterwards, and beyond that to reflect on what other key events besides Argentine ineptitude contributed to this being a close call.

Air Marshal Funnell: At the end of the study I gave a presentation at Whitehall, and I can remember remarking that perhaps the overriding conclusion I'd reached was something people have been saying in that part of the world for a very long time: God really is an Englishman.

Yes, random luck did have a lot to do with the British victory. In fact it was close in other respects as well. If the Argentine ground forces could have held out for another couple of weeks, I don't know how the British forces would have coped with the huge logistical problem that was building up for them. Many of their ships in the South Atlantic were barely operational. It would have been a very tricky business indeed.

If the *Atlantic Conveyer* had lost the Sea Harriers, that would have had a very serious impact, but I don't think it would have changed the outcome. But what I did learn in London was that if the *Canberra* had been lost on the way down—and it could well have been—the British would have abandoned the military operation. That was the significance of the *Canberra*, and as I said, it sat in San Carlos Water throughout the 21st of May and was not attacked. Since the war, some of the Argentine commanders—and I think this once again demonstrates their capacity for self-delusion—have said they deliberately didn't attack the *Atlantic Conveyer* or the Royal Fleet Auxiliaries because they "didn't do that sort of thing." My conclusion was that because the Argentine aircraft were operating at the extremes of their radius of action they would attack the first target they saw, and those targets naturally tended to be the pickets, not logistics support ships.

Professor Richard Overy: You've talked about this as an unnecessary war. I wonder whether you feel strongly that the reason it became a military conflict so early was because both Galtieri in Argentina and Thatcher in Britain had domestic political considerations which governed the choices they were making, rather than considerations based on military or international grounds. The second thing I wanted to ask is whether you could talk more about air intelligence. I think we haven't talked sufficiently about the development of air intelligence and the role it plays in operations. Is it that intelligence did not in fact govern the behavior of the two air forces very much in the Falklands conflict, or is it something that we don't know enough about yet?

Air Marshal Funnell: On the unnecessary war. There's no doubt that for both sides it's difficult to interpret international actions without understanding the domestic forces and the interplay between diplomacy and domestic politics. The Australian historian Geoffrey Blainey has examined that as a general proposition and thinks that the relationship is some-what overemphasized as an explanation of why wars occur. However, there's little doubt that the Argentine junta was in domestic trouble at the time, and they perceived the retaking of the Malvinas as something which would attract strong domestic support and that's the way it turned out. The initial Argentine plan was that they were going to take the islands bloodlessly—which they succeeded in doing, the only life lost was on their own side—and with very little harm to civilians, just to force the British back to the negotiating table. They then were going to withdraw. But, of course, the invasion was received with such acclaim in Argentina, in comparison to the riots the junta had had on their hands the week before, that there was no way in the world they could ever have withdrawn.

On the British side, as I mentioned, this was the most unpopular government of the twentieth century. In an opinion poll published in the *Times* in the middle of April 1982—this was after the task force had sailed—Margaret Thatcher was rated as the worst prime minister in history. She even beat Neville Chamberlain, who had held that position for the previous 50 years. So there also was an extremely unpopular government faced with major domestic problems. In the House of Commons the prime minister met with the chief of naval staff. He told her something like, "I can fix this, I can retake these

Islands, I've got a task force I'm putting together, and it can sail in 48 hours." That, I think, shows the way in which domestic politics can interact and bring about a decision which you might personally rationalize in other ways.

On intelligence. It was a war fought without good intelligence on either side and that's in a range of areas, not only on the air side. For example, the Argentines had only one submarine in operation, and it was scurrying around the South Atlantic, only occasionally coming in contact with British ships. The one occasion it did fire torpedoes against British shipping, it appeared they malfunctioned. Yet, because of the mere presence of the submarine, and mainly in reaction to false alarms, the Royal Navy task force had all but expended every single antisubmarine weapon they had in their armory during those 50 or so days down there. They just didn't have the intelligence to work with. Similarly, because they didn't have airborne early warning, their intelligence on incoming Argentine air raids was poor. Also, the British got very little intelligence from satellite systems. In the main, the information they got was very broad and didn't have the detail they sought. By contrast, they used signals intelligence very well after their landings on the 21st.

Another interesting thing about intelligence is that as soon as something like this comes along, you just do not have the staff to cope with it. The British forces brought in intelligence officers and reservists from everywhere, but now instead of operating in a peacetime environment—9 to 5, Monday to Friday—now it's 24 hours a day, seven days a week, and the volume of material coming in has expanded hugely. I can recall talking with some of the intelligence people. They were setting up camp stretchers in the hallways because people couldn't afford to go home: there was no one to handle the intelligence for them if they weren't there all the time.

One last comment on intelligence, although I don't know how much weight you can put on this. After the war, the Argentines maintained that their chief source of intelligence throughout the war was the BBC World Service. The BBC came in for a lot of flak in that war, and some of it I think was deserved. For example—although once again it appears that the Argentines didn't take advantage of it—the attack on Goose Green was announced by the BBC before it occurred. Lt Col H. Jones, who was in charge, said that when he got back to the UK he was personally going to initiate legal action against the BBC. Unfortunately, as you may recall he was killed. In like fashion, it was the BBC who informed the Argentines that their bombs weren't exploding.

Notes

1. G. M. Dillon, *The Falklands, Politics, and War* (Houndsmill, Basingstroke, Hampshire: Macmillan Press, 1989), viii.

2. South Georgia Island is about 800 nautical miles east-southeast of the Falklands. It is administered separately from the Falklands. It is also claimed by Argentina, but the claim is of post-World War II origin.

3. HMS *Sheffield* was subsequently lost while under tow.

4. Sandy Woodward and Patrick Robinson, *One Hundred Days: The Memoirs of the Falklands Battle Group Commander* (London: HarperCollins, 1992), 68.

5. John E. Marr, *War in the Falklands: Perspectives on British Strategy and the Use of Air Power*, Air War College Research Report (Maxwell Air Force Base, Ala.: Air University, 1988), 18.

6. Ibid.

7. Peter Calvert, *The Falklands Crisis: The Rights and the Wrongs* (London: Frances Pinter, 1982), 59.

8. Dillon, 130–31.

9. Interview with Miss Oriana Fallaci, *Times*, 12 June 1982, cited in Sir James Cable, "Surprise and the Single Scenario," *RUSI Journal*, March 1983, 33.

10. Woodward, xviii.

11. Anthony H. Cordesman and Abraham R. Wagner, *The Lessons of Modern War*, vol. 3, *The Afghan and Falkland Conflicts* (Boulder, Colo.: Westview Press, 1990), 243.

12. Rodney A. Burdon et al., *Falklands, The Air War* (London: Arms and Armour Press, 1986), 145.

13. The information in this section is drawn mainly from a number of sections within Burdon.

14. Information in this section has been extracted from numerous sources with most reliance being placed on the accounts in Burdon.

15. Burdon, 121.

16. Cordesman and Wagner, 253.

17. Lawrence Freedman and Virginia Gamba-Stonehouse, *Signals of War: The Falklands Conflict of 1982* (London: Faber and Faber, 1990), 359–60.

18. Ibid., 369.

19. Freedman and Gamba-Stonehouse.

20. Ibid., 402–6.

21. Jeffrey L. Ethell and Alfred Price, *Air War South Atlantic* (London: Sidgwick & Jackson, 1983), 65.

22. Ibid., 165.

23. Cordesman and Wagner, 326.

24. M. J. Armitage, *The Royal Air Force: An Illustrated History* (London: Arms and Armour Press, 1993), 238. See also Burdon, 389.

25. Woodward, 319.

26. Ibid., 323–24.

27. Cordesman and Wagner, 267.

28. Michael Eliot Howard, *The Lessons of History* (New Haven: Yale University Press, 1991), 115.

29. Ibid.

30. Adm Harry D. Train, "An Analysis of the Falklands/Malvinas Islands Campaign," *Naval War College Review*, Winter 1988, 50.

31. Ibid.

32. Maj Gen Sir Jeremy Moore and Adm Sir John Woodward, "The Falklands Experience," *RUSI Journal*, March 1983, 31.

33. Ibid.

34. Cordesman and Wagner, 329.

35. Ibid., xvii.

36. Adm Harry Train believes that, as a case study, it is one that is also rich in political and military mistakes. Train, 33.

37. Air Marshal R. G. Funnell, "The Essential Place of Conventional Air Power in an Uncertain 21st Century," in *Smaller but Larger: Conventional Air Power into the 21st Century: The Proceedings of the Conference held by the Royal Australian Air Force in Canberra, 25 March to 27 March 1991*, ed. Alan Stephens (Canberra: Australian Government Publishing Service, 1991), 15.

38. Howard, 108.

39. A fact which is often overlooked in studies of this conflict is that, despite the low level of effort expended by the Argentine navy, British air attacks against Argentine shipping resulted in the destruction of two patrol craft, two transports, a trawler, and a submarine and damage to two further patrol craft and two transports. This was accomplished without the loss of a single British aircraft.

40. Cordesman and Wagner, 312.

41. The information is gleaned from Burdon, 34–38.

42. Ethell and Price, 245.

43. British Ministry of Defence, *The Falklands Campaign: The Lessons* (London: Her Majesty's Stationery Office [HMSO], 1982), 25.

44. Cordesman and Wagner, 352. In this same period, Australia, having vacillated over the issue for decades, decided to acquire a tanking capability.

45. Of at least equal importance was the intelligence support provided by the United States to the British.

46. Armitage, 237.

47. A total of 35 such missions were flown. Cordesman and Wagner, 303.

48. Armitage, 237.

49. Two missions were flown to and from Stanley on that night, the last departing at 2335Z (2035 local time) carrying 72 sick and wounded. Burdon, 81–82.

50. Ethell and Price, 175.

51. For this exercise, we assume that the Argentine national aim is to force the British to negotiate seriously on the issue of sovereignty with the end in mind of transferring it to the Argentine.

52. The numbers are approximate rather than precise. Exactly how many aircraft of these types were available to the Argentines in the war is the subject of much speculation. However, for this exercise, the important factor is conceptual not numerical.

53. Alan Stephens and Gary Waters, *Operational Level Doctrine: Planning an Air Campaign*, Air Power Studies Centre, Paper no. 18 (Fairbairn Base, Australia: Royal Australian Air Force Air Power Studies Centre, October 1993).

54. Train, 39.

55. Burdon, 418.

56. Train, 39.

57. Cordesman and Wagner, 313.

58. Dillon, 230–31.

59. Baron Oliver Franks, *Falklands Islands Review: Report of a Committee of Privy Counsellors* (London: HMSO, 1983). The committee, under the chairmanship of Lord Franks, was appointed by Prime Minister Thatcher to review the way in which the government discharged its responsibilities in the period leading up to the Argentine invasion.

Airpower in Peripheral Conflict: From the Past, the Future?

Dennis M. Drew

The stellar lineup of papers for this symposium would seem to leave little to discuss, even under the nebulous heading, "Airpower in Peripheral Conflict," provided by the conference organizers. Nearly every conflict of note during the airpower age has received special treatment, and the organizers of the symposium have even commissioned a look at the future of airpower. But as interesting and enlightening as these major conflicts of the airpower age may be, they may provide few insights to the future employment of airpower. The era of thousand-bomber raids is long past, doomed by the economics of modern airpower and the destructive efficiency of modern weapons. Further, some noted analysts, such as Richard Simpkin[1] and Martin van Creveld,[2] argue with fervor and considerable logical justification that the entire concept of major military contingencies involving large, sophisticated military forces may be a thing of the past, or at least an aberration.

Although this observer does not entirely agree with Messrs. Simpkin and van Creveld, their observations about the possible future of armed conflict cast some degree of doubt upon the relevance of the most commonly studied past conflicts. The purpose of this paper is to briefly examine the role of airpower in recent but often overlooked conflicts which may have more relevance to the future if the theses of Simpkin and van Creveld prove accurate.

To accomplish this purpose I have chosen three conflicts in which airpower played an important, sometimes dominant role. One stands alone in terms of its future relevance. The Malayan Emergency, and how the British quelled that post–World War II uprising, provides a classic example of successful counterinsurgency and the defeat of an enemy using strategies based on Maoist principles. Although the Malayan Emergency was unique in many ways and thus not easily compared to Vietnam, Algeria, El Salvador, Nicaragua, or many other insurgent situations, it still provides some pithy lessons, particularly in regard to the use of airpower in counterinsurgent operations.

Insurgent warfare is the classic ploy of the weak against the strong, of those out of power against those holding power. At this writing there are a number of insurgencies of various stripes underway (e.g., Peru, Angola) and others which may or may not be finally settled (e.g., El Salvador, Nicaragua). Given the number of ongoing insurgencies and the perceived potential for many more in the future, the inclusion of the Malayan Emergency in this paper seems particularly important and appropriate.

The remaining two conflicts examined herein provide contrasting examples of very different kinds of warfare. The Israeli air strike on the Iraqi nuclear facility at Osirak (also spelled Osiraq) in 1981 and the strike by the United States on various targets in Libya in 1986 provide two examples of discrete air attacks designed to produce very limited and specific objectives. In the case of the former, the objective was to interrupt and delay the production of nuclear weapons by an archenemy. In the latter case, the objective was to "send a message" about the price one must pay for sponsoring international terrorist acts. The threat of nuclear proliferation, particularly to so-called rogue states, and the continued use of terrorism as an instrument of power indicate that the requirement to use airpower for such discrete purposes may be all too commonplace in future.

Focus and Limitations

This paper concerns airpower, and an analysis of its use, utility, success, and/or failure in the cases under examination. As such, the paper will not provide a comprehensive examination of the cases considered. The US strike against Libya and the Israeli strike against the Iraqi nuclear plant also raise particularly contentious political, legal, and moral issues. Although those issues may be exceedingly important, they are only tangentially related to the purpose of this paper and thus will not be examined.

A serious limitation of this paper concerns source material. Much of the source material concerning the US operations in

Libya remains classified. The same holds true for much of the source material concerning the Israeli raid on Osirak. The author has been forced, in those cases, to rely heavily upon published reports from reputable news organizations.

The Malayan Emergency

Background

The surprisingly rapid defeat of British forces in Malaya by the Japanese created the opportunity for the Malayan Communist Party (MCP) to assert itself as the principal opponent of the Japanese occupation. The MCP took to the jungle-covered backcountry and formed the Malayan People's Anti-Japanese Army (MPAJA). Eventually trained and armed by the British, it was never a serious threat to Japanese control although it harassed the invaders and provided a rallying point for the people.

The equally sudden collapse of the Japanese in 1945 created another opportunity for the MCP. After the Japanese surrender, MPAJA units quickly took control of much of the interior country. Seizing the moment, they took full credit for the collapse of the Japanese. As Edgar O'Ballance put it, "The Japanese were beaten and bewildered, and the Europeans discredited and humiliated."[3]

The British were slow to react. The first elements of the British military administration did not return to Kuala Lumpur until nearly mid-September. Once established, however, the British methodically spread their control to the interior areas.[4] The British were aided in reestablishing control by the composition of the MCP and its military arm, both of which were almost totally Chinese. Chinese had immigrated into Malaya since the 1850s to work the tin mines and later to work the rubber plantations. Because they were never accepted by the Malays as first-class citizens, they were susceptible to the blandishments of Marxism and the MCP. But the racial divisions and tensions between the Chinese immigrants and the native Malays which gave rise to the MCP also meant that the MCP would have little appeal for the majority of Malays.[5]

After the British regained control, they attempted to finesse the thorny MCP problem by negotiating a peaceful "disbandment" of the party's military arm. The MPAJA had rapidly increased in size after the Japanese surrender to over 10,000, as those who had not been a part of the underground army sought to be part of the "winning team" that had "beaten" the hated invader. However, only 6,800 were officially disbanded—the remainder being the most important and experienced personnel who retained a significant supply of arms in secret jungle hideouts.[6]

The insurgency got under way in mid-1948 following a secret meeting of MCP leaders during which they determined to overthrow the British colonial rule by force of arms, riding on the wave of growing communist strength throughout Asia, particularly in China and Indochina.[7] Led by Chin Peng, the secretary general of the MCP, and by the party's senior military leader Lau Yew (a student of Mao Tse-tung's writings), they sought to follow the basic teachings of Mao by developing a successful rural-based insurgency in careful stages.[8]

In the long run, the insurgency was probably doomed to failure for three interconnected reasons. The first was the aforementioned racial antagonism between the Chinese-dominated insurgent movement and the dominant Malay population. Expanding the insurgent movement into the general population would be difficult. It was made more difficult by the fact that the Malayan administration was neither corrupt nor widely disliked. The final problem the insurgents brought upon themselves. The MCP continually ignored Mao's teachings that the most important aim of the insurgent was to win over the loyalties of the population, thus gaining strength for the insurgency and reducing the government's credibility and capability. As a result, the MCP's misguided terror tactics failed to discredit the government and alienated the general population.[9]

Even though the long-term goals of the insurgency may have been doomed from the outset, there was much potential for dangerous and destructive mischief, particularly with a total Chinese population in Malaya numbering nearly four million (by 1960), of whom 500,000 were landless squatters and among whom the MCP program might gain great support.[10]

Facing potential problems of this magnitude, British counterinsurgent strategy was of critical importance, providing the coup de grâce for the MCP insurgency.

Key to the British victory was their clear and accurate understanding of the nature of the war. Almost from the beginning, the British authorities realized that the key to their counterinsurgent effort was to separate the rebels from the population that might support them, control that population and provide appropriate security (thus cutting off any support), and combine these efforts with military operations designed to find, harass, demoralize, and kill the insurgent fighters.[11]

Although some early progress was made during the tenure of High Commissioner Sir Henry Gurney, the British counterinsurgency program began to take definitive shape when Lt Gen Sir Harold Briggs arrived in Malaya as the first director of operations in April of 1950. The so-called Briggs Plan combined civil and military action. It exploited the dependence of the rebel forces on money, supplies, intelligence, and recruits from the local population, particularly from the clandestine civil arm of the insurgents, the Min Yuen, which operated among the landless Chinese squatters to whom the objectives of the insurgency had some appeal.

The Briggs Plan sought to control the vulnerable portions of the population, destroy the Min Yuen elements within that population, prevent the flow of important supplies from the Min Yuen into the hands of the insurgent fighters, raise the confidence of the population that the government had the situation under control—and then concentrate on military action to destroy the guerrilla forces.[12]

By mid-1951 the government had resettled about 80 percent of the Chinese squatters, provided them with security, schools, land, and self-determination which effectively isolated the insurgent movement from its potential base of popular support.[13] On the military side, intelligence activities were increased, and coordination with local police improved. However, large-scale military sweeps in search of insurgents proved a disappointment, and terrorist activities continued to increase, including one ambush which killed the high commissioner.

In early 1952 Gen Sir Gerald Templer became the high commissioner replacing the assassinated Gurney. Virtually every source credits Templer for reinvigorating the Briggs Plan, continuing the dual military/nonmilitary pressure on the insurgents, moving toward more effective small-unit military operations, and waging effective psychological warfare. The upshot was steadily decreasing support for the insurgency, continually declining morale among the insurgent fighters, and a continual depleting of their ranks through death, desertion, and surrender.

The insurgent forces, cut off from their sources of support, subjected to intense psychological warfare, harassed, ambushed, and killed, eventually gave up the effort. By 1958, the so-called Year of Mass Surrender, less than 300 insurgents remained in Malaya, and for all practical purposes, the insurgency was over. The Malayan Emergency was officially declared ended on 31 July 1960.

The price of victory and defeat was high, belying the modern characterization of "low-intensity conflict." The numbers vary by source, but the general consensus is that the insurgents lost over 6,000 killed and nearly 3,000 wounded. Government forces, including local police, lost nearly 2,000 killed and over 2,500 wounded.[14]

Airpower in the Malayan Emergency

As the emergency began to unfold, the Royal Air Force (RAF) found itself in a poor position to wage a significant air campaign against the insurgents. In mid-1945 Air Command Southeast Asia was comprised of some 70 squadrons with over 1,300 operational aircraft. As the emergency began in 1948, only a skeleton force remained, some 11 squadrons with just over 100 aircraft. Further, this force was concentrated on Singapore Island. The British had closed the former Malayan mainland base at Kuala Lumpur as part of the postwar demobilization.[15]

The RAF, often ably assisted by the Royal Australian Air Force (RAAF) and the Royal New Zealand Air Force (RNZAF), was confronted with a triple problem. The most obvious was a paucity of resources with which to conduct operations over an area about the size of England and Wales combined. The second problem was lack of experience. Far different from most of the aerial campaigns in World War II—even those conducted against the Japanese in other parts of Southeast Asia—and far different from the air control and policing campaigns pioneered by the RAF between the two world wars, the RAF would have to learn on the job how to effectively conduct operations in a counterinsurgency campaign. The third problem, intertwined with the first two, was simply the task of finding the insurgents. Less than 10,000 (normally considerably less) insurgents, operating in groups of less than 100, were spread over a large area of which 80 percent was covered by dense jungle. These problems, and a steep learning curve, would shape the air campaign.[16]

To understand the air campaign over the entire length of the emergency, the most logical organizational scheme is to sequentially discuss four of the major roles played by airpower—air attack, air transport, psychological warfare operations, and aerial spraying. In each role airpower had differing degrees of success and impact on the overall counterinsurgent effort.

Aerial Attack. It was in this role, direct attack on insurgents, that the airmen faced their biggest challenges, received their greatest criticism, and in the aftermath generated the greatest debate. The challenges have already been alluded to in terms of resources, area, jungle growth, and dispersed enemy formations. As the official RAF history of the campaign noted: "Successful air strikes normally depend on a number of factors, including high grade intelligence information giving the exact location of an identifiable target, an accurate method of pinpointing this target and an attacking force capable of accurate navigation to the target and carrying a weapon suitable for its destruction. In Malaya all these conditions were problematical."[17]

Two main types of offensive air attack were used—both with the basic intention of killing as many rebels as possible. The first type was against pinpoint targets, particularly insurgent campsites in the jungle. The second type was against area targets in which intelligence had reported concentrations of guerrilla forces. In the early days of the emergency, the former were lucrative targets, but as the insurgent forces realized the danger they faced from air attacks on their camps, they took elaborate and effective measures to disperse and hide their camps, which made detection particularly difficult. This resulted in moving to area attacks.

Area attacks might result in direct casualties among the insurgents, but these were often, at best, fortuitous. More effective was the indirect elimination of the enemy by combining area attacks with prepared ground ambushes, driving the guerrillas into the hands of the ground forces. However, success in such efforts required careful and close coordination with ground forces, something that was often difficult to achieve.[18]

It was not long before the airmen realized that one of their traditional air attack missions, close air support, simply was not practicable in the Malayan context. The featureless jungle terrain, fleeting targets, often long response times, and the inability of pilots to see friendly or enemy troops beneath the jungle canopy made close support a proposition laden with risk to friendly forces combined with a low probability of inflicting significant casualties on the enemy.[19]

The criticism and controversy over aerial attack missions comes into play when attempting to evaluate its effectiveness and contribution to the overall counterinsurgent campaign. Clearly, the effort and treasure expended on aerial attacks cannot be justified in terms of enemy casualties. During the first two years of the campaign, intelligence credited aerial attack with killing only 126 of the enemy, less than 10 percent of guerrillas eliminated in the overall campaign to that point.[20] As the RAF official history put it:

> The contribution made by offensive air support . . . cannot be evaluated solely in terms of the material results for any estimate of the number of casualties inflicted and the immense expenditure of bombs, ammunition and flying effort would suggest that air-strike action in this type of campaign was simply not worthwhile. For example, the eight Lincolns of No. 1 (RAAF) squadron dropped 17,500 short tons of bombs between 1950 and 1958 . . . and were credited with killing only sixteen terrorists and destroying twenty to thirty of their camps.[21]

Beyond killing the insurgents, there is also controversy as to the value of offensive air strikes used as a tool to continually harass the guerrillas and thus destroy their morale. Robert Jackson, for example, notes that "continual harassment from the air had a fearfully demoralising effect on terrorists who were already suffering from the rigours of life in the jungle, and was the agent that persuaded many to surrender."[22] The RAF official history supports Jackson's contention by noting that "testimonies of captured or surrendered terrorists bore witness to the effect it had and the fall in surrender rate after the cessation of area bombardments in 1953 substantiated their claims."[23]

Jackson goes on to claim that offensive air strikes also had a salutary impact on civilian morale in that they provided "a demonstration of power that persuaded many civilians to resist the terrorists and cooperate with the security forces."[24] Philip Towle agrees citing an after action report on a bombing raid which stated, "It was most stimulating for the local population and has raised their morale considerably. The air strike is still one of the main topics of conversation in the coffee shops and everyone is convinced that if the strike is repeated . . . the bandits will soon lose heart."[25]

However, that sanguine appraisal is not held universally. Gen Richard Clutterbuck, for example, noted: "Hundreds of tons of bombs were dropped on the jungle every month, particularly in 1951–52; they probably killed fewer than half a dozen guerrillas a year—more by accident than design. Such senseless swiping induced a feeling of contempt for the power of modern weapons, and the enemy made full use of this contempt in their propaganda among the villagers and aborigines who had heard all the noise."[26]

Clutterbuck was a veteran of the emergency and spoke from at least some firsthand knowledge of the controversy. His opinion is seconded by Air Marshal Michael Armitage and Air Commodore R. A. Mason when, after noting that 35,000 tons of bombs and nearly 10 million rounds of cannon and machine-gun ammunition were expended in over 4,000 sorties, they judge that "in terms of firepower delivered by air on to terrorist targets . . . the meagre results were out of all proportion to the extensive effort engaged."[27]

A final point in this controversy is left for the reader to interpret, because the meaning of the data is anything but clear. During 1952 air operations in Malaya were subjected to intensive statistical research. The research concluded, in summary form:

- those battalions which eliminated the most insurgents made the most use of airpower,
- that battalions which eliminated the fewest insurgents used a disproportionately large amount of available air strikes,
- air support assisted in about 50 percent of total guerrilla eliminations of which strikes comprised 33 percent and air supply drops the remaining 17 percent, and
- of the strikes carried out, 36 percent assisted in the elimination of one or more insurgents.[28]

Air Transport. Although there remains considerable debate about the effectiveness of aerial strike missions during the emergency, there is total agreement about the importance of air transport to the counterinsurgency effort. The ability to insert government forces into remote jungle areas the insurgents used as sanctuaries and to resupply ground units tracking and harassing insurgents provided the government forces with an advantage that the insurgents could not counter.

Air transport came into its own during the emergency in late 1951. As a result of the success of the Briggs Plan, many of the insurgent forces moved away from the populated areas and deep into the jungle. Without the ability to resupply by air, army and police patrols could not have chased the insurgents more than five to 10 miles from the jungle fringes.[29] Patrols normally carried only five days of supplies, and as the insurgents moved deeper into the jungle, most patrols would receive at least one airdrop, facilitated by an RAF forward air controller who often accompanied the patrol.[30]

Deeper penetrations into insurgent sanctuaries required paratroop drops and, somewhat later in the campaign, the widespread use of helicopters for troop insertion. Aerial delivery of ground troops considerably increased the offensive potential of the government forces by overcoming the need for exhausting jungle marches.[31]

Although helicopters were very useful as a method to insert troops in distant areas, the need for cleared landing zones and their preparation often meant that the element of surprise was lost. The British Special Air Service (SAS) regiment maintained the element of surprise by developing a method of parachuting into the jungle treetops, which did away with the need for a prepared landing zone. Originally developed by forest fire fighters in North America, the technique called for each man to steer himself into the densest foliage and then lower himself to the ground with a length of strap made of canvas webbing.[32]

The crushing operating tempo of the RAF transport squadrons indicated the importance of the aerial transport mission—a crushing tempo even though the RAF squadrons were assisted at intervals by RAAF and RNZAF squadrons stationed near Penang at Butterworth. So intense was the pressure that RAF crews spent a maximum of six months on flying duty before rotation. Three RAF squadrons took turns bearing the burden, and during the emergency dropped more than 25,000 short tons of food, medicine, clothing, ammunition, and other equipment. Often they had to contend with very small drop zones (less than 200 feet in diameter) surrounded by jungle trees of 150 or more feet in height.[33]

The net result of these aerial transport efforts was the continual harassment of insurgent forces, the infliction of casualties which the guerrillas could not replace because of the success of the nonmilitary portions of the Briggs Plan, and the destruction of insurgent morale as they realized there were no sanctuaries. Towle, with the advantage of 30 years of hindsight, goes so far as to declare that air transport was the RAF's key role in the Malayan Emergency.[34] The evidence indicates that Towle has not reached an unwarranted conclusion.

Psychological Warfare Operations. The government, understanding the nature of the enemy it faced, waged a massive psychological warfare campaign as part of the Briggs Plan. Briggs and his successors understood that both insurgency and counterinsurgency are essentially struggles for the hearts and minds of the population.[35] Airpower played a significant role in that struggle in many ways, but most directly through the delivery of government propaganda to the insurgents in both printed form and via voice communication.

The earliest and most widespread use of airpower in this psychological role was in the distribution of leaflets designed to convince guerrilla fighters to surrender. The leaflets—which were supposed to withstand tropical rains and remain readable[36]—were dropped by the millions from the air. Beginning in 1948 with 30 million leaflets, the number rose to an annual figure of over 100 million from 1954 through 1957. Even after the emergency was officially declared to be over, leaflet dropping continued. In all, some 500 million leaflets were dropped during the emergency by some 2,500 air sorties.[37]

The leaflets had such an affect that guerrilla commanders forbade their troops to read them. To overcome this guerrilla stratagem, the RAF began using aircraft to broadcast messages directly to the insurgents over loudspeakers—aircraft called "sky shouters" by the insurgents. Operation Loudhailer experiments began in October 1952. Technical problems abounded but were overcome in the end.

More important to success than the technical problems was technique. Flying at 1,000–2,000 feet, Valetta, Dakota, or Auster aircraft equipped with loudspeakers would broadcast recorded messages in Chinese (Malay was much more difficult to broadcast because of its high pitch, and anyway most of the insurgents were Chinese) spoken by a female voice (experiments proved the female voice to be most effective). Often this was done immediately following a successful encounter by government forces on the ground in order to take advantage of low enemy morale and thus further exploit insurgent setbacks.[38]

Even with technical problems solved and the technique of application perfected, the message itself remained the most important aspect of "sky shouting." As Jackson notes, "Most importantly, all statements had to be true. The principle was rigidly adhered to in Malaya, and it was noticeable in statements by surrendered terrorists that they never doubted the information delivered by voice aircraft. Threats were not used unless the authorities intended to carry out the threatened action and were capable of doing so. The messages had to be brief and clear, with words and phrases carefully chosen."[39]

As to overall success, it appears that a significant percentage of insurgents who surrendered to the government authorities were influenced by the sky shouters. There is some disagreement as to the exact impact,[40] but it is clear that voice aircraft—along with leaflet distribution—contributed significantly to the overall counterinsurgent effort.

Crop Spraying. A key element in the Briggs Plan was to separate the insurgents from their base of support within the population and, thereby, cut their flow of food, money, intelligence, and recruits. Resettlement of the Chinese squatters accomplished this purpose. The insurgents, cut off from their supply source and forced ever deeper into the jungle-covered backcountry, attempted to grow their own food. To counter this adaptation by the insurgents, the RAF began spraying insurgent crops with toxic chemicals.

At first, the insurgents brought trouble on themselves by planting their crops in tidy rows, a pattern easily spotted by RAF reconnaissance aircraft. Eventually realizing their mistake, the insurgents began planting in random "non-arrangements." However, in the long run RAF reconnaissance aircraft would usually spot many, if not most of the plantings.[41]

Sodium arsenite was the first toxic potion used to kill the insurgent crops. Although effective, it was also poisonous to humans, which posed a considerable risk to the native population among whom the insurgents often lived. The risk to the native population was politically unacceptable in a battle for "hearts and minds." As a result, sodium arsenite was replaced by a mixture of trioxene and diesoline, which was not only an effective herbicide but also made the ground temporarily unusable for cultivation.[42]

There is some controversy about the contribution of crop spraying to the counterinsurgent effort. To the extent that crop spraying denied the insurgents their food and kept them on the run, the spraying program was a boon to the overall Briggs Plan. Jackson, for example, contends that crop spraying was a "significant" factor in the overall counterinsurgent campaign.[43] Towle, on the other hand, notes that because the insurgents often lived among the native jungle dwellers, the spraying program led to some highly undesirable results. Further, Towle claims SAS teams were more successful in denying food to the enemy by "winning them over to the government side thus stopping them supplying the guerrillas with food."[44]

Summary

A more complete appreciation of the role of airpower in the Malayan Emergency and its implications for the future of warfare will be presented in the final section of this paper. However, it is appropriate at this point to present a few interim observations.

First, it is clear that the RAF, ably assisted by other Commonwealth airmen, played a significant role in the victory of the government forces. Just how decisive that role was remains a matter of some conjecture. Suffice it to say that without airpower, government victory would have been much more difficult, would have taken considerably longer (and to those directing a Maoist-based insurgency, time is an effective weapon, particularly when used against a democratic society), and probably would have involved the expenditure of more lives—perhaps on both sides.

Second, it is interesting that the more controversial airpower missions executed in Malaya were again executed and were again controversial during the Vietnam War. The controversy over the bombing of North Vietnam is well documented. But there were also significant misgivings about the bombing, particularly massive B-52 raids, on suspected jungle hideouts of the Vietcong. Some analysts believe many of the raids did little but churn up the jungle and kill monkeys. On the other side of the coin, interviews with captured or surrendered enemy soldiers consistently revealed that B-52 raids were the most feared American tactic.

The widespread use of herbicide, in this case the infamous Agent Orange, was also very controversial both during and after the Vietnam conflict. The primary purpose of spraying in Vietnam was to defoliate areas and thus deny them as hiding places for the enemy. The long-term effects on the ecology, the health of the Vietnamese natives, and the health of soldiers exposed to the herbicide may be the most important legacy of the defoliation effort. The final judgment has not yet been rendered.

The Israeli Raid on Osirak

Background

Israel has been in a precarious strategic situation since it became an independent state. For much of its short history, Israel has been surrounded on three sides by sworn enemies who have often combined themselves in various shifting alliances. This strategic problem is compounded by the fact that in facing such coalitions, Israel is outmanned and out-gunned (quantitatively if not qualitatively) and lacks any kind of strategic depth.

Faced with such perilous circumstances, the Israeli government has not been loath to take aggressive military action to forestall what it perceived to be particularly threatening situations. This "offensive defensiveness" was demonstrated both in the 1956 Sinai campaign and again (and more famously) in the 1967 Six Day War. Such was also the case in the air raid on the Osirak nuclear reactor.

The danger the Israelis attempted to avert was the acquisition of nuclear arms by the hostile Iraqi government. With nuclear arms mounted on readily available theater ballistic missiles (most notably the Scud missile originally developed by the Soviet Union), all of Israel would be hostage to the Iraqis. And there was considerable evidence, gathered by the Israeli intelligence organization, Mossad, that Iraq was attempting to develop its own nuclear capability.

Alarm bells sounded in 1976 when Iraq's Atomic Energy Commission budget increased to $70 million per year from $5 million. Saddam Hussein turned to two of the biggest customers for Iraqi oil, France and Italy, for sophisticated nuclear technology, including a powerful research reactor and a plutonium-separation plant that would enable Iraq to develop weapons-grade plutonium. France signed a contract with the Iraqis for $275 million to build the Osirak reactor and bring it on-line by 1981.[45]

The Osirak reactor was to be a materials testing reactor and would be among the largest of its kind in the world. Although a poor choice for a peaceful nuclear program, it was a good choice for producing weapons-grade fissionable material. To the Israelis, the French-Iraqi contract completed a clear pattern of attempts by the Iraqis to gain nuclear weapons. Earlier, in 1974, the Iraqis approached the French about purchase of a gas-graphite power reactor. Such reactors are not efficient sources of electricity but are superior producers of large quantities of plutonium—just the material needed to produce nuclear weapons. Iraqi intentions were confirmed in 1975 when Saddam Hussein announced that his attempts to obtain a nuclear reactor were "the first Arab attempt at nuclear arming." Two years later, a leading member of Iraq's Central Revolutionary Command noted in a public statement that "the Arabs must get an atomic bomb."[46]

Just how well Israeli intelligence had penetrated the Iraqi plan is at least somewhat open to question. The Mossad and its activities are tightly controlled state secrets. Its actual capabilities and activities remain clouded by an aura of ruthless efficiency that the Israelis have not seen fit to dispel. One Israeli official is reported to have boasted that they had obtained engineering blueprints for the reactor. In any case, it is reasonably clear that the Mossad began gathering a combat file on the proposed reactor.[47]

On 5 April 1979, barely three days before it was to be shipped from France, unknown saboteurs (suspected to be Mossad agents) penetrated the French nuclear facility at La Seyne-sur-Mer near Toulon and attempted to blow up the core of the French-built reactor. Reports on the extent of the damage vary, but apparently the damage delayed considerably shipment of the reactor. Other instances of suspected Mossad intervention include the assassination of Yahia El-Meshad, the Egyptian-born head of Iraq's nuclear program, in his room at the Hotel Meridien in Paris; the death of a key witness to the Meshad assassination at the hands of a hit-and-run driver in Paris; and the bombing of SNIA Techint, an Italian nuclear company working in Iraq. How many, if any, of these instances can be attributed to Israeli intelligence may never be known. However, the Mossad was suspect in each case.[48]

The stories of Israeli intelligence prowess and involvement have grown to almost legendary proportions. It is widely held that on 30 September 1980, Israeli Air Force F-4 Phantom jet fighter-bombers were over the Osirak site during the confusing early days of the Iran-Iraq War. One account indicates that the aircraft bore Iranian markings and launched an ineffective attack on the reactor, and although ineffective, the aircraft gathered important intelligence about the site. Another account claims that unmarked Israeli aircraft flew over the site on an intelligence-gathering mission and that the attack on the reactor was launched by Iranian aircraft. Whatever the truth may be, any and all of these incidents added greatly to the mystique of the Mossad and the Israeli Air Force.[49]

Preparations[50]

An air raid deep into Iraq to destroy the Osirak reactor would require superior intelligence, detailed planning, and flawless execution—not to mention considerable chutzpah (the Yiddish term seems particularly appropriate in this instance). Planning for Operation Babylon began in earnest as early as 1979.[51]

If indeed the Israelis were in possession of Osirak's engineering blueprints, they would have been able to locate the precise position of the reactor's core, the computer control facilities, and the appropriate stress points that would be most vulnerable in the concrete cupola which protected the core. From those plans and aerial reconnaissance photos, the Israelis built a full-scale concrete model of the facility in the Negev desert against which hand-picked aircrews flew practice bombing runs from the nearby Etzion air base. According to one senior officer, before the raid the Israeli pilots knew "every tree and house" on the route of attack.[52]

Getting to the attack site posed the most vexing problems. Any realistic route to Baghdad from Israel required overflight not only of Iraq but also of either Saudi Arabia, Jordan, or Syria. Further, American airborne warning and control system (AWACS) aircraft were orbiting over Saudi Arabia as part of the defense package provided to the Saudis during the Iran-Iraq War. AWACS, too, would have to be avoided. Extensive practice flights over the desert found holes in the radar coverage and developed tactics and techniques to confuse air defense capabilities along the ingress route.[53]

The Raid[54]

Sometime shortly after 1600 hours on 7 June 1981, the Israelis launched the raid from Etzion air base. The force consisted of eight F-16s, each carrying two 2,000-pound bombs of Israeli manufacture mounted on special bomb racks, in addition to an array of air-to-air missiles for self-defense, and six F-15 fighters which would provide protection for the bomb-laden F-16s. The route to Baghdad apparently took the aircraft into both Jordanian and Saudi Arabian airspace, attempting to exploit gaps in radar coverage along the Saudi-Jordanian border. Apparently also, after leaving the border area the route crossed well into northwestern Saudi Arabia before entering Iraq.

Sources agree that the F-16s flew at very low levels to avoid radar detection with the F-15s flying somewhat higher. One source indicates that the aircraft used some sort of a weaving pattern which the Israelis had found reduced radar visibility.[55] Another source fails to mention a weaving flight pattern but does claim the F-16s flew in an extremely tight formation designed to make the formation appear to be a large commercial airliner.[56]

The flight went flawlessly. At one point the strike force was picked up on radar (probably the Jordanian radar at Ma'an) and challenged. Stories conflict somewhat, but apparently, when challenged, an Israeli pilot either replied in Arabic that they were Jordanian aircraft or replied in English (the international language of commercial aviation) that the blip on the radar scope was a civilian airliner. The ruse—whichever version is accurate—worked, and the strike mission pressed on unmolested. At 1710 hours the aircraft entered Iraq. At 1730 the target, 12 miles southeast of Baghdad, was in sight.

Each F-16 made one pass at the target. The first bombs punched a hole in the protective concrete cupola while later bombs detonated within the interior. The roof collapsed and buried the reactor core under hundreds of tons of concrete and other debris from the explosions. The damage was such that US experts estimated that at a minimum, the Iraqis would require 18 months to recover. In reality, the reactor had been destroyed.[57] The bombing was so precise that many believe some version of "smart" weapons was used. However, the Israelis have denied that they used anything other than iron "dumb" bombs.[58]

After one pass by each F-16, the entire strike force headed back to Israel. Apparently a much more direct route was taken on the return flight, but sources disagree on whether or not aerial refueling was required. No Iraqi fighters gave chase, no surface-to-air missiles (SAM) were fired, and only light anti-aircraft fire was encountered at the target—all of it off the mark. Nor did any Jordanian or Saudi (depending on the egress route) fighters try to intercept on the outward leg of the mission, even though one would think that by this time both would have been fully alert and realized that their airspace had been violated.

Aftermath and Results

There is no question that the Israeli raid on Osirak was a serious setback for Iraq's plans to build a nuclear weapon. However, rather than discourage Saddam Hussein, he seems to have redoubled his efforts to reach the nuclear goal.[59] It is also likely that if the Israelis had not struck, the Iraqis would have possessed nuclear weapons when they invaded Kuwait and faced the US-led Coalition a decade later.[60] If true, the implications are very significant.

The raid had almost predictable diplomatic results. It was roundly condemned by nearly everyone, including the United States.[61] However, given the stakes involved and the distrust of Saddam among many Arab states, some of the condemnations would appear to be pro forma. On the other hand, at least one analyst claims that the raid heightened Arab apprehensions and distrust since "the Arabs are convinced that Israel is a nuclear power, the raid . . . also signified that Israel was asserting an exclusive right to nuclear weapons in the Middle East."[62]

The United States Raid on Libya

Background

In retrospect, the early to mid-1980s era was in many ways dominated by fears of terrorism. A contagion of terrorist acts was abroad on the globe, committed by various groups espousing a long list of causes, grievances, and retributions. Although there seemed to be no nation that was unaffected by the bombings, hijackings, assassinations, and other such atrocities, the United States was particularly vulnerable because of its worldwide political, economic, and military interests. Moreover, as a superpower often supporting the political status quo, the United States was viewed in many terrorist circles as the archenemy.

The list of terrorist provocations which eventually led to the attack on Libya is a long one. At the very least, the American perception of being under siege by terrorists goes back to 1983 when the US Embassy in West Beirut was bombed killing 63, the Marine compound in Beirut was bombed killing 241, and the American Embassy in Kuwait was bombed. In 1984 and 1985 the terror attacks not only continued but increased.[63]

Libya and its strongman Col Muammar al-Qaddafi were linked to a good many of these incidents, either directly or indirectly, by US and various European intelligence sources and by the revelations of terrorists captured in foiled attempts. Qaddafi, anxious to promote his role as a champion of radical Arab causes, did not duck responsibility but rather often taunted the West in general and the United States specifically. In a speech on 11 June 1984, he called Americans "the sons of bitches" and urged people "to ally even with the devil against America." Further, he said, "We are capable of exporting terrorism to the heart of America. We are also capable of physical liquidation, destruction, and arson inside America." On 3 March 1985 he publicly warned the United States, Great Britain, and West Germany that they would be attacked if they attempted to stop "legitimate and sacred action—an entire people liquidating its opponents at home and abroad in plain daylight."[64]

Three particularly despicable events seemed to have been the factors which convinced the Reagan administration that the United States must take action against Libya. The first was the suspected Libyan involvement in the terrorist seizure of the cruise ship *Achille Lauro* in the Mediterranean on 7 October 1985. Next, on 27 December, came nearly simultaneous attacks on the Leonardo da Vinci airport in Rome and the Schwechat airport in Vienna which left a total of 20 dead and over 100 wounded, including several Americans.[65]

The immediate result was to increase US naval presence in the area to conduct operations (Operation Prairie Fire) near the Gulf of Sidra, which Libya had claimed as territorial waters since 1973. Although operating under rules of engagement (ROE) that forbade firing unless fired upon, it was clear that the United States was baiting the Libyan strongman. On 25 January 1986, Qaddafi responded theatrically from the deck of a Libyan patrol boat where he declared the parallel 32º 30' north latitude (the approximate northern boundary of the Gulf of Sidra) to be a "line of death where we shall stand and fight with our backs to the wall."[66]

Beyond nonviolent aerial intercepts, the situation remained reasonably calm until 24 March when a US surface action group steamed across the "line of death." The Libyans ineffectually fired SAMs at long range against the group's supporting combat air patrol, an action that satisfied the ROEs and provided clearance to fire. Within about a 12-hour period beginning on the night of 24–25 March, US carrier aircraft sank two Libyan missile patrol boats and attacked shore-based surface-to-air missile sites with high-speed antiradiation missiles. No further contact with the Libyans resulted, and the surface action group retired north of the line of death on 29 March.[67]

The longer term Libyan reaction was to foment further terrorist violence which culminated with the bombing of the La Belle Discotheque in Berlin, a favorite gathering place for US troops. The bomb exploded at 1:49 A.M. on 5 April when about 500 people were crowded into the nightspot. Amazingly, only three died (two American servicemen) while over 200 were wounded, including 79 Americans. The United States believed it had solid evidence that Libya was behind the attack.

Qaddafi had cast the die, and the stage was now set for a much stronger US response—an air attack on Libya, Operation El Dorado Canyon. President Ronald Reagan, at a National Security Council meeting on 7 April, said the United States must "try to make the world smaller for the terrorists."[68]

Planning and Preparation

No military option other than air strikes was ever seriously considered. President Reagan ordered that plans should minimize risks to US pilots and to Libyan civilians on the ground. Further, the damage inflicted upon the Libyans had to be significant, high-visibility damage that would send a clear and strong message to the Libyans and to other sponsors of international terrorism. Light damage could send exactly the wrong message—a message of weakness and vacillation on the part of a superpower.

Operating under those guidelines, it was clear that attack would have to take place at night to reduce the threat of Libyan antiaircraft fire and to reduce the possibility of unwanted casualties on the ground. Further, the strike force would have to hit all targets simultaneously. Returning for subsequent strikes would only expose US aircrews to more risks, particularly from Libyan air defenses which would then be on full alert.

These requirements meant that the strikes could not be an all-Navy operation. The two carriers operating in the region could not put enough night-capable strike aircraft into the air to hit all the intended targets simultaneously with enough bomb tonnage to cause high-visibility damage. US Air Force F-111 aircraft stationed in Great Britain would be ideal for the mission in conjunction with the available naval aircraft.[69]

The targets that would produce the high-visibility damage included Bab al Azizia army compound (a command center and sometimes residence of Qaddafi), the military portion of Tripoli International Airport (which housed Libya's fleet of Il-76 transport aircraft), and the commando training facility at the naval port of Sidi Balal. All of these targets were in the immediate vicinity of Tripoli. Meanwhile, on the eastern shore of the Gulf of Sidra, two targets were selected in the Benghazi area—the Jumahiriya army barracks (an alternate command center) and the Benina military airfield (which housed MiG-23 interceptors).[70]

There is some controversy over the selection of these targets and the results the United States hoped to obtain. There is no quarrel with the concept of inflicting "high-visibility" damage at Benghazi, Benina, Tripoli International Airport, and Sidi Balal. However, the amount of attention lavished on the Bab al Azizia barracks has drawn attention because it was a principal residence of Qaddafi. Originally nine F-111s, each dropping four 2,000-pound laser-guided bombs, were targeted on the complex. However, for a variety of reasons ranging from mechanical failures to navigational errors, only two F-111s found the target. The United States flatly denied the target selection and original weight of effort were made in an attempt to kill Qaddafi, noting that Bab al Azizia was the headquarters of Qaddafi's loyalist guard and a nerve center for his entire command and control structure. However, unofficially, administration officials admitted the target was selected with a reasonable expectation that Qaddafi might have been there. One official reportedly said that if Qaddafi had died in the raid, "I don't think it would have been considered collateral damage."[71]

Beyond the high-visibility damage, Secretary of State George Shultz noted that the president hoped the air raid would "encourage Libyan officers to overthrow their leader."[72] Although this latter result might seem somewhat far-fetched, there had been as many as 10 internal efforts to remove Qaddafi from office in the years leading up to the air raid. Further, the economic situation in Libya was rapidly deteriorating. Libya's oil production was at half the levels it had been at six years previously, its exports had been reduced by 50 percent, and the country was deeply in debt thanks to Qaddafi's profligate spending on foreign military hardware.[73]

What should have been a rather straightforward operation was severely complicated by a diplomatic failure. Only Great Britain of the US's major European allies backed the use of force against Libya. France went so far as to deny overflight rights for the F-111s and tanker aircraft stationed in Great Britain. Spain followed suit. The result was a roundabout flight pattern for the F-111s skirting to the south of Spain and then east across the Mediterranean. The result nearly doubled the one-way route to the target to 2,500 nautical miles versus a 1,300-mile route available had the French cooperated. Suddenly the aerial refueling effort required magnified, as did worries about en route mechanical problems and, of course, aircrew fatigue. The British did cooperate although politically it was a very difficult decision.[74]

The Raid[75]

Operation El Dorado Canyon began at 12:13 P.M. (EST) on Monday, 14 April 1986, with the departure of 28 US Air Force tanker aircraft (KC-10s and KC-135s) from air bases RAF Fairford and RAF Mildenhall. Most of the KC-10s had staged to Great Britain from their home bases in the United States. Thirteen minutes later, 24 F-111F strike aircraft and five EF-111A electronic warfare aircraft began departing air base RAF Lakenheath. Most of the F-111Fs were equipped with four GBU-10 Paveway 2 laser-guided 2,000-lb bombs although some carried twelve 500-lb bombs.

The circuitous route south over the Atlantic and then east over the Straits of Gibraltar into the Mediterranean required four aerial refuelings en route (only two on the return trip), all of them carried out in total radio silence to preserve security and achieve surprise in the target area.[76] After the first refueling, seven aircraft (six F-111Fs and one EF-111A), which had been launched to cover any mechanical failures en route, returned to their base in Great Britain. The remainder of the aerial armada flew on through the afternoon and night sky toward Libya. Along the route, the armada was apparently sighted by French, Portuguese, and Spanish radar, none of whom did or said anything. However, upon reaching the central Mediterranean, an Italian radar operator demanded identification but was greeted with silence. The Italians notified the island of Malta that unidentified aircraft were approaching. Malta, in turn, notified the Libyans that unidentified aircraft were approaching North Africa about half an hour prior to the raid.

At about the same time the US Air Force aircraft were taking-off in Great Britain, two US Navy aircraft carriers (*Coral Sea* and

280

America) cruising in waters off Sicily began a high-speed passage through the Strait of Messina south toward Libya and their launch positions. Five hours later, at 00:20 A.M. Libyan time, the carriers began launching 70 Navy and Marine Corps aircraft. Included in the naval air armada were A-6 strike aircraft, EA-6B electronic warfare aircraft, and A-7E and F/A-18 defense suppression aircraft, as well as other support and fighter cover forces.

The melding of the Air Force armada and Navy airpower worked exceedingly well, even with tightly controlled radio communications and other electronic emissions. About 10 minutes prior to the scheduled bombing attack (H hour), the radio waves were filled with Libyan chatter about confusing radar returns as heavy electronic countermeasures began to take effect. Defense suppression (suppression of enemy air defenses—SEAD) aircraft launched devastating attacks with antiradiation missiles on Libyan SAM sites. The result of all of this preattack preparation was that

- the Libyans were taken almost completely by surprise, even though they had received warnings from Malta,
- there were no passive defensive measures taken by the Libyans—in the cities, street lights continued to glow and even at the military airports, the runways were fully illuminated,
- SAMs were launched but in unguided modes and to no effect, and
- the Libyans did not launch a single aircraft in defense of the two target areas.

In the Tripoli target area, the attacking F-111s split into three groups as they crossed the Libyan coast at 200 feet and 540 miles per hour. Two groups turned quickly to the east to attack Sidi Balal and Bab al Azizia. The third group continued inland and then circled around to approach the military side of the Tripoli airport from the south. The F-111s made their bombing runs after climbing quickly above 500 feet to acquire their targets. Damage at all three targets was extensive, in spite of the fact that several of the aircraft did not deliver their ordnance because of very restrictive rules of engagement designed to limit collateral damage.

At the Benghazi target area, six Navy A-6 aircraft attacked the Jumahiriya barracks area using Snakeye retarded delivery bombs. Simultaneously, six A-6s armed with Rockeye cluster bombs and Snakeye weapons attacked the Benina airfield. Three Navy aircraft had aborted from this double raid because of equipment failure or due to the restrictive rules of engagement. Damage was heavy at both targets.

In just 11 minutes, the raid was over, and the raiding aircraft were heading out to sea, either to their carriers or toward the first refueling point on the grueling roundabout return flight to Great Britain. The only aircraft lost was one F-111. How and when it was lost remains somewhat of a mystery in the unclassified sources. Some reports indicate the aircraft went down prior to reaching its target—others indicate that the aircraft crashed after leaving the target area. Some reports indicate that the aircraft may have crashed because of battle damage, while others indicate that the loss may have been due to mechanical failure. In any event, attempts to find and rescue the crew were fruitless.

The Aftermath

It is clear that the raid inflicted significant high-visibility damage. Early damage estimates were disappointing, but subsequent damage photos and interviews with diplomatic personnel on the ground told a different story. Targeted buildings at each site were heavily damaged, and runways were badly cratered. At least two Il-76 transports were destroyed and another 10 heavily damaged. At least three, and perhaps as many as 14, MiG-23 aircraft were destroyed along with two Mi-8 helicopters and several small transport aircraft. Another 10 to 15 helicopters were badly damaged along with two Boeing 727 transport aircraft. The raid destroyed one SA-5 SAM site and inflicted serious damage on the tracking facilities of other SAM sites. This was, indeed, "high-visibility" damage.

Qaddafi added to the visibility in the aftermath by claiming that US bombs had killed his 15-month-old adopted daughter and wounded two of his six sons. There are at least some indications that these claims were either entirely or partially a hoax staged for propaganda purposes.[77]

282

There was, however, unfortunate collateral damage near both target sites. The most highly publicized damage was in the middle-class Bin Ashur district which included the French Embassy. The Libyan government claimed 17 died in that area. Nearly a month after the raid, the Defense Department admitted that bombs intended for Bab al-Azizia had caused the damage in the Bin Ashur district, apparently because the aircrew had picked up the wrong offset point on its radar. The Libyans also claimed much more widespread damage to civilian areas, but much of this was probably due to Libyan anti-aircraft ordnance. Indeed, one Libyan "showpiece" of collateral damage included what the Libyans claimed was wreckage of a downed US aircraft. It was later identified as a booster stage of a Libyan SA-3 surface-to-air missile.[78]

The world reaction, both officially and unofficially in newspapers, et cetera, was extremely negative. Only a handful of governments supported the US operation including Great Britain, Israel, Singapore, Australia, and Canada. However, a significant number of governments refused to take a position publicly, the most notable being Japan.

The more important question in the aftermath has to do with reaction in Libya, particularly in relation to the sponsorship of terrorist activities. Unfortunately, it is nearly impossible to correlate terrorist activities (or the lack thereof) to the Libyan air raid. In the first two weeks following the raid, there was a small flurry of terrorist attacks, but there is some evidence that many of these had been in work well before the raid. After that two-week period, things seem to have quietened considerably on the terrorist front. It is also true that Libyan-sponsored terrorist activity, particularly against US targets, declined significantly during the remainder of 1986 and all of 1987. It is also evident that the boldness of the US attack encouraged European security officials to take stricter measures in opposition to terrorism—particularly the expulsion of many Libyans from various "People's Bureaus" throughout western Europe. But again, a direct cause and effect relationship is impossible to prove and can only be suggested by juxtaposition of events. However, Brian Jenkins, renowned expert on international terrorism, stated, "Clearly the bombing of Libya changed the equation. It suggested to nations that use terrorism as an instrument of policy that they risk retaliation. They may choose to dismiss that risk or to accept it, but they're going to have to take it into account."[79]

Conclusions and Implications

The Malayan Emergency was not a large-scale affair. The guerrilla fighters never numbered more than 10,000 at any given time. The insurgents faced insurmountable problems which, in retrospect, probably doomed their movement from the beginning. However, the method with which the British approached the problem displayed shrewd insight that is instructive as we look to the future.

Many Western military establishments, including the US military, have muddled their thinking in regard to the so-called low-intensity conflict arena. Under the low-intensity rubric, we have lumped tactics (e.g., guerrilla tactics, terrorism), police operations (peacekeeping, peace enforcement), small wars, and short-term peacetime contingency operations (i.e., raids, rescues, etc.). Lost among all this flotsam, and thus not receiving the attention it deserves, is Maoist-based insurgency, also known as protracted revolutionary warfare.

As practiced by Mao, Giap, Che, and others, this form of warfare has been extraordinarily widespread, principally because it embodies an effective method for the "have nots" to confront the "haves," for those out of power to combat those in power, and for the weak to combat the strong. All of its many forms employ somewhat different techniques, but at the same time, they have more commonalties than they have differences. Insurgents take much of what we commonly understand about warfare and turn it on its ear. They create parallel and mutually supporting military and nonmilitary struggles, which produce a built-in advantage for the insurgents. The government under siege must win both struggles to survive while the insurgents need win only one of the contests to achieve victory. Insurgents draw their strength from the population of the society they target, which means that both the government and the insurgents have the same center of gravity. This phenomenon casts in doubt the conventional military strategy of attacking an enemy's center of gravity by putting fire and steel on target. Finally, insurgents use time as a weapon to sap the strength of governments which must have quick victory to preserve their popular support.

Protracted revolutionary warfare is a fundamentally different kind of warfare that has been exceedingly difficult to defeat. In its various forms it succeeded in China, in Vietnam twice, and in Cuba. The issue remains somewhat in doubt in Nicaragua, El Salvador, Peru, Cambodia, and Angola among other places. And yet, despite its widespread use and despite its widespread success, for the United States and many others in the West, it remains lost among the debris we have cast into the stewpot of low-intensity conflict. Thus we should look on the British experience in Malaya with admiration and renewed interest.

Unlike the French and Americans in Vietnam, the British understood the nature of the conflict they faced from the very beginning. Their strategy suited the situation and provided an apt counter to the unique "duality" of Maoist-based insurgencies—isolate the guerrilla fighters from their base of popular support (e.g., resettle the Chinese squatters), co-opt the populist goals of the revolution to defeat the nonmilitary portion of the insurgency (e.g., provide the squatters with security and the title to land), and then relentlessly pursue the guerrilla fighters with shot, shell, and propaganda. Eventually, those guerrilla fighters who survived just gave up and went home. The emergency ended with a whimper, not a bang.

The British use of airpower during the Malayan Emergency sat well with the overall strategy. British and Commonwealth airmen did not try to refight World War II European air campaigns in the jungles of Malaya. Rather, they tailored the use of airpower to fit the situation, the strategy, and the enemy. The military side of the British strategy did not overwhelm the nonmilitary side, and the application of airborne firepower, although important, was not the central thrust of the military side of the strategy.

There is little doubt that airlift was of prime importance to the successful application of force against the insurgents.

Without air transport the pursuit of the guerrilla forces would have been a much longer, more difficult, and bloodier affair. Psychological warfare waged from the air, either through cleverly done leaflets or through sky shouting was also effective, especially once the insurgents were cut off from their base of popular support, were hungry, and were on the run from government forces. The overall success of aerial spraying used to deny the insurgents locally grown food supplies is much more questionable. Whether or not the pain inflicted on the insurgents outweighed the difficulties inflicted on the indigenous jungle dwellers is a question which may never be resolved.

The major question about the use of airpower in Malaya and other wars of this type has to do with the value of aerial firepower. As discussed in the body of this paper, opinions vary. There is no question that it was difficult to deliver what we would now call close air support. Intelligence problems, targeting problems, response times, and weapon accuracy all played a role in making close air support less than totally effective. The same problems often plagued attempts to hit pinpoint targets such as insurgent encampments. Area bombing was even more controversial, causing few direct enemy casualties and, in the view of some, demonstrating weakness to the insurgents and their potential allies as hapless airmen flailed about wildly killing only innocent jungle creatures. Others believe that the constant harassment from the air, and the combination of area bombing with ambush operations on the ground, not only caused considerable enemy casualties but also had a deleterious impact on insurgent morale.

Many of the problems that British and Commonwealth airmen faced when applying aerial firepower in Malaya have been overcome or at least ameliorated by the advance of technology. Improved communications, improved navigational systems, sophisticated overhead intelligence gathering systems, improved weapons accuracy (including smart weapons), and improved air-to-ground coordination have increased the capability of airmen to provide effective close support in the most difficult circumstances. During its struggle in Vietnam, the US military used close air support extensively and effectively, and it became vitally important to ground forces.

Area bombing, too, became more directly effective in Vietnam if we put any credence in the reports coming from captured enemy soldiers. The technological improvements cited above helped in this effort. However, the major improvement may well have been in the load-carrying capacity of the B-52 bomber, particularly the Big Belly modification of the B-52D, which allowed the aircraft to carry as many as 105 500-lb bombs. Often flying in cells of three at altitudes too high for the enemy to see or hear their approach, their attacks could have a shocking and deadly impact on insurgent forces in the area.

Although technological advances may make the role of aerial firepower much more effective in future insurgencies than it was in the Malayan Emergency, the reader must remember that it will never be the dominant factor. The unique duality of Maoist-based insurgencies requires a dual military/nonmilitary counterinsurgency strategy in which both halves of the strategy have equal importance. Airpower can only play a significant role in half of the overall strategy, no matter how effective a weapon it becomes. The British understood this fundamental tenet and wove the use of their airpower into a much broader tapestry of counterinsurgency strategy.

The raids on Osirak and Libya illustrate what might become the most common use of airpower in the new world disorder. The proliferation of nuclear weapons, particularly to so-called rogue states, may be the plague of the twenty-first century. The Cold War—with both sides armed to the teeth with nuclear weapons—was a dangerous game for all to play. It was made safer by the fact that those who possessed nuclear weapons understood the dangers, understood the unwritten rules of international power politics, and played by those rules. This was particularly true after the Cuban missile crisis in 1962. After both sides approached the edge and peered into the nuclear abyss, neither side seriously tested the other. The Cuban experience chastened everyone. After 1962 the "delicate balance of terror" was much less delicate.

In the political chaos of the new world disorder, nuclear capabilities threaten to spread to those who may not understand the rules of international behavior or, worse yet, may not care about the accepted norms. Driven by unbridled ambition, religious extremism, or racial and ethnic hatreds, these rogue states have in many cases proven themselves a threat to others. North Korea, Iran, and Iraq are just three cases in point. It may well be that the international community as a whole, or coalitions within the community, or individual nations will find intolerable the prospect of nuclear weapons in the hands of rogue states. If so, the solution will almost certainly be a counterproliferation policy and strategy with military teeth to enforce the policy. The Israeli raid on Osirak illustrates just such a counterproliferation policy in action.

The possession of nuclear weapons by those who would use or threaten to use them irresponsibly is the ultimate form of terrorism. Terrorism has become the plague of the modern world. Whether state sponsored or the work of independent radical groups, it has ravaged civilized society. When terrorist attacks cross the threshold of outrage, the public will demand action against those who perpetrated the attacks. Whether or not military action can deter terrorist activities becomes an almost irrelevant question. The public will demand action which will likely result in future raids such as the 1986 attack on Libya.

Airpower will likely be the weapon of choice to enforce counterproliferation and counterterrorist policies for at least three reasons. First, airpower will often be the only military means capable of striking at the heart of the problem. Second, air strikes generally are over with quickly, creating less exposure and risk to the participants. In the Osirak case, once the Iraqis were actually building their reactor an air strike presented the best possibility for crippling destruction with minimum risk to those involved. Except for the possibility of infiltrating saboteurs (with the attendant risks of such an operation), airpower was the only way to reach the object of Israeli concern.

The third reason that will make airpower the weapon of choice in future is time. As with all international disputes, one would hope to solve proliferation problems through diplomacy, negotiation, mutual agreements, inspections by international organizations, and other such peaceful methods. Under normal circumstances the use of military force would be considered only as a last resort. However, in the case of proliferation this may not be the case. If, during prolonged diplomatic maneuvering, the state in question actually produces a nuclear weapon or brings a reactor on line, it may be too late for military reaction. Weapons in hand mean that nuclear retaliation is possible if military action fails to destroy all of the weapons available. Attacks on an operating nuclear reactor may result in a catastrophic nuclear incident affecting not only those in the target area but also those who undertook the attack. In either case, waiting to use military force as a last resort after the weapons are produced or until fragile reactors are on-line could result in exactly what the use of military force was trying to prevent. In short, the use of military force may not be the last resort in counterproliferation situations. Further, once the decision to use force is made, time may be critically important. Airpower, of all the military forces, is the most time sensitive in terms of both force preparation and mission execution.

The Libyan case illustrates that even when other forces could perform the required function, airpower often remains the means of choice. Significant "high-visibility" damage could have been brought to Qaddafi by having surface ships bombard Libyan coastal targets. The naval battle groups stationed in the Mediterranean had already demonstrated they could enter the Gulf of Sidra at will, and important Libyan targets would have been in range of naval gunfire.

But why put ships of the line in needless jeopardy? Why risk attacks by Libyan torpedo boats, submarines, and aircraft? Why put all of those sailors at risk (no matter how small the risk) when airpower—land and sea based—could deliver the blow with minimum risk to US blood and treasure? The answers to these questions were obvious, and airpower became the weapon of choice.

The Libyan raid also demonstrated the inherent limitations of both sea- and land-based airpower. Sea-based airpower is limited by the capacity of the ships upon which it is based (i.e., numbers of aircraft that are available), design limitations of aircraft which must take off from and land on carrier decks (i.e., generally shorter range and smaller payloads), and priority missions that limit the type of aircraft available (i.e., the priority given to fleet defense which limits the attack aircraft available). The result was that the Libyan raid became a very complex joint operation.

Just as the limitations of sea-based airpower all relate to its floating bases, so too are the limitations of land-based airpower related to its bases. In this case, the lack of political support from NATO allies prevented what could have been a simple, short-range strike launched from bases in the southern NATO area. Because political problems made these bases unavailable, the land-based portion of the Libyan strike became a very large, very complex, very grueling affair with many opportunities for things to go awry.

Taken together, the limitations of both land- and sea-based airpower meant that to mount the Libyan raid would require two carrier battle groups including some 17 ships, more than 150 aircraft, and nearly 15,000 sailors, plus Air Force F-111s, EF-111s, KC-10s, and KC-135s. This was a force larger than that employed by Great Britain during the entire Falklands campaign.[80] Taken together, the limitations of both land- and sea-based airpower illustrate the need for both kinds of airpower. The nearly flawless execution of the mission also illustrates how well both kinds of airpower can work together and the effective synergies they can produce.

The raids on Osirak and Libya also illustrate at least two other important points worthy of consideration as we look to the future. The first is the importance of meticulous planning. Air raids designed for very limited and specific purposes are not simple exercises, particularly when significant defenses must be overcome, collateral damage limited, and friendly lives protected. They become even more difficult when success must be achieved on the first attempt—second attempts being so potentially costly as to be out of the question. The Israelis spent nearly a year in preparation for Osirak, as best we can tell from an operation still shrouded in secrecy. The result was a near perfect mission which achieved its objectives at minimal cost both to the Israelis and in terms of collateral damage. The United States spent only three weeks in serious planning for the Libyan raid and had only one week from the president's decision to strike until execution of the raid. The raid was successful and was a model of complex planning and interservice cooperation. However, it was costly in terms of lives (two F-111 crew members) and treasure (one aircraft lost). Further, although the raid did result in the desired high-visibility damage, it resulted in less damage than desired on some targets and more collateral damage than desired. The luxury of more planning time might have been put to use profitably.

The second point is the importance of intelligence. Neither of these raids would have been possible without timely, accurate intelligence. It is almost a truism that airpower is targeting, and targeting is intelligence. But the intelligence required goes far beyond accurately identifying targets. Detailed knowledge of hostile defense systems is an absolute requirement if costs in blood and treasure are to be kept at acceptable levels. Intelligence becomes of paramount importance in a raid such as that on Osirak, where the Israelis planned to penetrate to the target with a very small force that depended on daring, stealth, and a detailed understanding of the air defenses of Saudi Arabia, Jordan, and Iraq. The raid on Libya also depended on daring and stealth, but the force was large enough and powerful enough to fight its way to its targets and, in fact, did so with its defense suppression efforts. But, effective defense suppression also relies on superior intelligence.

Although the military future of the new world order may continue to contain the possibility of large-scale conventional conflict, it is conceivable that the more probable use of military forces will be in very different circumstances. So long as those out of power seek power, so long as there are haves and have nots, so long as there are the weak who oppose the strong, there is the strong possibility that protracted revolutionary warfare will flourish. As demonstrated by the British in Malaya, there are effective counterinsurgent strategies, and airpower can play a significant role. The importance of airpower may go far beyond that achieved by the British because so many of the problems they faced have been overcome by technology. However, even the most powerful and sophisticated airpower employment will come to naught if it is not applied as part of a comprehensive military/nonmilitary strategy designed to combat the peculiarities of Maoist-based insurgencies.

In our new world order, the discrete use of airpower to achieve very specific and limited objectives may also be commonplace. So long as terrorism is seen by some as a viable and legitimate tactic in international power politics, airpower may be the weapon of choice to strike back at the sources of terrorist activities. Air raids on the sources of terrorism may not solve the problem, but they can provide the retribution the public will demand and in doing so may also provide considerable deterrent value.

The ultimate form of terrorism may stem from the proliferation of nuclear weapons into the hands of those whose motivations we only vaguely understand and who are willing to use any means to seek their desired ends. Counterproliferation—including military capability and the will to use it in a timely fashion—may be an absolute policy requirement in the new world order. If that is true, it is very likely that the only effective military capability we will be willing to use is airpower.

With all of this in mind, it appears to this observer that study of the Malayan Emergency and air raids such as those on Osirak and Libya may provide a window through which we can catch a glimpse of the future. These cases provide valuable food for thought—"lessons" if you prefer—that can stand airmen in good stead in the new world order.

Discussion

Air Commodore C. H. Spurgeon: I was the commanding officer of No. 1 Squadron in March 1956, and those 16 CTs [communist terrorists] that were knocked off by air action were mine. I'd been up there for 12 months, and we were officially credited with one dismembered elephant and countless monkeys. We had also destroyed about 35 percent of the foliage in Malaya by flying around in circles at night at low level dropping one bomb every 30 minutes. What the hell that did to anybody I don't know. Suffice to say that the operation referred to was singularly successful because we managed to hide the intelligence completely from the army. No one in the army knew that those CTs were there except for the sole special forces fellow who had found them. The mission was set up at 6:30 A.M., and we used one flare as an aiming point, or as a run-in point, and the bombs straddled that target perfectly. Sixteen people were killed, including Goh Peng Tuan who was the head of the Malayan communist organization in southern Johore. It's significant that two days previously, Chin Peng, who was the head of the whole Malayan communist organization, had made his first appearance in public in the north ready to parley. I think it was in a matter of five or six weeks thereafter that the final talks leading to the cessation of what had been called the emergency were held.

Air Commodore Garry Garrisson: First of all may I congratulate Colonel Drew on a wonderful presentation of the situation in Malaya and the use of airpower during the emergency. I take issue with Air Commodore Spurgeon and would like to make a few comments. First of all, the plan was to protect the villages so that the insurgents were not able to get any help from the people. The other thing was that airpower—the air bombing—kept the CTs off balance all the time. If a campsite was discovered, we'd go and bomb it, and after the bombing raid, we'd go down and strafe it. The idea was to keep the CTs on the move all the time. Also, as Colonel Drew mentioned, we could drive the terrorists into the hands of our army forces. Finally, I would say that a key to success in Malaya was the establishment of areas which were deemed "black" or "white," depending on whether or not they had been cleared of CTs, and which were in fact methodically cleared and made safe through joint air/land operations.

Colonel Drew: That's interesting, particularly when you look at the Vietnam experience. In Vietnam we never had a secure operating base anywhere. They were always insecure. Areas were cleared and then immediately infiltrated again once our troops left. We did not fight that war very smartly, and we didn't learn a lot from what went on in Malaya. I appreciate that the two situations were very different, but I don't think we did a very good job in trying to translate the lessons from one war to the other.

Dr. Iain Spence: Colonel, you suggested that airmen are not particularly keen on looking at campaigns like Malaya, perhaps because they feel they haven't much of a role to play. Perhaps also, airmen don't like to come too firmly under the command of soldiers. I wonder if you might comment on the command and control of air forces in Malaya compared to Vietnam.

Colonel Drew: During my research I didn't go into the command and control arrangements in Malaya. But I can't imagine they could have been any worse than was the case in Vietnam. In Vietnam we had as many as seven separate air wars going on at the same time, none of them under any kind of centralized control at all. The strange thing was, the air war over the North was centralized control run amok. It was centralized in Washington at the Tuesday afternoon lunch group, at which there wasn't even a military officer present until 1967. The rest of the air war was broken up into small fragments, and the command and control system frankly was a mess. There was no joint force air component commander. I think we've made a lot of progress since then.

Lieutenant General Ghani: Just two points. The fundamental difference between Malaysia and Vietnam was that in Malaysia 99.9 percent of the communist insurgents were Chinese immigrants, who in turn constituted less than 30 percent of the total population. That's a big difference and that's the reason the "sky shouting" psychological warfare broadcasts were done in the Chinese language. The insurgents didn't speak Malay.

My other point deals with the notion that the insurgency died with a whimper. In 1965, when the British left, there were still 3,000 insurgents under arms, many of them in southern Thailand, and the fighting did not end until 1989. The insurgency continued as an ember, but we would not let it become a major forest fire. The most critical part of the operation was the tremendous amount of psychological warfare and the widespread intelligence network. Neither of those activities would have succeeded without airpower.

Notes

1. Richard E. Simpkin, *Race to the Swift: Thoughts on Twenty-First Century Warfare* (London: Brassey's Defence Publishers, 1985). See in particular chap. 18, "The Relevance of Organised Forces," 283–96.

2. Martin L. van Creveld, *The Transformation of War* (New York: Free Press, 1991). Although this notion lies at the heart of van Creveld's thesis, it is perhaps best summed up in a short chapter entitled "Postscript: The Shape of Things to Come." In that postscript van Creveld cleverly states, "If no nuclear holocaust takes place, then conventional war appears to be in the final stages of abolishing itself; if one does take place, then it will already have abolished itself."

3. Edgar O'Ballance, *Malaya: The Communist Insurgent War, 1948–1960* (Hamden, Conn.: Archon Books, 1966), 64. For other sources of background information, see Daniel S. Challis, "Counterinsurgency Success in Malaya," *Military Review*, February 1987, 56–58.

4. O'Ballance, 63.

5. Challis, 57.

6. O'Ballance, 66; and Challis, 57.

7. Challis, 58–59.

8. O'Ballance, 78–79.

9. Challis, 60; and O'Ballance, 129. In Vietnam, both the Vietminh and later the Vietcong used terror tactics with considerable success. The difference in success had to do with the careful planning and targeting of terror. Rather than random violence, in Vietnam the terror was targeted to punish those who cooperated with the government. The result was that it became very unhealthy to be a village chief or other local official loyal to the government, or an agent of the government stationed in the countryside. To widen the terror, common villagers were also killed or kidnapped in those villages that resisted Vietcong infiltration and control. See George McTurnan Kahin and John Wilson Lewis, *The United States in Vietnam*, rev. ed. (New York: Dell Publishing Co., 1969), 137–39; Bernard B. Fall, *Viet-Nam Witness, 1953–66* (New York: Frederick A. Praeger, 1966), 279–83; and Guenter Lewy, *America in Vietnam* (New York: Oxford University Press, 1978), 88.

10. Philip Towle, "The RAF and the Malayan Insurgency," *Air Clues*, August 1989, 290.

11. The British level of understanding about the nature of Maoist-based insurgency is in sharp contrast, according to many analysts, to the US failure to understand the nature of their struggle during the Vietnam War, particularly during the period from 1965–1968. See Mark Clodfelter, *The Limits of Airpower: The American Bombing of North Vietnam* (New York: Free Press, 1989); Lewy; Earl H. Tilford Jr., *Setup: What the Air Force Did in Vietnam and Why* (Maxwell Air Force Base [AFB], Ala.: Air University Press, 1991); and the author's *Rolling Thunder 1965: Anatomy of a Failure*, CADRE Paper (Maxwell AFB, Ala.: Air University Press, 1986).

12. Air Publication (AP) 3410, *The Malayan Emergency 1948–1960*, Royal Air Force, Ministry of Defence, June 1970 (hereinafter referred to as AP 3410). Also see Towle, 286; O'Ballance, 106; and Challis, 62.

13. In Vietnam, the strategic hamlet program was designed to accomplish the same ends. However, the situation was entirely different and the program was, to a large extent, a failure. In many cases the program actually alienated those affected. Lewy writes, "The peasants resented having to leave their homes and gardens and being herded into fortified stockades which the government forced them to build without compensation." Lewy, 25. Kahin and Lewis address the differing results directly, "American advisors in Vietnam were initially highly enthusiastic over prospects of the strategic hamlets because of the success of the British a decade earlier in the resettlement program in Malaya. Having little knowledge of the very different social and political conditions governing the Malayan experience, they jumped to the quite mistaken conclusion that what had worked in Malaya ought to work in Vietnam. . . . the British . . . had undertaken to move recently settled alien Chinese squatters. . . . in South Vietnam those who were forced to resettle were indigenous peasants, with strong local roots, living in socially cohesive communities, where family ties with the land went back as much as two centuries."

14. O'Ballance, 177; and Challis, 68.

15. Robert Jackson, *The Malayan Emergency: The Commonwealth's Wars, 1948–1966* (London: Routledge, 1991).

16. AP 3410, 39.

17. AP 3410.

18. O'Ballance, 133–34; and AP 3410, 39–40.

19. E. D. Smith, *Malaya and Borneo*, Counter-Insurgency Operations Series (London: Ian Allan, Ltd., 1985); AP 3410, 41; and O'Ballance, 133–34.

20. Jackson, 78.

21. AP 3410, 72.

22. Jackson, 78.

23. AP 3410, 74.

24. Jackson, 78.

25. Towle, 286.

26. Brig Richard L. Clutterbuck, *The Long War: Counterinsurgency in Malaya and Vietnam* (New York: Frederick Praeger, 1966).

27. M. J. Armitage and R. A. Mason, *Air Power in the Nuclear Age*, 2d ed. (Urbana, Ill.: University of Illinois Press, 1985), 67–69.

28. John Coates, *Suppressing Insurgency: An Analysis of the Malayan Emergency, 1948–1954* (Boulder, Colo.: Westview Press, 1992), 172–73.

29. AP 3410, 77.

30. Coates, 171.

31. AP 3410, 85.

32. Clutterbuck, 159; and Towle, 288. However, Towle notes that an SAS study indicated that "the accumulation of casualties from this type of parachuting was such that no training jumps were permitted."

33. Smith, 41.

34. Towle, 288.

35. O'Ballance notes, "Templer's policy was to gain the hearts and minds of the people. . . . This was indeed taking a leaf from the communist insurgent handbook. Mao Tse-tung had always insisted that the most important aim in the struggle was to win a person's mind, which was far more important than military victories." O'Ballance, 129.

36. Towle, 287.

37. Jackson, 110–11.

38. Towle, 288; Jackson, 112–13.

39. Jackson, 112–13.

40. Towle (page 288) states, "Some 70 percent of the guerrillas who surrendered said that their decision to do so had been influenced by the skyshouters." Jackson (page 114) says, "70 percent of all surrendered terrorists who had heard an aerial broadcast stated that it had influenced their decision to give themselves up, *and in many cases it had been the major factor involved.*" [Emphasis added.] These are two very different statements about the overall effectiveness of the loudhailing program.

41. O'Ballance, 136; and Towle, 287.

42. Jackson, 102–3.

43. Jackson.

44. Towle, 287.

45. "What Israel Knew," *Newsweek*, 22 June 1981, 25.

46. Lucien S. Vandenbroucke, "The Israeli Strike against Osiraq: The Dynamics of Fear and Proliferation in the Middle East," *Air University Review*, September–October 1984, 36–37.

47. George Russell, "Attack—and Fallout," *Time*, 22 June 1981, 26.

48. Russell, 26; "What Israel Knew," 25. Russell maintains that the damage done to the nuclear reactor core was so extensive that the reactor's delivery was delayed for two years. The editors of *Newsweek* maintain that the bomb only caused "minor damage."

49. Russell, 26; "What Israel Knew," 25–26. The US Department of State believed the actual attack on the reactor on 30 September was carried out by the Iranian air force. House, *Israeli Attack on Iraqi Nuclear Facilities: Hearings before the Subcommittees on International Security and Scientific Affairs, on Europe and the Middle East and on International Economic Policy and Trade of the Committee on Foreign Affairs*, 97th Cong., 1st sess., 17 and 25 June 1981, 17.

50. The reader should note that the actual preparations for the raid remain shrouded in secrecy and disinformation. The news sources cited in the following paragraphs are both reliable and knowledgeable and have used extensive on-the-scene sources. Further, the author has attempted to cite only material that seems plausible given the stunning success of the raid and to identify those issues over which the news reports provided conflicting information.

51. One source ("What Israel Knew," 26) indicates that serious planning did not begin until the summer of 1980, when Israel took delivery of the first F-16 fighter-bombers it had ordered from the United States in August of

1977 and after the delivery of an unsatisfactory French reply to an Israeli diplomatic protest. On the other hand, Russell, 27, indicates that preparation began in 1979 and that the Israelis originally planned to use F-4 Phantom fighter-bombers which were already in the Israeli Air Force inventory. The 1979 date seems much more likely to be accurate given the scale of preparations required.

52. "Two Minutes Over Baghdad," *Newsweek*, 22 June 1981, 22; and Russell, 27.

53. "Two Minutes Over Baghdad," 22. Avoiding AWACS did not pose a difficult problem because the AWACS aircraft flew patrol orbits far enough to the south that the route into Baghdad was beyond the effective range of the airborne radar.

54. The following paragraphs which outline what is known about the details of the raid itself were derived from the sometimes conflicting accounts in *Newsweek*, "Two Minutes Over Baghdad," 23–24; Russell, 27–28. Conflicting information is highlighted in the following notes.

55. Russell, 27.

56. "Two Minutes Over Baghdad," 22–23.

57. That the reactor was actually destroyed was the judgment 10 years later of Efraim Karsh and Inari Rautsi in *Saddam Hussein: A Political Biography* (London: Brassey's Defence Publishers, 1991), 128.

58. Attempting to determine whether or not "smart" weapons were used is very tricky. One might think that it would be good for the Israelis to let their hostile neighbors know that they had and could use such sophisticated weapons. On the other hand, in the Byzantine world of Mid-East politics, it might be better for the Israelis to impress their neighbors with the consummate skill of Israeli airmen by denying that they used smart weapons.

59. Karsh and Rautsi, 128.

60. A Congressional Research Service report prepared for congressional hearings in the wake of the Israeli raid concluded that it was possible for the Iraqis to have had a plutonium device in just over a year of the Israeli raid or a uranium-based device within a few months. House, *Israeli Attack on Iraqi Nuclear Facilities*, appendix 2, Congressional Research Service, "How Long Would it Take for Iraq to Obtain a Nuclear Explosive After its Research Reactor Began Operation?" 18 June 1981, 88–90.

61. Typical of articles in various journals condemning the raid was B. A. Hamzah, "Israel Flouts International Law," *Asian Defence Journal*, August 1981, 82–83.

62. Vandenbroucke, 44.

63. Brian L. Davis, *Qaddafi, Terrorism, and the Origins of the US Attack on Libya* (New York: Praeger, 1990), 58–69. Davis includes a litany of bombings, kidnappings, hijackings, and assassinations that is far too lengthy and detailed for this paper. Many, of course, were not aimed at the United States, but in many of these cases American casualties resulted. The result was a growing sense of both fear and outrage.

64. Davis, 66–67.

65. Konrad Alder, "An Eye for an Eye, A Tooth for a Tooth," *Amada International*, January 1987, 35; and Davis, 76–78.

66. Lt Comdr Robert E. Stumpf, "Air War with Libya," US Naval *Proceedings*, August 1986, 42–48; Alder, 35; and Davis, 89, 101–4.

67. Stumpf, 46–47; and Alder, 36.

68. William R. Doerner, "In the Dead of the Night," *Time*, 28 April 1986, 28; and Davis, 115–19.

69. Davis, 119–20; and Doerner, 28.

70. Doerner, 29; "US Demonstrates Advanced Weapons Technology in Libya," *Aviation Week & Space Technology*, 21 April 1986, 19–20; and "Reagan's Raiders," *Newsweek*, 28 April 1986, 26–27.

71. "Getting Rid of Kaddafi," *Newsweek*, 28 April 1986, 18; Doerner, 29; and Davis, 36.

72. "Getting Rid of Kaddafi," 18.

73. Anthony H. Cordesman, "After the Raid: The Emerging Lessons from the US Attack on Libya," *Armed Forces*, August 1986, 36.

74. Doerner, 28–29; and "A New Kind of War," *Newsweek*, 28 April 1986, 16–17.

75. The following paragraphs which outline the details of the air raid execution are compiled from the following sources: Davis, 133–34; Doerner, 28–31; "Reagan's Raiders," 26–28; Adler, 37–39; Stumpf, 48; "US Demonstrates Advanced Weapons," 19–21; and Cordesman, 360.

76. The difference in the number of refuelings required was caused by (1) a lighter load on the return trip because of expended ordnance and (2) some legs of the flight inbound to the targets were flown at very low level while the return trip was flown at much more fuel-efficient altitudes.

77. Davis, 141–42.

78. Richard Stengel, "So Close, Yet So Far," *Time*, 28 April 1986, 32; Ruth Marshall, "A View From the Bull's-eye," *Newsweek*, 28 April 1986, 30; "Reagan's Raiders," 26; Davis, 140–42; and Doerner, 30.

79. Brian Jenkins quoted in the *Los Angeles Times*, 11 October 1987, and in Davis, 168.

80. Cordesman, 358; and Doerner, 28.

Soviet Airpower in the
New Russian Mirror

Benjamin S. Lambeth[1]

In his masterful account of the Red Air Force's epic rise from near-disaster following the German onslaught in the summer of 1941 to its triumphant recovery four years later as the world's largest tactical air arm, Von Hardesty ably described how this trial by fire had the ironic effect of providing Soviet combat aviation with "an accelerated passage to modernization and power."[2] In the immediate wake of the Soviet Union's sudden implosion in December 1991, almost exactly five decades after the start of Operation Barbarossa, the Soviet air force (*Voenno-vozdushniye sily*, or VVS) experienced an all too similar, if less apocalyptic, trauma. Almost overnight, it plummeted from its lofty status as a giant of some 20,000 pilots and 13,000 aircraft to become a new, and greatly impaired, organization of 13,000 pilots and only 5,000 aircraft, mostly of obsolescent design.[3]

To make matters worse, the VVS, like the other four services of the former Soviet Union, found itself possessed of few resources with which to catalyze and sustain a prompt recovery. To this day, more than two years later, it remains embarked on an uncertain quest for renewed vitality and a new operational role in the post-Soviet and post-Cold-War world. For its current leaders, as for their predecessors in 1941, the crucial question concerns whether the blend of crisis and opportunity that circumstances forced upon them portends a fate of inexorable decline or, in Hardesty's formulation, offers a fortuitous springboard from which they might discover anew "an accelerated passage to modernization and power."

The abortive coup attempt of August 1991 that started the clock ticking toward the collapse of communism four months later affected the VVS much as it did the other Soviet services—and Soviet society across the board. With the old order roundly discredited and stripped of any lingering claim to legitimacy, the path was cleared for "new looks" at all aspects

of the VVS's repertoire that had been driven by the idiosyn-
crasies of the Soviet state. At the same time, most remaining
strictures against freedom of expression within the military
were lifted. As the VVS's monthly magazine later commented
in this regard, "glasnost continues to uncover an interminable
stream of problems that used to be kept silent in the life of our
armed forces."[4]

The first consequence of note for the VVS was a change in
leadership at the top. From his first days as commander in
chief starting in July 1990, Col Gen Yevgeny Shaposhnikov
had shown ample signs of being a reform-minded leader with
little patience for the hidebound ways of communist bureaucracy. Even Alexander Zuyev, the former VVS captain who
defected to the United States via Turkey by flying a stolen
MiG-29 from his base at Mikha Tskhakaya in Soviet Georgia
to Trabzon on the Black Sea in May 1989, later remarked that
Shaposhnikov was well regarded among squadron pilots.
Commenting on Shaposhnikov's role in thwarting the 1991
coup attempt, Zuyev characterized the VVS chief as "a real
reformer, a patriotic professional officer who knew where his
true loyalties lay."[5]

This impression was validated when, among all the Soviet
military chiefs, Shaposhnikov drew the line most forcefully
against Defense Minister Dmitri Yazov and others on the high
command who had supported or sympathized with the plot-
ters. For refusing to abide the coup attempt, Shaposhnikov
was selected to replace the disgraced Yazov once the back of
the putsch was broken. Shortly thereafter, he was elevated to
the rank of marshal of aviation.[6] To take over his vacated post
as VVS commander in chief, he picked his first deputy, Col
Gen Petr Stepanovich Deinekin.[7]

Unlike many previous VVS commanders, whose background
had been in fighters, Petr Deinekin rose through the ranks of
the Soviet bomber community. The son of a fighter pilot who
died in 1943 while flying a LaGG-3 during the Great Patriotic
War, he aspired to the Balashov VVAUL (*Vysheye voennoye
aviatsionnoye uchilishchye letchikov*, or Higher Military
Aviation School for Pilots) and eventually earned his wings as
a bomber pilot, later serving on squadron duty and, in time,

commanding a Tu-22M Backfire regiment. After that, he commanded an air division, an air army, and ultimately Long-Range Aviation (LRA) before being tapped by Shaposhnikov to become first deputy VVS commander in chief in 1990. During his career progression, he attended the Gagarin Air Academy and later graduated with honors from the Voroshilov General Staff Academy. He has 5,000 hours of flying time, including an initial qualification checkout in the Tu-160 Blackjack.

What kind of new Russian Air Force, under General Deinekin's command, is now emerging from the wreckage of communism and the old Soviet system? A full treatment would explore planned VVS reorganization, force development, pilot training, unit operations, and roles and missions as Russia's air arm slowly rebuilds itself for the post-Cold-War world. This chapter is mainly an initial damage assessment aimed at addressing those preoccupations that weigh most heavily on General Deinekin's mind as he seeks, first and foremost, to ensure his air force's survival as an institution. Because of its high-technology orientation and the special demands on resources that this focus naturally entails, the VVS is arguably hurting more than other services from Russia's economic crisis. It bears noting, however, that much of what will be etched out below regarding the VVS's post-Soviet tribulations can be said of the Russian armed forces as a whole. In this respect, General Deinekin is scarcely alone among his fellow service chiefs in the many difficulties he faces.

The Soviet Legacy

Military aviation has enjoyed a long and prominent tradition in Russia, predating—and thus far surviving—the 74-year intercession of Soviet communism. To note some of the high points, the world's first loop maneuver was performed by Maj Petr Nesterov in 1913. Russia developed and successfully flew the world's first four-engine strategic bomber, Igor Sikorsky's *Ilya Muromets*, over the eastern front in World War I. Valery Chkalov commanded a pioneering flight in 1937 from Moscow to Vancouver via the North Pole.[8] Soviet airmen fought valiantly in World War II and played a key role in the defeat of Nazi Germany.[9]

303

The Union of Soviet Socialist Republics (USSR) led the way in jet aviation as well, with the introduction of the MiG-15 fighter in 1948. This was the world's first high-performance combat aircraft by modern standards, and it proved to be at least a technical match for the American F-86 in the skies over Korea. In 1961, a Soviet fighter pilot, Yury Gagarin, became the first man to orbit the Earth. Throughout the Cold War, the VVS was uniformly recognized by Western defense experts to be a formidable fighting force. By any measure, it and the Soviet aircraft industry, from their austere beginnings in the early 1920s to the enthralling flight demonstrations of the MiG-29 during its Western debut at the 1988 Farnborough Air Show, earned the USSR—and now Russia—legitimate pride of place as an aviation giant.

Despite this rich background, most Westerners were only able to follow developments in Soviet military aviation from a distance until recently because of the Communist Party's obsession with secrecy and societal closure. To all intents and purposes, the VVS was a denied area, a central component of the Soviet threat, and thus an object, first and foremost, of Western intelligence concern. Other observers had to view it darkly in an effort to understand what was going on beneath the often tantalizing, but rarely satisfying, appearances provided by the Soviet press and by periodic Western threat portrayals.

Because of this indistinctness, two noted British aviation experts pointed out as recently as 1986 that "any attempt to describe the way aircraft are incorporated into the Soviet Air Forces, how they train, how they contribute to Soviet operational doctrine, and above all, how militarily effective they are, must be circumscribed again and again by conditions that apply in few other areas of military study."[10] These analysts offered four compelling reasons why any sweeping statements about the VVS needed to be advanced with the greatest care:

> First, Russia goes to great lengths to conceal evidence of a kind which in the West may be found in technical journals, obtained from conversations, and observed on airfields. Second, much of the evidence which does become available is fragmented, sometimes contradictory, and frequently open to varying interpretations. Third, interpretation of that evidence, like any other, is susceptible to the preconceptions of the analyst. Finally, even if the evidence was comprehensive and the

analysis always well judged and objective, the factors making up the equation of Soviet military effectiveness are so variable that a wide range of solutions would still be possible.

That was wise counsel at the time it was written. Today, however, with the Cold War over and the Soviet Union a fading relic of history, such obstructions to analysis have substantially receded. As a result, we are now increasingly able to study airpower developments in Russia much as we would study military aviation in any other country. The Russian media, including the military and technical press, have more and more become an open book. More important yet, Russia's military and industry leaders have become increasingly accessible to their foreign counterparts and have shown a steadily expanding willingness to engage in dialogue with Western defense experts.

These newly opened doors have revealed a Russian Air Force in the throes of a painful but determined metamorphosis. It is unmistakably embarked on a course of post-Soviet reform, yet it remains uncertain of its future as it strives to embrace the twenty-first century as a renewed institution. Even before the collapse of communism, there were gathering signs that the VVS, like the Soviet military as a whole, was entering its most turbulent time since its wartime trials in the early 1940s. Foremost among its challenges was adjusting to the radically changed setting of the post-Cold-War world at a time of deepening domestic political and economic duress.

For one thing, the end of the Cold War and the demise of the Warsaw Pact had left the VVS with no obvious threat and no clear mission beyond homeland defense. The "Warsaw Pact Air Operation," for which Soviet pilots and commanders had purportedly planned and trained for years, had become moot almost overnight. At the same time, the fact that air defense was now obliged to begin at Russia's western edge meant that the VVS and VPVO (*Voiska protivovozdushnoi oborony,* or Air Defense Forces) had assumed new responsibilities for which they were ill configured or prepared.

Beyond that, the freedom of expression made possible by President Mikhail Gorbachev's policy of *glasnost* introduced in 1986 had prompted an unprecedented venting of complaints throughout the armed forces. As a result, the VVS found itself besieged by a multitude of pressures from below. Among the issues with which its leadership now had to contend were declining aircrew morale and retention, the eroding quality and number of recruits to flight academies, severe housing shortages and an appalling quality of life for pilots and their families, a growing acknowledgment of deficiencies in tactical air training, mindless administrative detail and paper-chasing at the squadron and regiment level, problems of honesty and integrity within flying units, increasing concerns about the quality and reliability of the equipment provided by the aviation industry, and a mounting recognition among Soviet pilots of the substantial inequalities between their own and Western equipment and training.

Fortunately, the information explosion occasioned by *glasnost* and the collapse of the Soviet state has made developments in the armed forces of the former USSR much easier to read in detail. In the case of the VVS, the result has been to bring to the surface a number of issues concerning aircrew training, tactics development, and flight operations at the squadron and regiment level that had long simmered but remained largely suppressed by the Communist Party's intolerance of open dissent. In the process, some questions that were hotly debated among Western analysts in the 1980s without resolution have been put to rest by the frank admissions that Soviet—and now Russian—airmen have freely offered in more recent years. For much of this, we can thank the honesty and candor of the VVS leadership itself.

A Growing Crisis in Soviet Fighter Training

To review that background briefly, Western fighter pilots and threat assessors began paying serious attention to Soviet air combat training for the first time during the mid-1970s, when the United States Air Force's (USAF) Aggressor squadrons became operational and Red Flag was introduced as a routine training activity at Nellis Air Force Base, Nevada. For most of the decade that followed, Soviet tactical air activity remained an object of intense interest, as well as extensive guesswork, in Western tactical air circles. It was commonly assumed that the Soviet pilot was bound by a heavily scripted tactical repertoire that was all but completely dominated by ground control. This, it was generally thought, left him little room for the free-form initiative and adaptability that had long been a hallmark of Western tactical air practice.

Because first-hand information on Soviet training and tactics was largely unavailable, this impression was based heavily on the observed practices of the air forces of Moscow's military clients, notably North Vietnam, Egypt, and Syria. It gained further reinforcement from the informed comment of occasional defectors and from various inferences one could draw from a careful reading of articles appearing in *Aviatsiia i kosmonavtika*, the Soviet air force's monthly journal, and other military publications.[11]

There was anything but agreement, however, over the extent to which this assumed deficiency in Soviet tactical air prowess was an inherent condition of Soviet fighter aviation, let alone a weakness that mattered much in a military organization that was widely believed to be ready as a matter of practice to trade high loss rates for victory. Intense debates ensued among Western fighter pilots and threat assessors as protagonists for various points of view sought to justify their respective interpretations of the Soviet tactical air challenge. Each school of thought was able to draw sustenance from the inherent ambiguity surrounding much of the hard data on the Soviet tactical air arm and its operational activities.

A pointed attempt to discredit the view widely held among American and NATO European pilots took sharp exception to their inclination to dismiss their Soviet counterpart as "virtually a puppet, rigidly controlled by GCI [ground controlled intercept] and acting as little more than flying artillery."[12] This argument maintained, "The situation has changed considerably in the last few years. The Soviets have entered a period of intense study and discussion of their theory of tactics and are beginning to implement changes in their operational training." A similar contention was reflected in the claim of a US Defense Department publication in 1983 that "the Soviets have recently made significant changes in their air combat tactics and training programs. Pilot independence and initiative are now stressed."[13]

A starkly contrasting view was this appraisal offered by a USAF Aggressor squadron commander no less well informed on Soviet fighter weapons and tactics: "Exactly how good is the enemy? Is he a ten-foot giant? Not exactly. In fact, without exaggerating, one could place him in the mediocre to poor category when it comes to air combat capability. Certainly his equipment has not improved at nearly the rate ours has. Most important, however, Soviet training is so inferior to ours that this could well be the deciding factor in the outcome of the next conflict."[14]

This latter appraisal was based in part on the poor Soviet showing a decade earlier, when five Soviet-flown MiG-21s were summarily downed by Israeli F-4s and Mirages, with no Israeli losses, in an intense aerial engagement over Suez during the 1970 War of Attrition. It was further supported by the known fact that Soviet air doctrine required most sorties to be flown under the close control of a ground-based mission supervisor, with the added proviso that if contact with the controller were lost, the mission was to be aborted.[15]

Such was the evidence that largely informed the prevailing Western view that the typical Soviet fighter pilot was an acknowledged professional in his basic flying skills, yet remained largely untutored in the ingrained situation awareness, free-form tactical moves, and ability to think ahead in a dynamic, multiparticipant engagement that made the crucial difference between winning and losing in aerial combat.[16] Contention persisted among American fighter pilots and threat assessors, almost up to the demise of the USSR, over the ultimate meaning of that fact for Soviet war-fighting capability. Most American pilots, however, seemed ready to accept as axiomatic this characterization offered by a US naval reserve F-4 pilot: "I have found that asking two US pilots for their tactics in a given situation elicits three different answers. By contrast, it is my understanding that three Russian fighter pilots will all give the same answer."[17]

That impression gained powerful backing from an account in 1986 by a British aviation writer based on interviews with

Indian air force pilots, who spoke freely of their experiences and frustration while undergoing MiG-21 conversion training in the USSR during the early 1970s.[18] Although those interviews reflected dated information, they dovetailed nicely with the picture offered by more current indicators, including periodic veiled complaints voiced by operational pilots in the VVS's monthly journal. The essence of that picture was that continuity far outweighed change during the intervening years.

According to this report, the VVS followed a syllabus approach throughout the service life of the MiG-21 which assumed that the student had an almost complete lack of understanding of fighter aircraft, as well as an entrenched incapacity to learn other than through repetitive instruction over a prolonged period. This was most unsettling to the Indians, who were experienced pilots brought up in the manner of the Royal Air Force. Although they did not "buck the system," they were facing an imminent war with Pakistan and needed to know the MiG-21 to its limits. Yet they literally had to beg to try anything of tactical relevance or value.[19] All in all, they said, the Soviet approach was to instruct "rather in the way small children learn multiplication tables," with students frequently "chanting the correct answers in unison. Any deep thought about how to get the best out of one's aircraft, or even hack an unusual situation, was simply not part of the syllabus."[20]

Fortunately for our understanding of this once-elusive subject, the fruits of *glasnost* and democratization have more and more made Soviet—and now Russian—operational style an open book to attentive outside observers. In so doing, they have helped break down much of the mystery that, in previous years, shrouded all but the broadest outlines of Soviet fighter employment practice.

The Enduring Importance of Russian Airpower

Why should anyone care today about an air force that has been declared to be no longer a threat to Western security—and, indeed, that finds itself operating in virtually a survival mode? For one thing, the frank admissions of VVS pilots and commanders at all levels since the beginning of *glasnost* give us an unprecedented chance to update and, where necessary, correct our past impressions of the VVS. Beyond that, better knowledge of where the air arm of the former USSR stands today can shed useful light on the future course it may take once the current post-Soviet reform effort establishes an even keel. Whatever difficulties and transition pains the VVS may be experiencing today, there is little doubt that Russia will eventually emerge from the collapse of communism as a strong nation. There is also little doubt that the VVS will constitute an important part of its military capability.

By far the greatest value to be gained from the recent opening up of the Russian armed forces, including the VVS, however, is the prospect that this unprecedented access offers us for becoming better acquainted with a potential fellow air force at a time when markedly improved, if still turbulent, East-West relations portend closer contacts between the VVS and its former adversary air forces around the world. To cite one notable example, the current tone in the relationship between the US Air Force and the VVS was established by the two service chiefs in separate interviews during a visit by the USAF chief of staff, Gen Merrill A. McPeak, to Moscow in October 1991. General Deinekin remarked first that "it is important today to strengthen friendship not only among ministers, commanders in chief, and generals, but also among officers. [General McPeak] and I talked about the fact that pilots are a special fraternity. . . . I am in favor of beginning visits with the US Air Force in the future."

When later asked for his thoughts on when "friendship and exchanges among our aces will become commonplace," the USAF chief replied:

> I believe it will be some time before we arrive at that point. But I hope that relations between the air forces of our countries will become stronger. We constantly exchange pilots with France, Great Britain, Germany. . . . I am confident that your country will be no exception. There is a respectful attitude toward Soviet military pilots, and we could learn a lot from them. I do not see any obstacles to improving relations. We will treat each other with mutual respect and even, I hope, become friends.[21]

Against the reasonable chance that such contacts will become more and more routine in the months and years ahead, it behooves Western airmen to do as much as possible now to become better informed about their Russian counterparts.

This argument takes on added strength in light of the striking similarity between many of the problems currently faced by the VVS and its most advanced Western counterparts. Among the most acute concerns confronting the VVS today are a need to harness new technology to mission requirements at an affordable cost, enlisting and retaining high-quality people, keeping the defense industry accountable to the expectations of VVS planners, sustaining the morale and motivation of VVS personnel, especially aircrews, at a time of major budget and force reductions, and assuring that the VVS develops the organizational adaptability it will need to survive as a healthy institution in the twenty-first century.

These problems are not, in their fundamentals, all that different from those facing most Western air forces today. Indeed, they are compounded many times over in the case of the VVS by Russia's continuing political and economic crisis. All the more so for that reason, it may be instructive for Western planners to observe how the Russians are grappling with familiar challenges in a much more demanding situation than anything we have had to confront, at least so far.

Many of the complaints expressed by Russian pilots and unit commanders since the onset of *glasnost* sound remarkably similar to those voiced for seemingly time immemorial by their Western counterparts. Indeed, they tend to bear out the popular notion that some such complaints simply go with the trade. These include, among other things, such perennial vexations as overly intrusive higher-headquarters meddling in day-to-day flight operations, seemingly endless paperwork and bureaucratic overlay at the squadron and regiment level, burdensome additional duties for line pilots, and the continuing tension between the demands of flight safety and the often conflicting imperatives of operational realism in peacetime training.

Russian pilots and commanders have also become increasingly outspoken with regard to more fundamental concerns, such as misplaced service priorities, rampant careerism and compromises of integrity by commanders looking mainly to "get ahead" within the system, and a consequent loss of vision and sense of purpose by the institution as a whole. These, too, are problems of a sort not unknown in other air forces around the world. To varying degrees, they seemed to dominate VVS practice right up to the end of the Soviet experience in 1991.

The one problem that remains unique to the VVS, however, is the top-down rigidity in both operations and thought which the communist system, for years, imposed on line pilots and commanders, who knew better but were obliged to pretend otherwise. *This* is the legacy of the now-discredited Soviet approach to operations and training that Russian airmen will have to work the hardest to overcome.

New Priorities and Concerns

General Deinekin faces an array of headaches and challenges as least as thorny as those besetting any other air chief in the world today. Upon his assumption of command of the Russian Air Force, he inherited a near-total inversion of the priorities that typically concern a peacetime military aviation establishment. Matters like force modernization, training and tactics, and similar mission-related preoccupations have taken a back seat to the more pressing demands of simply housing and caring for badly deprived personnel. Among other vexations, General Deinekin has been saddled with a severely curtailed procurement and operations budget, a fuel shortage of crisis dimensions, a bloated pilot-to-aircraft ratio further aggravating the insufficiency of available flying hours for Russian aircrews, widespread maintenance problems caused by a dearth of spare parts and the failure of the conscription system, a rising aircraft accident rate as a result of these negative influences, and a precipitous drop in the former prestige and respectability of air force service, with potentially grave implications for future officer recruitment.

The Collapse of State Financing for Defense

During the final days of its existence in late 1991, the Soviet Defense Ministry reported that outlays for weapons and associated procurement had fallen by 23 percent, or by 7.2 billion rubles, from the previous level in 1990. It anticipated that a comparable reduction would occur in 1992, meaning that defense production would be effectively halved from the baseline 1989 level.[22] In the end, the VVS received only 15 percent of the allocations for research and development (R&D) and procurement that it was expecting in 1992. This forced it to buy equipment at the barest minimum level required to ensure that Russia's aircraft industry would not become completely moribund. Even such elementary provisions as flight suits and helmets are in critically short supply.[23]

> Shortly before his appointment as first deputy minister of defense, Andrei Kokoshin, then-deputy director of the USA and Canada Institute, predicted that Russia's defense industry would receive virtually no production orders in 1992, since all available funds had to be used to clothe and house military personnel.[24] By late 1993, promised funding allotments from the Ministry of Finance had fallen so far behind, complained Kokoshin, that the Defense Ministry was a full trillion rubles in arrears to the defense industry for goods and services already delivered.[25]

The inertia of the old Soviet system, which routinely favored strategic missiles and armor, still dies slowly. Today, according to General Deinekin, aviation equipment accounts for only 12 to 15 percent of Russia's arms purchases, as contrasted to an asserted 25 to 30 percent in the United States. Since the USSR's collapse, the VVS has been forced to cancel any further purchases of the MiG-29. It has also had to defer production of several improved variants of the Su-27, which have been designated by the VVS as the intended mainstays of Russia's fighter inventory for at least the remainder of this century. Galloping inflation since President Boris Yeltsin's elimination of state price controls in January 1992 has driven up the cost of current-generation aircraft more than 20-fold. Research, development, test, and evaluation (RDT&E) on new aircraft have largely been frozen, and the financing of several promising prototype programs has reportedly been halted.

A Growing Pilot Surplus

The VVS's pilot-to-aircraft ratio has more than doubled since the collapse of the USSR. General Deinekin stated in early 1992 that it had risen to three pilots for each flyable aircraft because of force reductions and accelerated unit withdrawals from Eastern Europe and the former Baltic republics.[26] He later remarked that in some units, the ratio had become as severe as *five* pilots per aircraft.[27]

This pilot glut is especially concentrated in fighter and ground attack units. One approach toward grappling with the problem that has been aired at VVS headquarters has been to encourage fighter pilots who wish to remain on flight status to volunteer for other aviation branches or to accept navigator assignments. As a "triage" technique for managing its aircrew reduction plans, the VVS is treating those pilots who have served three to four years in a given assignment as a "reserve" pool for potential selection to higher positions. Others, with five or more years in the same posting, who are considered poor prospects for promotion will most likely end up being released into the reserve.

The VVS is striving to reduce its pilot contingent to a stabilized norm of three pilots for every two aircraft. In the meantime, the pilot surplus is imposing a perceptible burden on day-to-day continuation training in operational squadrons. A case in point was the instance of a senior lieutenant who described taxiing out for a long-awaited range mission to reestablish his mission currency, only to experience an avionics system failure immediately prior to takeoff. The result was a noneffective sortie. The lieutenant later remarked:

> The aircraft situation here is really like a free-for-all. You should see how emotions flare up when we are preparing our little "plan." Each pilot and flight commander thinks that his problems are the most important. What happens is that everyone keeps pulling the blanket over to his side. . . . All these gyrations are prompted by the growing number of pilots arriving from VVS units undergoing reductions and, for other reasons, from various areas of the former USSR. But the aircraft pool remains the same.[28]

The Crisis in Flying Hours

Following President Yeltsin's lifting of price controls in January 1992, fuel costs escalated 2,000 percent just during the remainder of that year alone.[29] The first deputy head of the Defense Ministry's Main Budget and Finance Directorate reported that because of reduced appropriations for fuel, pilots were typically getting less than one-third of their annual flying norm.[30]

General Deinekin confirmed in early 1993 that largely because of the fuel shortage, VVS fighter pilots were averaging 40 flying hours a year, bomber pilots 80 hours a year, and VTA (*Voenno-transportnaia aviatsiia*, or Military Transport Aviation) pilots 150 hours (the differences reflecting variations in mission type, with LRA and transport crews flying fewer sorties of longer duration).[31] General Deinekin further reported that the VVS has roughly two assigned pilots for each single-seat aircraft, since "several thousand" fighter pilots stationed in the former republics had returned home following the USSR's collapse.[32] In most cases, the fuel shortage has required regimental commanders to preclude their headquarters staff officers from flying altogether so as to assure the most rational distribution of their meager fuel allotments to their neediest line pilots.

Conditions are scarcely better with those few remaining VVS fighter units awaiting final withdrawal from eastern Germany. The air commander for the Western Group of Forces (WGF), Lieutenant General Tarasenko, remarked that to give each pilot an equal chance to fly in such circumstances would be, in effect, to provide an opportunity to no one, since "letting everyone fly, but no more than once or twice a month, would mean taking everyone to the brink of losing his professional skills."[33]

WGF sorties in 1992 were apportioned at the regimental commander's discretion such that those pilots representing the VVS's core talent pool were given the greatest amount of time. Other Band-Aid fixes included reducing the average duration of scheduled sorties, eliminating repeat passes at the weapons range, combining multiple mission events on a single sortie, curtailing afterburner use and flight into marginal weather to save fuel, and greater reliance on flight simulators, even though Russia's defense industry has radically curtailed their manufacture and technical support.

A later account of WGF training indicated similar currency and proficiency concerns as forward-based VVS units approached the midpoint of their three-year phased withdrawal from former East German territory. The deputy commander of

Russian forces in Germany, Maj Gen Nikolai Selivorstov, reported that available flight time for WGF pilots had been cut back to the bone and that missions "in zone" had grown progressively more rudimentary as a result of the disappearance of any operational purpose behind the lingering Russian presence in Germany.

In a revealing snapshot of where things stand today, a military reporter provided an arresting account of VVS flight activity during a typical 24-hour day in the fall of 1993. A conversation with Maj Gen Aleksandr Slukhai, senior duty officer in the central command post at VVS headquarters in Moscow on the day in question, indicated that VVS flight schools and fighter aviation recorded 845 sorties that day for a total of 459 flying hours, with LRA registering 183 sorties for 115 hours and VTA logging 117 sorties at training centers for 58 hours in the air. The total came to slightly more than 1,000 VVS flights, for an average sortie length (including in LRA and VTA) of around one-half hour each. The reporter tried hard to put the best possible spin on these figures: "There is no basis for the idle conjectures of certain mass media that the VVS has neglected combat training. . . . A total of 1,145 training flights in a 24-hour period—is that not combat training?" The bitter truth, however, was laid bare in General Slukhai's more disquieting observation, "Some days the flying time for the entire VVS adds up to the number of hours the regiment I previously commanded would have flown in a 24-hour period."[34] In a telling contrast, General Deinekin earlier reported that on a typical flying day in August the *preceding* year, the VVS had registered 6,798 sorties.[35]

Maintenance and the Accident Situation

Aircraft maintenance in all services has suffered notably as a result of the failed conscription system in post-Soviet Russia. This has occasioned a drop in noncommissioned manning to the 50 percent level or below in many VVS and VPVO units. "This is an alarming indicator," said the VPVO's commander in chief, Col Gen Viktor Prudnikov, "because it was always felt that a unit was not operationally ready if it fell below 70 percent. We have now crossed that line."[36] Even before the August 1991 coup, the VVS's deputy commander for logistics complained that maintenance manning remained hung up at approximately 1972 levels. He said that as a result, the VVS was able to provide only some 60 percent of its needed rear service support for training and readiness.[37]

Cannibalization of parts from some aircraft to keep others flying has become common in many fighter units, even though it is in direct violation of safety rules. Such reliance on so-called donor aircraft (a polite term for hangar queens) was bound to happen sooner or later as a result of the declining availability of assemblies and spare parts. The impetus behind this flouting of published rules and good judgment has been to keep the greatest possible number of aircraft flyable at any cost, since flying hours are meted out according to the number of serviceable aircraft in a given unit. Even *with* cannibalization, considerable flight time has been lost to many units as a result of delays in the delivery of petroleum, oil, and lubricants (POL), tires, and other consumables.[38]

All of this has had a predictable impact on the VVS's flight safety situation. A report in June 1992 declared that "the aircraft accident rate is threatening to shift from isolated instances to a landslide."[39] It noted that there were 26 major mishaps in VVS operating units in 1991, with eight mishaps recorded during the first three months of 1992 alone. The article added that in some regiments, pilots were not even getting a minimal allocation of 40 flying hours a year and that it was precisely in those units where the accident rate was most disturbingly on the rise. It implored the VVS to take a hard look at proven foreign aviation safety practices in search of a better way to ramp down the incidence of flight mishaps. It also stated that in 1968, the Soviet air force roughly matched the USAF in the number of accidents per 100,000 hours, whereas today the VVS exceeds the USAF's number by a factor of two, even with "many times" fewer flying hours.

The Declining Quality of VVS Life

Six months before the coup, then-VVS commander Shaposhnikov attacked the inadequate provision of housing and social amenities for the families of VVS officers. Some of this he blamed on the return of Soviet units from Eastern Europe at an unexpectedly rapid rate. However, General Shaposhnikov complained that responsibility for the VVS's housing conundrum lay primarily with local civilian councils, which had failed to make good on their pledges to provide housing for the VVS. To take up at least part of the slack, the VVS committed 80 percent of its capital construction funds in 1991 for family housing. It also established a Main Engineering Administration to accelerate the resolution of the housing problem.[40] Yet today, over 22,000 VVS families remain without living quarters. More than 3,500 of these are families of pilots.

Even for those VVS families lucky enough to be blessed with adequate living accommodation, all too often their daily existence is bleak. Shortly before the coup, the VVS's chief political officer noted that around one-half of all officers' wives possessed special work qualifications, yet lacked any realistic chance of finding gainful employment in the often remote parts of the country where their husbands were stationed.[41] Such deprivation has had a predictable impact on morale. Acknowledging that many officers have remained hardworking and devoted professionals in the face of mounting adversity, the deputy commander of the Chernigov VVAUL confessed that "one feels frankly ashamed to reproach people for their deficiencies" when they sit at their workstations on air bases for up to 12-14 hours a day.[42] Much the same sentiment was reflected in a Defense Ministry poll of 1,100 officers in all of Russia's services, including the VPVO and VVS, indicating that many "are losing their social and moral reference points and values, and their confidence in tomorrow is dying away."[43]

At the time of the coup, a Moscow bus driver typically got paid more than a trained Soviet fighter pilot. Since then, Russia's economy has deteriorated to a state where operational pilots now have to work the fields on weekends to help bring in the crop. VVS officers are being forced to harvest their own agricultural produce. Base commanders must cultivate plots and maintain subsidiary farms on their airfields. Even at prestigious Kubinka, fighter pilots often spend their weekends weeding and hoeing. The former commander of the VVS's Su-27 flight demonstration team, Col Vladimir Basov, said, "All of us are forced to tend our kitchen gardens because we don't have any other source of food." He added, "It's a shame our pilots get lower pay than a plumber or a mechanic."[44] General Deinekin himself has commented that cadets at the Barnaul VVAUL live in such austere conditions that they are forced to use parachutes as blankets during winter time.[45]

Sadly to say, Russia's pilots are watching their professional pride slowly leach away as a result of these pernicious influences. Smoking is said to be the rule among them, and drinking to excess has become more and more commonplace. "The whole country drinks, after all, and do they ever!" wrote one disgusted pilot. "Why should aviation be any better?"[46] Only a few officers reportedly take part in regular physical exercise, and many work out only enough to get ready to pass their semiannual evaluation—if it is given. Even these tests are typically a charade because of the widespread prevalence of cheating.

Faltering Service Prestige and Pilot Recruitment

During the banner years of the Soviet Union, appeals to patriotism and the romance of high-performance flight were nearly all it took to entice the best of Soviet youth to seek a VVS career. Today, squalid living conditions and rapidly dwindling opportunities for pilots to fly have become increasing barriers to VVS recruitment. Consistently low pay for officers and the badly tarnished image of a military career in post-Soviet Russia, set against the precipitous decline in the quality of service life, have resulted in a virtual disappearance of competition for pilot training slots in both the VVS and VPVO. Even before the USSR's collapse, the commandant of the Kharkhov VVAUL reported that "the influx of young people into flight academies has recently fallen drastically." He noted that 790 applicants were accepted to Kharkhov in 1989, whereas only 312 cadets entered the program in 1990. He added, "There was practically no competition after the medical board's findings. In some cases, we were even forced to reexamine those who received 'twos.'"[47]

During the early 1970s, six to eight applicants typically vied for each available pilot training slot nationwide. Today, the VVS is forced "to accept adolescents who have shown only fair

319

knowledge on the entrance exams. The criterion for their enrolment is just good health, and even that with certain allowances." One colonel complained, "There is essentially no weeding out after psychological testing. There is no one to choose from!"[48] Another pilot cynically joked that VVAUL acceptance standards had fallen to such a low state that there are now only two criteria: "The applicant must be able to hear thunder and see lightning—and one of these is waiverable!"

Many junior officers have simply quit out of disillusionment.[49] In July 1992, for example, all 48 graduates of the Barnaul VVAUL declined to honor their service commitments because of "no prestige and no prospects." Upon being awarded their commissions and aeronautical ratings, they were immediately released into the reserves.[50] In trying to come to honest grips with this arresting trend, the VVS's chief of education, Major General Yanakov, frankly conceded, "Today's youth have begun looking harder and deeper into life's questions. They can no longer be won over simply by slogans and appeals. Firm assurances of a dignified social status of officership are now required."[51]

Trends and Prospects

In light of the daunting problems outlined above, coupled with continued uncertainty over the long-term prospects for political and economic change in Russia, one might fairly ask whether the sun is rising or setting on General Deinekin's VVS. To this question, General Deinekin would almost certainly answer with cautious optimism born of conviction. He has repeatedly declared that the VVS has the needed talent, an appreciation of its past failings under communist rule, a vision of what needs to be done to correct them, and an abiding determination that, in due course, Russian aviation will recover to full health. The hard reality, of course, is that the main factors that will determine the ultimate course and outcome of the VVS's resurrection lie largely beyond General Deinekin's control. At bottom, the fate of the VVS, like that of the military establishment as a whole, is inseparably tied up with the fate of post-Soviet Russia.

One of the first hints of the new course the VVS will follow in its quest for post-Soviet reform may have been reflected in a statement by General Deinekin while he was still first deputy commander of the Soviet air force. In an interview in early 1991, Deinekin remarked that the sharp rise in the pilot-to-aircraft ratio prompted by force reductions and wholesale unit withdrawals from Eastern Europe had occasioned "a harsh need for converting combat training from extensive methods to intensive ones. Every minute of flight time," he said, "should be used for maximum return," with the main emphasis being placed "on the quality of assimilating the training programs."[52]

General Deinekin pleaded for patience and cooperation up and down the command hierarchy in the interest of weathering the turbulent times yet to come: "Intelligent initiative and a creative approach to realizing military reform are most important during this difficult period. One cannot simply sit and fold one's arms, waiting for all the answers to hard questions to emanate from the center. The High Command will do everything within its power. But supervisors must themselves analyze the situation and take appropriate steps." He added, "I believe that the air force will emerge from this difficult situation with honor. The main thing is not to yield to pessimism and despair."

Later, after the August 1991 coup attempt fell apart, General Deinekin left no room for doubt about where he felt the blame belonged for the many years of stagnation in VVS practice. He said, "The processes of de-partyization and de-politicization . . . that have been initiated actively reflect the long-standing attitude of most military fliers. The party political structures that existed interfered constantly and quite persistently in the conduct of virtually all aspects of our combat training, tying the hands of commanders and specialists."[53] Asked later what he felt the effects would be on the VVS as a result of the dismantling of these structures, General Deinekin replied: "Regardless of the final shape the reform will take, the air force will benefit from it. This country's air force suffered the burden of communism for 74 years. Now that burden has finally ceased to exist."[54]

With the communist system firmly repudiated and a new horizon looming ahead, the VVS now stands on the threshold of *potentially* the most radical departure from its familiar ways of doing business since the earliest days of the Soviet state. As the deputy chief of the VVS's higher educational institutions, Major General Yanakov, remarked in late 1991, "The events of August 1991 have accelerated the process of radical change in the country's armed forces. It is gratifying to note that commonsense is returning to us, albeit slowly."[55]

This reflection bears out the important fact that throughout the history of the VVS, *the main problem was communism, not the man or his equipment.* The Soviet pilot was selected by exacting criteria, and he represented the best talent for his calling that Soviet society had to offer. For their part, Soviet aircraft and air-to-air missiles have always been respectable threats from a technical standpoint. Especially today, the fourth-generation MiG-29 and Su-27 and the Alamo and Archer missiles, properly used, are a match for any comparable systems the West currently operates. In some respects, they command a definite performance edge. The reason the VVS has long had such trouble getting the most out of these assets is that the Soviet pilot was, inevitably, a product of his training environment. Naturally, his techniques and skills were heavily conditioned—and circumscribed—by the inhibiting effect of a uniquely "Soviet" operational culture.

Given the many restrictions on pilot initiative that hampered the VVS's operational adaptability throughout the long years of the Cold War, it was all but inevitable that the Soviet MiG-21 pilots who were lured into battle by the Israeli Air Force over Suez in July 1970 would be so completely outmatched. The difference was not in the quality of the *people* who were pitted against one another in that engagement, but rather in their diametrically opposed approaches to training and force employment. With their heavy dependence on GCI close control and their unfamiliarity with anything beyond the broadest essentials of free air combat maneuvering, the Soviets lacked the situation awareness and implicit knowledge of appropriate moves and countermoves that are crucial for surviving and winning in a highly dynamic, multiparticipant air battle. That said, it is a safe bet that a typical Russian fighter pilot today could be picked virtually at random from squadron service, detrained of his most counterproductive habits acquired through exposure to Soviet influence, enrolled in a USAF F-15 conversion course or its equivalent, and emerge with creditable air-to-air skills by any standard.

Exactly how the VVS will respond to its unprecedented opportunity for change remains hard to say with assurance. Much will depend, in the near term at least, on the extent to which Russia's weakened economy will permit the channeling of enough funds into the VVS's operations and maintenance accounts to underwrite a training program commensurate with the new latitude for improvisation the VVS appears to have acquired. Farther down the road, much will also hinge on the extent to which the dismantlement of the old communist order will yield a permanent change in the daily pattern of organizational life for Russian pilots and commanders.

It remains too early to predict what the future holds beyond the broadest of generalizations. With respect to force modernization, General Deinekin and other VVS leaders have openly stated their near-term intentions and goals through the year 2000. These goals are not unreasonable for the sort of VVS that would seem appropriate for post-Soviet Russia, given its likely operational challenges in the immediate years ahead. Yet, because of the continuing budget crisis, it is hard to see how the VVS can take more than the first steps in this direction, when it is having trouble just providing its pilots with enough monthly flying time to keep from killing themselves.

On the books, the VVS has a declared requirement for a follow-on to the MiG-29 and Su-27. As recently as late January 1994, the deputy VVS commander in chief, Col Gen Viktor Kot, reported that the main efforts of VVS acquisition planning were being targeted on "the priority development of fifth-generation aviation complexes and the procurement of spares."[56] Yet, given the bleak outlook for financing of new systems and the problems the VVS currently faces in funding even the improvement of *existing* types, that may be a pipe dream, at least for the near term. This holds particularly true in light of a pronouncement only a few weeks earlier by First Deputy

Defense Minister Kokoshin that upcoming R&D and procurement for *all* the services would focus mainly on reconnaissance, command and control, supply to mobile forces, and precision-strike munitions.[57]

Much the same can be said with regard to training and tactics development. Without question, the VVS has been freed of the organizational choke hold that limited its capacity to innovate under communist rule. In principle, it is now at liberty to cast aside its old ways and develop a new operational repertoire aimed at extracting the fullest leverage from its highly capable equipment. Yet, with a shoestring operations and maintenance budget that forces unit commanders to bend every effort simply to maintain their pilots' basic aircraft handling proficiency, it defies logic to imagine how they might conduct anything even remotely like the sort of graduated and structured training, from the simple to the complex, that would be required, at a minimum, to bring Russia's pilots up to accepted Western mission readiness standards.

Finally, with respect to doctrine and concepts, the VVS has discarded its canonical Warsaw Pact Air Operation Plan (if, indeed, it ever paid more than lip service to that plan in its day-to-day training) and now confronts a need to develop new strategies consistent with the emerging mission requirements of post-Soviet Russia. However, Russia has yet to develop a coherent and fully articulated foreign policy, or, for that matter, even an agreed set of national interests upon which such a policy might be based. Accordingly, its much-vaunted "new military doctrine" published in late 1993 remains little more than a statement of broad principles for an ideal world. In the absence of a clear threat or readily definable operational challenge, any attempt to produce a more detailed repertoire for Russian airpower would come close to putting the cart before the horse.

There is no clearer testament to the acuteness of the many problems the VVS faces today than its continued inability to do much beyond intellectualize about the implications of the 1991 Persian Gulf War. As the fall of communism neared, the VVS had a ringside seat from which to watch the allied Coalition's successful air campaign against Iraq. That campaign opened the eyes of Soviet airmen not just to what

Western aviation could accomplish, but to what airpower in general (including *Russian* airpower) could do if properly equipped, configured, and applied.[58] Unfortunately for the VVS, however, that realization dawned precisely as its own operational and institutional moorings had become cast almost completely adrift by the winds of international and domestic change.

The powerful role model provided for Russian air tacticians by the Coalition's performance in Desert Storm, coupled with the subsequent lifting of many of the former inhibitions that blocked any serious effort at tactical reform in the VVS, makes it fair to speculate that at least some of the impending changes in Russian operational practice, once they take root, will show a heightened Western orientation. The air-to-air arena warrants special attention in this regard. Since improvement in air combat prowess is *relatively* inexpensive (in that it turns largely on altered procedures for sorties that will be flown in any case, rather than on new equipment), the VVS is now positioned to begin applying whatever inclinations its best tacticians may long have harbored by way of desired changes in air-to-air training.

One constraint here, possibly a serious one in the near term, entails the extent to which even seemingly "low-cost" changes in tactical training may be preempted by a diversion of already scarce operations and maintenance funds toward providing housing and other needed quality-of-life improvements for officers and their families. Another constraint has to do with where the VVS's Combat Training Directorate will find a suitable homegrown experience pool from which to develop and pass along to Russian pilots a fundamentally new air combat repertoire. Such skills cannot be acquired simply by reading the right books.

Despite the difficulties outlined above, the VVS's situation is far from hopeless. For one thing, it has been granted a decisive end to political controls, new individual liberties and freedoms of expression, active encouragement of initiative and independent judgment from below, and an easing or elimination of the most odious former Soviet operating rules and restrictions. All of this has been expressly geared toward enhancing opportunities for talented pilots and commanders to achieve their fullest potential. The system remains slow to change, and old habits linger on. But at least the door to reform is now open.

There is good news for the West as well. Old patterns of Soviet secrecy are gradually yielding to a new interest in dialogue. President Yeltsin's military adviser during the early months following the coup, Gen Konstantin Kobets, expressed the readiness of *all* Russian services to reach out and embrace proven practices of other military establishments around the world. He admonished each to "apply the experience of all civilized countries which have undergone reforms at one time or another in their own fashion, adopt the best and least expensive things, and apply these with the greatest possible effect."[59] General Deinekin likewise acknowledged the value of going to school on the West's experience: "There is something to adopt from abroad. We must train our pilots to world standards."[60]

However the VVS's current leaders and their successors will eventually choose to exercise their new options, they are entering a historic phase in their professional growth. The best of its new leaders, first and foremost General Deinekin, have freely admitted their problems and indicated what they believe needs to be done to start fixing them. This has removed a major obstacle from the road to recovery. It has also set the stage for a time of creative ferment that could begin at any moment once the Russian armed forces emerge from their current crisis with a measure of fiscal solvency.

Discussion

Air Marshal David Evans: Will the changes in Russia's situation call for a different structure in their air force? Did you get a feel for their future strategic thinking? For example, are they going to need a long-range strike force?

Dr. Lambeth: The central theme of Soviet doctrine for conventional war in Europe was the offensive, based on mass, on surprise, on shock, and sheer weight of numbers. It was a war-winning strategy from beginning to end. With the demise of the Cold War, that's all gone and they are looking now at a fundamentally new mission set that has to do mainly with the projection of power into remote areas around the periphery of the former Soviet Union. They talk about the former republics as the principal hotbeds of tension that may call for the application of Russian power in a peacemaking role. That raises some questions about whether the requirements the Russian Air Force has put on the table are really entirely appropriate to the operational needs the political leadership is likely to feel in the near term, which are mobility, projection, and heavy airlift. They face a severe shortfall in those capabilities right now. They lost, as I mentioned, one-half of their best transports to the other former republics. Why the Russian Air Force would want to continue to operate the very costly and technically troublesome Blackjack bomber is an interesting question. Why it really needs a fifth-generation fighter, other than to just remain at the leading edge of technology, is another fair question. But, clearly, you will not see anything like the numbers or the weight of airpower in Russia 10 years down the road that we grew up with for two generations. Apart from the cost, the operational requirement is simply no longer there.

Air Vice-Marshal Peter Squire: We in NATO are now working toward opening a program under the title of Partnership for Peace as a way of trying to bridge the gap with the Russians, particularly in terms of the way we operate, because clearly with systems which are poles apart, it will be very difficult to do more than simply offer encouragement at the moment. What do you think the Russians' greatest aspirations will be for the program?

Dr. Lambeth: You've raised a very important question. I believe it is absolutely essential that we, not just in the United States but the Western powers generally, reach out and seek to bring the Russians into a community in which they are regarded as, and encouraged to act as, a normal player in world affairs. Much as we did with Germany and Japan after World War II, I believe we have both the opportunity and the obligation to try to do the same with Russia today. A critical difference, of course, is that, despite those who insist that the West "won the Cold War," Russia is not a defeated power. It is a proud country in profound domestic turmoil over which the West has very little direct control.

To your specific question of what's in it for them, I believe first and foremost what they're looking for is nothing more demanding than acceptance as fellow professionals. They want to be taken seriously. They want to be respected. The West has a tremendous opportunity to rise to that challenge and show both the Russian high command and rank-and-file Russian operators that they are regarded as brother warriors. That alone, I think, would take us a long way toward establishing a common hailing frequency from which we could then develop common procedures for interoperability and for getting to know each other better.

Quite apart from the premature political symbolism, I think we're a long way yet from the point where, for example, we might want to invite the Russian Air Force to participate in Red Flag, not least of all because they could make for an accident hazard of the first order with their current shortcomings in operational proficiency. I don't believe they're in a position today even to begin to assimilate the richness and intensity of what goes on in that kind of training environment. But short of that, there are a number of things that can be done, such as sharing insights into the way we train undergraduate flight instructors and helping them with aircraft maintenance and their mounting accident problems. The sky's the limit in this regard, and Partnership for Peace offers an ideal framework in which to develop those kinds of ties. This is, of course, a counsel of hope to some degree. But I believe that if these kinds of initiatives are pursued, we'll be pleasantly surprised at the kind of response we get. I would encourage you in your NATO capacity to do all you can to press for that.

Back to Air Marshal Evans's question. The Russian Air Force last year conducted an exercise, which it called *Voskhod* '93, in an effort to validate its emerging power projection strategy.

328

It involved a package of eight Su-24 Fencer fighter-bombers, plus a number of Tu-95 bombers with tanker support. General Deinekin was aboard an airborne command post for two days, and they generated that package all the way from the western part of Russia out to Lake Baikal. There were also six or eight Flanker escorts. They all went out and delivered simulated weapons at a range and came back. I think there were at least two rationales for that. First, to demonstrate both to the Russian Air Force and to everyone else that they were very serious about developing this projection capability; and second, to attempt a first-order validation of their new strategy. General Deinekin later said that this was the most complex strike package that had been put together in the Russian Air Force in over 10 years. It wasn't even a shadow of what takes place at Red Flag on a regular basis. So they've got a long way to go yet. What matters is that they are trying hard in a situation of great adversity.

Professor Robin Higham: Ben, I liked your paper very much. Perhaps you'd like to comment a little about what's happening to the aircraft industry, since that's going to be one of the fundamental bases of airpower.

Dr. Lambeth: The aircraft industry today is moribund. It really is in danger of going under because of the financial crisis. The head of the Mikoyan Design Bureau, Rostislav Belyakov, is a personal friend of mine, and he's been very candid in lamenting the lot of his people. The chief of their advanced development division also told me that out of 120 engineers, he had lost around 40 of his best in just a year. There is no easy way to replace them. You can make more money today selling Coca-Cola off Red Square than you can as a salaried engineer in the aircraft industry.

It doesn't necessarily require the mass production of aircraft to keep the aviation industry alive. At some point soon, they really are going to have to face up to the excesses and the slack that were permitted by the communist system, which were inexcusable. They employed three times as many people as they needed. If they intend to be serious competitors in the international aviation market, they're going to have to develop much more efficient standards of design and production management. That won't happen overnight.

Beyond that, Mr. Belyakov was our guest at RAND in the fall of 1989, before the USSR collapsed. He stated then, and I believe this was a harbinger of things to come, that given the increasing cost of major weapons systems, it will be harder and harder for industry to persuade the air force to buy new systems without an ironclad requirement. However, he added, it will be essential to maintain the R&D effort, because that's where new ideas come from. They can manage, in the near term at least, to weather the crisis in *production* funding. What they *can't* afford, even for a very short time, is a continued lapse of support for research and development, without which there may be no follow-on systems produced for a generation or more. Here again, they're facing a very steep uphill climb.

Mr. Carlo Kopp: Can you please elaborate on the influence of Luftwaffe doctrine on the development of the post-World War II Soviet air force, particularly on Frontal Aviation? Also, the Soviets deployed the Su-27 Flanker during the 1980s, an aircraft which arguably has the capability to function as a strategic fighter escort with a combat radius in the order of several hundred nautical miles. Have you seen any evidence to suggest that the Soviet air force would in fact capitalize on that capability?

Dr. Lambeth: There are people better qualified than I to take your first question, including Robin Higham, who is here today. I think the short answer regarding the Luftwaffe is that the Russians learned the hard way in 1941 what a massed, combined-arms offensive can do, and they went to school on it in a determined way, in the wake of recovering from the Nazi onslaught, in developing their own operational concepts for the Cold War. I would assert as a point for discussion that, shorn of its ideological trimmings, Soviet military doctrine for conventional warfare in Europe was almost a mirror image of the doctrine that animated Operation Barbarossa in 1941.

With regard to the Su-27, this is a most interesting airplane. I think of it almost as a fighter-equivalent of Battlestar Galactica. The airplane carries 22,000 pounds of fuel internally. It is not even configured to carry external tanks, because it doesn't need them. When the airplane went to the Paris Air Show in 1989, it flew nonstop from Moscow clean and landed with fuel to spare.

How would the airplane be employed? It's operated by both the Air Defense Forces and the air force. The airplane was conceived as a counterpart to the F-15. Russian designers have repeatedly stated over the past few years that it took a development in the West to spark a comparable development in the former Soviet Union. There really was an almost pure action-reaction phenomenon at work here. The Su-24 was an answer to the F-111, and the Su-25 was a reaction to the A-9/A-10 development. It's interesting that they would react to an aircraft type rather than to a mission need, but that's the way their requirements have been generated. The operational application of the Su-27, first and foremost, was in a home defense role, particularly in the far north. I'm speculating a bit here now, but one of its principal missions, I believe, was to force SAC [Strategic Air Command] bombers down to low altitude far enough out that they would not be within range to release their cruise missiles.

With regard to Frontal Aviation's use, would Su-27s have been employed to escort Backfire bombers, for example, in a war in central Europe? You can probably find doctrinal writings that would suggest the possibility of that. They spoke repeatedly of *soprovozhdeniye*, or "accompaniment." But don't forget that the Backfire and the Flanker are operated by separate service branches in the air force. There is not a great deal of cross-communication between those two communities. To my knowledge there has not been, until recently at least, anything like the kind of escort role demonstrated in practice that's been occasionally hinted at in the doctrinal literature. The Su-27s that the Soviets deployed in central Europe, in Poland, for example, were mainly there in a battlefield air support role. I believe their mission was to provide offensive CAP [combat air patrol] for the Fencers that were targeted against NATO air bases in Western Europe.

Group Capt Andrew Vallance: Ben, just one comment and then a question. The comment concerns Partnership for Peace. In my previous appointment, I was chief of military cooperation at SHAPE [Supreme Headquarters Allied Powers Europe] and therefore responsible for the military element of the Partnership for Peace program. I would have to say that for two years we worked very hard with it, but that we produced a lemon. We knew that, first of all, we had to engage Russia as the key to those 22 countries in central Eastern Europe. That was the key to it, but finding a center of gravity for meaningful military cooperation proved elusive. The second element, finding concrete proposals for future cooperation, again proved elusive because it's very difficult to find something substantial which is acceptable to the 16 NATO nations and also acceptable to the 22 nations of the central Eastern European bloc. I think from that point of view, Partnership for Peace is going to continue to be a very difficult program to mount, particularly if we can't identify a center of gravity that we can deal with in Russia itself.

My question concerns threats that the Russian Air Force sees and, in particular, the potential threat from Ukraine. Do they see a threat? And if so, how do they intend to cope with it?

Dr. Lambeth: First on your comment. I can appreciate how, as an operator who had to deal with such things on a daily basis, you would encounter the experiences you described. I received a letter a couple of weeks ago from the US defense attaché in Moscow commenting on some work I had done espousing the development of an East-West strategic partnership. He remarked that it's all well and good to talk at a macro level about these great ideas, but that as he'd learned from his day-to-day experiences, the devil will be in the details. We don't readily appreciate these difficulties until we've had to deal with them face to face.

One of the problems the Western democracies confront in trying to nurture this kind of a dialogue with the Russians is getting over some profound institutional paranoia that has developed over a lifetime of conditioning. The Russians are still operating very much in a mode in which old secrecy habits die hard. One of the biggest hurdles I've worked hard to surmount in my own dealings with Russian military aviation professionals has been to be completely above board and honest about what I'm trying to accomplish, lest I project a false impression that I'm out there working someone else's collection requirements list. Clearly, that's not what it's all about, but those kinds of suspicions are going to take time to get over. I would venture to guess that this lies partly at the root of the problem you've described.

With regard to threats, you've got to have threats to justify forces, and the Russians will develop notional adversaries to the extent necessary to justify their budget requests. I believe, however, that the problem with Ukraine first and foremost is a political and strategic one rather than one that would, in the foreseeable future, call for the application of force. The Russians are rightly concerned over Ukraine's retention of nuclear weapons. Nobody wants more than the Russians to see those forces stood down and returned to Russia. I am not a closely read specialist in Russian-Ukrainian political relations, but what I see is a Ukraine tottering today on the brink of economic and political collapse. One possibility we could observe over the next couple of years is a slow but steady process of economic reintegration of Ukraine with Russia. In other words, Ukraine's lack of autarky could drive the threat away. Whatever the case, it is a turbulent cauldron of political chemistry right now. Anybody who would venture to speculate on the outcome would be rolling the dice.

Notes

1. This chapter is an excerpt from a more extensive study on the outlook for military aviation in post-Soviet Russia that is now being written by the author under the auspices of RAND's Project Air Force. Any views expressed

are solely those of the author and should not be attributed to RAND or any of its governmental or private research sponsors.

2. Von Hardesty, *Red Phoenix: The Rise of Soviet Air Power, 1941–1945* (Washington, D.C.: Smithsonian Institution Press, 1982), 7.

3. Because of the USSR's western strategic orientation, much of the best of its combat equipment had been fielded on Ukrainian soil. As a result, Ukraine emerged from the union's collapse, among other things, as the possessor of over 1,000 military aircraft, including between one-quarter and one-third of the former Soviet air force's MiG-29s and Su-27s, one-half of its 40 Il-78 tankers, almost one-half of its Il-76 transports, and all but two of its serviceable Tu-160 bombers. These assets instantly endowed Ukraine with an air force considerably larger than that of any West European country, including Britain, France, and Germany.

4. Col (Res.) V. Dudin, "Through a Mass of Stereotypes," *Aviatsiia i kosmonavtika*, no. 1, January 1992, 4–6.

5. This notwithstanding the fact that as first deputy VVS commander, Shaposhnikov reportedly headed the inquiry into Zuyev's theft of the MiG-29. See Alexander Zuyev, with Malcolm McConnell, *Fulcrum* (New York: Warner Books, 1992), 354. Later, Shaposhnikov even claimed his readiness to attack the Kremlin had the putschists sought to take the white house by force. See Michael Evans, "Marshal Was Ready to Bomb Kremlin," *London Times*, 13 September 1991.

6. By far the richest English-language account is David Remnick, *Lenin's Tomb: The Last Days of the Soviet Empire* (New York: Random House, 1993). Shaposhnikov has told this story himself in a remarkably honest retrospective on his experiences during the coup and the subsequent collapse of communism in his recently-published *Vybor: zapiski glavnokomanduiushchego* (*A Time for Choice: Notes of a Commander in Chief*) (Moscow: Nezavisimoye Izdatel'stvo PIK, 1993).

7. See Foreign Broadcast Information Service (FBIS), Eurasia Report, 3 September 1991, 54.

8. That event and its background are chronicled in Georgy Baidukov, *Russian Lindbergh: The Life of Valery Chkalov* (Washington, D.C.: Smithsonian Institution Press, 1991). See also Valery P. Chkalov, *V. P. Chkalov* (Moscow: Izdatel'stvo Planeta, 1984).

9. For a particularly engrossing memoir, see Marshal of Aviation E. I. Savitskii, *Polveka s nebom* (*A Half-Century With the Sky*) (Moscow: *Voenizdat*, 1988).

10. R. A. Mason and John W. R. Taylor, *Aircraft, Strategy and Operations of the Soviet Air Force* (London: Jane's Publishing Co., 1986), 9–10.

11. To cite but one example from the pre-*glasnost* era, the air commander for the North Caucasus Military District, in criticizing an exercise failure that stemmed from blind pursuit of rote procedures and an incapacity for improvising, faulted his pilots in 1976 for having "simply not thought out the situation. How can one go into real combat," he lamented, "without the necessary skills?" Lt Gen A. Pavlov, "The Inexhaustible Reserve," *Krasnaia zvezda*, 4 August 1976.

12. Capt Rana J. Pennington, USAF, "Closing the Tactics Gap," *Air Force Magazine*, March 1984, 83. A year later, Captain Pennington similarly wrote that "rather than painting the Soviet pilot as ten feet tall, we have consistently depicted him as a midget—a dwarf at best. It has long been a matter of reassurance to the Air Force that no matter how many aircraft the Soviets had, the poor skills of their pilots would significantly hamper their ability to use those aircraft effectively." "Another Look at the Soviet Fighter Pilot," *Air Force Magazine*, April 1985, 83.

13. *Soviet Military Power, 1983* (Washington, D.C.: Government Printing Office, 1983), 43.

14. Lt Col Mike Press, "Aggressor Reflections," *USAF Fighter Weapons Review*, Summer 1981, 4.

15. Michael Skinner, *USAFE: A Primer of Modern Air Combat in Europe* (Novato, Calif.: Presidio Press, 1983), 122.

16. This image was reinforced by the manner in which Soviet air defense forces downed Korean Air Lines Flight 007 in September 1983. As indicated in detail by the published transcript of air-to-ground communications between the Su-15 pilot and his GCI controller, the intercept was a model of confusion and directed behavior from start to finish. It took the pilot a full 14 minutes to down the 747 after his initial reported visual contact. During this period, he was vectored all over the sky by his controller even as he had the aircraft in sight. At one point during the intercept, he closed to within 6,000 feet of the target. But he never positively identified it or showed any other sign of initiative in the situation. See "US Intercepts Soviet Fighter Transmissions," *Aviation Week & Space Technology*, 12 September 1983.

17. Robert L. Shaw, *Fighter Combat: Tactics and Maneuvering* (Annapolis: US Naval Institute Press, 1985), x.

18. Bill Gunston, *Mikoyan MiG-21* (London: Osprey Publishing, 1986), 36, 47, 64, 88–92.

19. The Finnish air force, which also acquired (and continues to operate) the MiG-21, reports a similar experience. According to its current commander, Maj Gen Heikki Nikunen, introductory training on the aircraft for the initial Finnish cadre at Lugovaya included no tactical flying and proceeded so slowly that the Finnish team leader finally called a halt to it and brought the group home to complete the process on its own. The MiG-21 was thoroughly evaluated at the Finnish air force flight test center, and optimum tactics were then developed based on those results (letter from General Nikunen to the author, 16 April 1993).

20. This aspect of the Soviet approach to flight training has more recently come under criticism. As one instructor wrote in 1987, "Obviously the 'grandfather' approach, which entails drilling students with the notorious 'do as I do' principle, is a significant shortcoming in cadet training. Experience shows that in flight training, the instructor pilot should devote more attention to letting the cadet develop his habits independently under the instructor's supervision." Lt Col N. Litvinchuk and Maj V. Kozlov, "How Do You Adapt to an Airplane?" *Aviatsiia i kosmonavtika*, no. 11, November 1987, 17.

21. Col Gen Petr S. Deinekin and Gen Merrill A. McPeak, interviewed by Yelena Agapova, "The Skies Are the Same—the Concerns Different," *Krasnaia zvezda*, 26 October 1991.

22. Radio Moscow Domestic Service, 30 November 1991.

23. Lt Col V. Rudenko, "Russia Scrambles the Tu-160," *Krasnaia zvezda*, 4 August 1992.

24. John Lloyd, "Sharp Cut in Soviet Defense Orders," *London Financial Times*, 28 October 1991.

25. Nikolai Poroskov, "The Time for Stating Problems is Past. Initiatives and Quests for Reserves Are What Is Needed," *Krasnaia zvezda*, 9 December 1993.

26. Colonel General Deinekin, interviewed by Yu. Dmitriyev, "A Country Without Wings? No," *Trud*, 10 March 1992.

27. Lt Col A. Vetakh, 'Waiting for an Aircraft: Combat Pilots Await Their Turn," *Krasnaia zvezda*, 15 May 1992.

28. Quoted in Vetakh, "Waiting for an Aircraft."

29. *Aviation Week & Space Technology*, 11 January 1993. With the military's loss of its privileged position and the fuel industry increasingly starved for funds, the VVS's fuel costs probably rose in parallel with those of the civilian airline industry.

30. Maj Gen Vasily Kuznetsov, interview in "Inflation Devours the Military Budget Before It Can Be Approved," *Krasnaia zvezda*, 15 October 1992. Kuznetsov also noted that there were delays in pay raises and paycheck deliveries due to inflation, which had made it impossible for the Defense Ministry to make good on decisions approved by the Supreme Soviet. He further stated that there were no immediate savings to be had from the massed discharge of officers, since it would cost R500 million to cover terminal allowances for 10,000 officers released to the civilian sector.

31. General Deinekin has stated that in the best of times, he used to fly 500 hours a year when he was a line pilot in LRA. That would be a dream of any LRA pilot today. After I flew a MiG-23UB with the Mikoyan Design Bureau at the Zhukovskii Flight Test Center in August 1993, my pilot, Col Vladimir Gorbunov, told me that there was no shortage of jet fuel per se in Russia today. The problem, he said, was a shortage of adequate financing to pay for it.

32. Report by ITAR-TASS correspondent Vadim Byrkin, 16 February 1993.

33. Lt Gen A. Tarasenko, interviewed by Colonels V. Markushin and S. Pashayev, "In a Holding Pattern: Comments on Problems of the 16th Air Army," *Krasnaia zvezda*, 27 March 1992.

34. Quoted in Aleksandr Manushkin, "Things Are Never Boring for the Duty General," *Krasnaia zvezda*, 23 October 1993.

35. Weather may have been an extenuating factor here, at least at the margins, considering that the sortie number provided by General Slukhai was recorded in October, while that given by General Deinekin was in August, when flying conditions in Russia are best. Nevertheless, the difference speaks for itself. General Deinekin further noted that on that same

flying day in August 1992, 980 sorties were reported by VPVO, 409 by the Strategic Rocket Forces, and 432 by the navy. Deinekin, interviewed by Yelena Agapova, "A Russia Without Wings Is Not Russia. It Does and Will Have Them," *Krasnaia zvezda*, 15 August 1992.

36. Colonel General Prudnikov, interviewed by Col A. Belousov and Maj A. Ivanov, "A Unified System Is Needed," *Krasnaia zvezda*, 11 April 1992.

37. Militarywide, Russian operational units today are reportedly manned at only around 60 percent of their assigned strength on the average. Statement by the chief of the General Staff, Col Gen Mikhail Kolesnikov, cited in Viktor Litovkin, "The Army Pins Hopes on the Help of Legislators . . . and Women," *Izvestiia*, 17 October 1992. During the first half of 1992, nearly 70 percent of Russian youths who were eligible for service dodged the draft. Sergei Ostanin, ITAR-TASS, 15 October 1992.

38. Lt Col A. Vetakh, "Donor Aircraft," *Krasnaia zvezda*, 15 April 1992. Colonel General Kalugin singled out the Tu-160 as a maintenance nightmare because of its unusual complexity. The aircraft requires a dedicated air base equipped with special ground-support equipment, high-pressure hydraulics, and an extensive supply train. General Kalugin complained that it is still being debugged of design problems and that a more user-friendly and less expensive bomber is needed.

39. Comment on a letter to the editor from a Zhukovskii Air Force Engineering Academy student by Col A. Andryushkov, "We Are Flying Less and Less. We Are Crashing More Often. Will Russia Become Wingless?" *Krasnaia zvezda*, 19 June 1992.

40. Colonel General Shaposhnikov, interviewed by Yelena Agapova, "So When Will Pilots Get Apartments?" *Krasnaia zvezda*, 3 March 1991.

41. Lt Gen Gennady Benov, interview on the program "I Serve the Soviet Union," Moscow television, 18 August 1991.

42. Col V. Sobolev, "Stop Teaching in a Retrograde Way," *Aviatsiia i kosmonavtika*, no. 3, March 1991, 4–6.

43. Lt Col Nikolai Pechen, "With What Do We Fill the Void?" *Vestnik protivovozdushnoi oborony*, no. 9, September 1993, 30.

44. Daniel Schneider, "Russian Fighter Pilots Wax Nostalgic for Days of Top Gun Status," *The Christian Science Monitor*, 5 August 1992. Defense Minister Grachev has tried hard to do something about this. In early 1993, he announced that pay for junior officers had been increased six-fold, and 12-fold for those posted in the far north. Grachev interviewed by V. Starkov in "General Grachev on the Military and on the Soldier," *Argumenty i fakty*, no. 5, February 1993. Grachev also revealed a becoming disdain for "looking good" for show in his barbed comment that "as VDV [Airborne Troops] commander, I got them out of the habit of painting everything for my arrival. Whenever I smelled fresh paint, I would give the unit commander hell."

45. General Deinekin, interview in *Krylia rodiny*, March 1993.

46. Lt Col V. Vysotskii, "A Stumbling Block, Or Problems of Combat Training," *Aviatsiia i kosmonavtika*, no. 11, November 1991, 4–7.

47. Col V. Shevstsov, interview in, "Pilots Who Never Developed: Can We Halt the Outflow of Cadets from Military Schools?" *Krasnaia zvezda*, 12 March 1991.

48. Things at the end of 1991 were a little better in VPVO. According to its chief of fighter aviation, then-Lt Gen Vladimir Andreyev, there was a maximum of 1.5 applicants competing for each position. But this was not much of an improvement over the VVS's situation. General Andreyev said that in 1966, when he entered the VPVO flight school at Armavir, he had already flown 40 hours on light aircraft in the Lugansk DOSAAF aero club and that the VVAUL only accepted applicants with prior DOSAAF training. He also noted that the competition then was seven applicants per slot. Lt Gen Vladimir I. Andreyev, interviewed by Col A. Andryushkov, "We Need to Know the Threat By Sight," *Krasnaia zvezda*, 22 November 1991.

49. General Deinekin told me in December 1991 that he would not hold back any officer who wished to leave the VVS.

50. "Military Pilots Are Reluctant to Serve," *Izvestiia*, 4 July 1992.

51. Maj Gen Ya. Yanakov, "From the Retrograde to the Modern," *Aviatsiia i kosmonavtika*, no. 1, January 1992, 2–3.

52. Col Gen of Aviation Petr S. Deinekin, interview in "A Time for Fundamental Solutions," *Aviatsiia i kosmonavtika*, no. 2, February 1991, 2–3.

53. General Deinekin, interviewed by N. Belan, "Gaining Altitude," *Sovetskaia Rossiya*, 6 September 1991. General Deinekin recalled how in earlier days the VVS might wish to advance a promising young officer, only to hit a brick wall in the party's Central Committee, where "some young man in a gray suit and blue shirt would pick up a special telephone and say that this candidacy did not suit them."

54. Quoted in Alexander Velovich, "Soviet Forces Face Restructure," *Flight International*, 25 September–1 October 1991. Later, Deinekin added with pride that "the spirit of democracy is inherent in aviators." Interviewed by Yelena Agapova, "The Skies Are the Same." He also affirmed, during a press interview in Germany, that the new leadership in Moscow had broken with communism once and for all. Rudiger Moniac, "All Commitments Regarding Germany Will Be Precisely Honored," *Die Welt*, 12 December 1991.

55. Yanakov, 2–3.

56. Col Gen Viktor Kot, interviewed by Sergei Babich, "The Air Force Acquires a New Image," *Krasnaia zvezda*, 27 January 1994.

57. ITAR-TASS World Service, 24 December 1993.

58. A detailed assessment of the Soviet and Russian reaction to the Gulf War is presented in Benjamin S. Lambeth, *Desert Storm and Its Meaning: The View from Moscow*, RAND Report R-4164-AF (Santa Monica, Calif.: RAND, 1992).

59. Gen Konstantin Kobets, interview in "The Future of the Armed Forces," *Voenniye znaniye*, no. 1, January 1992.

60. Colonel General Deinekin, interview in "Who Will Take Up the Sword?" *Krylia rodiny*, March 1993.

Air Operations in the Gulf War

Sir Patrick Hine

First, let me say how pleased I am to have this opportunity to address you on air operations in the Persian Gulf War. My own role as joint commander of the British forces came right at the end of 40-plus years service in the RAF, and it was particularly gratifying to take part in a war that was won principally through the effective application of airpower.

Most of you will have heard of Gen Jan Smuts—a South African. In 1917 he commented with great prescience that "the day may not be far off when aerial operations become the principal operations of war to which the older forms of military and naval operations may become secondary and subordinate."

However, airpower has not until recently become the dominant factor in modern warfare that Smuts foresaw. That is because technology hitherto could never quite match adopted concepts of air operations. But there can be no doubt following the Gulf War that airpower, correctly applied, can now enable wars to be won, even against enemies with large forces, quickly, decisively, and cheaply in terms of friendly lives lost. Certainly, it is no longer possible to conduct effective land or naval operations without first creating air superiority. Airpower is pervasive, and at last it is beginning to realize its full potential.

The initial reaction amongst the Gulf states to Saddam Hussein's invasion of Kuwait on 2 August 1990 was one of deep shock. But on 6 August, by which time Iraq was beginning to mass some of its 11 divisions and 200,000 troops in Kuwait along the border with Saudi Arabia, King Fahd asked both the United States and United Kingdom to deploy forces. Thus began Operation Desert Shield, or Operation Granby as the British called it.

The American response to the wider threat from Saddam was rapid and impressive, with both air and ground forces arriving in Saudi Arabia within 48 hours of the decision to deploy. On 9 August the first (15th) wing of F-15s began flying combat air patrols, having flown nonstop from the United

States for more than 14 hours and with seven aerial refuelings. Initial British forces consisted of a squadron of Tornado F-3s (air defense) and a squadron of Jaguar ground attack aircraft. The Tornados were flying combat air patrols within two hours of arrival at Dhahran.

Central Command's forward headquarters, under Gen Charles "Chuck" Horner pending the arrival of Gen Norman Schwarzkopf later in the month, was set up in Riyadh in the Saudi Ministry of Defense and Aviation, with its much smaller British counterpart being located nearby.

Time was needed to build up the Coalition's ground forces to a level where Norman Schwarzkopf could be confident of defending Saudi Arabia against an Iraqi attack, and thus for the first two months of the crisis, the allies would have had to rely very heavily on airpower to stem any Iraqi advance. That it would have succeeded, I have no doubt for the American build-up of air forces (including those on two aircraft carriers) was quick and effective. Moreover, the RAF deployed two squadrons of Tornado GR-1s with their JP 233 specialist airfield denial weapons in the early weeks of the crisis.

Planning of an air campaign to defeat Iraq and to oust Saddam's forces from Kuwait began very early on and by the end of August was well advanced. The responsibility for drawing up and developing the air campaign plan (ACP) in theater was vested by General Horner (the joint force air component commander) in one general (now lieutenant general), Buster Glosson. He and his number two, Lt Col David Deptula, did a splendid job.

The *objectives* of the ACP were simply stated but very clear:

- Establish air superiority
- Isolate and incapacitate the Iraqi leadership
- Destroy Iraq's nuclear, biological, and chemical (NBC) warfare capability
- Eliminate Iraq's offensive military capability
- Eject the Iraqi army from Kuwait

The *planning* concepts adopted by Buster Glosson and his team were as follows:

- Create strategic paralysis among the enemy leadership

- Destroy the enemy's will and capacity to fight
- Conduct the campaign over a relatively short time span (weeks not months)
- Target the Saddam regime, *not* the Iraqi people
- Minimize civilian casualties and collateral damage
- Pit Coalition strengths against Iraqi weaknesses

The aim was to create strategic paralysis by making it impossible or very difficult for the Iraqi leadership to communicate with or influence either its military forces or the civilian populace, followed by the destruction of the enemy's capacity and will to fight. Successful prosecution of that aim through intensive air attacks, day and night, would, it was thought, limit the war to no more than 60 days. There was no intention, unlike in Vietnam, of applying airpower (or any other combat power) against Iraq incrementally—force would be used massively from the outset in order to maximize the shock effect.

It was the Iraqi regime that was targeted, not the Iraqi people with whom the Coalition had no quarrel. In fact, the planners went to great lengths to minimize civilian casualties and collateral damage. Finally, it was important to pit allied strengths against Iraqi weaknesses and, by observing Suntzu's guidelines for warfare, not to allow the enemy to fight the battle he wanted.

It is interesting to observe that the focus of the air campaign planners was consistent with some principles of airpower drawn up by Marshal of the Royal Air Force Sir Hugh (later Lord) Trenchard when he became the RAF's first chief of the air staff in 1918:

- Obtain mastery of the air, and . . . keep it
- Destroy the enemy's means of production and communications by strategic bombing
- Maintain the battle without any interference by the enemy
- Prevent the enemy from being able to maintain the battle

Iraq's critical nodes were judged to be its leadership, military, and infrastructure. Large and quite well-equipped armed forces, and a huge military infrastructure, including the capacity to develop and produce nuclear, biological, and chemical weapons, had been built up over the previous decade

341

or more, together with extensive command, control, and communication (C^3) and integrated air defense systems. However, C^3 was highly centralized under Saddam himself, which was a major weakness that was exploited to the full in the early hours and days of the air war.

It was against this background then that the ACP was drawn up. By mid-September it was ready and had been briefed to Schwarzkopf and in Washington. It was basically a three-phased plan:

- Phase 1: Strategic air operations against Iraq
- Phase 2: Suppression of enemy air defenses (SEAD) in the Kuwait Theater of Operations (KTO)
- Phase 3: Destroying the battlefield

General Glosson's instructions were to prepare an ACP that was stand-alone and not associated with any Coalition ground campaign. But when I first saw General Schwarzkopf around the beginning of September, he briefed me in outline on an ACP that had a fourth phase, which was "Air support of ground operations." He also referred to phase 3 as "Preparation of the battlefield"—a small but not unimportant difference from "Destroying."

I formed a close relationship with Schwarzkopf over the months that followed. I both liked and respected him, and I know that he understood the importance of airpower and how vital it was to him as the overall commander. I remember asking him at that first meeting how he saw an offensive operation going if political pressure and economic sanctions failed to persuade Saddam to withdraw from Kuwait. He answered that if the president required him to mount such an operation, then he would insist on:

- Having sufficient ground forces available, and properly supported logistically, to complete the task quickly, and
- To achieve that objective with minimum allied casualties, the air force would be required to reduce the enemy's combat strength—and here he specifically mentioned tanks and artillery—by some 50 percent during the preparation of the battlefield phase.

He added that, once his overall operational plan had been approved by the president, he would insist on minimal political interference with its execution and look to Gen Colin Powell, chairman of the US Joint Chiefs of Staff in Washington, to shield him from such pressures. Schwarzkopf never wavered from these conditions, although at times he came under considerable pressure to do so from the Washington end.

By the end of October, the American force level in the Persian Gulf had built up to its planned 230,000 level. The British 7th Armoured Brigade Group and many other Coalition forces were also in theater. At a meeting I had with Schwarzkopf towards the end of October, I discussed with him the operational plan to regain Kuwait.

I explained that we, in my headquarters in the United Kingdom, had been doing some serious thinking about this. Options we had considered included a wide "left hook" maneuver by the land forces, with the disposition of Saddam's elite Republican Guard forces a key consideration there. We did not favor amphibious operations because of the possible high casualties. Overall, there were risks associated with a precipitate land action because of the adverse force ratios and the difficulty of protecting our flanks, notwithstanding the assumption that we would have air superiority. General Schwarzkopf's response was that he held similar views. The risk was that the Coalition could get bogged down in a war of attrition with mounting casualties.

There was a growing realization in Washington that economic sanctions were unlikely to work within a realistic timescale and that any Coalition military operation would need to be mounted during the coming winter.

But there was reluctance by some in the US administration (Scowcroft) to authorize further extensive reinforcements. Schwarzkopf asked: Couldn't the air forces weaken Saddam Hussein to the point where only mop-up operations would be required? What was my view?

I replied that airpower might well defeat Iraqis without the need for a ground campaign, but was it sensible to rely on that? Saddam Hussein had proved to be an obdurate leader who had shown that he was prepared to sustain high casualties and to use chemical weapons. He might not buckle under a heavy weight of air attack, and then the Coalition would have to go in with the ground forces available and could face mounting casualties. What would the effect be on public support for the war, particularly in the United States? Frankly, while I was confident that allied airpower would prove very effective, if not decisive, I felt that the risks of going to war with such an adverse ground force ratio were too high. We would almost certainly only get one shot at removing Saddam from Kuwait. We had to take advantage of the winter window of opportunity—before Ramadan and before temperatures rose significantly (which would increase the chemical threat)—and we also had to win quickly and with minimum loss of Coalition lives. So I favored further reinforcement.

Schwarzkopf had already come to the same conclusion and had secured Colin Powell's support for major US reinforcement of the gulf, and notably by armored forces. He thought that despite some still conflicting views, the president would agree, which he did two days later. As for a further British contribution, Schwarzkopf put as his top priority a second armored brigade and then yet more Tornado GR-1s.

The British government agreed to both requests a few days later, and our ground forces were brought up to divisional strength.

The allied reinforcements, which included the powerful US VII Corps from Germany, could not be all in theater before mid-February.

Diplomatic activity and the embargo operations continued but failed to persuade Saddam to withdraw from Kuwait. The UN deadline of 15 January passed. There was concern that Saddam might announce a partial withdrawal or just start to withdraw. President George S. Bush did not want to delay, so air operations began on the night of 16–17 January.

The Coalition had very clear advantages in the air:

- The Iraqi air force had no track record.
- The Coalition had better aircraft, weapons, command and control (C^2), doctrine, tactics, training, and a 3:1 numerical advantage.

- The advanced technology developed during and since the Vietnam War, particularly with regard to precision-guided munitions (PGM), stealth, electronic warfare (EW), and SEAD, was clearly going to be a big plus. Also in the Coalition's favor was the high reliability of allied aircraft and their round-the-clock/night capability.

Despite these advantages in the air, the threat faced by the Coalition was numerically formidable. At H hour, we faced a threat array twice as dense as Eastern Europe during the Cold War including:

- Seven thousand radar missiles
- Nine thousand infrared (IR) missiles
- Eight hundred fighter aircraft
- The fourth largest army in the world
- Chemical and biological weapons
- Ballistic missiles

It was *not* a benign environment.

Table 1

Strike Forces

United States		United Kingdom		Other Allied	
98	F-14	18	Tornado F-3	85	F-5
96	F-15C	40	Tornado GR-1	82	F-15
48	F-15E	12	Jaguar	12	F-16
210	F-16	6	Buccaneer	24	CF-18
162	F/A-18			70	Mirage
64	F-111			8	Jaguar
36	F-117			57	Tornado
105	A-6			20	A-4
22	A-7				
60	AV-8				
144	A-10				
42	B-52				
4	AC-130				

Against the threat, the Coalition had almost 1,750 fighter, ground attack, and operational support aircraft. The cutting edge of the offensive element was the F-117s, F-15Es, F-111s, and Tornado GR-1s, especially for the strategic operations against Iraq, while the EF-111 Ravens, F-4G Wild Weasels, and Alarm-equipped Tornados were amongst the key support assets.

Table 2

Support Forces

United States		United Kingdom		Other Allied	
48	F-4G	6	GR-1 (Alarm)	5	E-3
18	EF-111	6	GR-1A	20	C-130
50	EA-6	9	VC-10	7	KC-130
7	EC-130	7	C-130	5	C-135
10	E-3	4	Nimrod		
6	RC-135				
9	U-2R/TR-1				
18	RF-4				
224	KC-135/10				
128	C-130				
40	SOF				

For several weeks before the war started, Iraq was shown the same allied air activity picture every night, which included quite regular force packages, including tankers, that flew to within about 25 miles of the Saudi-Iraqi border. The idea was to achieve the maximum tactical surprise when the initial raids started on 17 January by presenting enemy radars with broadly the same picture. But there was, of course, a great deal more that he did not see.

The initial raids were as follows:

- H hour minus 30 minutes: Cruise missiles launched from the Persian Gulf and Red Sea.
- Ten minutes later: Eight Apaches took out two forward radar sites in southern Iraq to allow F-15Es through to attack static Scud sites (which were pretargeted against Israel).

- The F-117s went in—we believe totally unobserved—to drop the first bombs on key C^2 targets in and around Baghdad—at H hour.
- A few minutes later the cruise missiles began to arrive.
- Twenty to twenty-five minutes after that, the EW packages (there were two main ones) arrived to suppress enemy defenses in preparation for the strike aircraft.
- The raids by the initial attack packages.

The Iraqi integrated air defense system was severely disrupted—indeed almost neutralized as far as providing effective C^2 was concerned—within the first 24 to 36 hours. Furthermore, the SAMs were rendered virtually ineffective by a combination of hard- and soft-kill SEAD.

The Iraqi main operating bases were attacked by force packages that included Tornado GR-1s dropping JP 233s from very low level—the aim being to disrupt operations and to reduce sortie rates, rather than to close the airfields altogether which, given their size, was beyond the capability of the resources available.

The Iraqi air force virtually failed to show, except for a few air defense fighters. Lacking any kind of effective control, they were quickly picked off by Coalition fighters, mainly F-15s directed by AWACS. After three to four days, it was clear that Saddam was holding his air force back for the ground battle, which he expected to begin within a week or so. His ploy was almost certainly to draw the Coalition into a battle of attrition, inflict high casualties, and then withdraw with honor.

The Coalition's response was to bring forward its attacks against Iraqi air force hardened aircraft shelters (HAS), using smart bombs. As the HAS destruction rate mounted, many of Iraq's remaining most capable aircraft were flown to Iran, never to return. The air superiority quickly attained became air supremacy.

After that, there was a change of emphasis in the follow-on air attacks that were sustained until the end of the war. The aim was to dismantle as much of the huge Iraqi military infrastructure as we could—NBC facilities, C^3 nodes, the power grid, petroleum refineries and storage, et cetera—while in parallel interdicting the KTO and preparing the battlefield—what General Powell appositely called "cutting him off and killing him."

There were, of course, some problems, particularly with the weather, which in terms of cloud cover below 10,000 feet was about three times worse than normal (39 percent of the time), and suppressing the Scuds. The main difficulty here was locating the mobile Scud launchers and then attacking them before they had fired and retreated to some kind of hiding place. However, a combination of keeping up an intensive effort against the Scud, the deployment to Israel and perceived success of the Patriot missile, intense diplomatic pressure on Israel to stay out of the war and not play into Saddam's hands, and the notable part played by British and American special forces in western Iraq, enabled us to contain this largely "political" weapon threat.

The progressive attrition of Iraq's ground forces in the KTO gathered pace in the two weeks leading up to the commencement of the land battle. The B-52s did an excellent job in undermining the morale of enemy troops, particularly those in the forward infantry divisions, whilst the smart bombers steadily took their toll of his armor and artillery. It was, however, very difficult to get accurate bomb damage assessment (BDA) from overhead imagery—to assist in determining whether or not we had reduced the combat strength of the key Iraqi divisions, notably the Republican Guard, down to General Schwarzkopf's stipulated 50 percent. This was particularly frustrating, but by 21 February the general judgment was that the air forces had adequately prepared the battlefield, and the decision was taken to launch the ground campaign. It began on 24 February and was all over in four days. Very considerable direct air support of Coalition land forces was given, despite at times very poor weather.

The Gulf War is sometimes referred to as the 100-hour war, but in reality it was the 1,100-hour air war that enabled the Coalition to defeat the world's fourth largest army and sixth largest air force in only six weeks and with the loss of only 240 allied lives. This war clearly illustrated the tremendous impact that modern airpower can have in major conflict. There is no other way to keep casualties down which, given the glare of publicity today from the media, especially TV, is essential to maintain public support.

I should like to finish off by touching on what I saw as the main air lessons to emerge from the Gulf War.

But first, let me pay tribute to the Americans for providing outstanding leadership and higher direction of the war. That they were able to lead such a disparate Coalition so successfully throughout a lengthy crisis and a major conflict was a tribute to skillful diplomacy and to General Schwarzkopf's qualities as the overall commander. From the president downwards, through Secretary of State James Baker, Secretary of Defense Dick Cheney, and Chairman Powell of the Joint Chiefs, the administration functioned very efficiently—helped, it has to be said, by some gross misjudgments by Saddam Hussein who, if he had had six feet, would have shot himself through each more than once! But without that firm American leadership, and the clear articulation of political objectives and military aims, the Coalition's forces would not have been anything like as cohesive and successful as they were.

At the operational level, we saw a classic example of centralized and effective planning and control of air operations. The air effort was sharply focused, firmly directed, and well executed by professional operators whose skills had been developed and honed through realistic and varied training. The emphasis on flag exercises, air combat maneuvering, electronic warfare training, and tactical leadership courses really paid off. The lesson I draw from this is that we cut back on training at our peril.

Next, airpower certainly came of age, largely as a result of technology at last being able to underpin our air doctrine, tactics, training, and professional skills.

Through satellites, high- and low-flying reconnaissance systems, and ELINT and SIGINT aircraft, the Coalition was supplied at the strategic level with a diverse and virtually constant flow of intelligence. AWACS provided airborne early warning and control for our force packages over Iraq and Kuwait, and the new Joint Surveillance Target Attack and Radar System (JSTARS), together with ABC[3] Hercules, enabled us to allocate offensive air support aircraft in the KTO to best effect. The use of specialist EW and SEAD aircraft helped enormously to keep the attrition rate of allied aircraft down to an almost unbelievable figure of 0.035 percent over about 110,000 offensive sorties. Thirty-nine aircraft were lost. The breakdown is given in table 3.

Table 3

Aircraft Combat Losses

US Air Force	US Navy	Royal Air Force
3 A-10	5 A-6	6 Tornado
1 AC-130	1 F-14	
1 F-4G	2 F/A-18	
2 F-15E		
5 F-16		
2 OA-10	*US Marines*	*Other Allied Forces*
	6 AV-8	1 A-4
	2 OV-10	1 F-5
		1 Tornado
Totals: 30 US		
6 UK		
3 Other		

The extensive use of precision-guided weapons enabled the allied air forces to inflict high levels of destruction and damage against key point targets, with minimum loss of civilian lives and collateral damage to civilian property. One interesting statistic: 10 percent of the munitions (all smart) did 75 percent of the damage.

Stealth, through F-117s which flew over 1,250 sorties without loss, proved its value. They were the only aircraft to attack targets in downtown Baghdad, and on the crucial first night, they achieved total surprise and, albeit representing only 2.5 percent of the force, hit 31 percent of the targets. While stealth technology is likely to become cheaper in real terms over the next 10 to 20 years, very few nations can at present afford it. Moreover, it may be that effective counters to stealth—or some facets of it—will be developed.

And so, force packaging and SEAD will remain essential when mounting raids against versatile, layered, or point air defenses. But SEAD, unless it is totally effective, has the disadvantage of signaling the approach of the force package (or gorilla as it is known), especially if used against point defenses; and thus it needs to be applied with care if the attacking aircraft are forced to operate at low level, as was the case with the Tornado GR-1s when on JP 233 offensive counterair missions early on in the gulf air campaign.

Although a number of Coalition aircraft delivered dumb bombs from medium altitude with praiseworthy accuracy, it was only those with a precision-guidance capability that achieved more damage. Without smart weapons, it is simply not possible to conduct effective offensive air operations from medium altitude or to obtain the full cost benefits of airpower. That and the need to design as much flexibility as possible into weapon systems, so that they can be effectively dropped or fired from either low or medium altitude, were two of the main lessons to come home to me from the Gulf conflict. Moreover, if they can be afforded, standoff smart weapons confer further advantages in terms of reducing vulnerability to target defenses or, alternatively, of extending effective range.

It is already possible, by using a combination of inertial and GPS, to achieve standoff weapon accuracies of around five meters without any in-flight correction by the crew; in short, we are getting close to acquiring the adverse/all-weather "smart" weapons capability for which the Gulf War clearly showed the need. Yet greater accuracies can only be achieved with some form of terminal seeker, such as laser radar, millimeter wave radar, synthetic aperture radar, double-imaging IR, or IR-laser radar. I am confident that we will see this near total all-weather precision-bombing capability in service in the next five to 10 years.

The need to improve warhead effectiveness, particularly against very hard concrete targets, was another requirement to emerge from the Gulf conflict. And here, I believe that the Royal Ordnance Division and BAe [British Aerospace] have something promising to offer. I will not go into any detail, but suffice to say that I expect to see a warhead developed before the year 2000 that will enable a single 1,000-lb laser-guided bomb to penetrate up to three meters of reinforced concrete.

There are other lessons to emerge from the air operations in the Gulf War, but time does not permit me to mention them all. However, we can pursue any that are of particular interest to you, either collectively or individually, during the question period. I will cite but four.

First, the importance of space systems, be they for warning, C^3, weather, navigation, the cuing of ground-based weapon systems, or intelligence. Second, the importance of tactical reconnaissance. The ball in the sky is not a panacea, and the few all-weather tactical reconnaissance aircraft that we had in the Persian Gulf more than proved their worth. Third, the need to improve our BDA techniques and dissemination of the results to the combat forces. Finally, the vital importance of mobility in all its aspects—through air transport, both fixed wing and rotary, and air-to-air refueling.

Let me conclude by saying that it was a privilege and honor to command the British forces committed to the Gulf War and to witness the total vindication of airpower. It was applied with imagination and skill, exploiting in the process the capabilities that advanced technology has at last provided. I can just see Jan Smuts smiling with satisfaction from across the ether.

Discussion

Air Vice-Marshal Gary Beck: Could I ask you to elaborate on the relationship between the air objectives for the campaign and the overall strategic objectives?

Air Chief Marshal Hine: The strategic air campaign objectives were established as early as August 1990. Air superiority is of course a sine qua non for any further operations. That, and the isolation and incapacitation of the Iraqi leadership, both political and military, was always seen as something that would be extremely important to do if we could, early in the operation. The need whilst we were at war to do our best to take out the NBC capability, both in terms of research and storage facilities, was another top priority. The reduction of the Iraqi ground forces' offensive capabilities by 50 percent was an extremely important consideration for Schwarzkopf. And the final strategic objective, of course, was what was achieved: the ejection of the Iraqis from Kuwait. For all objectives, those strategic objectives of the air campaign plan never varied. There was a difference of view between the air commanders, and maybe even Schwarzkopf, on the one hand, and the corps commanders on the other, concerning how air should be allocated in the final few days, in particular, to attacking targets within the KTO. The air force wanted to continue to pound the Republican Guard, whereas I think the corps and divisional commanders were very concerned about pounding the forward artillery and the Iraqis' defensive positions, which we thought were well prepared and through which, of course, our own breakthrough would have to take place. So I think it would be fair to say that there was some difference of view there which was resolved.

I have heard one army commander say that when they went in through the breach, they found that something like 80 percent of the Iraqi artillery had been destroyed by the Coalition ground force's organic firepower from MLRS. Where the truth lies I'm not too sure. But there was an awful lot of effort put into the preparation of the battlefield and, through close examination of all sorts of intelligence, Schwarzkopf and Horner were, I think, quite convinced by the 20th of February that the combat effectiveness, if not the numbers, of tanks and artillery pieces was below the 50 percent level.

Squadron Leader Owen Hammond: You alluded to reports which stated that despite an extensive air and special forces effort, not one mobile Scud launcher was destroyed. Because the Iraqis moved and buried chemical agents, the amount destroyed by air could be measured in kilograms while the stocks amounted to hundreds of tonnes. These unsuccessful efforts can be extended to include biological and nuclear facilities. The survivability of the Iraqi assets speaks volumes for the passive defense tenets of mobility and concealment. You spoke of the need to improve hardened target construction, but could you comment on passive defense and its use by the Iraqis?

Air Chief Marshal Hine: You're quite right in saying that airpower was relatively ineffective in suppressing the mobile Scuds, and since then a great deal of thought has gone into how that might have been improved. We didn't have too much trouble in finding and attacking those NBC facilities which our intelligence had already located. I think you were implying there was quite a lot found after the war that we didn't actually know about during the war itself. I wasn't quite sure about your question concerning passive defense. What are you after there?

Squadron Leader Hammond: The lessons you drew were all based on active defense. I was wondering if you could draw any lessons regarding passive defense. I know we had to develop a new penetrator bomb to replace the I-2000 for bunkers; for example, at one location there were eight bunkers and only one was actually destroyed although three others were extensively damaged. So hardened shelters were one form of passive defense that was perhaps effective. Dispersal, redundancy, concealment, deception, and mobility were used quite effectively by the Iraqis, and I think that we often miss this lesson by concentrating on our own side, as opposed what happened on the other side.

Air Chief Marshal Hine: Well, the hardened aircraft shelters did not, of course, prove to be effective as a passive defensive measure. The deeper bunkers were extremely difficult to take out, as you indicated, and it was only right at the end of the war, actually the last day, that the Americans dropped the two GBU-28 5,000-lb bombs which had been developed very quickly over a matter of weeks and flown from the continental United States to the theater. One of those two bombs actually hit its target and took it out. I did refer during my presentation to the need to develop warheads which are more capable of deep penetration into these very hard targets.

Dispersal, yes, the Iraqis used dispersal as one method of hiding their aircraft. They tended to put them into villages or towns and close to schools where they knew it would be more difficult for us to attack them, and indeed we let them go when they were so located. Dispersal can be effective, particularly in forested areas, although infrared systems should help you find what you're looking for unless it's been cold for many days. Deception, yes, they were extremely successful with the mock Scud launchers that they had, and we have some wonderful gun-sight film of these mobile Scuds being destroyed by both fixed-wing aircraft and helicopters, only to find out after the war that they were only dummies. So I think there is scope there for us to learn some lessons.

Passive defense is something to which we in NATO have paid a great deal of attention, particularly survival against chemical or biological attack. I think it behooves all military forces to take that kind of threat seriously. I was very surprised, frankly, that chemical weapons were not used during this war. I was convinced that Saddam might well use them during the actual breach operations, chemical artillery against our concentrated forces in much the same way that he had previously in the Iran-Iraq War. But this was a classic case of deterrence working. Saddam and his generals had worked out that if they were to inflict very high casualties on Coalition forces through using chemical weapons, they would get something back in spades.

Mr. Maurice Horsburgh: I'd appreciate a few comments about the handling of the media. If I could go back firstly to the Falklands War, we were subjected nightly to a barrage from a civil servant who was capable of making any major victory sound like the greatest defeat the British military had ever suffered. However, it seemed in the gulf that the military had got their act together, and we saw excellent presentations nightly. I would be interested in your comments on how the media were handled during the Gulf War.

Air Chief Marshal Hine: Basically, in theater we had two levels of media presence, one in Riyadh itself where there were the daily press briefings to which you refer. The Americans held one and the British held their own, and I think we were generally pretty successful in giving the media what they wanted. The other level was the mobile reporting teams where you had media syndicates covering radio, television, and the newspapers out with the operational forces. They would be with a brigade headquarters, for instance, or on board a ship or at an air base, and they were free with little censorship to report on what had happened and to interview the combat people, the commanding officers, and so on and so forth. So I think on the whole, the media this time were very much happier with the way they were treated by the military than had been the case in the Falklands.

The problem modern commanders face with the media is that given the speed with which bad news can be relayed through satellites into capitals, it can often be the case that the public are seeing what is happening on some part of the battlefield before commanders in the rear area, or certainly back in the UK, or politicians back in the UK know what is happening. In my case I had a very nervous secretary of state for defence who was concerned about being bounced in the House of Commons if something awful had happened, and he was not in a position to make a statement. I had to say to him: don't phone up the brigade commanders or the battalion commanders, they're in the middle of a battle; we will find out as soon as we can for you exactly what's happened, and in the meantime you'll just have to face any press at home or colleagues in the House of Commons and say you've only just heard about it, you don't know, but as soon as you get the information you'll make a statement. There's no doubt that the politicians are very nervous about the media portraying things that could be happening in theater almost immediately and before they can be properly briefed. This is a fact of life, and all commanders in future are going to have to fight modern war in the full glare of publicity.

Air Marshal Ray Funnell: Firstly a comment on the last question, and I bring this out in my paper on the Falklands War. It's a comment from Sandy Woodward, and it's something we all should contemplate. What Sandy had to say came out of the Bluff Cove disaster: one of the unfortunate side effects of having a battle fought out in your living room is the impression it creates that what television shows is important and what it doesn't show must be unimportant. That isn't necessarily the case.

My question is that while wars of the future may be fought in very different geographic, diplomatic, and political circumstances to the Gulf War, two aspects are likely to be common to almost any conflict. First, we are likely to fight as part of a coalition; and second, the use of airpower is likely to be central to achieving the coalition's operational and strategic aims. The Americans find it difficult even to get their four air forces to work together effectively, and in the gulf a number of other air forces had to be integrated into a coherent whole. From what I've read it wasn't quite as easy, quite as simple, or quite as effective as some people believe.

Air Chief Marshal Hine: I have no doubt there were one or two cases where one or more of the junior partners within the Coalition were not entirely happy with the way their squadrons were tasked, but I think that would be the exception rather than the rule. Certainly the Royal Air Force was involved very closely with the planning of the daily task order. The RAF commander in theater had to be entirely happy with all of the missions he was going to be tasked with. In other words, you weren't just given a task; there was a consultative process so that the capabilities and limitations of your aircraft and crews were taken into account. And the junior members of the Coalition only undertook those sorties which they were perfectly happy to undertake. So I thought on the whole, it worked pretty well, and I know of no major disagreements from any of the other members of the Coalition with the way that the Americans put the air campaign and the daily task order together.

Air Marshal Funnell: Let me follow up. You mentioned the RAF's experience. Did the system work as smoothly for other air forces like the French and the Italians? Also, I wondered about the use of Marine air assets. In the past, Marine air has tended to be reserved solely for Marine surface forces. What was the arrangement in the gulf?

Air Chief Marshal Hine: Again, if they were unhappy with what Glosson and Deptula wanted them to do, they could hold up the red card and there would be no acrimony. The smaller air forces only undertook those tasks that they were happy with and which they were competent to undertake.

As far as Marine Corps aviation was concerned, it was brought under Horner and, in fact, contributed to the overall air campaign objectives. The nature of Marine aviation, particularly the AV-8Bs, limited them to operations within the Kuwaiti Theater of Operations, but they were part of the daily ATO. It was not until the last few days before the ground campaign started that they became intimately associated with specific Marine Corps objectives. During those last three or four days, if I remember correctly, they were swung onto targets which would be immediately in front of the two US Marine Corps divisions which were going in to one of the better-defended parts of Kuwait. But it was much more the case in this war than any previous war that the Marines put their aviation under the operational control of an overall air commander, who happened to be light blue. It was something they, perhaps, were not comfortable with, but were quite clearly directed to do by Schwarzkopf.

Air Vice-Marshal Alan Reed: It's apparent that intelligence played a major role in both targeting and damage assessment. You had platforms varying from aircraft to satellites. Obviously an air force like the RAAF has a limited budget. If you had a limited budget, where would you put your money? And if I may ask another quick question, the RAF had the job of attacking runways with the JP 233. Following the Gulf War, is that still an RAF role?

Air Chief Marshal Hine: If you have very limited funds, I would go for the tactical reconnaissance capability. Now that can be provided either by manned aircraft, in our case the Tornado GR-1A, or by unmanned aircraft or a combination of the two. Regardless of which you choose, I don't think you can fight a ground campaign of this sort effectively without tactical reconnaissance. It also is critical to find out exactly what damage you've caused with deeper penetration air missions, be they interdiction or offensive counter air. If you are relying solely on satellites and you have got cloud cover, as we had much of the time, you will not get the battle damage assessment intelligence you're looking for. For smaller air forces, which may become involved in coalition warfare, they're almost certainly going to have to look to the Americans to provide the strategic intelligence from satellites and other sources. So modest investment, in my view, should go on tactical reconnaissance aircraft and/or drones.

Your second question was on the RAF's Tornado GR-1s and the JP 233 attacks. Those were successful. The loss rate was of some concern; as you know, we lost four aircraft during the first five days of the war. These were some of the more demanding operations, carried out at very low level at night, and they were very dark nights. We lost two of the aircraft to SAMs, and the other two aircraft, we believe, actually flew into the ground. Only one aircraft, incidentally, came back with antiaircraft artillery damage, so there wasn't an impenetrable wall of fire, although it must have looked like that to the crews with tracer coming up and so forth. It remains a role which we would have to conduct in certain wars if we're involved in the future. There is no alternative but to drop JP 233 from low level, and it can be extremely effective for interdicting airfields for a matter of hours, if not days. But in this particular war, after four or five days, it was quite clear the Iraqi air force was not going to show; they were laid up inside the hardened aircraft shelters. There was no point in continuing these disruptive attacks against runways and taxiways, so we moved the Tornados up to medium altitude, initially doing radar bombing at night and then day bombing, and, ultimately after about a week, bombing with laser designation provided by Buccaneers. But the low-level option is one of those which will remain in my view. There will be certain circumstances where it is preferable and actually makes the aircraft less vulnerable than medium-level attack.

Air Vice-Marshal Tony Mason: I have two questions if I may. What if any intelligence did we have on 23 February about the imminent withdrawal of Iraqi forces from the Kuwait sector before a single soldier had crossed the start line? The second question is looking to the future. What are we going to do about looking and striking below big, wet trees?

Air Chief Marshal Hine: I don't think we had any good intelligence that the Iraqis were about to withdraw on the 23d. There had been some statement made by Saddam Hussein in Baghdad, setting out certain preconditions for withdrawal, and this stemmed from negotiations that continued throughout the early weeks of the war between the Russians and the Iraqis. But Saddam attached certain conditions to the withdrawal which were quite unacceptable to the Coalition, by which I mean linkage into the broader Arab-Israeli question, and there were other conditions which we found unacceptable. So nobody took any notice of it, and the ground campaign began the following day.

The second one is very difficult. I honestly don't have an immediate answer to it other than that you have to get intelligence from one source or another which pinpoints the target. Once you know the position, it can be attacked from the air using systems like precision-guided munitions and GPS.

New Era Warfare

Charles A. Horner

Air Marshal Gration, ladies, and gentlemen. It's an honor for me to be here. [This paper was the conference after-dinner speech.] I think that what you're doing in holding this series of conferences is admirable and something that we need to do. We must always examine how we do business in the military because what we do is so important to our nations. Quite frankly, it's the survival of our nations that we're about.

I talk a little about Operation Desert Storm everywhere I go because I think that it is very, very interesting. It represents what I call *new era warfare*. I coined that phrase because if you don't have a catch phrase then people don't catch on. When I talk about new era warfare, it doesn't mean that I have any great insights. We have some great historians present. I think they would agree with me that you need about a hundred years to study an event in order to get the proper perspective. So, some of you younger people will be able to get a full account of Desert Storm. I don't think I'll make it. But I do think there are things in Desert Storm that are worth examining. They're glimpses of the future for military operations. There are things that are as old as Napoleonic operations, but there are others that are much different. They are primarily things like the timeliness and the strategy and the political aspects of modern warfare. Gen John Baker used a term today that I'm going to steal, which was *knowledge warfare*. Everybody wants to talk about information warfare, but, in fact, it is knowledge warfare. I think we learn everywhere we go.

To understand Desert Storm from the American side, I think you must also study Vietnam. They're inseparable. We came out of Vietnam confused in terms of putting a title on it. We said Vietnam was *low-intensity conflict*, and quite frankly I never understood that. Because to me getting shot at is *high-intensity conflict*. It didn't really make sense. But I think some of the things that we did in Desert Storm were a direct result of our Vietnam experience. So, if you want to draw a line on the big historical board, maybe Vietnam is the place to draw it and not Desert Storm. Desert Storm is just the logical outcome.

But what are we talking about? Is it a product of technology? I think the answer to that in some cases is "yes." Technology cannot be ignored. Precision munitions, global navigation systems, computers, communications, the range, speed, and survivability of modern aircraft, stealth, and the use of space have changed warfare.

There's no doubt about it, Desert Storm indicated that the nature of warfare has altered. Some of the changes are worth examining. First of all, there is some measure of efficiency. I think we all know that war is horrible, setting aside the moral aspects, setting aside the pain and suffering. War is horrible because it is inefficient. It's obscene to people who want to do things in an orderly fashion. We have brought to modern warfare some measure of efficiency. I talk about timelines, which relate to the decision-making process. We must understand that in war now we must be decentralized. It's absolutely necessary. In World War I, we were decentralized where sergeants and captains were making decisions. Our system wasn't deliberately designed that way; we did it because there were gas attacks, no communications, and because of the fog of war. In Desert Storm we decentralized consciously, and we did that because it's the only way you can accommodate the timelines of modern warfare. Our longest timeline in air operations in Desert Storm had to do with retargeting the B-52s. That was three minutes. Anything inside of that we would never hesitate to change the plan in order to get more efficiency or to take advantage of information if something became available. So, when we talk about modern warfare, we talk now in terms of seconds—not days, months, or years that characterized war in the past. And I think that it's important we keep that in mind.

There are other things in terms of data demands. For example, in the past you wanted to know where the tanks were stored. Now you want to know where the load-bearing wall is in the building where the tanks are stored. You want to know—is the overburden on the bunker 26 feet of concrete or 26 feet of earth? The data demands of modern warfare are just going out of sight, but it's important.

I think it's important to talk about these things at your airpower conference because airpower is the one force that is really capable of taking advantage of these new elements of modern warfare—because of its speed, its lethality, its flexibility of employment.

I think it is also important though that we not concentrate solely on the military. The political aspects of modern warfare have really come into their own. I think one of the main reasons for this is that the human race is mature. I do believe that people—I realize this is a dangerous thought—are growing up. I believe they are recognizing that war is a horrible thing and shouldn't be glorified. It shouldn't be sought after as a means of political will. It may come to that, but it is abhorrent and ghastly. If you're involved with war—and I think the military people in this room understand that better than anyone—when it's all over with, you're the ones that somebody has to face at the graveyard.

Another thing is that our public has a much lower acceptance of war than in the past. That probably comes from two reasons: one, the world is obviously a much smaller place because of jet travel, because of television, things of this nature. The other is of course the media. We all know the impact of CNN on modern warfare. Quite frankly, I think those of us in the Persian Gulf War spent as much time watching CNN as the people at home. People all over the world watched the war, not just any one country. You got things like the "Highway of Death"—a perfectly legitimate military operation, conducted very efficiently and in terms of loss of life very low. Nonetheless, it also meant that we could not sustain the war. The bombing of the command bunker in Baghdad is an example. We believed it to be a command and control facility, while in fact it was being used as an air raid shelter. We probably killed 200 to 400 civilians. It had a profound impact on our targeting thereafter.

Now to understand the political reasoning in modern warfare, you must understand something about setting goals. I'll ignore the goal of survival for the nation whose survival is at stake. In the case of the Gulf War, it was Kuwait. There's no getting around that. You're going to fight with everything you have, anyway you can. That's understandable. But I think the rest of us, particularly countries like Australia and the United States, which have large oceans, are unlikely to be involved in a national survival war. We've got to keep in mind that first of all our entrance into combat should have some selfish aspect to it. As much as we'd like to be seeking the greater good, we wind up with things like Somalia, chasing after the images of starving children on television, and suddenly find ourselves in a very difficult situation. In fact, we have withdrawn. So, I think, first of all the nation needs to pick a side, which is self-serving as well as altruistic, as we did in Desert Storm. It was all right to take up the cause of Kuwait, which was overrun and being tortured, raped, and plundered. On the other hand, it was also right to protect access to oil vital to our industrial society. There is nothing immoral about protecting your nation's vital interest. We need to do that.

There is one crucial issue that we in the military must train our political leadership to understand. This is a big step because it involves all kinds of nuances that are antidemocratic if you're not careful. But we must always insist that the goals we're given by our political leadership are militarily achievable. In Desert Storm we were blessed. George Bush gave us the job of ejecting the Iraqi army from Kuwait and, while we were at it, crippling the nuclear, biological, and chemical operations in Iraq. He did not give us the job of fixing Iraq. People back in the United States love simple answers to complex problems. We're very much like Australia. People said, "If we just had gotten Saddam Hussein that would have solved the whole thing." Well, it would be like wiping out the head of the Mafia. It really wouldn't solve things. We would have had our people still controlling the streets of Baghdad getting shot at by people who were concerned about their homes, their families, and their children. It would have been an absolute mess. So, none of us had a problem when it came time to stop the offensive operation. We were all relieved. We'd done the job that we could do, and the problem with Iraq is going to have to be solved by the Iraqis. They've had 300 or 400 years of this kind of internecine warfare between the Shiites and the Kurds. They're going to have to take care of it themselves.

One thing we really didn't do well in Desert Storm was termination of conflict. It was presumed by the military, when we were planning the offensive operations in August, September, and October, that somebody in the State Department was burning the midnight oil writing out the peace treaty. The day we stopped offensive operations against the Iraqis, we had a call from Washington, and they said, "Would you please go and negotiate a meeting some place." We sat down with a yellow pad—Norman Schwarzkopf, John Yeosock, and myself—the three of us sat there and said, "What do we negotiate?" And then we said, "Well, first thing from Vietnam—prisoners and MIAs—full accounting—and also, the return of Kuwaiti citizens who had been kidnapped and imprisoned." And next, "How do we separate the forces so we don't bump into each other with loaded weapons and continue the killing and things of this nature?" Eventually, I will say this, the diplomatic corps caught on and very rapidly after Safwan there were negotiations that led to substantial agreements which were very, very important. Unfortunately, we made some mistakes at Safwan. That could have been avoided. So, to all of you who are in the military, if you get involved in one of these situations, you should demand that you know what the "end-game" should look like before you begin the "game."

There are practical aspects of Desert Storm that were brought to us, primarily to me, by President Bush at Camp David. We went out there on Saturday morning—the invasion had occurred Wednesday night. There was a great deal of confusion as to what should be the proper course of action. The cabinet sat around the table, and Schwarzkopf presented ground options and I presented air options. We then sat down and people started questioning us. Bush didn't say a thing. He sat there and held his own counsel. I was watching him. The rest of them were firing questions. Then President Bush started asking questions after they all finished. His questions first had to do with the loss of life. He was absolutely fixated on the concept of how do we avoid the loss of life. Obviously, we were all thinking "body bags/Vietnam/American lives." But he wasn't talking only about American lives. He wasn't even talking only about allied lives. He was talking about the loss of lives on both sides, Iraq and Coalition. Believe me, it colored everything we did thereafter. Every target was examined on how to approach it with minimum loss of life.

We could have bombed the Iraqi army to death. Instead, we went after their equipment. Normally before we would strike their tanks and artillery, we would drop leaflets that would say, "Get away from your tanks." After the war we talked to the Iraqi generals. They would say things like, "In the Iranian War, the tank was my friend because I could put my troops in it, and they would be safe from artillery strikes. In this war, the tank was our enemy. The minute we would park it, we would get away from it." You'd see them on the film digging slit trenches about one-half a kilometer away. If we didn't hit the tank that night, we got it the next day or the next night.

The other thing that I think is very instructive in modern warfare, in new era warfare, is the international relationships. I don't want to go into World War I or World War II, but I think Vietnam tended to be mostly an American show. The strongest ally we had other than South Vietnam was Australia. But Bush in his questioning kept asking the cabinet, particularly Jim Baker, "What do other nations think about this? What do they think should be done?" In the high councils of America, that question was not asked often enough. I don't know where it came from. I don't know whether it came from his time as ambassador to China, or his time with the UN, or his time with the CIA, but President Bush really pushed that point hard. There's a book out called *The Commanders*. I just read it. It's exactly wrong on this subject. At that table Bush turned to Cheney and he said, "Dick, I want you to talk to King Fahd. He has the most at stake in this." So, Secretary Cheney flew to Riyadh to do that.

What did we gain from this experience? What did we find significant, of interest, in the planning and execution of Desert Storm? I think one thing that we must keep in mind is that planning must be done in theater. There's lots of data flow that must come from the outside. But Washington, D.C., is the perfect example of what can go wrong with out-of-theater planning. They call Washington "Ants on the Log." It's a giant log floating up the Potomac River with 10 million ants on board, and each one of them thinks it's steering the log. We must be careful about headquarters not in the theater running the war. Again, in Vietnam, the president picking the targets in Washington and our flying them in Vietnam was just a ludicrous way to fight—a terrible waste of life. We were bound and determined that was not going to happen. The problem we have is that historically our intelligence in peacetime gets centralized. Because if you're an intelligence person, the way you get promoted is taking pictures and putting them in front of the prime minister or the president, and then everybody says what a good boy you are and promotes you. So, as a result, intelligence people flock to Washington. The trouble is, they don't work to meet the war fighters' requirements. Instead, peacetime intelligence does things like national estimates, technology analysis, and economic estimates. So, we had a rule. The targets had to be picked in the theater. We made that an article of faith. It did not mean we did not get good targeting from Washington or elsewhere. We did, but the targets had been picked in theater.

Another thing I wouldn't let them do was to plan the war beyond the first two days. The captains and majors who did the planning wanted to take it through the first weeks. But the problem is that modern war is so uncertain and so fluid that you must develop the capacity to react. If we had built that plan beyond the first two days, we would have become slaves to it, and we would have missed all the opportunities. So what happened was our efficiency in air operations was very high the first two days, dropped off drastically the third and fourth days, and then began to gradually go back up. We then achieved levels of efficiency which would not have been possible if we hadn't given people the chance to learn how to operate in this uncertainty called war. So, you must do that for your planning.

In terms of the Coalition, I can tell you that you must recognize that national prerogatives are important. We had a whole variety of vastly different nations there. Now with the NATO people, we work together in Europe and have common ways of doing business and common training. But on the political side, for example, some of the European nations sent combat forces, some sent support forces, some sent equipment, and some just sent monetary support. That was fine. We could accommodate all that, and it helped make a strong coalition in terms of being there—being a participant whether it was risking life or risking resources. Participation is important. You must be able to recognize the prerogatives of each nation.

You also must have some flexibility in your operation of a coalition. People want to create command chains. And, particularly, land forces live for command chains. They love boxes with lines. By contrast, airmen like unity of effort. What we do is we sit down and ask, "What needs to be done?" We decide on an approach. Then what airmen do, is they say, "OK, well my kind of airplane flies best at night, flies these kinds of distances, has these kind of munitions." So they just divide up the workload. It's like a big job jar. You just pull out what's appropriate to your capabilities. Before the war—I'll never forget this—we were always getting all this heat about "Why don't you have the usual command organization?" and "Its all going to come unglued." Absolutely false, wrong, and dumb. We never had a single problem. We all worked very well together. We also had an advantage because airmen all speak English. It was more difficult on the ground side because many of the countries could not communicate with one another.

I talk about decentralization and execution. It is the fundamental way you release the initiative of thousands of people. If one person tries to run things, you get one person's initiative. What we did is we said, "The most important place where things are happening is over the target." So we pushed decisions as close to that as we could. The air tasking order was constructed in detail, but it was only a plan from which people could depart, so when they made a decision they had some basis for that decision. And that's a big one. It's very difficult for military people to learn to let go. We want to be in control. The generals want to be generals. I'm going to tell you something. Generals don't amount to a hill of beans. It's the captains and the sergeants who do. When that sergeant goes out to load bombs, and he's "fragged" to put 2,000-pound bombs on an F-16 and he gets out there and there's no more 2,000-pound bombs, if you have a very centralized system, he will sit down and do nothing. If you have a decentralized system he says, "Those guys are so dumb, I can't believe it. We're going to put eight, 500-pound bombs on the airplane." Well, the mission takes off and the target is destroyed—not as efficiently as planned, but the job gets done.

I have a statement I use; I stole it from Bill Creech. It's called "nose in, hands off." The commander, the leader, must know in detail what's going on, but he cannot tell people how to do it. One of the best cases was Dick Cheney. He knew in detail everything we did. For example, we needed to bomb the biological storage area. We were in a terrible dilemma. There were two white papers—one from England and one from the United States—that said if you bomb those biological storage areas in Iraq, every living thing on the peninsula of Saudi Arabia would die. Since we were located there, we tended to think that was a serious business. Cheney came in and I had 15 minutes to discuss with him the decision to bomb those sites. After three hours of intense discussion, it was decided that we should attack the target. The discussion involved detailed data on weapons effects designed to preclude the fallout of hazardous material. He knew in detail what we were doing, approved what we were doing, but left the tactics up to us.

On the other hand, with modern communications it's very easy to distribute information; therefore, the risk is to centralize decisions. The best example I can think of is the "Joint STARS picture" that was being plugged into various command centers around the theater. The Joint STARS picture is the big radar that shows moving objects on the ground. It's for tanks, trucks, and things like that. One night I got a phone call from Schwarzkopf, and he said, "There are 20 trucks at such and such location." I said, "We'll get on it," and I just turned to the duty officer next to me and said, "Divert this flight here onto that target." He did that. They got through, and there was nothing there. And, of course, if you divert a flight lead onto a target and there's nothing there, you have one angry flight lead who proceeded to give me a phone call. That's pretty interesting, for a captain to chew-out a three-star general. However, it was appropriate. So then I looked into it. What had happened was the picture had come in and had gone hard copy off the TV screen, and a young corporal looked at it. The corporal gave it to his sergeant and said, "Look at this, look at all these trucks." The sergeant says, "Hey, I can make points with the captain." He went running and found a captain who just came back from dinner. They looked at it and the captain said, "I'll bet the colonel will be interested in this." So, he waited around for the colonel, who gets up from his nap, and showed him. The colonel, wanting to be a brigadier general, went right to Schwarzkopf and said, "Look at this." And Schwarzkopf said, "Hit that thing." Only now it was four-hours old. So after that, every time Schwarzkopf called about a Joint STARS picture, I said, "We will go after it if it's valid." And he said, "I accept that."

Another example involves the AWACS. I would sit there and have the air picture of everything that was going on from the Mediterranean to Teheran and from Turkey to Riyadh. I could see the minute an Iraqi aircraft broke ground. I can't tell you the number of times I wanted to reach for that microphone and call the AWACS and put "Eagle Flight" onto those two Iraqis who just broke ground. I didn't do it, and it was always some other flight that got vectored on, and the targets always got shot down. It's a very, very difficult thing to learn to let go, but we have to do it.

The other thing is that in modern warfare, there's something you cannot overlook and that's the environment you're in. When you sit in a tactical air control center, you hear things. Things that wash over you. As you walk into your post, you go by the search and rescue center, and you're checking on the Tornado guy who got shot down or on the A-10 guy who's missing in action. The individual in the theater, when he or she sits down, has an attitude, a feeling, a sensitivity for the game you don't get outside the theater. We lose sight of that because we have wars so seldom, thank God. I think my best example is when [USAF Chief of Staff Merrill A.] "Tony" McPeak would call me up. He always wanted to know what was going on. We would chat, usually in the afternoon—it was morning in Washington, D.C. We'd talk about how things were going, and pretty soon he'd say, "What we need to do is this and this." I would listen, and I'd listen carefully. Not because it was Tony McPeak, but because you're always looking for good ideas. One day he was talking to me and said, "You're not saying anything." I said, "I'm listening." And he said, "No you're not, you're telling me I'm not in charge."

Let me give you another example—and I share this with you because I think it is very instructive concerning something we came out of Vietnam with—of this business of the theater versus the rear echelon. We felt in some ways betrayed by our leadership in Vietnam because they did not stand up. It's fun to criticize the generals of the past, but then one day you're a general and then criticism starts coming close to home. In this case, I had a wing commander call up, Rick Parsons, from up in northwest Saudi Arabia. They had just shot down two airplanes about 30 miles inside Iran. What had happened was that two Iraqis had taken off from the Baghdad area to go to Iran for asylum. Rick got vectored onto them, turned in, lit the burners, and they finally caught these guys, splashed them both. When they got back home and looked at their inertial navigation system (INS) coordinates, they were a good 30 miles inside Iran. In Vietnam our first casualty was integrity—we didn't talk. We didn't ever tell the ugly things. But Rick Parsons called me and said, "Boss, I hate to tell you this, but we just shot down two Iraqi airplanes in Iran, and we know we weren't supposed to be there." So I said, "OK." I called Schwarzkopf and said, "We just shot down two Iraqi airplanes in Iran. We know we weren't supposed to be there. I will try not to do it again. The guys know what the rules are. These things happen." And he said, "No problem." And he called [Chairman of the Joint Chiefs of Staff Colin] Powell, who told Cheney.

Well, I knew inside the Pentagon there would be someone who would say, "No good deed can go unpunished" and would conjure up something called a "buffer zone" because we had one in Vietnam. It worked wonderfully in Vietnam in terms of making us inefficient. So, I sat there and suddenly my criticisms of the generals in Vietnam came to haunt me. Because now I was faced with trying to refute this buffer zone that they were going to put up. There wasn't enough room to have one—the distance from Baghdad to the Iranian border is very, very short. I was marshalling my arguments, getting them all lined up and ready to go. But I knew I'd fail because I'd be arguing with the Pentagon. So, what I had to do was draft my letter of resignation. Here I was at the epitome of a professional military career, and I was going to have to quit. I was going to have to resign. I was going to have to walk away. I had no other choice. Fortunately, the phone call never came. After the war I asked, "How come we weren't told to establish a buffer zone?" I was told it was brought up, but it was decided that the guys in theater will know what to do; if they need a buffer, they'll go make one.

Two areas where all the military people in this room have failed are in exercising logistics and intelligence. They're the two most important aspects of warfare you will face when the real time comes. So, pay attention to that.

Friendly fire—I'll talk a little about it. Probably over one-half the casualties ground-to-ground were friendly fire. In the case of air, we had one where we destroyed a Marine vehicle, marines bombed a Marine column, and two A-10s shot two British vehicles. In terms of absolute numbers, friendly fire incidents were very, very low. In terms of percentages of the casualties, they were very high because the casualty base was so low. I think that we have not paid enough attention to this problem. In the past, that was probably acceptable and probably had to do with the inefficiency of warfare. In Vietnam, if you bombed a friendly convoy, you probably disabled a truck and may have killed somebody. If you put a modern Maverick missile into an armored vehicle, you're going to kill everybody inside that vehicle because today's weapons are so lethal. So, the friendly fire or fratricide, or whatever term, must be worked absolutely assiduously. You must pay absolute attention in detail to it because of the lethality of modern weapons. And, remember, if you have casualties, you lose the war.

The media. The media are everywhere and cause military people a lot of problems. We, as a group, are intimidated by the media. Particularly because if we do something stupid, they tell the whole world we did something stupid. The other thing is they're always seeking information, and they're always asking probing questions. In Desert Storm, they wanted to go with the body count thing because people wanted to know how we were doing. We live in a statistical age. So, they wanted to know how many people did you kill—like it was something to be proud of. We refused to do that. We never hesitated to tell the media where we believed we had good facts and it did not reveal our plans. Sometimes we were wrong afterwards, and that's kind of hard to swallow and admit. The thing about the media that we in the military must understand is that, in our societies, the media are fundamental, and we must not be afraid of them. If you don't want to answer a question, you don't answer a question. If you think it is a stupid question, you say, "Well, that's the dumbest question I ever heard, Sam. You got another one?" And it's amazing how they retreat when you stand up to them.

Don't always try to please the media. They are people trying to earn a living. Help them earn their living. They're just like the rest of us. They have children to feed and people to educate. Always deal with them from a position of confidence and on a factual basis. Another thing that is fundamental in the media is this: understand if you do something stupid and they identify it as stupid, in some ways they're helping you because you can correct your mistakes or say you were wrong and you won't do it again. That's good. If you've done something right, you can stand up for it. You can't trust the media to always have integrity, but I can tell you that you can trust 95 percent of them to have integrity. Because integrity to the media is just as important as it is to a historian or a military officer. They are lost without it. But the basic thing about the media is this: if you distrust the media, it isn't the media you are condemning. It's the people who read the papers, who watch the television programs—the very people who pay your salary. They're the ones you've lost faith in. So, let the media take their most savage shot. Let them have their worst, most unjust shot at you and just keep faith in the people you work for—the people who pay your wages, the people you're serving. Because they're also the same people the media are really serving and representing.

If Saddam Hussein had one thing that worked in Desert Storm, it was the Scud missile. I think that we failed to learn a lesson from that. It had no military value. It had lousy accuracy, and he did not have a fuse for a gas warhead. In fact, he would have been wise to put poisonous material in front of the Scud because the Patriot missile would have dispersed it for him. So, we dodged a bad situation there. We will not continue

373

to be able to dodge that situation, as evidenced by what is going on in North Korea. Believe me, the impact of the ballistic missile is not understood by military people. It is only understood by civilians. In the city of Riyadh, in Bahrain, in Israel, they understood it in spades. I asked after the war, "Why didn't we learn that lesson?" The other night they had the F-117 film here on TV. In the film, the guy who did the stealth technology was an English fellow who had grown up in London during World War II. He had learned the lesson—he said, "I can imagine how terrifying it is to have the F-117 fly over your country. You don't know it's there, and suddenly you have a bomb explode. It's like the V-2 over London." We must come to grips with the ballistic missile threat, particularly when it's coupled with nuclear, biological, or chemical warheads.

I'm traveling around our country and talking about the war that's going to replace the Cold War. It's the war of nonproliferation. It's going to become the most significant struggle we'll face internationally. It must be fought as a coalition, not necessarily on a battlefield, but in terms of deterrence, defense, diplomacy—those kinds of things.

Now, I've come to the conclusion that war has profoundly changed. I think that airpower is equal to land and sea power. I don't think it's superior. I think it has the things like speed, lethality, and flexibility to take advantage of modern warfare, so it's very, very important and very significant. But each war must be determined on the circumstances involved in that war—the environment, the aims, the political goals, the nature of the enemy forces, and the nature of the friendly forces. But there are those who still believe that airpower is subservient, particularly to land, and also to sea power. That is absolutely wrong. I think we proved that in Desert Storm.

The political aspects of war are still crucial. We must have a good leadership. We must understand the limits of military power, and we need adequate forces. It's too late when the crisis begins. You lose your options. Then, the situation becomes as it was in Korea or in World Wars I and II. And we paid for it with the blood of our men and women. Every military person in this room has an obligation to go through his or her chain and demand credible, capable military forces. You owe it. You can't wait until the last minute.

I think there are drastic changes in conflict. Every target in Desert Storm was reviewed by a lawyer. The law of armed conflict is something that all military people need to know. I never found it constraining. There were some targets we wanted to hit that we couldn't. But nonetheless, we must abide by some level of morality because the nations that are involved in a war are still going to be left on the earth together. They're still going to have to live together. You're still going to have to think about what's going to happen 300 or 500 years from now. The nature of war doesn't change—but the efficiency of operations, the importance of information, and the importance of command and control have changed. The need to decentralize the way you do business is most important. You must give people decision authority; give them room to make the right decision. You must have adequate planning and be able to take decisive action on the battlefield. And before the war you must emphasize joint and coalition training.

The things that the military are doing in Australia will serve this country well into the far future, not necessarily on the battlefield, but in nations working together, building ties, trust, and confidence. You must understand that modern warfare has to be quick and lethal—that aspect does not change. And that all of us, when we prepare for war—as horrible as it is—must keep in mind that we have really one major obligation in our military profession, and that is to be loyal to those people we send into battle to die—that we send them prepared, equipped, and well led. That is our reason for having conferences like this and that's why they're so important. Thank you very much.

The Future of Airpower

Richard P. Hallion

It is a great pleasure to be speaking to you today on the subject of the future of airpower.[1] We have heard some distinguished authorities on its evolution, from both historians and practitioners. Therefore, it is with some trepidation that I stand before you. The business of prediction is, after all, a dangerous one.

I'll just offer you two examples. The first is from Lord Kelvin, president of the Royal Society, who wrote to Maj B. F. S. Baden-Powell of the Aeronautical Society of Great Britain (later the Royal Aeronautical Society) in 1896, after having been invited to membership. "I have not the smallest molecule of faith in aerial navigation other than ballooning," he less-than-graciously replied.[2] The second example is from the noted futurist and science fiction author H. G. Wells. In contrast to Lord Kelvin, Wells was an aviation enthusiast. He wrote in 1901, "Long before the year 2000 A.D., and very probably before 1950, a successful aeroplane will have soared and come home safe and sound."[3]

What both these statements reveal—one from a skeptic, one from a true believer—is that very often the state of technology and the state of societal development can move so rapidly that even highly regarded experts can be woefully wrong. Neither Kelvin nor Wells, for example, recognized that the state of aeronautical inquiry was so advanced that the Wright Brothers—already busily at work when these two men were writing—would fly within a few short years. Indeed, a mere 10 years after Wells made his statement, the Italians would carry out the first bombing campaign in military aviation history, against rebelling tribesmen in Libya. Wells himself lived to see the widespread use of airpower in both world wars. And by 1950 (four years after Wells died), the first ballistic missile, the first jet fighter, the first jet airliner, the first air-delivered atomic bomb, the first cruise missiles, the first guided bombs, the first surface-to-air missiles (SAM) and air-to-air missiles

(AAM), the first antishipping missiles, and the first supersonic airplanes had all made their appearance. So the task of the prophet is a daunting one.

There are some striking continuities that one notices when looking at defense matters. For example, let's cast our minds back to the heady days of late 1989 and the fall of the Berlin Wall. I daresay many of you remember some of the bolder pronouncements in academe, the media, and by certain politicians who chided the West for having wasted the economic resources of various nations by building massive defense organizations over the previous 40 years, organizations now without a purpose or reason for existence. Many of these individuals proclaimed a millennial age of peace or, even, the "end of history." Yet less than a year later, there were over one-half million troops deployed to confront Saddam Hussein, and prepared to fight a war very much like that which had dominated European and American defense thought for nearly one-half century. The millennial age of peace had lasted about nine months. Indeed, many smaller conflicts had continued unabated by the end of the Cold War, or have followed since, from the Horn of Africa to the shambles of the former Yugoslavia. Today, not quite 80 years after Sarajevo first came to public prominence, we find an eerily reminiscent quality to what is happening there, with a pastiche of national identities attempting to sort themselves out, in the shadow of Slavic interest. Indeed NATO, only recently held by some to be an organization without purpose, fired its first shots in anger a few weeks ago, when two F-16 pilots offered the Serbs a lesson in airpower application. It seems, then, that the new world order is increasingly more like the old; history, while it may not repeat itself, sure does rhyme: The most notable enduring certainty about defense affairs is their basic and inherent uncertainty.

We are three years beyond the most successful air war in military history, yet still within the first century of powered flight. Over the last 90 years of winged aviation, we have seen the airplane transformed from a crude hopping machine to a globe-girdling engine of societal change. In this period of time, the rocket has gone from a firework to an arbiter of global nuclear deterrence, and the bomb has evolved from a crude shell with fins to a sophisticated precision munition capable of hitting a target within a negligible distance from its aiming point.

The reputation of airpower itself has changed, from the myths and misunderstandings surrounding its use in earlier wars to the more positive sentiments often echoed today. Consider the following: A popular history on the Vietnam War written in the 1980s concluded that "over and over again we have to learn the lesson that airpower cannot win wars."[4] In the fall of 1990, primarily because of this "conventional wisdom," official skepticism regarding airpower was a constant concern of airpower planners, who believed—not without reason—that it might act to limit the military options being presented to the president.[5] Media portrayals and images of airpower stressed "carpet bombing," "friendly fire," and massive civilian casualties. In January 1991, on the eve of the Persian Gulf War, an outspoken airpower critic, John Kenneth Galbraith, stated that Americans "should react with a healthy skepticism to the notion that airpower will decide the outcome of a war in Kuwait and Iraq," even though the United States Strategic Bombing Survey that he himself had participated in 45 years earlier had taken a far more optimistic view of air warfare.[6]

Then came the war itself, and virtually at once the tenor of airpower discussion changed. President George S. Bush remarked, "Gulf lesson one is the value of airpower."[7] Numerous other spokesmen—including those from the non-aerospace community—opined that air had been the dominant force in the war. As a result, even if there was a debate over whether or not a "revolution" in military affairs had occurred (my personal opinion is that yes, there was, and one a long-time coming), airpower nevertheless had a credibility and an awareness in the minds of decision makers that it lacked for decades previously.[8] A cautionary recent assessment of American airpower concludes that it has a deservedly earned "mystique," noting that "airpower dominated the Persian Gulf War as no other conflict since World War II. . . . In the end airmen were probably correct in their belief that this war marked a departure."[9] What does all of this say for the future? Is faith in airpower a justifiable mystique or a dangerous mistake?

The easy answer, of course, is that it is situational and depends upon what one is trying to do and what the circumstances surrounding the use of airpower are. There is a strong theme of continuity in airpower application going back to its very roots. We should remember, for example, that the contemporary missions of air forces today are those first promulgated, explored, and then standardized in the First World War—air superiority, bombardment, reconnaissance, maritime operations, to name just a few. We still fulfill them, and we are likely to do so well into the future. Technology has transformed them, has changed their capabilities, but not the basic intent of the missions themselves. For example, the Second World War gave us our first experience with electronic, turbojet, and atomic warfare, and it shaped the nature of the postwar world. But the missions remained the same. The revolutions and revolutionary techniques since midcentury—the afterburning turbojet/turbofan, the supersonic breakthrough, the liquid-and solid-fuel rocket, "avionics," aerial refueling, the practical helicopter, nuclear weaponry, computers, electronic controls, composite structures, stealth—added ever-increasing capabilities to military and commercial aircraft systems. But the missions have remained the same.

One of the greatest challenges we face in the airpower community is education of the non-airpower specialist, particularly those individuals charged with responsibility for maintaining the national defense. When one is contemplating a field of military endeavor in which, literally, lives, treasure, and national security are at stake, it is obvious that this is a serious responsibility for us all, particularly, I think, for historians. It is not one, I may say, that we have done particularly well. The price of failure to adequately undertake such analyses can doom an air force to obsolescence. The failure to appreciate the need for an air force, or to understand what an air force brings to a fight, can doom a nation—look at Nazi Germany or, more recently, Hussein's Iraq.

In the post-Cold-War era, these are not idle questions. Right now, the United States is poised on the brink of a return to the roles and missions debates of the post-World War II years. In the exchanges that will no doubt accompany those debates, salient points and perspectives on both the current state of airpower and its legacy of use should be kept uppermost. In particular, I recommend a provocative group of 10 propositions derived from historical experience by Col Phillip S. Meilinger, the commander of the Air Force's School of Advanced Airpower Studies (SAAS) at Maxwell Air Force Base, Alabama.

- Whoever controls the air generally controls the surface.
- Airpower is an inherently strategic force.
- Airpower is primarily an offensive weapon.
- In essence, airpower is targeting, targeting is intelligence, and intelligence is analyzing the effects of air operations.
- Airpower produces physical and psychological shock by dominating the fourth dimension—time.
- Airpower can conduct parallel operations at all levels of war, simultaneously.
- Precision air weapons have redefined the meaning of mass.
- Airpower's unique characteristics necessitate that it be centrally controlled by airmen.
- Technology and airpower are integrally and synergistically related.
- Airpower includes not only military assets but also an aerospace industry and commercial aviation.

Certainly, there will be those who quibble and question some of these, but they constitute, I think, an important beginning. For my own part, airpower attributes that I think are of particular importance include the following; I present them in no particular order lest they be construed as "rank orderings."[10]

First: Airpower today, and for the foreseeable future, possesses some innate synergistic qualities and advantages that have matured over a one-half century of development and refinement, which add new vigor and value to the traditional missions air forces have prosecuted and which offer a nation a unique and special ability to project power and presence. In June 1990 these were recognized and enumerated in a United States Air Force white paper under the rubric "Global Reach— Global Power," and they were important underlying assumptions in the subsequent revision of Air Force Manual 1-1,

Basic Aerospace Doctrine of the United States Air Force, March 1992 edition.[11] They consisted of "virtues" associated with air-power, most from the beginnings of air warfare—speed, range, flexibility, precision, and lethality.

Speed and range were generally mature concepts by the mid-1950s, as hinted earlier, but even they benefited from the expansion of turbojet technology, refined high-speed aerody-namic design, and aerial refueling after that time. Interestingly, the implications of the air weapon's reach were enunciated in 1945 by the distinguished military theorist J. F. C. Fuller, who noted that range was, throughout military his-tory, "the characteristic which dominated the fight."[12] In the airpower era, he believed, the "fulcrum of combined tactics" had to be shaped around the airplane. Such indeed, as exem-plified by the Gulf War, has come to pass.

Reach today is critical, for it means not only global power but global presence. The air-refueled aircraft of the present day exert a power and presence previously attainable only by expensive overseas basing of troops, aircraft, and fleets, and, in most cases, without the vulnerabilities to enemy action and terrorism that accompanied such foreign basing. Through them, one can exert presence, demonstrate will, and obtain influence from a home-based force.

The others—flexibility, precision, lethality—had been at best imperfectly realized. The flexibility of airpower only came of age in the era of air refueling, coupled with more reliable engine and systems technology, though occasionally it had manifested itself in earlier conflicts, such as the strategic implications of fighters in World War II or the tactical applicability of long-range bombers. Precision had undergone the greatest change. In World War II, examples existed of precision attack, but it was always the exception, never the rule. One thinks of the Royal Air Force's (RAF) Mosquitoes—surely the F-117s of their day—against Amiens prison and various Gestapo headquarters or George Kenney's skip-bombing B-25s or the use of dive-bombers (with their attendant disadvantages) by the Luftwaffe and various navies. The daily reality of the war, however, was imprecise dumb bombing. In the Second World War, only 7 per-cent of all bombs dropped by B-17 bombers fell within a thousand feet of their aim point—and this was not only considered acceptable, but good.[13] In the late 1980s—on the eve of the Gulf War—self-designating, precision bomb-droppers such as the F-117, F-111F, and F-15E were routinely placing laser-guided bombs (LGB) less than 10 feet off target.

Coupled to precision weapons was, of course, precision navigation which, by the time of the Gulf War, not only meant reliance upon both mature radio navigation aids and more recent technologies, such as the ring-laser gyro, but also space-based navigation, such as the now-famous Global Positioning System (GPS). Hand-in-hand with precision came lethality—the ability of air attack to deliver overwhelmingly destructive force against pinpoint targets via air weapons. By the onset of the Gulf War, the ability existed for air forces and other airpower projection organizations to strike a range of targets with sophisticated autonomous or near-autonomous munitions. For example, in that war, the Air Force's Maverick and the Army's Hellfire missiles both proved devastating against mechanized forces, even when they were on the move. One Apache helicopter unit, for example, scored 102 hits for 107 missiles fired, a rate of better than 95 percent.[14]

In sum, then, the synergistic coupling of these five attributes ensures that an air force today can undertake the traditional missions discussed earlier with a certainty of success that our predecessors—the Trenchards, Burnetts, Joneses, Harrises, Spaatzs, and, yes, the Goerings—would have found remarkable. To place this in context, a global jet airlifter, supported by air refueling, can rapidly deliver precision munitions into a theater, hand them off to an air-refueled strike aircraft, and, scant hours later, those munitions can be applied to a high-value target. This is not some dream from a techno-thriller. Rather, that exact scenario was played out in the Gulf War when a C-141 delivered two 4,700-lb GBU-28 LGBs, whose casings were still warm from their freshly poured bomb mix when two F-111Fs took off with them for delivery against a deep bunker at Taji.[15]

This particular example also indicates a second important attribute: The time compression inherent to airpower. Airpower, as our distinguished RAF colleague Air Vice-Marshal

"Tony" Mason has noted, is "war in the third dimension."[16] But I would also suggest that in its ability to respond quickly to a crisis and to respond in such a fashion that it counters an enemy's ability to react by non-airpower means, it is really "war in the fourth dimension"—time—as well.

This flows from the inherent qualities of aerospace technology itself. Two-dimensional surface forces—those moving on land or sea—operate at a mobility disadvantage compared to three-dimensional air and space forces. This relates to the physical environment in which they operate: the viscosity and turbulence of the sea or the convoluted terrain of land, as well as the nature of movement while restricted to a geometric plane. In contrast, atmospheric flight systems are constrained only by the dynamic pressure (q) limits of the vehicle itself and by its designed range, speed, and altitude limitations. Space systems above the atmosphere are constrained only by the natural laws of Newtonian and Keplerian physics governing spatial movement.

To put this in military terms, in the deployment phase of a crisis, airpower reacts in hours versus weeks. For example, land-based airlifters and combat aircraft deployed directly from the continental United States to the Gulf region in nonstop 8,000-mile, 15-hour journeys. In contrast, aircraft carriers took an average of three weeks to a month to reach the Gulf region from East Coast ports, and even designated "fast" sealift ships took 10 days.[17] This is the difference of late twentieth century rates of mobility and engagement—the airplane—with rates more typical of the turn-of-the-century—exemplified by the steam-turbine-powered ship.

The difference is even more dramatic when compared to land combat rates of movement and engagement.[18] In several seconds, an aircraft can orient itself to confront a mechanized surface opponent who has taken several hours to shift position. In the attack phase, an aircraft can have as much as a 10 or 12:1 velocity advantage over a surface vehicle. (Again, essentially late twentieth century versus early twentieth century rates of engagement.) Against individual troops, this advantage is as much as 200:1. (Late twentieth century versus third century B.C. rates of engagement.) The rates of engagement of aerospace missile systems—for example, air-to-surface or surface-to-surface weapons—are even more extreme, in the order of 60 or even 80:1 against moving surface vehicles. The implications are clear: Once such a weapon is unleashed, the opportunity for a two-dimensionally constrained surface opponent to detect, assess, and evade such a threat is essentially nonexistent. In the Gulf War, Iraqi mechanized forces intuitively recognized this. Confronted by air attack, they reacted in the best possible way for their survival—they simply abandoned their vehicles under attack, even while those vehicles were on the move.[19]

Thus, an opponent unable to confront an attacker in the air finds eventually that he is operating out of sequence with his enemy. His decisions take longer; his pace of operations (as compared to his foe) is diminished. In Boyd "Observation-Orientation-Decision-Action (OODA) Loop" terms,[20] this is the natural result of a more capable attacker taking advantage of his higher rates of operation to achieve effects or results that increasingly slow his opponent's ability to function within his own OODA Loop. Eventually, the summation of the cumulative differences in operation generates dramatic disparities and discontinuities, rather like comparing the operations of a late-1980s Cray supercomputer to, say, a 1960s-vintage IBM 360. Even more apt, it is as if an individual uses a virus-free computer while another "makes do" with a similar one inflicted by a virus that increasingly slows its operations.

These effects of air attack were evident as early as the Second World War—even at that relatively primitive stage of airpower utilization. For example, the Nazi general, Frido von Senger und Etterlin, complained that Allied air attacks had reduced him to the level of a chess player able to make only one move to an opponent's three.[21] The same situation recently occurred in the Gulf War, when communications attacks denied Hussein the ability to effectively control or move his forces, preventing him from exercising the various nuances of control required to confront the rampages of the Coalition's air and land assault on multiple levels and in multiple locations.[22] Airpower is far more than the ability to put fire and steel on a target. It is relevant to a wide range of operations and concerns. Nevertheless, it is, of course, in combat operations that most of us think of an air force having to show its stuff. And this brings us to a third attribute: Only airpower has the ability to bring strategic and other high-value targets an enemy holds most dear under rapid attack in simultaneous or near-simultaneous fashion. It is, in the words of Col John A. Warden, USAF, "death by a thousand cuts," for even if any one particular sortie by a strike aircraft is not of great significance, in and of itself, the combination is deadly. Once again, this is only possible because of the maturity of modern airpower, particularly precision navigation and attack, and stealth.

The best example of this in practice was the Gulf War, typified by the opening night strikes across Iraq.[23] In earlier air wars, because of the immaturity of precision, air attacks had to be sequential rather than parallel. For example, the strikes by the Eighth Air Force against Nazi Germany in 1943 and 1944 were complex, unwieldy, unfocused, and characterized by a slow pace of operations. An entire bomber stream of up to 600 B-17s operated essentially against one aiming point. In all of 1943, the Eighth Air Force hit less than 50 targets, causing weekly damage equivalent to, say, a destructive tornado in the American Midwest. Yet, in the Gulf War, in one 24-hour period, there were 150 targets hit, roughly equivalent to a major earthquake every day. Nearly 700 attackers on opening night struck hundreds of different aim points with literally shattering effect.[24]

The implications of this particular attribute for a nation's ability to achieve its war aims are significant. There are, of course, many different kinds of war, and it is a truism that airpower works best against a high-technology opponent, for such an enemy is particularly vulnerable to the kind of devastation that air warfare can wreak. (This is not merely a lesson of modern airpower, but one that goes back in time as well; it was recognized even by De Seversky as early as the 1940s.) Nevertheless, historical experience from multiple conflicts involving national survival indicates that as a war continues from weeks to months to years, the potential of casualties and collateral damage increases dramatically, while the likelihood of a nation achieving the aims it set out to fulfill declines as an enemy adapts and friendly losses mount. Conversely, in a short war, the likelihood of achieving war aims is at its highest, as is the expectation of suffering minimal losses. Recent experiences suggest that nation-states that possess high-technology, robust air forces operating to insightful doctrine can greatly increase the expectation of achieving the goal of a short war, and with it, the rapid, overwhelming destruction of an enemy force.

Fulfillment of this parallel, simultaneous attribute of airpower requires information mastery of such magnitude as to constitute a fourth attribute itself: Airpower is dependent upon the power of information. Information has a value and a worth all its own, and, without it, modern airpower cannot function effectively. Indeed, one could go so far as to say that, in the modern postindustrial nation-state, information constitutes its own "center of gravity."[25] To a degree, of course, this is not a modern lesson, but one that dates to the dawn of warfare—it involves knowing one's craft, knowing one's abilities, being able to communicate easily and understandably, and knowing one's enemies. The lack of information has always been costly in air warfare, both tactically and strategically. The Battle of Midway is probably the best example of how communications limitations, prior knowledge, and knowledge deficits combined to hamper and help both American and Japanese operations. Fortunately, their implications were more serious for the Japanese side than for the American one.

Today, the amount of information available to commanders has increased in direct relationship to the growth and widespread distribution of data-processing systems. To show how the pace of information generation has grown, one need only do a (very) rough comparison of just the print data available to American air commanders from the Second World War and the Gulf War. Second World War US Army Air Forces (USAAF) air operations generated a combined average of 220 documents per day from all theaters, a total of approximately 26,000 pages of material. In the Gulf War, from one theater of operations, the Air Force generated a daily average of 340 documents totaling nearly 49,000 pages of material.[26] Given the time constraints upon modern commanders, and the speed and rapidity with which events can change, it is obvious that information mastery becomes a considerable challenge. To this end, modern airpower requires the internetting of intelligence, administration, and communications to a degree unknown in previous conflicts. But while this challenge is great, if successfully met, the resulting increase in operational efficiency generates benefits all its own, as one opponent achieves information dominance over another.

The extraordinary success of two particular airborne platforms—the E-3 airborne warning and control system (AWACS) and E-8 joint surveillance target attack radar system (JSTARS)—offers a powerful confirmation of what information dominance means in modern war. AWACS deconflicted the air war, preventing "blue-on-blue" fire even as thousands of daily sorties were flown by aircraft from several different air forces. JSTARS—even though a rudimentary brass-board system hastily kluged together for operational use—constituted an AWACS for the ground war. The two E-8 aircraft in theater played a decisive role in the outcome of the Battle of Khafji and the rout of the Iraqi occupiers of Kuwait.[27]

Conversely, the rapid pace of war in the face of information generation can induce its own problems. For example, one of the major disconnects in the Gulf War was the poor turnaround time of intelligence information from sensor systems through the analysis process and back to the operators. In part, this was driven by the tempo of the air war—it was, essentially, a 24-hour war, with no time for intelligence to "catch up" as it had in previous conflicts when air operations generally slowed at night. Another weakness highlighted in the war was the slow pace of data transmission from classified fax machines, though the data they sent were critical, particularly during the early deployment phase of the confrontation. One of the real strengths, however, was the widespread availability of secure telephones.

In sum then, to wage a modern air war successfully, commanders must have access to reliable, secure communications, the best possible intelligence, streamlined administration, the most exacting information on their own forces, and the ability to exchange and use information without undue meddling from organizational elements that are not directly involved in the decision-making and combat-operations process.

The acquisition, exchange, and exploitation of knowledge in the modern world have been revolutionized by the onset of the space age, not yet 40 years old. Thus, a fifth aspect of modern airpower is that airpower is really air and space power. The demarcation between *air* and *space* is increasingly irrelevant, for a modern air force must be prepared to operate in both.[28] I'm not alluding here to Buck Rogers or Flash Gordon fantasies. We must recognize that we have already fought our first space war, even though the current state of space operations could be compared to, say, the use of submarines or aircraft in the First World War: Just a hint of what is to come.[29]

In the Gulf War, the Coalition forces relied upon space-based communications, space-based navigation, real-time weather analysis, intelligence from space, and space-based cuing for Patriot SAM ground-defense systems. These capabilities will be even more significant for us in the future than they have been in the past, particularly as space takes up the challenge of confronting theater missile defense (TMD) issues. Further, the benefits of space-based information dominance run across the spectrum of conflict from low- to high-intensity war.[30]

An air force that can call upon space-based assets is one that can dramatically improve its efficiencies and abilities to prosecute a war quickly and with minimal risk. For that reason, it is disturbing to note the dependency we have upon aging space systems. For the most part, the launch vehicle technology employed by the United States today and for the future dates to the dawn of the "space age," the precomputer, preelectronic, presystems, precomposite structures era.[31] The three primary launch vehicles—the Atlas, Titan, and Delta—are derivatives of early ballistic missile systems (Atlas, in fact, predates the space age by three years). Further, the space community needs—as United States Space Command (USSPACECOM) commander, Gen Charles Horner, has noted—to develop an operational mind-set as opposed to a research and development one. Only then will the space community have legitimacy as a full-fledged war-fighting player. To do this will require a significant investment in a space-based future, precisely at a time when calls continue for a steady decline in apportionment of national resources to defense. With a proliferation of nations operating in space, some with cheap and reliable launch systems, we must remember—to paraphrase an old science-fiction movie— "We are not alone." Finally, there is yet another cautionary note. High technology builds in its own high-tech dependencies and vulnerabilities. An air force accustomed to having the advantages that space assets offer could find itself having to scramble to maintain its efficiency if those assets were, somehow, negated or denied by enemy action or misfortune. Confronting threats to space assets—whether from surface- or air- and space-based platforms—is thus one issue requiring major consideration now and in the future.

A sixth attribute of airpower is its duality, for both combat and humanitarian purposes. In some situations, one has to do both—for example, today, the airlifters of Operation Provide Promise into Bosnia-Herzegovina are capped by NATO fighters which, in turn, are controlled by AWACS. They make use of all the accoutrements of modern warfare—secure communications, GPS, et cetera. Given this, one could be flippant and say that one of the messages of modern airpower is "Bread or bombs: We do both." Air-refueled airlifters bring munitions or humanitarian food rations at transonic speeds into a crisis region. Weapons can be handed off to strike aircraft. Food can be delivered directly, or handed off to theater airlift. In any case, the message here for our air commanders is that the United States Air Force must be prepared to do both combat and noncombat missions: the major regional contingencies (MRC) as well as military operations other than war (MOOTW), perhaps even multiple ones at the same time. It cannot justify itself exclusively only in combat projection terms.

This duality has, of course, existed for quite a while. (For example, this year—1994—marks the 75th anniversary of American humanitarian air operations, and many will recall the efforts at the end of World War II by the RAF and USAAF to air-drop supplies to the Dutch, as well as the better-known Berlin Airlift.) But the combination of the large-capacity jet airlifter coupled with air refueling has given it more significance today than at any previous time. This dual war-and-peace capability was never better demonstrated than after the fall of the Soviet Union, with the emergency food airlift into the former USSR, Operation Provide Hope. It is worth noting that the key individuals in initiating and organizing that food relief effort were, in fact, Air Force personnel detailed to the Department of State, because they appreciated what modern airlift could accomplish. As the food relief planning effort began, it was obvious that deficiencies in the Russian transportation infrastructure would limit the value of merely shipping food to Russian ports. Airpower offered a way out—direct flights from the continental United States or Europe to the Russian heartland. It was this flexibility that made the food resupply effort of substantive, as opposed to merely symbolic, importance.[32]

Yet, as extensive as that operation was, it could have been even greater still. (In the Gulf War, for example, airlifters delivered an average of 17 million ton/miles of cargo per day into the Gulf region.) But while the Air Force had the airlift capacity and global reach to make the resupply effort work, Aeroflot, on its own, did not. Had the crisis worsened, and had it been necessary to do so, the following scenario could have been played out: Assisted by KC-10s and KC-135s, massive airlift by C-5s and C-141s could have delivered key food items, such as canned goods, refined grains, and breads, directly into the former USSR, landing at airheads and then transferring cargo (if necessary) to C-130s and Aeroflot aircraft and helicopters for in-country resupply. In this scenario, Aeroflot would have functioned in the same "on call" role as the Civil Reserve Air Fleet (CRAF) did during the Gulf War. Such was not required. But, in any case, the Russian food supply effort of 1991–93 set an important post-Cold-War precedent for subsequent global humanitarian airlift operations. Last year, 1993, Air Force Air Mobility Command (AMC) aircrews operated in 96 percent of the world's countries: 186 out of a total of 193 nations.[33]

A seventh attribute of airpower is its dominance over other forms of warfare. Today and for the foreseeable future, it is no longer possible to state with any certainty that surface forces are the primary instruments whereby a nation secures victory in war. This has led to a recognition that there is a "new calculus" in military affairs, so that even in joint operations in far-flung regional contingencies, it is the air component that is the most critical and, indeed, the linchpin of victory. As RAND investigators have noted:

> The results of our analysis do indicate that the calculus has changed and airpower's ability to contribute to the joint battle has increased. Not only can modern airpower arrive quickly where needed, it has become far more lethal in conventional operations. Equipped with advanced munitions either in service or about to become operational and directed by modern C^{3}I [command, control, communications, and intelligence] systems, airpower has the potential to destroy enemy ground forces either on the move or in defensive positions at a high rate while concurrently destroying vital elements of the enemy's war-fighting infrastructure. In short, the mobility, lethality, and survivability of airpower makes it well suited to the needs of rapidly developing regional conflicts. These factors taken together have changed—and will continue to change—the ways in which Americans think about military power and its application.[34]

As Gen Michael J. Dugan, USAF, noted in 1989, "Modern warfare is joint warfare."[35] But while there will always be a need for joint combined arms forces to function in a war-fighting environment, surface warfare traditionalists are engaging in wishful thinking when they proclaim the dominance of older forms of sequential power-projection forces. In particular, air's ability to enter a crisis quickly and to employ high-leverage force against an enemy's centers of gravity means that military power has, at last, entered what might be termed the "post-Clausewitzian era."[36]

The command relationship implications are very significant, for a joint force air component commander (JFACC) thus emerges as the dominant arbiter of power simply by the power projection capability that he commands. In the future, it would be a wise theater commander in chief (CINC) who would defer to his JFACC the broadest possible latitude in the planning and execution of the air campaign. While this runs counter to the views of traditional surface force adherents, who argue that air operates only "in support" of a surface campaign, the JFACC can point to notable CINCs whose efforts were crowned by success when they adopted just such an approach: Montgomery in the Western Desert, MacArthur in the Southwest Pacific, Eisenhower in western Europe, and Schwarzkopf in the gulf. Conversely, where air has been tied too closely to ground commanders—

notably the French in 1940 or the Americans at Kasserine in 1943—the result has been disaster. Indeed, in the future it may well be increasingly difficult to argue for the appointment of a CINC or joint force commander who does not come from within the airpower community.[37]

This, of course, brings up an eighth attribute: Historically, airpower works best when it is projected by a genuine air force. While many military organizations can project limited forms of airpower, only a dedicated air force has the doctrinal underpinnings, mind-set, infrastructure, accumulated expertise, technological base, and ability to use it to its greatest effect. Surface forces using helicopters or other short-range aviation systems may use them profitably in land warfare or "across the beach" situations (for example, the dramatic use of helicopters in Iraq and Kuwait or the use of carrier-based aviation in Vietnam). Though these surface forces have also historically invested in longer-range technologies, including cruise missiles and battlefield missile systems such as the Army tactical missile system (ATACMS) and multiple launch rocket system (MLRS), these are at best poor substitutes for long-range, land-based stealthy or otherwise precision-strike platforms. They typically lack the accuracy of the manned aircraft, or its ability to undertake multiple mission taskings, or its ability to deliver devastating force or penetrating weapons capable of gutting an opponent.

But of more significance is the organizational structure itself: Surface forces traditionally think not in long-range theaterwide terms, but in shorter-range "front" or "beachhead" terms. This was evident in the Gulf War, in the near-constant battle between General Schwarzkopf and his corps commanders over the "proper use" of airpower and in the after-action examination of carrier aviation undertaken within the naval historical community.[38] Further, surface forces traditionally lack the infrastructure to support a fully robust and sustainable air campaign force because their assets have to be split among so many different war-fighting communities. Likewise, the deployment of airpower elements by surface warfare forces tends not to take fullest advantage of the capabilities of aerospace systems: They traditionally deploy at the speed of the surface force itself, not at the speed of the airplanes involved. As previously noted in this paper, this is the difference between 15-hour non-stop continental United States to theater deployments of land-based air and three-week cruises by carriers transiting the Atlantic, the Mediterranean, and the Suez Canal to get on station.[39] It is vitally important, then, that decision makers and military commanders alike recognize the difference between a service having an air branch and an air force. It is right and proper for all military branches to incorporate airpower elements within them—indeed, they would be remiss if they did not do so—but a nation, to take fullest advantage of the aerospace environment must have, first and foremost, an independent, well-led, and well-equipped air force.

The dominance of air warfare in the modern era reaffirms—if it were somehow yet still needed!—a ninth attribute: That in the airpower era, loss of air superiority equates to loss of the ability to exercise national prerogatives. Today, more than ever before, the penalty for losing air superiority is too great to risk. When a high-technology society is stripped of air superiority, it is utterly vulnerable to an enemy, which can attack it as it wishes. Put another way, the damage inflicted by precision weaponry to the Iraqi leadership and key military targets in Baghdad on opening night would have been virtually equally devastating against the capital of the United States. In the Iraqi case, loss of air superiority over its own homeland has forced Iraq's leadership to live with an "air occupation" that has exposed the very core of Iraqi military capabilities to outside inspection and destruction.[40]

The tenet—indeed, truism—that air superiority is, first and foremost, the most vital mission of an air force is increasingly questioned by defense analysts writing in the post-Cold-War era, many of whom suggest that modern air forces do not require the latest-generation fighter or strike aircraft technology. Yet it is equally arguable that (because of the extreme threat that loss of air superiority poses and because of the proliferation of advanced air-to-air missiles that can, when married to older-generation aircraft, act as "force multipliers," enabling these older generation aircraft to successfully confront current-generation ones) the quest for higher performance and more survivable aircraft—particularly fighters—is no less critical now than it has been in the past.

The dramatic surge in dangerous surface-to-air missile and antiaircraft artillery (AAA) threats—first dramatically highlighted by the experiences of the Israeli Air Force over the Golan Heights in 1973—forces its own concern upon planners. In the Gulf War, for example, 87 percent of losses came from radar and infrared SAMs and AAA.[41] Essentially, the low-altitude environment was "off limits" to the Coalition from opening night onwards, which degraded the ability of non-precision "dumb-bomb" droppers to do a credible job. Further, these systems have forced greater reliance upon night air war, in which advanced air forces now excel. But the proliferation of increasingly lethal longer-range SAMs and sophisticated night sensor systems will undoubtedly force a technology race for the future between defender and attacker.

This is particularly true of the air-to-air quest for "first look, first shot, first kill" systems blending sensors, stealth, and weapons in a synergistic package that can enable a small, deploying high-technology force to offset a more numerical enemy. One study, for example, suggests that the combination of an F-15C and AIM-120 advanced medium-range air-to-air missile—a force structure advocated by some defense analysts—offers no better than a parity of threat between the United States and potential foreign enemies after the year 2000, largely because of foreign missile developments. But the combination of the projected F-22 and the AIM-120 offers to maintain an air superiority edge for the United States beyond the year 2010.[42]

Why is it that the air superiority issue, in particular, is so difficult to "sell" to the defense analysis community or, worse, to many individuals who might have to evaluate, by dint of political or organizational position, contemporary military airpower capabilities? It may be because, to the untutored eye, one airplane or missile type more or less looks like every other airplane of the same type (think, for example, of a 1950's 707 and a 1990's A-340, or a 1970's AIM-7 Sparrow and a 1990's AIM-120 AMRAAM). This is, of course, dangerously misleading. For aircraft today, traditional parameters—speed, range, and payload—are increasingly less relevant or satisfactory than measuring the overall systemic benefits that the synergistic packaging of modern technology produces.

For example, the basic Mach 2 plus/60,000-foot envelope of the modern jet fighter was established by 1958, with the F-104. So we have an apparent—though illusory—plateau here: No production fighter aircraft since then, be it the F-4, the Mirage, the MiG-21, or the F-15, has really ventured beyond this. But would a fighter pilot today willingly choose an F-104 over, say, an F-22? Hopefully, the answer is obvious. The combination of low observables, electronics, modern air-to-air weapons, air refueling, maneuverability and agility, advanced structures, and high-performance propulsion systems weight this decision in favor of the modern fighter, even though the "top end" performance, on paper, does not seem all that remarkable or different.

The difficulty of selling counterair systems may also have to do with a misperception of airpower itself: That, somehow, the air-to-air war between opposing fighters is a "sideshow" compared to the "real war" occurring on the ground or over the front or somewhere else. Similar dangers lurk, incidentally, when simplistically looking at bombers, such as the B-52 versus the B-2, or airlifters, such as the C-17 versus the C-5, or some conventional widebody transport, such as a 747. In particular, the notion that bombers are, somehow, only creatures of strategic nuclear war (and thus negated by the new international order), is one that is dying hard. This myth gains apparent credence because of the long association of "fighters" with "Tactical Air Command" and "bombers" with "Strategic Air Command," and (by implication) the notion that *strategic* war must only mean *nuclear* war. Here, as in so much of airpower matters, education of decision makers is critical.

My tenth attribute of airpower is its inherently dynamic character and dependency upon high technology. The Gulf War reaffirmed the leverage that high technology offers a nation confronting a sophisticated opponent. And, contrary to the dire predictions of the "defense reform" community of the 1980s, there was essentially no difference in the mission-capability rates of high-technology (for example, F-15E) and low-technology (for example, A-10) aircraft: The rates were well above 90 percent for fighter and strike aircraft and, in the case of the two aircraft mentioned here, 95.5 percent for both.[43] In particular, airpower today benefits from not only the now-"ancient" revolutions of the turbojet and high-speed aerodynamics but from less obvious ones, such as the tremendous advances in miniature electronics, computational design tools, and composite structures.

In particular, the stealth revolution and the revolution in precision attack—both the precision of finding and fixing a target, and the precision of hitting it—have transformed military affairs in a way remarkable by the standards of military history. For example, in previous warfare, nations tended to develop comparable systems quickly or, at most, within a few years. The steam-turbine-powered ship, the dreadnought, the fighter, radar, the jet engine, jet fighters, supersonic aircraft, the atomic and hydrogen bombs, and earth satellites constitute relatively recent examples. But in the case of stealth, which "went operational" in 1983, the future seems clear of rival systems until well past the turn of the century. Thus, at the least, the F-117 will have given the United States a 17-year lead over any potential rival.

Technological development is, of course, inherently unstable, and the quest for antistealth systems is a vigorous one. But stealth proponents can take comfort in the experience of the submarine—an early stealth system—which, though engagable and sinkable even as far back as the First World War, has remained a viable and, indeed, most serious threat to surface systems ever since. Such will, I am confident, be true of stealth aerospace systems as well, despite the plethora of detection systems that may be arrayed against them.

In this characteristic challenge-and-response struggle between threat and counter, which in World War II was termed the *wizard war*, certain adjustments will have to be made. We will have to develop the ability to do greater distance stand-off attacks with precision munitions capable of destroying hardened targets. The combination of space-based navigation, precision seekers for terminal engagement, and, perhaps, hypersonic impact velocities courtesy of high-energy booster systems will, I predict, prove valuable. Hypersonic weapon velocities also potentially offer a high degree of survivability against SAM air-defense systems, something slower velocity systems, such as transonic nonstealthy cruise missiles already lack. Above all, we will have to equip more of our forces to deliver precision munitions, for in the war-fighting environments of the present-day and foreseeable future, dumb bombs move earth, not minds. This situation is particularly acute when one looks to confronting simultaneous or near-simultaneous multiple regional contingencies. In the Gulf War, for example, the United States Air Force deployed over 90 percent of its aircraft capable of self-designating and delivering precision munitions. Had a second crisis arisen—say, in Korea—we would have been hard pressed to meet the needs of both. Precision-attack aircraft, in this case, not weapons, were the potential limiting factor.[44]

We will have to extend far greater attention to nonlethal systems, which hold great promise both for military effect and for the humanitarian implications of their use. For the latter reason, if some of these nonlethal systems, nevertheless, cause egregious injury that smacks of cruelty—for example, the deliberate use of laser systems to blind or disable an opponent or systems that cannot themselves be precisely targeted—it will raise serious ethical issues that will—and should—force reconsideration of their development and use. The issue of nonlethal weaponry is an interesting one, insomuch as, in part, it stems from a growing concern within Western nations, in particular, to minimize both enemy and friendly casualties in war. The reaction to the Al Firdus bunker strike in Baghdad at the height of the Gulf War illustrated this perfectly; a single bomb, placed on a high-value and clearly defensible target, succeeded in forcing a redirection of the air campaign away from Baghdad almost until the end of the war, thanks to the casualties to civilians occupying it at the time it was hit. For this reason, in today's world, every bomb is potentially a "political bomb" or "media bomb" as well as a military one. Nonlethal weaponry capable of destroying an opponent's infrastructure—for example, airborne systems that enable the exploitation of an enemy's communications network, nonnuclear electromagnetic pulse weapons, or computer viruses capable of insertion in key enemy facilities—represent an evolutionary step in warfare that is potentially no less significant than the invention of gunpowder itself.

Now that airpower is firmly embedded in the information age, we will have to refine our ability to measure what we do. Measurement of airpower effects is directly related to apportionment of effort, and that, of course, is directly related to duration of conflict and intensity of attack. We saw in the recent Gulf War how deficiencies in the intelligence process—particularly the bomb damage assessment process—nearly derailed the air campaign in early February as a heated and, ultimately, pointless debate broke out between the intelligence community, the national political leadership, the military leadership, and the forces in theater. Fortunately, in this case, a strong-minded and insightful CINC, with the support of the chairman of the Joint Chiefs, the secretary of defense, and, ultimately, the president, made the correct decision. But will we be so fortunate in the future? We will if we plan for it now.

In closing, I wish to affirm the obvious: Wars are won by individuals and by individual will, heroism, and sacrifice. Certainly that has been true of all the air wars which have occurred to date. We have an obligation to educate ourselves about our profession so that we guarantee that the individuals who go to war are the best trained, the best led, and the best equipped.

I am disturbed, for example, at how few senior air leaders—from all nations—have addressed airpower issues since the Second World War, in contrast to the sometimes furious scribbling of their brethren in other, more traditional services. I personally feel that is why the expectations of many in the political leadership and media about what an air war in the Persian Gulf would mean were so wrong: They were thinking in terms of Berlin or Tokyo in 1945, not in the realities of post-Gulf-War Baghdad. It is also why today we face surprising difficulties persuading some in the political arena that aircraft are as much a vital part of the national industrial base infrastructure as, say, tanks, aircraft carriers, or submarines and must not be allowed to become an "endangered species." We must not risk that misperception again. We must not be—and cannot afford to be—a series of air forces that continue to draw our doctrinal and strategic sense from the great airpower prophets of the past—the Douhets and Trenchards and Mitchells—men who wrote over 60 years ago. We need to be as dynamic in our thought as our profession itself is. And that is why I am particularly honored to have been invited here to present this talk to you. I make no claim for it to be revealed truth. Rather, if it stimulates discussion and critique, I will be satisfied that it has served its purpose. Thank you all very much.

Discussion

Professor Richard Overy: I enjoyed your paper enormously. One rather intriguing thought occurred to me. If this paper had been given 50 or 60 years ago, I think that a lot of it would have been concerned with what we came to call the military-industrial complex, the idea that airpower could only be exercised effectively by states with a very large manufacturing capacity. There would be high losses, but those losses could be replaced fairly rapidly from the factory as they were in the Second World War, when a great deal of organizational and economic effort went into the production and supply of a continuous flow of weapons. But I'm struck by the fact that you didn't talk a great deal about economic and supply backup. Further, the kind of air war of the future that you're describing is one which will be very difficult to resupply quickly and effectively if for some reason or another, once you're engaged in war, you experience extremely high loss rates. Now I don't think this would affect the United States, and I think that your paper, in a sense, puts the United States right at the vanguard. A lot of smaller and weaker economies will remain extremely reliant on American technology. But imagine a war between medium or small states with limited airpower, sustaining fairly high losses as we heard the Egyptians did in the war with Israel. Without effective depths of production and supply, there's a danger that your airpower, on which you spent a great deal of money, may become virtually worthless in a matter of hours. Do you have a view on the future of supply and production and what sort of depth might be necessary?

Dr. Hallion: I think the issues you've raised are very insightful. We are in a very interesting situation now with modern airpower in that its lethality is so high it can very quickly wipe out an opponent's forces and accumulated stocks. We are dealing with high-technology systems in virtually all air forces now, even smaller ones, that cannot be rapidly replaced. There was a study done a number of years ago within the United States Air Force into what would happen if we decided to go to surge production on the F-16—how long would it be before we rolled out the first aircraft beyond what had been already planned in the pipeline. The answer was three years. Now by World War II standards, that's absurd. I think the point is a serious one because what it shows is that nations which may confront an air attack have to be able to fend off the attacker in such a way that they do not lose their investment. To highlight the problem, look at the difficulties Iraq faced with the immediate destruction of aircraft, war stocks, hardened aircraft shelters, and so on, things that previously would have been fairly easily protected.

However, the implication that only countries with very high technology bases can engage in this kind of war is flawed, I think. The combination of older aircraft and modern weapons systems which are readily available in the post-Cold-War environment—precision munitions, air-to-air weapons, air-to-ground weapons—means that even smaller powers can expect to have not only reasonable defense capabilities but also very reasonable attack capabilities. And for this reason you might see a Gulf War on a smaller scale but with the same sort of decisive outcome. But the problem you've alluded to, that we'll see airplanes that can be very quickly destroyed or put out of service, and because they are so complex and expensive are not readily replaced, is a serious issue.

Air Vice-Marshal Tony Mason: Could I endorse Richard Overy's comment. Thank you for a magnificent paper. It struck me also that when you were referring to air forces, you were in fact referring to one in particular, the United States Air Force. If we had met here in the 1920s, we could perhaps have had representatives from Britain, France, Australia, Germany, Italy, the United States, the USSR, Germany, Japan, and many more. And when they talked about airpower, they would have all been talking about the same thing. I'm not sure that we are all talking about the same thing any more. In my introduction to my own paper yesterday, I used the expression "differential airpower," because many of the applications you mentioned depend upon a synergy of advanced technology—space, stealth, information systems, and so on—which none of us in the foreseeable future can aspire to. If that supposition's correct, it poses three questions about airpower which the medium powers should be thinking about long and hard. The first one is how would we use airpower as a national instrument in cooperation with the United States? Second, how should we develop our own airpower as a national instrument to be applied independently, not necessarily with interests which were synonymous with those of the United States? And third, while most of us will be happy most of the time to harmonize our interests with the United States, it is by no means the case universally. There will be many countries who see the United States and the "new world order" as something antithetical to their regional interests. The lessons they take from the gulf will not be ours. Our lesson from the gulf, generally speaking, is: How can we apply those capabilities nationally and make them more effective? Other countries will ask, what lessons can we derive from the gulf which will discourage the United States from using its airpower in similar circumstances in the future? I think those three questions are worthy of more study.

Dr. Hallion: At any particular point in the history of aerospace development we have had a leader-follower relationship between certain nations in terms of what they were able to do, both commercially and militarily. Then because you have this leader-follower relationship, at some later point, those capabilities wind up being spread over a larger group of nations. For example, when the first supersonic jet fighters came out, they were really the province of only the United States, the Soviet Union, Great Britain, and France. But we very quickly got to the point where we were exporting those aircraft, so eventually other nations developed the capability to design and build their own jets. Sometimes that development was undertaken within a very constrained industrial or economic base. So my feeling here is that while countries like the United States, Great Britain, and France might have an advantage in technological capabilities right now, it will not last. It will very quickly change. It will change as a result of the commercial exploitation of systems, and it will change as a result of increased access for all countries to technological education through the Western university system.

Now the three questions you raised. First, how should a small or medium state plan to use airpower in cooperation with the United States? I think it would be foolish for any nation to seek a particular form of airpower application—say maritime patrol or army cooperation—and rely on the United States for air superiority, airlift, and so on. My belief is that nations understand their own geostrategic environment very clearly. They should plan to undertake all the missions appropriate to that environment, with the necessary adjustments of scale. For example, in Australia your needs in many ways are very much like ours. You need to have the ability to operate at very long ranges. You also have a very small military force, therefore, that would tend, at least in my mind, to drive you towards precision weapons platforms and systems. So you're looking right away at medium- to long-range airlift and, if necessary, medium- to long-range strike operations.

Second question. Assuming that a conflict became more serious or there were such strong regional or global implications that the United States had to become involved, your existing force structure presumably would be utilized to best advantage as part of a coalition air force.

The third question is the most intriguing. What lessons could other countries derive from the gulf about discouraging the United States from applying airpower at long range? Some of aspects of that question really relate to a larger issue, and I think it's one we have recognized in the United States since the Vietnam War. I refer to the criteria proposed by Caspar Weinberger in the mid-1980s, which stated among other things that the United States will not make a commitment to go to war without the support of the American people. In other words, the weapon of choice for a nation seeking to discourage the United States from getting involved in a war is to win the war of public opinion within the United States itself. I think you will find that within the United States there's a great deal of reluctance among our population to involve ourselves in what are perceived to be foreign adventures. The Gulf War debates were acute and absolutely critical. I think that if George Bush had tried to fulfill the United Nations mandate without first having had a public debate, major protests would have ensued. But this battle of public opinion may be the most effective way for a nation to try to influence American action.

Air Vice-Marshal Alan Reed: It seems that over the past three days the lessons we've derived are those that relate to air forces. Militarily, there is a much broader sense that I think we should accommodate. We heard yesterday from Air Marshal Funnell about the vulnerability of surface ships in the Falklands, and the example from the Gulf War indicates that ground forces also are very vulnerable. You alluded in your paper to some aspects of this, but would you comment about the navies and armies of the world: have they recognized that airpower has come of age, if so what are they doing about it?

Dr. Hallion: I'll give you some background from my own experiences. I taught at the Army War College at Carlisle Barracks in Pennsylvania for a year in the late 1980s, and I found a very interesting thing. I found that within the United States Army community there was a great gulf between Army aviators and Army nonaviators. Basically the tank, the infantry, and the artillery communities were very skeptical of the value of organic army aviation. More often than not, when we talked about the future of war and the role of airpower, I found that my natural allies were the Army aviators. I felt that I was in the Air Corps Tactical School in the 1930s.

404

The implication—and I believe that this is largely driven by physical science—is that a two-dimensional opponent has difficulty confronting a three-dimensional opponent. If you take a look at "Sandy" Woodward's book on the Falklands War, you'll find that he saw this from both ends. As a submarine commander, he was able to sneak up on surface ships with relative ease. As a surface force commander, he had very great difficulty dealing with 1950s aircraft and weapons technology, even though he had 1980s technology to confront it. You folks here saw this first hand: you saw it in the Battle of Coral Sea, in the fighting around New Guinea, at Milne Bay where the RAAF operated very successfully against Japanese surface forces, at the Battle of Bismarck Sea, which was a classic. Ultimately, as a result of those and other actions, an air blockade was essentially inflicted on New Guinea. The vulnerability of ships goes back a very long time. The vulnerability of surface mechanized vehicles goes back a very long time. Rommel in the Western Desert complained that air attack pinned him down so he couldn't move. He made the same complaint several years later at Normandy, where he said that enemy air attacks were so overwhelming that his army had become immobile, and there was nothing he could do about it. And yet when we look back, we realize that the aircraft systems that we are talking about from those days—the Typhoon, the Thunderbolt, the Hurribomber, things of that sort—were very immature systems. They were carrying at most two or maybe three 250- to 500-pound bombs, or they had small caliber cannon, and yet they were already having a powerful impact on surface forces. Now we are in the precision-munitions era, and air forces have an even greater leverage against mechanized surface forces, land and sea.

My personal feeling is that armies and navies need to think very seriously about what constitutes robust military force in the present era. For example, for an army to place priority on the development of armored fighting vehicles doesn't make much sense. Helicopter gunships, troop transports, observation helicopter systems—those make perfect sense—but to waste effort developing another main battle tank or something of that sort makes little sense. You do need a small number of those vehicles if you're in a Bosnia or a Somalia situation, basically to keep the small arms fire out so to speak. But to think that wars are going to be won by main battle tank encounters in the future is, I think, really somewhat ludicrous. This has gone beyond strategy and thought; it's now become in some army circles dogma and theology. Long-range power projection using army systems would be not an airlifter carrying a tank into a crisis area, but an airlifter carrying a helicopter gunship or something of that sort because you get the flexible attributes of airpower. And that ties in with a comment I made at the end of my paper, which was that all military branches have an obligation to exploit the air weapon consistent with their larger purposes. I happen to believe that the overwhelming use of airpower is best left in the hands of air forces, but it is absolutely obligatory that other military forces make the maximum use of air weapons, because the more traditional forms of power projection that they have relied upon—surface vessels with cannons, tanks, things of that sort—I think really represent an older paradigm of war.

Dr. Ben Lambeth: Let me take my cue from the last words in your presentation and ask you a question which I know does not have an easy answer. How can airpower theorists and professionals around the world better educate their principal constituencies, namely, the services? How do we get people to think of airpower in functional rather than service terms, and understand it as a supremely effective instrumentality of warfare rather than something that necessarily air forces do? And here I might take issue with your comment about air forces being the only appropriate repository of airpower. It seems to me that if airpower professionals can cross that bridge, we can go substantially towards getting beyond these parochial squabbles that we see over force structures and budgets, and think in terms of getting the done job rather than who gets the credit.

Dr. Hallion: A very good question. First of all, don't misunderstand what I've said. I didn't say that air forces should be the *only* repositories of airpower. I think they are the only repositories for the *decisive* use of overwhelming airpower, but everybody brings some airpower to the fight.

Turning to your question. This gets back to education. We have a very serious challenge confronting us; we can see it by looking around at the audience here; this is an air force audience. It would be far better if this was not an air force audience, it would be far better if the air force people here were in a minority.

I think that basically the emphasis in the air force has been on the operator as a pilot rather than on the operator as a thinker or a writer. With rare exceptions, we have not seen our own people carrying the message to the broader world on what air brings. And in fact that's also true for naval and army aviators. We need a lot more operators as thinkers and writers in our respective governments, with our respective political decision makers, and in our university environments, not just in the professional military education environment but also in civilian universities. There needs to be more of a debate; we need more of our senior officers writing pieces for newspapers. We need to get this message out. On the eve of the Gulf War I was working on Secretary Don Rice's staff group, and what really shocked me at that time was that peoples' expectations of airpower were so outdated. They were looking to a World War II model; they were looking to massive collateral damage, tens of thousands of civilian casualties, bombs wildly off target as a routine, the savaging of friendly forces by airborne friendly fire.

Incidentally, the preconceived notion about friendly fire was, I think, in some ways the most tragic aspect of the Gulf War. While the services were trained to deal with the problem of friendly fire in terms of air versus ground, they were not as well prepared for the far greater danger of ground versus ground friendly fire. Again, thinking was outdated. Ground versus ground friendly fire incidents in the Gulf War outnumbered the air versus ground friendly fire incidents by 250 percent and were much more lethal.

We have to take this education challenge very seriously. Once again that's why I think these conferences are so important, but looking around the audience I wish I were seeing less blue out there and a lot more green or tan.

Air Marshal Ray Funnell: I was taken by your remarks about the political aspect of war in the modern era. When you look at the interactions between and among public opinion, the mass media, and political will, you realize that even low-level conflicts, if they're protracted, will quickly exhaust the popular support base. It would seem to me that if we do have to use airpower, we should fully maximize the shock and the surprise it brings with it. So even at low levels of conflict, we should be thinking in terms of keeping the war as short as possible. And in particular, if we do have a major national interest at risk, we should apply our airpower with full force from the outset and never again try to build up pressure gradually, as was attempted in Vietnam. That approach makes it very difficult to sustain popular support and to keep political and military objectives aligned.

Dr. Hallion: I would second everything you said. Military power in general and airpower in particular works better when it's applied decisively and to maximum effect. There's that old joke, "If you want to send a message call Western Union." You don't use air to send messages; you use air to achieve decisive military results. Your comment on short wars is a very important one. There has been a cultural shift in the way nations look at war. I don't think we have the patience to put ourselves through a four-year, a five-year war, the will just is not there. Had the Gulf War gone on beyond the six-month point, I think there would have been a sharp increase in the number of people calling for some sort of settlement, anything to get out.

One consequence of the Gulf War that I think has not been fully thought through in some circles is the question of casualties. The casualty rates of the Second World War and Vietnam would no longer be accepted. But equally, the Gulf War may have created unrealistically low expectations. We lost

148 people to enemy action, and there is now a belief among some that we can always contain our losses like that. It's dangerous to think in those terms.

Notes

1. This paper should not be construed as representing or constituting an official position of the United States Air Force, the Department of Defense, or the United States government.

There are many definitions of airpower. For the purposes of this article I offer up one of my own: "Airpower is the various uses of airborne vehicles and forces to achieve national needs by the projection of military power or presence at a distance."

I wish to acknowledge the assistance of a number of individuals who provided insights, particularly Gen Charles Horner, USAF; Lt Gens "Jay" Kelly, Buster C. Glosson, and Thomas Moorman, USAF; Air Vice-Marshals R. A. "Tony" Mason and Ron Dick, RAF (Ret.); Cols John Piazza, John A. Warden III, Phillip S. Meilinger, and David A. Deptula, USAF; Group Capt Andy Vallance and Neil Taylor, RAF; Group Capt Gary Waters, RAAF; Lt Col Allan Howey, USAF; Maj William Bruner, USAF; Ellen Piazza, SAF/OSX; Dr. Christopher J. Bowie, Dr. Benjamin Lambeth, and Dr. Rebecca Grant of the RAND Corporation; and Dr. Alan Stephens, RAAF Air Power Studies Centre. The conclusions drawn and statements made are, unless otherwise cited, mine alone.

2. C. H. Gibbs-Smith, *The Aeroplane: An Historical Survey of its Origins and Development* (London: Her Majesty's Stationery Office, 1960), 35.

3. Charles M. Westenhoff, ed., *Military Airpower: The CADRE Digest of Airpower Opinions and Thoughts* (Maxwell Air Force Base [AFB], Ala.: Air University Press, October 1990), 51.

4. Loren Baritz, *Backfire: A History of How American Culture Led Us into Vietnam and Made Us Fight the Way We Did* (New York: Ballantine Books, 1986), 153.

5. In fact, as President Bush himself recalled with some amusement during a commencement speech at the Air Force Academy on 29 May 1991, when briefed on what airpower could do in the gulf, Bush—a former naval aviator himself—turned to his national security adviser and questioned whether the briefer—the Air Force chief of staff, no less—knew what he was talking about. See Richard H. Kohn, "Out of Control: The Crisis in Civil-Military Relations," *The National Interest*, Spring 1994, 10–11. I have also drawn on personal recollections from this time period.

6. Quoted in Jean Heller, "Air Power: Brutal, But Not Enough?" *St. Petersburg Times*, 12 January 1991. For example, *United States Strategic Bombing Survey (USSBS)* concluded, "Allied air power was decisive in the war in Western Europe," and the Pacific air campaign "supports the findings in Germany that no nation can long survive the free exploitation of air

weapons over its homeland. For the future it is important fully to grasp the fact that enemy planes enjoying control of the sky over one's head can be as disastrous to one's country as its occupation by physical invasion." See *USSBS, Summary Reports European and Pacific Theaters* (reprint, Maxwell AFB, Ala.: Air University Press, 1987), 37, 110–11.

7. George S. Bush, commencement speech, US Air Force Academy, 29 May 1991.

8. More disturbing than the "revolution" debate has been the incipient return of the "land power (i.e., tank and infantry) triumphant" wishful-thinking school of thought. For an example, see Brig Gen Robert J. Scales Jr. et al., *Certain Victory: United States Army in the Gulf War* (Washington, D.C.: Office of the Chief of Staff, US Army, 1993).

9. Eliot A. Cohen, "The Mystique of US Air Power," *Foreign Affairs*, 73, January–February 1994, 109–24.

10. Phillip S. Meilinger, *Ten Propositions Regarding Airpower* (Washington, D.C.: Air Force History and Museum Program, 1997).

11. Office of the Secretary of the Air Force, *The Air Force and US National Security: Global Reach—Global Power* (Washington, D.C.: Headquarters USAF, June 1991), passim. See also Air Force Manual (AFM) 1-1, *Basic Aerospace Doctrine of the United States Air Force*, 2 vols., March 1992.

12. J. F. C. Fuller, *Armament and History: A Study of the Influence of Armament on History from the Dawn of Classical Warfare to the Second World War* (New York: Charles Scribner's Sons, 1945), 7.

13. United States Army Air Forces (USAAF), "AAF Bombing Accuracy Report no. 2," Operational Research Section, Eighth Air Force, 1945, Chart 2, "Distribution of Effort and Results."

14. "Army Weapons System Performance in Southwest Asia" (Washington, D.C.: Department of the Army, 13 March 1991), 3–4.

15. Gen Ronald Yates, USAF, speech at the annual meeting of the East Coast Section, Society of Experimental Test Pilots, Alexandria, Va., 26 April 1991.

16. R. A. Mason, ed., *War in the Third Dimension: Essays in Contemporary Air Power* (London: Brassey's Defence Publishers, 1986).

17. Naval unit transit times are from the Office of the Chief of Naval Operations, *The United States Navy in "Desert Shield" "Desert Storm"* (Washington, D.C.: Department of the Navy, 1991), A-2–14.

18. For rates of advance of land combat forces, see Robert Helmbold, "Rates of Advance in Historical Land Combat Operations," CAA-RP-90-1 (Bethesda, Md.: Army Concepts Analysis Agency, 1990); and R. P. Mulholland and R. D. Specht, *The Rate of Advance of the Front Line in Some World War II Campaigns*, RAND Report RM-1072 (Santa Monica, Calif.: RAND, 1953).

19. For example, see Thomas A. Keaney and Eliot A. Cohen, *Gulf War Air Power Survey, Summary Report* (Washington, D.C.: Gulf War Air Power Survey Team, for sale by Government Printing Office [GPO], 1993), 117.

20. The Observation-Orientation-Decision-Action (OODA) Loop is a concept enunciated by John Boyd, the father of agility metrics and energy maneuverability.

21. Frido von Senger und Etterlin, *Neither Fear Nor Hope: The Wartime Career of General Frido von Senger und Etterlin. Defender of Cassino* (New York: E. P. Dutton, 1964), 224.

22. Precisely how effectively Iraqi communications were shattered is hotly debated. Interrogation reports of captured Iraqi commanders suggest that Iraqi C^3 was essentially destroyed, as does journalistic evidence from Iraqi citizens. The cautiously optimistic Gulf War Air Power Survey (GWAPS) will only state that communications were "greatly reduced" and that "common sense would argue that strikes against [Iraqi communications and leadership targets] must have imposed *some,* if not *considerable,* disruption and dislocation." (Emphasis in original.) Keaney and Cohen, 70.

23. Some of this also relates to the Warden notion of "five strategic rings," enunciated in his essay, "Employing Air Power in the Twenty-First Century," in Richard H. Shultz Jr. and Robert L. Pfaltzgraff Jr., *The Future of Air Power in the Aftermath of the Gulf War* (Maxwell AFB, Ala.: Air University Press, July 1992), 57–82.

24. I am indebted to Col John A. Warden, now commander of the Air Command and Staff College, Maxwell AFB, Alabama, for this analogy. Damage to "leadership targets," communications, and "transportation targets" by the recent Los Angeles earthquake was remarkably similar to damage inflicted by air attack in Iraq though without, of course, the randomness of damage (collateral damage) associated with an earthquake. For example, the earthquake destroyed key junctions on the Highways 2, 5, 10, 118, and 405 interchanges, essentially severing all major freeways into LA from the north and east, as well as the major east-west interchanges.

25. As indeed Maj Gary Crowder, USAF, of the Headquarters USAF Strategic Planning Staff does in his briefing, "Revolution in Military Affairs: A Geo-Strategic Assessment of Trends Affecting the US Military Through 2015," 22 March 1994.

26. This statistic was assembled by Mr. Joseph D. Caver of the Air Force Historical Research Agency, Maxwell AFB, Alabama, based upon its record holdings of World War II and Gulf War material.

27. Col George K. Muellner and Col George J. Cusimano, "Development Flight Test in Combat: Joint Stars at War," in *1991 Report to the Aerospace Profession* (Beverly Hills, Calif.: Society of Experimental Test Pilots [SETP], September 1991), 60–82.

28. For example, see the previously cited AFM 1-1, vol. 1, 2-1, 5.

29. Currently, there is a major space forecasting activity underway under the direction of Lt Gen Jay Kelley, commander of the Air University at Maxwell AFB, Alabama. This study, called *Spacecast,* is currently identifying technologies and missions to be pursued within the context of the anticipated global environment of the next century.

30. For example, reflecting on his experiences during Operation Just Cause, Gen Clark Steiner, commander of the US Army's XVIII Airborne

Corps, stated, "Space just doesn't help . . . I cannot go to war without space systems." See Headquarters USAF, *Report to the 102d Congress of the United States of America*, FY 1992/93 (Washington, D.C.: GPO, 1991), 25. I wish to acknowledge information and insights received from Lt Gen Thomas S. Moorman Jr., commander of Air Force Space Command (AFSPC), Peterson AFB, Colorado.

31. Though Robert H. Goddard flew his first liquid-fuel rocket in 1926, the space age is commonly held to have begun on 4 October 1957, with the launch of *Sputnik I.*

32. I have benefited from discussions with Col John Piazza, USAF; Col John Warden, USAF; and Lt Col Barbara McColgan, USAF, as well as having drawn upon personal recollections from meetings in the Air Force Secretariat.

33. This scenario was first presented to the Air Force secretary as one possible option in mid-November 1991. See SAF/OSX (R. P. Hallion), memo to SAF/OS, 13 November 1991, AF/HO files. Statistic on 1993 AMC operations from Ellen Piazza, SAF/OSX, 21 March 1994.

34. Christopher Bowie et al., *The New Calculus: Analyzing Airpower's Changing Role in Joint Theater Campaigns*, RAND Report MR-149-AF (Santa Monica, Calif.: RAND, 1993), 83–84.

35. Gen Michael J. Dugan, "Air Power: Concentration, Responsiveness and the Operational Art," *Military Review* 69, 7 July 1989, 21. On the necessity of jointness in war, see Joint Chiefs of Staff Publication 1 (Joint Pub 1), *Joint Warfare of the US Armed Forces* (Washington, D.C.: National Defense University Press, for sale by GPO, 11 November 1991; and Col Thomas A. Cardwell III, USAF, *Airland Combat: An Organization for Joint Warfare* (Maxwell AFB, Ala.: Air University Press, December 1992). An excellent survey of the jointness issue as applied to air warfare is James A. Winnefeld and Dana J. Johnson, *Joint Operations: Pursuit of Unity in Command and Control, 1942–1991* (Annapolis: US Naval Institute Press in association with RAND, 1993), passim.

36. An example of this "post-Clausewitzian" thinking would be Col John A. Warden III's influential book, *The Air Campaign: Planning for Combat* (Washington, D.C.: National Defense University Press, 1988). I use this term post-Clausewitzian to distinguish such thinking from the "neo-Clausewitzian" approach of thinkers such as Col Harry Summers, USA, retired, in works such as Summers' *On Strategy: A Critical Analysis of the Vietnam War* (Novato, Calif.: Presidio Press, 1982).

37. I have benefited from discussions with Dr. Diane Putney of the Center for Air Force History on this issue.

38. For an example of this—from a pro-corps commander and anti-Schwarzkopf perspective—see the previously cited Scales, passim; and Capt Steven U. Ramsdell, USN, report to Dr. Dean Allard, Naval Historical Center, 14 May 1991.

39. See endnote 17.

40. Based on looking at Iraqi targets and "translating" them into American ones, the following would have been destroyed or rendered

unusable: The White House and Blair House; the Capitol; the Pentagon; the Executive Office Building; FBI, CIA, DIA, and NSA Headquarters; command and key facilities at Bolling and Andrews AFBs; the Naval Air Test Center; the Navy Yard and Navy Annex; Quantico Marine Base; Forts Belvoir, McNair, Myer, and Meade; Camp David; the Suitland Federal Center; the Sprint, MCI, and AT&T regional communications centers; and all significant power plant and fuel storage facilities. (The source of this is a postwar analysis by Air Force Checkmate Operation.)

41. Keaney and Cohen, 61.

42. Bowie, 43–44.

43. For a discussion of reliability and maintainability issues, see the author's own *Storm Over Iraq: Air Power and the Gulf War* (Washington, D.C.: Smithsonian Institution Press, 1992), 3, 196–97.

44. F-15Es, F-111Fs, and F-117s.

Index

417